RELATIONAL DATABASE DESIGN

AN INTRODUCTION

RELATIONAL DATABASE DESIGN

AN INTRODUCTION

I. T. Hawryszkiewycz
University of Technology, Sydney

PRENTICE HALL

New York London Toronto Sydney Tokyo Singapore

Typeset by Keyboard Wizards, Professional Typesetters, Harbord, NSW.

Cover design by Norman Baptista.

Printed and bound in Australia by Macarthur Press Sales Pty Limited, Parramatta, NSW.

2 3 4 5 94 93 92 91

ISBN 0 7248 1045 5 (paperback)
ISBN 0-13-771791-1 (hardback)

National Library of Australia
Cataloguing-in-Publication Data

Hawryszkiewycz, I. T. (Igor Titus)
Relational database design.

Bibliography
Includes index.
ISBN 0 7248 1045 5

1. Database design. 2. Relational databases. I. Title.

005.756

Library of Congress
Cataloguing-in-Publication Data

Hawryszkiewycz, I. T.
A primer for relational database design : an introduction / by Igor Hawryszkiewycz.
p. cm.
Includes index.
ISBN: 0-13-771791-1

1. Relational data bases. 2. Data base design. I. Title.

QA76.9.D3H387 1990 90-36317
005.75'6--dc20 CIP

Prentice Hall, Inc., *Englewood Cliffs, New Jersey*
Prentice Hall Canada, Inc., *Toronto*
Prentice Hall Hispanoamericana, SA, *Mexico*
Prentice Hall of India Private Ltd, *New Delhi*
Prentice Hall International, Inc., *London*
Prentice Hall of Japan, Inc., *Tokyo*
Prentice Hall of Southeast Asia Pty Ltd, *Singapore*
Editora Prentice Hall do Brasil Ltda, *Rio de Janeiro*

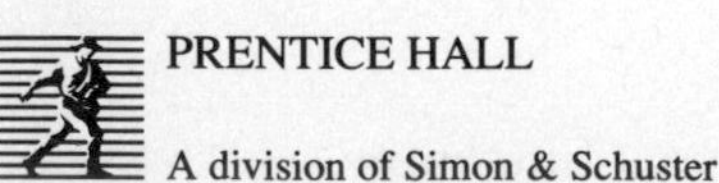

Contents

Preface

Databases have significantly changed in nature over the last few years. Early databases often supported single organizational functions and were used to provide regular pre-specified reports. Contemporary databases now play a central role in many information systems and support many organizational functions. Furthermore, they can be used to provide information on an ad-hoc and irregular basis. Consequently, both the software that supports such databases and the database design procedures have evolved over time to meet these changing needs. Many databases are now built with relational database software because it can adapt to change and provide good interface support. Systems such as DB2 or INGRES have meant that relational systems, no longer in the researcher's arena, are now becoming an accepted technology in the practice. Database design has also evolved from the ad-hoc methods used initially to design databases that supported simple systems to more formal procedures that can handle all the complex decisions that must be made to design corporate databases. The design processes have established the principles to be met by good databases as well as the design procedures and steps used to build databases. The book introduces the principles of design and shows how these principles can be used in design methodologies.

One of the major principles and theories of database design is relational theory. This forms the basis of most design processes by defining the constraints good database designs must comply with. Such constraints reduce database redundancy and databases that comply with these constraints are often said to satisfy relational normal forms. The first few chapters of the book thus describe relations and relational normal forms. This sets the goal for good database structure.

However, there is more to database design than good structure. Designers must also ensure that they capture all the database requirements correctly and build the necessary software to satisfy these requirements. The book thus continues by describing techniques used to describe user data structures and their implementation using database software. Chapters 7 to 10 describe methods used to describe user requirements, in particular, the semantics of the data and how the data will be used. The semantics are described using a semantic model. The book here concentrates on the Entity- Relationship (E-R) model, which is now widely used. After describing this model, the book shows how user requirements specified in terms of the E-R model can be converted to relational normal forms. It then describes how methods of data access are defined and how these can be used to modify the normal forms to satisfy performance requirements.

Once we have a database design, the next step is to implement the database on software to build application programs that use the database. Thus Chapter 11 describes the relational software that is now commonly available to implement database. The following chapters then describe languages and methods used to build programs. The emphasis here is on SQL (Structured Query Language) that has now become the standard for using relational databases. Chapters 12 to 14 concentrate on defining SQL and how it can be used both to formulate complex queries and update the database. The book then continues with application development and shows how SQL can be used to develop transaction systems using either high-level languages or application development systems. It concludes with two recent developments in database design, namely, distributed database systems and automated support tools for database design.

This book has benefited from the many courses the author has given to new students and to practitioners. It draws on the author's experience of the kinds of difficulties encountered by people new to database. It elaborates on such difficulties to simplify them, outlines good practices to follow, and identifies common errors often made by novices in the hope that readers will not repeat them.

The book thus serves two purposes. The first concerns teaching. This is an introductory text which introduces new techniques in their proper context, with many examples to illustrate them. It thus makes it possible to introduce database design early in students' study courses, thus preparing them to get away from ad-hoc approaches and begin to use proper methods right from the start. The book assumes some knowledge of computers and is most useful if it follows an introductory year of studying information systems, such as followed in the author's earlier text, *Introduction to Systems Analysis and Design*. This earlier book introduces some of the ideas but does not elaborate on them. The new book has a lengthier and more thorough treatment of design, but places much greater emphasis on relational languages and application development tools. Nevertheless, for those readers who believe in the database approach to design, an introductory semester studying systems analysis is not really necessary, as this book introduces all database concepts and can be used in a course that concentrates on data design techniques.

The book is also useful to computer professionals. It takes a very methodological approach to design and follows steps that would be followed by designers. Thus in many cases it can be used as a prescriptive approach to design.

Igor Hawryszkiewycz

1

Design methodologies

INTRODUCTION

A computer-based information system is made up of many components. It has a number of computers which store the system data. It also has programs to support user procedures that use this data. These programs allow users to access and change any data during their work. Computer systems that provide such support use a variety of software. The software includes database management systems to store and manage data. In addition, software includes application development tools to develop programs that manipulate user data. Designers must ensure that all needed data is in the database and that correct application programs are written to manipulate this data.

Relational database management systems (RDBMS) are increasingly used to develop computer-based information systems. Most users view the RDBMS as a collection of software used to manage user data. However, although initially RDBMS were used just to manage data, recent RDBMS also provide the software needed to develop application programs. Thus it is possible to purchase a RDBMS and use it to develop all the programs needed by user applications.

The kind of environment provided by RDBMS software is shown in Figure 1.1. It includes a number of components. The central component is the data manager, which supports a database. This database contains data needed to support user functions and activities. In addition most contemporary RDBMS also include software to help users or programmers develop applications that use this data. Some of these components are illustrated in Figure 1.1. One such component is software that supports ad-hoc enquiries

Figure 1.1 Components of a relational system

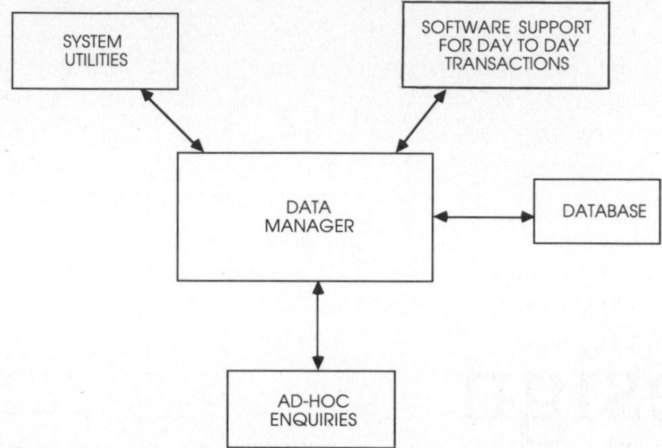

to the system. Another component is software that can be used to develop programs that handle everyday transactions. An RDBMS also includes utilities to ensure the security and privacy of the database.

However, RDBMS have not found wide acceptance simply because they include all these components. Many other systems manage data and provide software support for application development. There are two other reasons for the wide use of RDBMS. One reason is that relational systems use a natural tabular structure to store data and provide design guidelines for choosing good structures. Secondly, this natural structure results in an interface that makes relational systems easy to use when compared to many other database systems. This makes RDBMS attractive to those users who are increasingly taking an active part in system development.

This book describes how relational systems can be used to build applications. It covers two major aspects: the design processes needed to correctly analyze and design a system; the relational technology and how it can be used to implement the designs.

The book begins by describing database design, and approaches the whole idea of design by emphasizing design methodologies. Design methodologies are made up of sets of steps that support an orderly way for designing complex systems. They are now increasingly used in practice to build computer-based information systems.

The book then continues by describing the methods that can be used to design and build application programs that use the database. The emphasis in the second part is on SQL, a language that is central to relational system development. It is a standard language that is used both for ad-hoc enquiry and to develop software that supports predefined system transactions. The book describes how SQL can be used to retrieve ad-hoc information and to develop transaction systems using high-level procedural languages or application generators. The book then outlines some evolving trends in database systems, in particular distributed systems.

This introductory chapter gives a brief overview of all the steps that are used to design the database and develop programs that use the database. It describes the steps and shows why they are necessary. It also points out the chapters that deal with each of the issues or techniques described. The first part concerns design methodologies.

DESIGN METHODOLOGIES

It is now recognized that, to build good application systems, design must proceed in a set of orderly steps using proper techniques at each step. Such techniques must be chosen so that the output of one step can be used as the input for the following step. Design methodologies are collections of techniques organized into sets of steps that support an orderly way for designing databases. Design methodologies also provide the documentation necessary to record any design decisions. Many methodologies now provide software support or CASE (Computer Assisted Software Engineering) tools to support designers and maintain the documentation.

A design methodology usually follows the three steps shown in Figure 1.2. It commences with systems analysis. The analysis determines the requirements of the system and produces a system model. Analysis is followed by system design, which produces a specification of the system to be built. Then follows technical design, which specifies how available hardware and software is to be used to build the system.

The design process must produce both a database and a set program that can be used to access this database in a way needed by user applications. In many methodologies these two components are first modeled separately as shown in Figure 1.3. Usually different modeling techniques are used to model data and functions during requirements analysis. Then, during design, function requirements are used to modify data structures to fit particular function requirements. This modified model of user data becomes the database, whereas functional requirements become system programs.

Figure 1.2 Design methodology steps

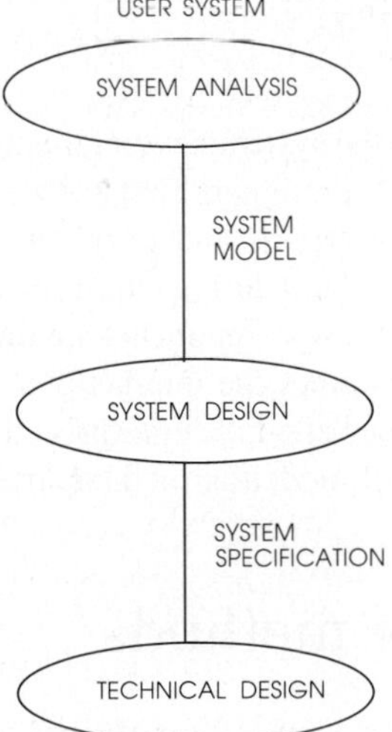

Figure 1.3 Combining data and functional analysis

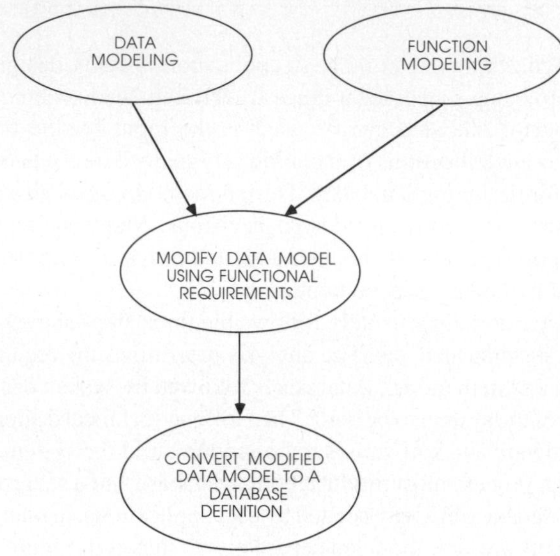

In many methodologies, analysis starts with data because data is the more stable of the two components. It is often the case that users think up new ways of using the same data rather than discover new data structures. Programs can be developed after the database is in place.

DATABASE DESIGN

Database design is part of the system development process and closely follows the three steps shown in Figure 1.2. Designers first gather database requirements through user interviews, examination of reports and forms, analysis of existing computer files and databases. A model of data is built during requirements analysis. This model defines major components of user data. These components are the data about the major system entities together with data that describes the interactions or relationships between these major entities. This model is often called the enterprise model or the conceptual model of user data. There are a number of modeling methods used in data analysis.

Data modeling methods

Data modeling methods are needed for a number of reasons. They are needed to clearly specify the user data structure and to produce a model that is understood by both users and computer professionals. Thus it should be possible to use the model as a communication tool in clarifying any misunderstandings, show sample values during any discussions, and

Figure 1.4 Techniques used in database design

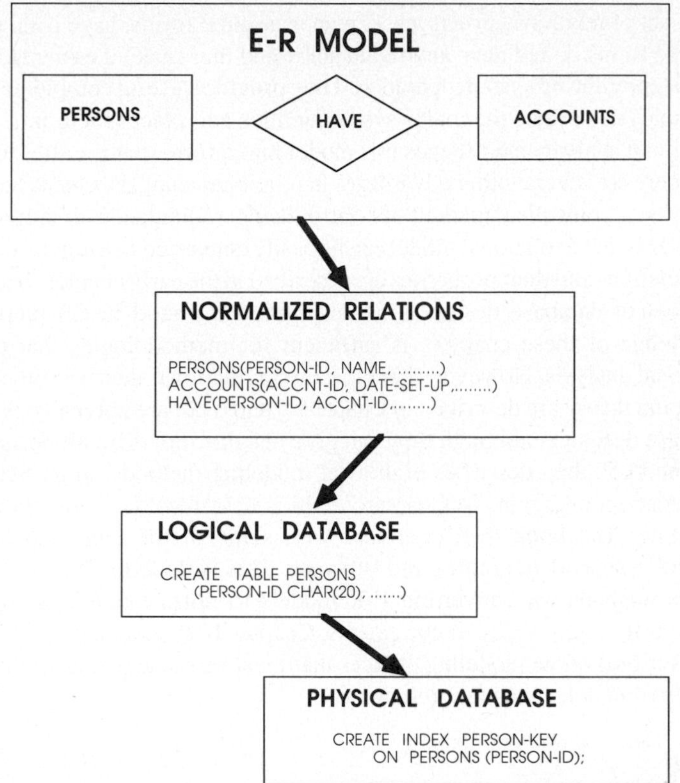

include criteria to check for data redundancies. Later this model is converted to a computer system.

Data modeling usually proceeds through a number of stages. These are shown in Figure 1.4. A high-level model of the system is developed first during system analysis. In Figure 1.4 this high-level model is an E-R (Entity-Relationship) model which defines the top-level data semantics. It identifies the most important entities and relationships in the data.

The next step is to construct a set of normalized relations. This set of relations removes any unnecessary redundancy. Then the logical database definition is created. The form of the definition depends on the database management software that is to be used to implement the database. It defines the database schema using the DBMS data definition language.

The advantage of relations

You may well ask, why should relations be used at all? Why not simply use the high-level modeling techniques and go directly from the high-level model to the logical definition?

Relational analysis is used because it has a strong theoretical basis that provides designers with clear guidelines for choosing database structures.

A set of relational structures, known as normal forms, have been defined. Relations in these forms do not have any redundancy and thus make it easier to maintain database consistency during system operation. They provide a useful complement to E-R analysis. E-R analysis defines the major system entities and places them in a high-level model. Relational analysis then shapes this model into a form that is easier to use.

There are several other advantages in relational analysis. One is that later in design it supports a controlled method for introducing redundancy to improve performance. Another is that a relational model can be easily converted to a logical database definition.

Relations and their properties are described in the early chapters because they provide the goal of database design. This description is found in Chapters 2 to 4. Usually knowledge of these chapters is sufficient for methodologies that combine E-R and relational analysis. However, there is more to relational theory. Some further aspects of relational theory are described in Chapters 5 and 6 but are not really essential reading for database designers although they can give insights into difficult design issues.

The book then describes high-level modeling methods, in particular E-R analysis. This description begins in Chapter 7, which describes the basic concepts used in E-R modeling. The book then continues with some of the more advanced concepts, in particular dependent entities and subtypes. This is done in Chapter 8. Then Chapter 9 covers methods for converting E-R models to normal relations and adjusting these relations to satisfy access requirements. Chapter 10 then concludes this part of the book by describing some modeling choices that must be made to ensure that E-R models are converted to non-redundant relations.

SYSTEM DESIGN

System design starts when the enterprise model is completed. System design is used to choose methods for storing data. It begins by shaping the data into form that is suitable for storage. Usually any data redundancies are removed during this step and the logical database definition is proposed.

System design must also look at further design criteria.

Design criteria

Database design must satisfy a large number of criteria. Analysis satisfies one class of criteria. These are user criteria that require all data about the system to be captured and stored. This is done by developing a clear and concise conceptual model of user data.

System design now considers another set of criteria. These criteria begin to place greater emphasis on how the system will be implemented and used. An important criterion here is response time to user inputs. It is essential to produce designs that eliminate unnecessary waiting times for users. Another criterion is to eliminate database redundancy unless it is needed to improve performance, use of minimal storage, and adequate performance.

Other criteria that appear during design are: data must be accessible from the most convenient locations using interfaces that are easy to use; any designs must be easy to change as most systems change over their lifetimes.

System design usually begins by eliminating all redundancies from the database using relational analysis. This non-redundant definition may be amended once it is known how the database is to be used. Such amendments are often necessary to ensure that the design meets important performance criteria. Data usage is determined during design. To do this, it is necessary to identify system functions and their data needs. Transactions and access needed by such functions are then determined and each transaction is analyzed to see how it will use the database. The results of this analysis are used to choose the physical access paths as well as introducing some redundancy to improve performance. Methods used to do this are described in Chapter 9.

Such analysis together with any proposed amendments completes the database design. The database can now be built and initialized with data to be stored in database. Then application programs are written and tested against the database.

USING THE DATABASE

After database design, the book turns its attention to using the database. It begins by describing how RDBMS software provides the facilities needed to develop applications. This is done in Chapter 11. This chapter also includes additional facilities provided by RDBMS to ensure database recovery in case of system failure. It also covers methods to ensure data privacy. Designers must use these facilities to ensure that users only get access to that data which they need to carry out their function.

Then the book continues by describing languages and programs that develop use applications.

Such program development and languages must take into account the method to be used. Databases can be used in two ways. First there are the repetitive kinds of operation often found in practice. These include updating an account, changing an inventory record or updating a personnel record. These predefined operations are supported by specially developed programs that support such routine transactions.

There is also a second kind of access. This is ad-hoc access where a user must access information in a way that has not been predefined. In that case some general software is needed to accept such ad-hoc queries.

Languages that support ad-hoc access must be both user friendly and also contain sufficient expressive power to retrieve information that meets even the most complex conditions. This is where the language SQL comes in. It has become the standard for accessing relational databases. It can be used to both specify the kinds of conditions often met in ad-hoc retrieval and for transaction program development.

Chapters 12 through to 14 describe the SQL language and how it is used in ad-hoc retrieval. Chapters 15 through to 17 then describe how SQL can be used to develop application programs. Chapter 15 describes report generation, Chapter 16 covers methods used to develop high-volume transaction applications, whereas Chapter 17 describes facilities provided for end-user development. Chapter 18 then follows with a description of distributed database systems that support high-volume repetitive transactions.

CASE TOOLS

Finally an introductory book on design would not be complete without some mention of CASE tools. These tools assist designers in a number of ways. They can act as repositories of data and store the models developed at all the levels shown in Figure 1.2. They can also assist some of the processes. For example, they can assist normalization and often automatically convert the set of relations or E-R model to a database definition.

SUMMARY

This chapter outlined design methodologies. It showed that system design is a staged process and how database design fits into this staged development process. The chapter defined the major steps in database design and the role of data modeling methods in these steps. It then described the advantage of relational models and outlined an alternative design methodology that uses relational analysis only.

2

Relations

INTRODUCTION

The relational model was introduced by Codd in 1971. Since then relations have played an important part in most database design methodologies. They are important in database design for three reasons. First, they make a good communication tool between users and designers. Relations represent data structures in a way that is readily understood by users and computer professionals. They do this by presenting a simple data structure which can include values to assist explanations.

The second important reason for using the relational model concerns meeting essential database design criteria. The relational model defines such criteria in terms of normal form relations. Normal form definitions are given in Chapter 4 after some preliminary discussion in this and the next chapter. These normal form definitions are then used to evaluate proposed designs.

Finally the relational model has one additional advantage. Data structures represented by relations can be readily converted to relational DBMS and implemented directly on computers that support relational database management systems (RDBMS). Thus once you have a relational design you can define it by languages provided by these systems.

This chapter will describe what relations look like and define some terminology associated with relations. It will then indicate the difference between good and bad ways for storing data using relations.

WHAT IS A RELATION?

Relations were first defined using mathematical relational theory. It is this theory that can be used to precisely define formal design criteria. Presentation of this theory has been simplified over time into a form that is acceptable to a wider community. Thus the simplest way to define a relation is as a table with data values stored in table rows. One such relation or table is illustrated in Figure 2.1. This shows a relation called WORK made up of three columns, named PERSON-ID, PROJ-NO and TOTAL-TIME-SPENT-BY-PERSON-ON-PROJECT. It stores the times spent by people on projects. Each row in the relation shows the time spent by one person on one project. Figure 2.1 also includes another relation, named PERSONS. This relation stores details about persons working on projects. A relational database is a collection of relations.

Figure 2.1 Relations WORK and PERSONS

WORK

PERSON-ID	PROJ-NO	TOTAL-TIME-SPENT-BY PERSON-ON-PROJECT
P1	PROJ1	20
P3	PROJ1	16
P2	PROJ2	35
P2	PROJ3	42
P3	PROJ2	17
P3	PROJ1	83
P4	PROJ3	41

PERSONS

PERSON-ID	DATE-OF-BIRTH	NAME
P1	Jan 62	Joe
P4	Feb 65	Mary
P3	Aug 33	Andrew
P2	Jul 48	Joe

Relational representations are useful because they are very similar to many data structures found in practice. For example, much data in practice has been presented as listings or stored on card indices. Such common structures are very similar to relations as illustrated in Figure 2.2. This Figure shows a payroll list of payments made to persons, and a card index that contains each person's personal details. Figure 2.2 also shows how the payroll sheet is easily represented as relation PAYROLL and how the personnel index file is easily represented by relation PERSONNEL. Such straightforward representations of common user structures make relations look like natural representations of user data and thus quite acceptable as a communications tool.

Terminology

Descriptions of relations and their properties need a much clearer and more formal set of definitions than those given in the previous section. These definitions are illustrated in Figure 2.3.

The most important definition is that of the *relation* or *table*. The word relation is more appropriate in formal mathematical work whereas the word table is now more used in practice as the alternative to the term relation. The term *relation attributes* defines *table columns* and the term *tuples* defines *table rows*.

Figure 2.2 Relational-like structures in practice

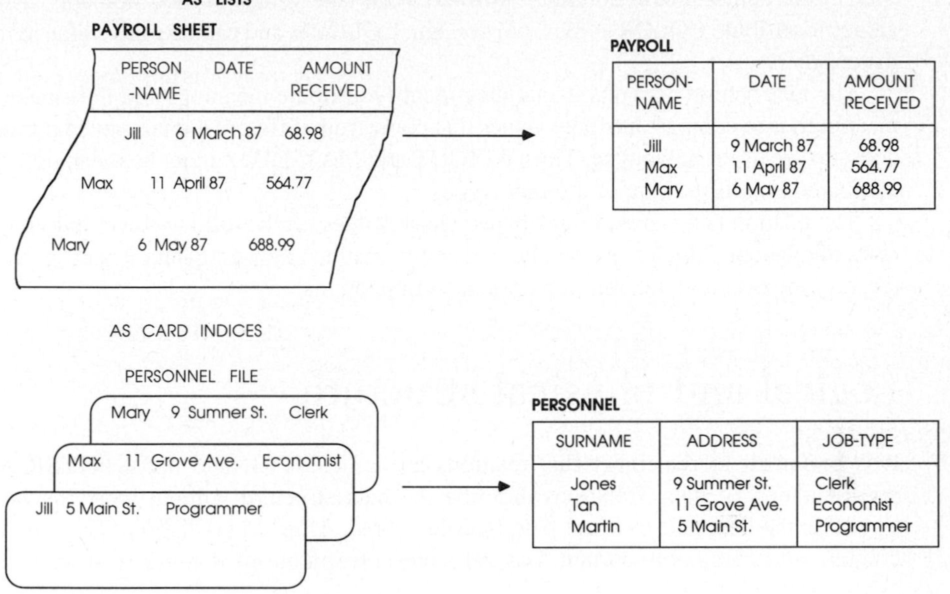

Figure 2.3 Terminology

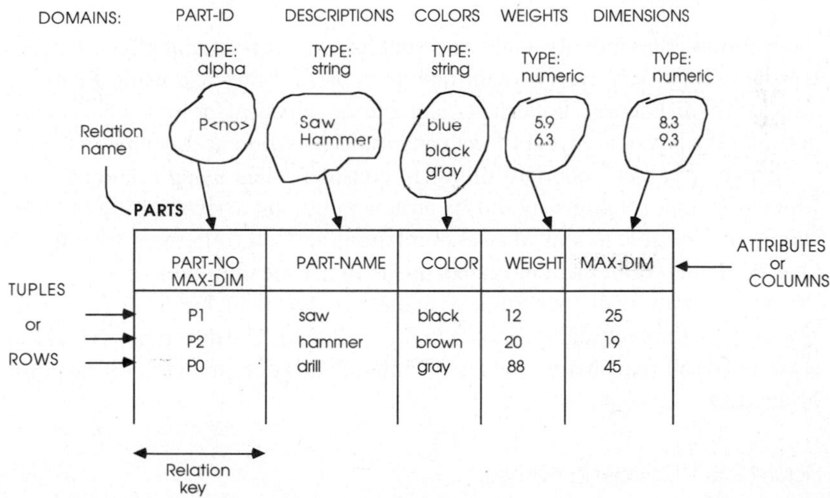

There are two other important terms, *domains* and *relation key*. Domains define the values that attributes can take, or alternatively, values that can appear in columns. Domains are not just types. The domain is actually a name that identifies a set of values, and those values are of some type. It is thus possible to have two domains that are of the same type but which are different domains. For example, in Figure 2.3 there are five domains, PART-ID, DESCRIPTIONS, COLORS, WEIGHTS and DIMENSIONS.

Some of these domains are of the same type. For example, WEIGHTS and DIMENSIONS are both numeric domains. Attributes can take values in their domains. Thus values in attribute COLOR come from domain, COLORS, and can take any value in the list of colors.

The idea behind domains is that they identify attribute meanings and thus make it meaningless to compare attribute values that come from different domains even if those domains are of the same type. Thus WEIGHT and MAX-DIM cannot be meaningfully compared even if they are of the same type.

The relation key is a set of attributes whose values can be used to select individual rows of relations. Much more will be said about relation keys in Chapter 3 because they are very important in determining normal form relations.

Logical and physical structure

It is important to remember that relations are a LOGICAL and not a PHYSICAL representation of data. Relations describe the data structure without worrying how to access the data and how the data is to be stored. Thus things like indices, row or column orders are not important. Logical representation means that in a relation:

- there are no duplicate rows;
- the order of the rows is not significant; and
- each column in a relation has a unique name in the relation.

It follows that initially analysts do not have to worry about physical organization of the data. They only worry about how to represent the data using relations. Physical structure will become important later during physical design when designers must consider the physical layout of data and indices used to access data in the relations.

There are other important things to consider when using relations to model data. Remember that relations should be an unambiguous representation of user data. One should thus be able to look at a set of relations and tell from them what the user data is. One essential requirement to realize this is to use meaningful names.

An illustration of meaningless names is shown in Figure 2.4(a). The preferred structure for the same data is shown in Figure 2.4(b). The difference is that Figure 2.4(b) tends to be self explanatory, whereas Figure 2.4(a) does not include the entire meaning of the data.

Figure 2.4 Choosing names

RELATION-A

X	Y	Z
P7	SALES	1June 83
P3	PRODUCTION	1 May 82
P5	SALES	1 Feb 81

(a) Unclear meaning

WORK-IN

PERSON-ID	DEPARTMENT	DATE-STARTED
P7	SALES	1June 83
P3	PRODUCTION	1 May 82
P5	SALES	1 Feb 81

(b) Meaningful names

Exercise 2.1

Construct relations to store the following information.

1. Orders (identified by ORDER-ID) are made for parts (identified by PART-NO). Any QTY of parts can be ordered in an order.
2. The BALANCE of accounts (identified by ACCOUNT-NO) and the BALANCE-DATE.
3. The GRADES received by students (identified by STUDENT-ID) in COURSES in different SEMESTERS.
4. The PRICE of cars (identified by REG-NO) in CAR-YARDS owned by a dealer.
5. The outstanding loans (including BORROWER-ID and DATE-DUE) of books (identified by ACCESSION-NO).
6. The DATE and AMOUNT of withdrawals and deposits on accounts (identified by ACCOUNT-NO).
7. The NUMBER OF MILES that cars (identified by REG-NO) were used by drivers (identified by DRIVER-ID) on various DAYS.
8. The WEIGHT of animals (identified by ANIMAL-NO) monitored on a daily basis.
9. Loan applications including APPLICANT-NAME, APPLICATION-DATE, AMOUNT-REQUESTED and the TIME and BRANCH at which the application was made.

GOOD METHODS FOR STORING DATA

So far nothing has been said about how attributes are combined into relations. It is possible to take any set of attributes and make a relation out of them. In fact it is possible to take all the data items in the system and put them into one relation. Hence one relation can describe the whole system. Such a relation is called the ***universal relation*** in theoretical work.

However, most relational databases contain a number of relations. It is necessary to store data as a number of relations rather than one universal relation to eliminate redundancy. It is easier to maintain consistency in databases with no redundancy. Consistency usually means that each row in a relation is independent of any other row. It is then possible to change any single row of any relation independently of any other row in any relation.

To further explain redundancy and consistency, it is necessary to elaborate on what is meant by the term fact. Informally a fact often associates some value with an object or associates two objects. In a system described by attributes, a fact exists when the value of one attribute determines at most one value of another attribute. Thus DATE-OF-BIRTH is a fact about a person. Because a person is identified by a value of PERSON-ID, then PERSON-ID determines a value of DATE-OF-BIRTH.

It is also common to informally distinguish ***single-valued*** facts from ***multi-valued*** facts. A single-valued fact takes only a single value. A multi-valued fact can take more than one value. Thus DATE-OF-BIRTH is a single-valued fact about PERSON-ID because a person only has one DATE-OF-BIRTH. SKILL on the other hand is a multi-valued fact because a person can have more than one SKILL.

It is also important to distinguish between ***derived*** and ***basic*** facts.

Derived and basic facts

Often one fact known about an object leads to some other fact about an object. For example, we know that a DATE-OF-BIRTH is a fact about PERSON-ID. We also know the DAY-OF-WEEK for each date (for example, 5 March 1985 was a Tuesday). From these two facts we can derive the fact that a person born on 5 March 1985 was born on a Tuesday. This is a derived fact. Logical databases should not store derived facts.

REDUNDANCY

One goal of logical database design is to avoid redundancy in the database. Redundancy occurs whenever the same fact is stored more than once or when derived facts are stored. Redundancy, apart from using unnecessary storage, tends to complicate update operations and leads to the possibility of database inconsistency. However, it should be pointed out that later in design redundancy may be introduced in a controlled manner for performance reasons. Methods for doing this will be discussed in Chapter 9.

There are two kinds of redundancy: multiple storage of the same fact or the storage of derived facts.

Redundancy by multiple storage of facts

Figure 2.5 illustrates relation PROJECT-DATA, which stores some facts more than once. In relation PROJECT-DATA, the PROJECT-BUDGET of a project is stored more than once. In fact it is stored as many times as there are persons working on the project. Such redundant storage of facts has many disadvantages. For example:

- If the PROJ-BUDGET for a PROJ-NO changes then we must change more than one row in the relation.
- Every time a new row for a person working on a project is added to a project it is also necessary to look up the project budget and include it in the new row.
- A project with no persons assigned to it, such as PROJ4, will only have a value PROJECT-BUDGET but no values for the other attributes. This means that some simple operations must be done differently, depending on the current database state. Thus adding a new person to PROJ2 requires the insertion of a new row. Adding a new person to PROJ4 requires two null values to be changed.

Figure 2.5 A relation with redundancies

PROJECT-DATA

PERSON-ID	PROJ-NO	PROJECT BUDGET	TOTAL-TIME-SPENT-BY-PERSON-ON-PROJECT
P1	PROJ1	20	20
P3	PROJ1	20	16
P2	PROJ2	17	35
P2	PROJ3	84	42
P3	PROJ2	17	17
P2	PROJ1	20	83
P4	PROJ3	84	41
–	PROJ4	90	–

Redundancy and duplication

You should not confuse the term redundancy with duplication of values. Duplication of values is sometimes needed in databases whereas redundancy should be avoided.

Figure 2.6(a) illustrates relation USE. This relation has more than one row with the same value of PROJECT-ID, for example PROJ1. It also has more than one row with the same value of PROJ2. It is necessary to store these values more than once because each project can use more than one part. Thus each storage of one value of PROJ1 describes a different fact. When PROJ1 is stored in the same row as P1 then it is part of the fact that states how many P1 parts PROJ1 used. When PROJ1 appears in the same row as P3 then it is part of the fact that states how many P3 parts PROJ1 used. Thus in relation USE there is some duplication of values but no redundant storage of facts.

Figure 2.6 Duplication and redundancy

USE

PROJ-ID	PART-NO	QTY-USED
PROJ1	P1	17
PROJ2	P2	85
PROJ1	P3	73
PROJ2	P3	80

(a) Non-redundant data

ASSIGNMENTS

PERSON-ID	DEPT	DATE-OF-BIRTH	DATE STARTED	DATE-FINISHED
P1	SALES	1 June 53	2 June 80	5 Aug 83
P2	SALES	3 July 51	5 Aug 81	9 Dec 82
P3	ACCOUNTING	8 Aug 60	3 Feb 79	17 Jul 82
P1	PRODUCTION	1 June 53	11 Mar 82	3 Feb 85

(b) Redundant data

In relation ASSIGNMENTS, a value of DATE-OF-BIRTH, say 1 JUNE 53, can also appear more than once. Each such occurrence in this case, however, is associated with the same person and thus describes the same fact. Thus relation ASSIGNMENTS contains redundant data.

You should now do Exercise 2.2 to get a better understanding of the meaning of redundancy.

Exercise 2.2

Examine the following to see if they contain redundant data.

1. PART-USE

PROJ-NO	PROJ-MANAGER	PART-NO	QTY-USED
P1	Jill	HAMMER	7
P2	Henry	HAMMER	11
P1	Jill	DRILL	3
P2	Henry	SAW	20

2. PERSONS

PERSON	ADDRESS	DATE-MOVED-IN
Jill	ADD1	1 June 79
Henry	ADD7	11 Aug 73
Jill	ADD5	22 Sep 80
Emma	ADD3	27 Mar 77

3. FAULTS

EQUIP-NO	DATE-OF-FAULT	REPAIR-PERSON	TIME-SPENT
E70	1 June 81	Jill	12
E12	7 July 81	Jane	6
E70	7 Aug 81	Jill	12
E70	20 July	Jill	15
E70	1 June 81	Jane	7

There is at most one fault on an EQUIP-NO on one day.

4. DELIVERIES

DELIVERY-NO	TRUCK-USED	DRIVER	DRIVER-ADDRESS
1	V6	Joe	PAGE
2	J22	Jill	ARANDA
3	V6	Vicki	HAWKER
4	N12	Joe	PAGE

Redundancy through the storage of derived facts

Figure 2.7 illustrates the storage of derived data. Here a person works for one department, each department has one manager, and the manager lives at one MANAGER-ADDRESS. These three sets of facts are stored in relations ASSIGNMENT, MANAGEMENT and LOCATION in Figure 2.7.

Figure 2.7 also includes the relation ADDRESSES. This relation stores the addresses of person managers. Relation ADDRESSES stores PERSON-MANAGER-ADDRESS, which is a single-valued fact about the person — it is the address at which the manager of the person's department lives.

However, you should note that all information in relation ADDRESSES can be derived from the other three relations. For example, Joe works in DEP1 and Mr. Beck is the manager of DEP1. Mr. Beck lives in Glebe. Thus Joe's manager lives in Glebe, which is exactly row 1 in relation ADDRESSES. Thus relation ADDRESSES stores derived facts and is redundant.

One problem with storing derived relations is that changes in one relation often affect other relations. For example, the contents of ADDRESSES are affected by changes to the other relations. Thus:

Figure 2.7 A derived relation

WORK

PERSON	DEPT
Joe	DEP1
Jill	DEP2
Mary	DEP2
Jim	DEP3

PERSONS

DEPT	MANAGER
DEP1	Mr. Beck
DEP2	Ms. Amis
DEP3	Ms. Tang

LOCATION

MANAGER	MANAGER -ADDRESS
Ms. Amis	Newtown
Mr. Beck	Glebe
Ms. Tang	Glebe

ADDRESSES

PERSON	PERSON-MANAGER -ADDRESS
Joe	Glebe
Jill	Newtown
Mary	Newtown
Jim	Glebe

- If a person moves from one department to another then a row in ASSIGNMENT will change. This change will also mean that the PERSON-MANAGER-ADDRESS in ADDRESSES for that person will change.
- If a manager of a department changes, then a row in MANAGEMENT is changed. This change will also mean that the PERSON-MANAGER-ADDRESS for all persons in the department will change.
- If a new manager moves to a new address then a row in LOCATION will change. This change will also mean that the PERSON-MANAGER-ADDRESS for all persons in the departments managed by that manager must change.

Now you should do Exercise 2.3 to see whether you can identify derived relations.

Exercise 2.3

Are any of the relations in the following sets derived?

SET 1

(a) OFFICES

OFFICE	BUILDING	FLOOR-NO
J30	HOWARTH	6
J97	JETTY	3
K70	HOWARTH	9

(b) LAST MOVEMENTS

PERSON-ID	OFFICE	DATE-MOVED -IN
Vicki	J30	June 80
Martha	J97	Aug 81
Andrew	J30	July 83
John	K70	March 82

(c) OCCUPANTS

PERSON -ID	BUILDING	FLOOR -NO
Vicki	HOWARTH	6
Martha	JETTY	3
Andrew	HOWARTH	6
John	HOWARTH	9

SET 2

(a) WORK

PERSON -ID	PROJ-NO	TIME -SPENT
P1	PROJ1	10
P2	PROJ1	72
P2	PROJ2	20
P3	PROJ2	15

(b) TASKS

PROJ-NO	TASK -NO	DATE -SET-UP
PROJ1	1	Jan 80
PROJ1	2	Nov 82
PROJ1	3	Feb 81
PROJ2	1	Oct 82
PROJ2	2	Feb 83

(c) TASK-ASSIGNMENT

PERSON -ID	PROJ-NO	TASK-NO	DATE-PERSON -ASSIGNED
P1	PROJ1	1	Feb 80
P2	PROJ1	2	April 80
P2	PROJ2	2	Nov 82
P3	PROJ2	1	March 83

Exercise 2.3 (continued)

SET 3

(a) FAULTS

FAULT-ID	EQUIPMENT	DATE-OCCURRED
F1	SWITCH 3	1 Feb 82
F2	LINE 80	17 April 83
F3	SWITCH 3	3 March 81

(b) REPAIR-WORK

FAULT-ID	PERSON-ID	TIME-SPENT -ON-FAULT
F1	P1	1
F1	P2	3
F2	P1	1
F3	P1	2
F3	P2	1

(c) EQUIPMENT-FIXING -EXPERIENCE

EQUIPMENT	PERSON-ID
SWITCH 3	P1
LINE 80	P1
SWITCH 3	P2

REMOVING REDUNDANCIES

Redundancies are removed in two ways. Relations that store derived data should be removed from the database. Redundancies caused by the multiple storage of facts are usually removed by decomposition.

Decomposition

A relation that stores facts more than once can be decomposed into relations that store facts once only.

For example, relation PROJECT-DATA in Figure 2.5 is decomposed into relations PROJECTS and WORK shown in Figure 2.8.

Note the problems that occurred in relation PROJECT-DATA in Figure 2.5 no longer occur in the new relations. Thus in the new relations:

Figure 2.8 Decomposed relation

PROJECTS

PROJ-NO	PROJECT-BUDGET
PROJ1	20
PROJ2	17
PROJ3	84
PROJ4	90

WORK

PERSON-ID	PROJ-NO	TOTAL-TIME-SPENT-BY -PERSON-ON-PROJECT
P1	PROJ1	20
P3	PROJ1	16
P2	PROJ2	35
P2	PROJ3	42
P3	PROJ2	17
P3	PROJ1	83
P4	PROJ3	41

- if a PROJECT-BUDGET is changed then only one row in relation PROJECTS must be changed;
- when a new row for a person working on a project is added to a project we need not look up the project budget;
- a project that has no persons does not require special treatment.

SUMMARY

This chapter described relations as a set of tables. It defined the terminology used in relational systems. Relations were defined as a logical representation of data. Such logical representations must eventually be converted to physical designs that support access to the data.

The goal is to define relations that store data without any redundancy. Redundancy occurs when some fact is stored more than once. The chapter showed some examples of redundant data. The next two chapters will describe how to design databases that do not contain any redundancies.

3

Dependencies and relation keys

INTRODUCTION

Relational theory includes methods for identifying various levels of redundancy in relations. The term used to define levels of redundancy is the relation's ***normal form***. There are in fact five normal forms. The relation proceeds to the next higher normal form as each kind of redundancy is eliminated. The goal is to convert each relation into the highest normal form.

Two important properties are needed to define normal forms. One property concerns dependencies between attributes and consequently the facts in the system. The goal of design is to ensure that no fact is stored more than once.

The other property is the relation key. The relation key is a set of attributes whose values identify unique rows in the relation. Relation keys are dependent on the attributes in a relation and the dependencies between these attributes. Later we will see that non-redundant relations only store facts about the relation keys.

This chapter describes ***functional dependencies*** and ***relation keys***. The next chapter will describe how these two properties are used to determine the normal form of a relation.

FUNCTIONAL DEPENDENCIES

Informally functional dependencies are a formal representation of single-valued facts. A fact, you might recall, has been defined as a value associated with some object or an association between two objects. In the mathematical sense, this fact is represented by a functional dependency, which shows that a unique value of one attribute is determined by a given value of another attribute. This dependence is defined by a functional dependence statement. As an example, the single-valued fact that a person has one DATE-OF-BIRTH can be represented by a functional dependency (FD) statement:

PERSON-ID → DATE-OF-BIRTH

This statement means that there is only **only one** value of DATE-OF-BIRTH for any given value of PERSON-ID. Functional dependencies can also be represented by functional dependency diagrams as the one shown in Figure 3.1.

Figure 3.1 A functional dependency

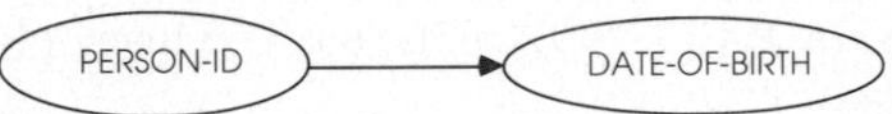

The left-hand side (LHS) of a functional dependency is called a **determinant**.PERSON-ID is a determinant of the above functional dependency. It is important to note that a value of the determinant determines **only one** value of the right-hand side (RHS) of the functional dependency. In the above example a value of PERSON-ID determines one value of DATE-OF-BIRTH.

It is equally important to keep in mind that if more than one value of one attribute can be associated with one value of another then there is no functional dependency. For example, if a person with a PERSON-ID has a number of ADDRESSES then it is not true that

PERSON-ID → ADDRESS

However, if a person has one address then:

PERSON-ID → ADDRESS

is true. Thus functional dependencies are determined by the nature of the information. A functional dependency statement may include more than one dependency. For example, if a person has one DATE-OF-BIRTH and one ADDRESS, then both of these dependencies can be shown by the one dependency statement:

PERSON-ID → DATE-OF-BIRTH, ADDRESS

It is also possible for two sets of attributes to be mutually dependent. If each project has one manager, and each manager manages one project, then the following two functional dependencies are true:

PROJECT-NO → MANAGER
MANAGER → PROJECT-NO

A double-ended arrow is used to describe such mutual dependencies and these two functional dependencies become:

PROJECT-NO $\leftrightarrow$ MANAGER

To get a better understanding of functional dependency try Exercise 3.1.

Exercise 3.1

Look at the following sentences and define any functional dependencies between the capitalized attributes.

1. Projects (identified by PROJ-NO) have a given START-DATE.
2. Parts (identified by PART-NO) can be used on many projects (identified by PROJ-NO).
3. Persons (identified by PERSON-ID) live in cities (identified by CITY-NAME). Cars (identified by REG-NO) have a NUMBER-OF-CYLINDERS.
4. Mountains (identified by MOUNTAIN-NAME) have a given HEIGHT.
5. Persons (identified by a PERSON-ID) own any number of cars (identified by REG-NO), but only one person can own each car. Each car is owned by one person.
6. Parts (identified by PART-NO) are sold in shops (identified by STORE-NO) and each shop has one ADDRESS.
7. Each sale (identified by SALE-NO) is made by one SALESPERSON and can include any QUANTITY of different items (identified by ITEM-NO).

Functional dependencies on more than one attribute

Sometimes facts are stored about combinations of two or more attributes. For example, the total time spent by a particular person on a particular project is a fact about the association between that person and the project. Here it is not sufficient to know only the value of PERSON-ID to get a single-value of TOTAL-TIME-SPENT-BY-PERSON-ON-PROJECT. This is because a person may be working on more than one project and the TOTAL-TIME-SPENT-BY-PERSON-ON-PROJECT will be different for each project for that person. Thus both a value of PERSON-ID and PROJ-NO are needed to get a value of TOTAL-TIME-SPENT-BY-PERSON-ON-PROJECT.

Dependencies on two or more attributes are represented as follows:

PERSON-ID, PROJ-NO $\rightarrow$ TOTAL-TIME-SPENT-BY-PERSON-ON-PROJECT

Now the determinant is composed of more than one attribute. Such functional dependencies can also be represented on functional dependency diagrams like that shown in Figure 3.2.

Figure 3.2 A determinant with more than one attribute

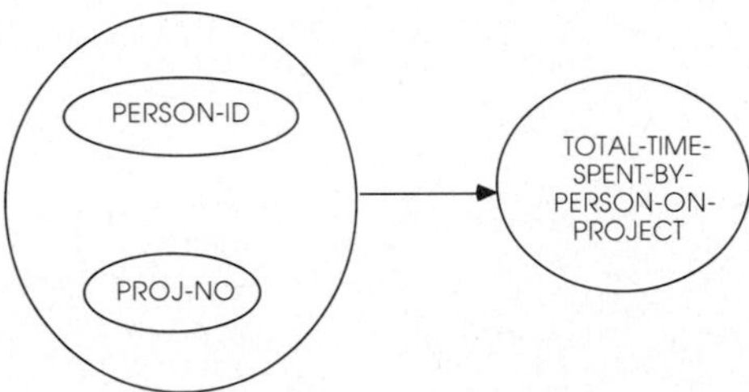

Now the two attributes in the determinant are enclosed and an arrow from the boundary of the enclosure terminate on attributes whose single-values are determined by the determinant.

Again you should be careful to use the rule that a functional dependency only exists if a value of one attribute determines one value of another. Thus it is not true that

PERSON-ID → TOTAL-TIME-SPENT-BY-PERSON-ON-PROJECT

because there may be many values for TOTAL-TIME-SPENT-BY-PERSON-ON-PROJECT for a person.

Try Exercise 3.2 to see the difference between dependencies on one attribute and those with more than one attribute.

Exercise 3.2

Select the true dependencies in each of the following sets.

SET 1

A person is assigned to one department. A department may have many persons assigned to it.

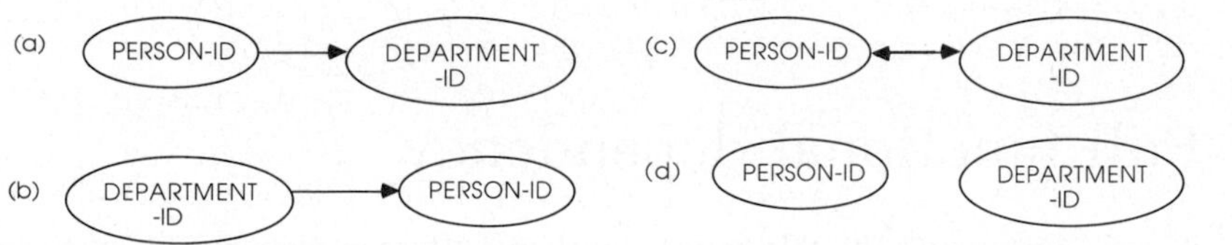

Exercise 3.2 (continued)

SET 2

A person can start on a project on a given start date. More than one person can start on the same project on the same date but a person can only start once on the same project and cannot start on more than one project on the same date. A person can work on more than one project.

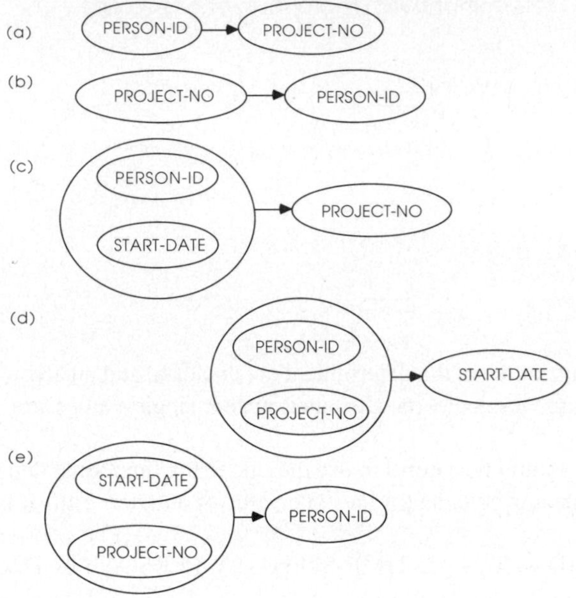

SET 3

Temperatures are recorded once an hour on the hour at a number of locations

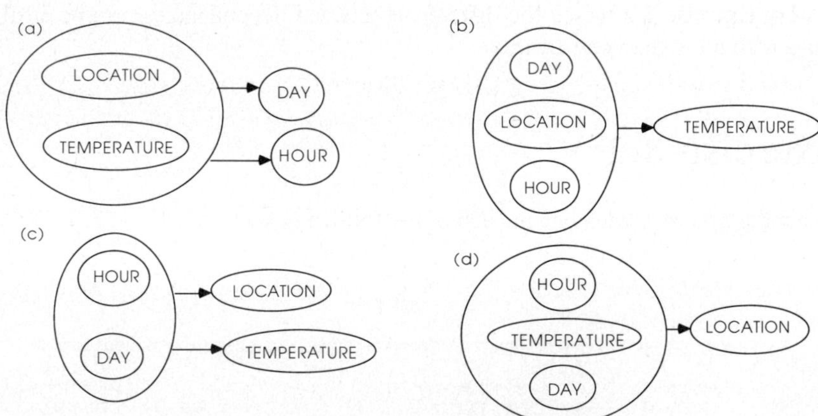

Full functional dependency

It is also important to be able to distinguish the difference between functional dependencies and full functional dependencies. A full functional dependency must not have unnecessary attributes in the determinant.

To see the difference between a functional dependency and a full functional dependency note that if

PERSON-ID → DATE-OF-BIRTH

then it is also true that

PERSON-ID, PERSON-NAME → DATE-OF-BIRTH

But we do not need to know PERSON-NAME to get DATE-OF-BIRTH; PERSON-ID is sufficient. Thus:

PERSON-ID, PERSON-NAME → DATE-OF-BIRTH

is not a full functional dependency because we do not need PERSON-NAME in the determinant. But

PERSON-ID → DATE-OF-BIRTH

is a full functional dependency.

Similarly if each project has one manager then

PROJECT-NO, PART-NO → QTY-USED

is a full functional dependency but

PROJECT-NO, PART-NO, MANAGER → QTY-USED

is not because we do not need MANAGER in the determinant to get QTY-USED.

Only full FDs are used in design. Now try Exercise 3.3 to specify some functional dependencies.

Exercise 3.3

Consider the following sentences. Show any functional dependencies between the capitalized attributes.

1. A student (identified by STUDENT-ID) obtained a GRADE for a COURSE in a given SEMESTER.
2. A QTY of parts (identified by PART-NO) in orders (identified by ORDER-NO) by customers (identified by CUSTOMER-NAME). Each order is placed by one customer.
3. The MAX-HEIGHT jumped by a high-jumper (identified by ATHLETE-NO) in athletic events (identified by EVENT-NAME).
4. The AMOUNT-REQUESTED by customers (identified by CUSTOMER-NAME)

in a loan-application (identified by APPLICATION-NO). Each application is by one customer.

5. Rooms (identified by ROOM-NO) are used by courses (identified by COURSE-NO) on a given DATE and TIME.
6. Tasks (identified by TASK-NAME within PROJ-NO) are assigned to departments (identified by DEPT-NAME).
7. Persons (identified by PERSON-NAME) board planes (identified by FLIGHT-NO) at AIRPORTS on a given DEPARTURE-DATE. A flight can only leave an airport once on a given day.

NOTATIONS FOR DESCRIBING RELATIONS

Instead of drawing tables, relations can also be described using mathematical notation. The mathematical notation includes both the relation attributes and the functional dependencies between them.

Figure 3.3 Relation ASSIGNMENTS

ASSIGNMENTS

PERSON-ID	DATE-OF-BIRTH	DEPT-NAME
P1	7 July 49	Accounts
P3	3 June 61	Sales
P2	11 Feb 65	Accounts
P4	22 April 64	Sales
P5	17 May 66	Sales

For example, suppose we take the relation, ASSIGNMENTS, in Figure 3.3. This relation shows how persons are assigned to departments. Relation ASSIGNMENTS is described in mathematical notation in two parts:

ASSIGNMENTS = ({attributes}, {list of functional dependencies})

which becomes

ASSIGNMENTS = ({PERSON-ID, DEPT-NAME, DATE-OF-BIRTH},
{PERSON-ID → DEPT-NAME, DATE-OF-BIRTH})

It shows that ASSIGNMENTS has three attributes, PERSON-ID, DEPT-NAME and DATE-OF-BIRTH. There are also two dependencies in the attributes. One is that PERSON-ID determines the DATE-OF-BIRTH and the other is that PERSON-ID determines DEPT-NAME. Both of these dependencies are shown by the one functional dependency statement. Many examples in this and other books use algebraic notation instead of actual names to reduce the amount of writing in examples. Using this notation, a relation with three attributes, A, B and C can be specified as

R1 = ({A,B,C}, {AB → C, B → C})

MULTI-VALUED DEPENDENCIES

Sometimes you may find that functional dependencies cannot express an association between attributes. For example:

Each person, identified by a PERSON-ID, can possess many skills, identified by SKILL. Each skill can be possessed by many persons.

In this case, neither

PERSON-ID → SKILL, nor
SKILL → PERSON-ID

is true.

Some methodologies use the concept of multi-valued dependencies to define that an attribute is always associated with a given set of values of another attribute. Thus, the fact that a person has many skills is expressed as

PERSON-ID →→ SKILL

Here →→ stands for multi-valued dependency (MVD).

Multi-valued dependencies were initially defined for relations only. In this way they differ from functional dependencies which are independent of relations.

Many methodologies, however, now use multi-valued dependencies in the same sense as functional dependencies, that is, out of the context of relations.

A multi-valued dependency says that a single value of a set of attributes, A, determines a set of values of other attributes. Furthermore, this set of values is the same independent of any other dependencies of attributes A.

An example of a multi-valued dependency of two attributes on another attribute is:

PERSON-ID →→ SKILL-ID, DATE-ACQUIRED

Here a PERSON-ID determines a set of SKILL-IDs together with the dates on which each skill was obtained by the person.

Relationship between MVDs and FDs

There is a relationship between functional dependencies and multi-valued dependencies. Often a functional dependency can express the same fact as a multi-valued dependency.

Example

The functional dependency

PROJECT-ID, PART-ID → QTY-USED

says that a given project uses a given QTY-USED of a part.

This can also be expressed as:

PROJECT-ID →→ PART-ID, QTY-USED

which says that for a given project there is a set of parts used by the project and quantities of those parts used.

Methodologies prefer to use functional dependencies whenever possible and not use multi-valued dependencies to show facts that can otherwise be shown by functional dependencies. Thus the rule is to draw all the functional dependencies first and then add multi-valued dependencies to show any missing information.

Thus you may come across statements such as a person has many vehicles, which tends to suggest the multi-valued dependency

PERSON-ID →→ REG-NO

However, if the DATE-PURCHASED is also stored for a vehicle, then the functional dependency

PERSON-ID, REG-NO → DATE-PURCHASED

is true. A dependency diagram would only include this functional dependency and would not include the MVD.

Exercise 3.4 should help you decide when to use FDs and when to use MVDs.

Exercise 3.4

Draw a dependency diagram for the following problem using multi-valued dependencies only in those cases where it is absolutely necessary.

1. Organizations identified by TRADING-NAME have many ADDRESSes and one OWNER.
2. Deliveries identified by DEL-NO include many parts (identified by PART-NO). There is a QTY-DELIVERED of each part, and each part has one WEIGHT and many COLORs.
3. Animals identified by ANIMAL-NO are weighed each day. The WEIGHT of the animal is recorded each day.
4. Subjects identified by SUBJECT-NAME use a number of texts. Each TEXT has one NAME and can have a number of AUTHORs. Each subject can be taught a number of SEMESTERs and there is one TEACHER for each subject each semester.

5. Vehicles identified by REG-NO are used during working days. The NO-MILES used by each vehicle each DAY are recorded.
6. Each person works on a number of projects. The TIME-SPENT each day by each person on each project is recorded. Each person has a PERSON-ID and each project has a PROJ-NO.
7. A department can occupy many buildings. The department has one DEPT-NAME and each building has one BUILDING-NAME.

RELATION KEYS

In addition to functional dependencies, the other property that must be understood about relations is the relation key. The value of the relation key identifies a unique row in a relation. The relation key is made up of one or more of the relation attributes. The attributes in the relation key have the following properties:

- A given set of attribute values identify only one row in the relation.
- No subset of the attributes in a relation key is also a relation key.
- Key attributes cannot take null values.

Figure 3.4 shows one example of a relation key. It shows that PERSON-ID is the relation key of the relation PERSONS. There is at most one row in the relation with a given value of PERSON-ID. Thus for example there is only one row in PERSONS with PERSON-ID = ‘P3’. NAME is not a relation key because there can be more than one person with the same name, hence more than one row can have the same value of NAME.

Figure 3.4 Relation PERSONS

PERSONS

PERSON-ID	DATE-OF-BIRTH	NAME
P1	7 July 49	Joe
P3	3 June 61	Mary
P2	11 Feb 65	Andrew
P4	22 April 64	Joe
P5	17 May 66	Jill

DATE-OF-BIRTH is not a relation key of relation PERSONS because more than one person can be born on the same date. Hence more than one row can have the same value of DATE-OF-BIRTH.

It is important to remember that the relation key is a key for any set of relation values and not only for the set of values at a given instant of time. Thus it may appear in the above relation that DATE-OF-BIRTH is a relation key because at this particular instant, each row has a different value of DATE-OF-BIRTH. However, it is possible that eventually there will be two people with the same DATE-OF-BIRTH in the database. Because two rows with the same value of DATE-OF-BIRTH can occur, then DATE-OF-BIRTH cannot be a relation key.

Relation PERSONS has a key with one attribute only. It is also necessary in many cases for keys to be made up of more than one attribute to identify unique rows. As an example, relation WORK in Figure 3.5 has a relation key made up of two attributes, PERSON-ID and PROJ-NO.

Figure 3.5 Relation WORK

WORK

PERSON-ID	PROJ-NO	TOTAL-TIME-SPENT-BY -PERSON-ON-PROJECT
P1	PROJ1	20
P3	PROJ1	16
P2	PROJ2	35
P2	PROJ3	42
P3	PROJ2	17
P2	PROJ1	83
P4	PROJ3	41

Values of both PERSON-ID and PROJ-NO are necessary to identify a unique row. It is not sufficient to use a value of PERSON-ID only or a value of PROJ-NO only to find a unique row.

You should now attempt Exercise 3.5 to obtain some practice at finding relation keys.

Exercise 3.5

Find the key of the following relations.

1. VEHICLE-OWNERS

MANU-FAC-TURER	REGISTRATION -NO	OWNER
FORD	JTY-751	JILL BROWN
FORD	JTZ-309	RICHARD WEIR
GMH	KWC-612	JENNY GREEN
TOYOTA	BCJ-012	JILL BROWN
VOLVO	FOI-392	ADRIAN NEWMAN

A person can own any number of vehicles but each vehicle has one owner.

2. JUMP-PERFORMANCE

MAXIMUM-DISTANCE-JUMPED	ATHLETE-NAME	EVENT	DATE-OF -EVENT
6.31	JENNY	NATIONAL TITLES	1981
6.21	BILL	WORLD CUP	1982
5.75	MARGARET	WORLD CUP	1984
6.05	BILL	NATIONAL TITLES	1982
5.92	JENNY	WORLD CUP	1984

A long-jumper can appear in any number of events. The longest jumps in the event for every jumper is the event is stored.

3. LOANS

CUSTOMER -ADDRESS	CUSTOMER -NAME	LOAN -NO	LOAN -DATE
ARANDA	Joe	75	APR 75
HAWKER	Jill	97	JUNE 76
ARANDA	Joe	102	MAY 77
ARANDA	Mary	12	JUNE 77

A finance company makes loans to its customers. Each customer can have any number of loans but each loan is made to one customer.

2. WAREHOUSE-WITHDRAWALS

WAREHOUSE -NO	PART -NO	PROJECT -NO	QTY WITHDRAWN	DATE WITHDRAWN
W1	PX7	PROJ1	17	1 June 85
W1	PX7	PROJ2	22	2 June 95
W2	PX1	PROJ1	17	3 June 85
W3	PX1	PROJ2	33	1 June 85
W4	PX7	PROJ1	19	1 June 85

Projects withdraw parts from warehouses. The quantities of parts withdrawn on each day by a project are recorded.

Exercise 3.5 (continued)

5. VEHICLE-USAGE

REGISTRATION -NO	MAKE	DRIVER	DATE	KILOMETRES-USED -ON-DATE-BY-DRIVER
YJ73	FALCON	Joe	060783	69
XY19	TOYOTA	Jill	070783	33
YJ73	FALCON	Mary	060783	73
YJ23	MAZDA	Joe	070783	86
YJ73	FALCON	Joe	070783	33

A driver can take out any number of vehicles each day and a vehicle can be used by many drivers on the same day.

6. EQUIPMENT-FAULTS

EQUIPMENT -NO	FAULT -NO	DATE -OCCURRED	REPAIR PERSON	TIME-SPENT -ON-FAULT
X3	33	060783	Joe	3
X3	33	060783	Bill	9
X2	6	070783	Joe	9
Y3	7	060783	Bill	6
Y3	7	060783	Mary	3
Y2	16	090983	Bill	3

All faults are numbered uniquely within the organization. More than one person can work on one fault.

Some relations can have more than one key

Relation CONSULTATIONS in Figure 3.6 describes consultations by doctors. It is assumed that each consultation involves one doctor and one patient. Relation consultation has two keys. These are {DOCTOR-NO, TIME-OF-CONSULTATION} and {PATIENT -NO, TIME-OF-CONSULTATION}.

Figure 3.6 Relation CONSULTATIONS

CONSULTATIONS

DOCTOR-NO	PATIENT-NO	TIME-OF-CONSULTATION
Dr. Jones	Ms.James	10.00 am June 5
Dr. Jones	Mr. Able	11.15 am May 25
Dr. Smith	Ms. James	2.00 pm Apr 11
Dr. Ajax	Mr. Able	12.15 pm Aug 17
Dr. Jones	Ms. James	3.00 pm July 7

{DOCTOR-NO, TIME-OF-VISIT} is a key because a doctor can only have one consultation at the one time.

{PATIENT-NO, TIME-OF-VISIT} is a key because a patient can only have one consultation at the one time.

You should also note that {DOCTOR-NO, PATIENT-NO} is not a relation key because the same patient may visit the same doctor more than once. Exercise 3.6 includes some relations that have more than one relation key.

Exercise 3.6

Find the relation keys of the following relations.

1. FILM SHOWING

SESSION	THEATER	MAJOR-FILM	PROJECTIONIST	DATE
MORNING	CENTER	BLACKJACK	Smith	3 Aug 81
EVENING	CENTER	QUICKHORSE	Jones	3 Aug 81
NIGHT	CENTER	QUICKHORSE	Smith	3 Aug 81
NIGHT	SUBURB	QUICKHORSE	Muns	3 Aug 81

Each session (of which there are MORNING, AFTERNOON, EVENING, NIGHT) has one MAJOR-FILM and one projectionist. Each projectionist attends only one theater on a given date and there is at most one projectionist at each session.

2. PRODUCTION

FACTORY	PRODUCTION -NO	ENGINE-NO	DATE-MADE	PRODUCTION -RUN
NO-1	1	XJ70	1 June 84	2
NO-1	2	XJ71	1 June 84	2
NO-2	1	XY60	1 July 85	2
NO-2	2	XY61	1 July 85	2
NO-1	1	XJ72	2 June 84	3
NO-1	2	XJ73	2 June 84	3
NO-2	1	XY62	2 June 84	3
NO-2	2	XY63	2 June 84	3
NO-2	3	XY64	2 June 84	3

Each ENGINE-NO is unique in the organization and has a unique PRODUCTION-NO in a FACTORY. Factories produce engines on a series of PRODUCTION runs. A PRODUCTION-RUN is made of an arbitrary number of engines and each engine is completed in one production run. PRODUCTION-NUMBERs are sequential numbers within a PRODUCTION-RUN.

3. TASK-MANAGEMENT

PROJECT-NO	TASK-NO-IN-DEPT	DEPT-NO	DEPT-MANAGER	DATE-TASK -STARTED
P1	1	D1	Joe	1 Aug 85
P1	1	D2	Jill	12 June 95
P2	2	D1	Joe	1 Sep 86
P2	1	D3	Jack	8 Nov 85

Here TASK-NO-IN-DEPT is a unique number assigned to each task managed by a department. Each project is assigned to one department and all tasks in the project are managed by that department.

4. JOB APPLICATIONS

APPLICATION -NO	OFFICE-RECEIVED	POSITION-ADVERTISED	DATE-ADVERTISED	APPLICANT NAME	APPLICANT -ADDRESS	DATE APPL'N RECEIVED
11	HOBART	PS17	110583	Jones	MELBOURNE	110683
11	MELBOURNE	PS17	110583	Williams	MELBOURNE	050983
23	HOBART	PS23	050583	Jones	MELBOURNE	060383

Here applications are numbered chronologically within offices in the order that they are received and independently of advertised position. Position numbers are unique within the organization and applicants (each of whom has one address) can apply for any position but only once for each position.

5. FLIGHTS

FLIGHT -NO	DEPARTURE -AIRPORT	DEPARTURE -TIME	FLIGHT-CAPTAIN	ARRIVAL AIRPORT	ARRIVAL -TIME
FLO1	BRISBANE	11 am FRI	Jones	SYDNEY	12 am FRI
FLO1	SYDNEY	1 pm FRI	Black	MELBOURNE	2 pm FRI
FLO1	MELBOURNE	3 pm FRI	Andrews	SYDNEY	3 pm FRI
FLO1	SYDNEY	5 pm FRI	Jones	BRISBANE	6 pm FRI

Each FLIGHT has one FLIGHT-CAPTAIN, but the FLIGHT-CAPTAIN of a FLIGHT can change during a stopover at an airport. A flight can have any number of stopovers.

Functional dependencies and relation keys

It is important to remember that facts or functional dependencies are properties of a system. They arise from the nature of the data. Relation keys are also determined by the nature of data in the relation. For example, the fact that a person has only one DATE-OF-BIRTH and NAME would mean that PERSON-ID is the relation key in relation PERSONS in Figure 3.4.

Similarly the fact that a doctor can hold at most one consultation at a time led to the relation keys in relation CONSULTATION in Figure 3.5. Thus it should be possible to determine relation keys from functional dependencies. How this is done is described in Chapter 6.

Foreign keys

The term foreign key is also increasingly used in design. A foreign key is a set of attributes in one relation such that this set of attributes is not a key of this relation but a key in another relation.

Thus, for example, suppose the two relations in Figures 3.3 and 3.4 make up the one database. In that case PERSON-ID is the relation key of relation PERSONS. It is not a relation key of relation ASSIGNMENTS but it is a foreign key of relation PROJECT-DATA. Note that PERSON-ID is part of the relation key of ASSIGNMENTS. It is important to note that being part of a relation key does not stop a set of attributes from being a foreign key of that relation.

SUMMARY

This chapter defined two important properties that are used to design normal relations: functional dependencies and relation keys. Functional dependencies define properties in the information itself whereas relation keys are properties of relations.

These properties are used to determine the normal form of relations. How this is done, is described in the next chapter.

4

Normal forms

INTRODUCTION

The design goal is to construct relations that have no redundancy. To do this it is necessary to define conditions that must be satisfied by non-redundant relations. These conditions are defined in terms of normal relations. Relations should be in the highest possible normal form, and progression from one normal form to the next eliminates one kind of redundancy. This chapter describes these normal forms.

NORMAL FORM RELATIONS

The whole idea of normal form relations revolves around relation keys and dependencies on these keys. Simply stated, relations should only store facts about relation keys. Thus it is important to be familiar with relation keys and the way that dependencies represent facts.

There are five normal forms. The first three normal forms concern redundancies that arise from functional dependencies. The fourth and fifth normal forms concern redundancies that arise from multi-valued dependencies.

A relation is in normal form if all its attribute values are simple. In fact all relations illustrated so far in this book have been in normal form. Figure 4.1 illustrates the difference

Figure 4.1 Normalizing a relation

ORDERS

<table>
<tr><th>ORDER-NO</th><th>ORDER-DATE</th><th colspan="2">ORDER-CONTENTS</th></tr>
<tr><td>T20</td><td>6 July 1987</td><td>ITEM
-NO

PC6
BW3
TY6</td><td>QUANTITY
-ORDERED

24
83
37</td></tr>
<tr><td>T33</td><td>20 May 1987</td><td>ITEM
-NO

PC5
BW3
TY6
HJ7</td><td>QUANTITY
-ORDERED

89
15
33
45</td></tr>
</table>

(a) A relation not in normal form

ORDERS

ORDER-NO	ORDER-DATE	ITEM-NO	QUANTITY -ORDERED
T20	6 July 1987	PC6	24
T20	6 July 1987	BW3	83
T20	6 July 1987	TY6	37
T33	20 May 1987	PC5	89
T33	20 May 1987	BW3	15
T33	20 May 1987	TY6	33
T33	20 May 1987	HJ7	45

(b) Normalized relation

between a normal relation and one that is not normal. Figure 4.1 shows two relations that contain information about orders made for parts. However, the relation in Figure 4.1(a) has one column, ORDER-CONTENTS, whose attribute values are themselves relations. Thus ORDER-NO is the number of an order, ORDER-DATE is the date on which the order was made. ORDER-CONTENTS contains all the lines in an order. Each line is for a quantity of some part.

The relation shown in Figure 4.1(b) contains the same data as the relation in Figure 4.1(a). However it does not have any attributes whose values are themselves relations and all attribute values in this relation are simple values. The relation in Figure 4.1(b) is constructed from the relation in Figure 4.1(a) by taking each row in ORDER-CONTENTS and combining it with ORDER-NO and ORDER-DATE to make a row in the relation in Figure 4.1(b). You should, however, note that the relation in Figure 4.1(b) contains redundancy as it stores the ORDER-DATE for a given order more than once.

There are of course other forms of non-normal relations. One such form is illustrated in Figure 4.2(a). Here the attribute CHARACTERISTIC stores combinations of attribute name and value. This can be reduced to the normal relation shown in Figure 4.2(b).

A relation whose attribute values are all simple is in normal form. It is at least in first normal form. However, relations in first normal form can still contain redundancies.

Figure 4.2 Normalizing PERSONS

PERSONS

PERSON-ID	DATE-OF-BIRTH	CHARACTERISTIC
PER35	7 Dec 1965	HEIGHT 173cm WEIGHT 69KG HAIR Brown
PER88	11Jan 1965	HEIGHT 170cm WEIGHT 61KG HAIR Black

(a) Non-normal form of PERSONS

PERSONS

PERSON-ID	DATE-OF-BIRTH	HEIGHT	WEIGHT	HAIR COLOR
PER35	7 Dec 1956	173	69	Brown
PER88	11 Jan 1965	170	61	Black

(b) Normal form of PERSONS

Relations with no redundancies satisfy additional requirements and are in higher normal forms. They can be in second, third or optimal (BCNF) normal forms.

Some additional terms

Two more terms are needed to define these higher normal form relations. These are prime attributes and non-prime attributes. A prime attribute in a relation is an attribute that is at least part of one relation key. A non-prime attribute is not part of any relation key. Relation WORK in Figure 3.5 has two prime attributes: PERSON-ID and PROJ-NO. It has only one non-prime attribute: TOTAL-TIME-SPENT-BY-PERSON-ON-PROJECT. Relation CONSULTATIONS in Figure 3.6 only has prime attributes. It has no non-prime attributes because each of its attributes is in at least one relation key.

SECOND NORMAL FORM RELATIONS

Being normal is not a sufficient condition for non-redundancy. For example, relation PROJECT-DATA in Figure 4.3 is normal because all its attributes take simple values. However, it contains redundancies because project budgets can be stored more than once for a given project. The reason for this redundancy is that the relation key of PROJECT-DATA is {PERSON-ID, PROJ-NO} and BUDGET is a fact about PROJ-NO only. It follows that BUDGET is functionally dependent on part of the relation key. Relations that contain facts or dependencies on part of the relation key are only in first but not second normal form. To be in second normal form (2NF), relations should not store facts about parts of a relation key. Formally to be in second normal form a relation:

- must be in first normal form; and
- all its non-prime attributes must be fully functionally dependent on each relation key.

Figure 4.3 Relation PROJECT-DATA

PROJECT-DATA

PERSON-ID	PROJ-NO	PROJECT BUDGET	TOTAL-TIME-SPENT-BY-PERSON-ON-PROJECT
P1	PROJ1	20	20
P3	PROJ1	20	16
P2	PROJ2	17	35
P2	PROJ3	84	42
P3	PROJ2	17	17
P2	PROJ1	20	83
P4	PROJ3	84	41
-	PROJ4	90	-

Relation key

Let us now see how this definition is used to explain why relation PROJECT-DATA in Figure 4.3 is not in 2NF. The relation key of PROJECT-DATA is {PERSON-ID, PROJ-NO}. Its non-prime attributes are PROJECT-BUDGET and TOTAL-TIME-SPENT-BY-PERSON-ON-PROJECT. In this relation, one non-prime attribute, TOTAL-TIME-SPENT-BY-PERSON-ON-PROJECT is fully functionally dependent on the relation key. Another non-prime attribute, PROJECT-BUDGET, is not fully functionally dependent on the whole relation key. It is only dependent on PROJ-NO, which is part of the relation key. However, the definition requires that in a relation that is in 2NF all non-prime attributes are fully functionally dependent on the relation key. For this reason, relation PROJECT-DATA is not in second normal form.

Relations in first but not second normal form can be converted into 2NF relations by decomposition. As an illustration, relation PROJECT-DATA in Figure 4.3 can be decomposed into the two relations shown in Figure 4.4. These two relations are in second normal form.

You should now attempt Exercise 4.1 to become familiar with the difference between 1NF and 2NF relations.

Figure 4.4 Decomposing relation PROJECT-DATA

PROJECTS

PROJ-NO	PROJECT-BUDGET
PROJ1	20
PROJ2	17
PROJ3	84
PROJ4	90

Relation key

WORK

PERSON-ID	PROJ-NO	TOTAL-TIME-SPENT-BY-PERSON-ON-PROJECT
P1	PROJ1	20
P3	PROJ1	16
P2	PROJ2	35
P2	PROJ3	42
P3	PROJ2	17
P3	PROJ1	83
P4	PROJ3	41

Relation key

Exercise 4.1

Which of the following relations are in 2NF and which are only in 1NF?

1. PROJECTS

PROJECT	BUDGET	START-DATE
PROJ1	70	June 83
PROJ2	63	May 84
PROJ3	82	Oct 83

2. ORDERS

ORDER-NO	ITEM-NO	QTY-ORDERED	ORDER-DATE
ORD1	17	16	OCT-80
ORD1	19	17	OCT-80
ORD2	133	8	NOV-81
ORD2	19	39	NOV-81
ORD2	111	83	NOV-81

Each order has one ORDER-DATE but may include any number of items.

3. APPLICATIONS

APPLICATION -NO	CUSTOMER -NO	CUSTOOMER -ADDRESS	DATE APPROVED
X97	Joe	CANBERRA	29 Jun 80
X99	Vicki	SYDNEY	3 May 80
Y72	Joe	CANBERRA	17 Aug 81

Each loan application is by one customer but each customer may make many applications.

4. SHOPS

SHOP-NO	ITEM-NO	DATE	QTY-SOLD
S1	MODEL2	3 Jun 70	3
S1	MODEL3	8 Jun 71	4
S2	MODEL2	3 Jun 70	4

Each shop sells a number (QTY-SOLD) of items on each day.

You should have noticed in Exercise 4.1 that any relation whose relation key contains one attribute only is always in 2NF. If the relation key has only one attribute then no other attribute can depend on part of the relation key only (as we cannot split attributes). Thus the second requirement of 2NF relations is always satisfied.

THIRD NORMAL FORM RELATIONS

Relations in second normal form can still contain redundancies. For example, consider relation PROJECTS in Figure 4.5. This relation is in second normal form. However, because a manager can manage more than one project, the relation contains redundancies because a manager's DATE-OF-BIRTH can be stored more than once.

Let us first show that PROJECTS satisfies the conditions of 2NF. The key of relation PROJECTS is PROJ-NO and PROJ-NO is a prime attribute. MANAGER and DATE-OF-BIRTH are both non-prime attributes of relation PROJECTS. Let us look at each non-prime attribute in turn. MANAGER is fully functionally dependent on the whole relation key. The non-prime attribute, DATE-OF-BIRTH is also fully functionally dependent on PROJ-NO although this may not be quite as obvious. DATE-OF-BIRTH is naturally dependent on MANAGER and MANAGER is dependent on PROJ-NO. Thus once we

Figure 4.5 Relation PROJECTS

PROJECTS

PROJ-NO	MANAGER	DATE-OF-BIRTH
P1	Joe	Jan 63
P3	Vicki	March 57
P2	Joe	Jan 63
P4	Marilyn	July 57

Relation key

know PROJ-NO we know MANAGER and once we know MANAGER then we know DATE-OF-BIRTH. In this roundabout way we know that there is only one value of the MANAGER's DATE-OF-BIRTH for each project and hence DATE-OF-BIRTH is fully functionally dependent on PROJ-NO. Now each non-prime attribute is fully functionally dependent on the relation key and relation PROJECTS is in 2NF.

A relation in second normal form does not store any facts about parts of relation keys. It can, however, still have redundancies if it stores facts about non-prime attributes. This is the case in relation PROJECTS. Here DATE-OF-BIRTH is dependent on MANAGER, which is not part of the relation key. You should note that a given manager's date of birth can be stored as many times as there are projects managed by the manager. Thus PROJECTS contains redundancies and is in second but not third normal form. Third normal form relations do not store facts about non-prime attributes. Formally a relation is in third normal form if:

- it is in second normal from, and
- it does not contain any functional dependencies between non-prime attributes.

The second condition does not hold for relation PROJECTS because DATE-OF-BIRTH is determined by MANAGER.

Relation PROJECTS can be decomposed into the two relations shown in Figure 4.6. Both of these are in third normal form.

Figure 4.6 Decomposing relation PROJECTS

PROJECTS

PROJ-NO	MANAGER
P1	Joe
P3	Joe
P2	Vicki
P4	Marilyn

Relation key

MANAGERS

MANAGER	DATE-OF-BIRTH
Joe	Jan 63
Vicki	March 57
Marilyn	July 53

Relation key

You should now do Exercise 4.2 to become familiar with the idea of third normal form relations.

Exercise 4.2

Which of the following relations are in 3NF and which are only in 2NF?

1. LIVES-IN

PERSON-ID	SUBURB	POSTCODE
P79	PAGE	2614
P63	HAWKER	2614
P95	PAGE	2614

Each person lives in one suburb and each suburb has one postcode.

2. REPAYMENTS

PERSON-ID	RECEIPT-NO	AMOUNT -RECEIVED	CUSTOMER	CUSTOMER -ADDRESS	RECEIPT -DATE
Z23	35	201.30	Joe	PAGE	3 Aug 83
Y72	39	173.12	Vicki	ARANDA	15 July 82
Z23	27	8.60	Joe	PAGE	12 Sep 83
X11	32	93.82	Joe	PAGE	22 Feb 81
Y72	41	11.91	Vicki	ARANDA	7 Apr 82

Each customer has one address and there is one customer for each account. The receipt is made out to the customer when a payment is received. Each receipt is for one account only. Each customer has one CUSTOMER-ADDRESS.

3. PAYMENTS

PERSON-ID	PAY-DATE	AMOUNT-RECEIVED	PAY-OFFICE
P79	Oct 79	612.70	X1
P79	Nov 79	612.70	X4
P63	Aug 79	715.82	X1
P63	Sept 79	715.82	X1
P63	Oct 79	715.82	X2

Persons may receive their pay at different pay offices on different dates.

Again you should note that any 2NF relation with no or one non-prime attribute is automatically in 3NF. Furthermore, any relation with no non-prime attributes is in 3NF. However, there is a problem when a relation has more than one relation key. It is possible for such relations to be in 3NF but still contain redundancies.

NORMAL FORMS AND RELATIONS WITH MANY KEYS

So far all normal forms have been illustrated with relations that have only one relation key. These definitions, of course, are also applicable to relations with more than one relation key.

Figure 4.7 A 3NF relation not in BCNF

ATTENDANCE

TEACHER	SEMESTER	SUBJECT	SECTION	ATTENDANCES
Joe	1/88	COBOL	SECTION1	35
Jenny	1/88	MATHS	SECTION1	40
Gregory	2/88	UNIX	SECTION2	33
Jenny	1/88	MATHS	SECTION2	42
Gregory	2/88	UNIX	SECTION1	47
Joe	1/88	COBOL	SECTION2	50
Joe	1/88	COBOL	SECTION3	12

However, problems arise when relations have more than one relation key. In these relations it is possible for an attribute to be part of one key but not another. By definition such an attribute is a prime attribute. This attribute can also be dependent on part of the key of which the attribute is not a part. However, 2NF and 3NF definitions formally use prime attributes. Thus the dependency of an attribute on part of a key of which the attribute is not a part is not used in the test for second normal form, because the attribute is a prime attribute. The relation is thus in 3NF although it contains a dependency on part of one relation key. The relation in Figure 4.7 illustrates this problem.

Relation ATTENDANCE in Figure 4.7 describes attendance in sections of each subject. It is assumed in this relation that each teacher teaches one subject each semester, and each subject only has one teacher each semester, although that teacher can take any number of sections. Thus:

TEACHER, SEMESTER → SUBJECT, and
SUBJECT, SEMESTER → TEACHER.

Relation ATTENDANCE has two relation keys. One key is {TEACHER, SEMESTER, SECTION} and the other is {SUBJECT, SEMESTER, SECTION}. The only non-prime attribute is ATTENDANCES. This is fully functionally dependent on each relation key and there are no dependencies between non-prime attributes, because there is only one non-prime attribute. Thus relation ATTENDANCE is in 3NF. However, relation ATTENDANCE has redundancy because the teacher for a subject in a semester can be stored more than once.

The reason for the redundancy is that an attribute (TEACHER) in one relation key is dependent on part of a key (SUBJECT, SEMESTER, SECTION) of which it is not a part. To overcome this problem it is necessary to define the optimal or the BCNF (BOYCE-CODD normal form).

BCNF

One way to redefine 3NF to cater for relations with more than one relation key is to add a condition:

- Each prime attribute will be fully functionally dependent on each key of which it is not a part.

However, there is a simpler definition. This states that:

- A relation is in BCNF (or optimal) normal form if every determinant between the relation attributes is a relation key.

Informally stated a relation is in optimal form if, whenever facts are stored about some attributes, then these attributes are a relation key.

Thus ATTENDANCE is not in BCNF because (SEMESTER, SUBJECT) is a determinant and not a relation key. Relation ATTENDANCE can be decomposed into the two relations shown in Figure 4.8.

Figure 4.8 Decomposing courses

ATTENDANCE

SEMESTER	SUBJECT	SECTION	ATTENDANCES
1/88	COBOL	SECTION1	35
1/88	MATHS	SECTION1	40
2/88	UNIX	SECTION2	33
1/88	MATHS	SECTION2	42
2/88	UNIX	SECTION1	47
1/88	COBOL	SECTION2	50
1/88	COBOL	SECTION3	12

TEACHERS

TEACHER	SEMESTER	SUBJECT
Joe	1/88	COBOL
Jenny	1/88	MATHS
Gregory	2/88	UNIX

You should now do Exercise 4.3 to see the difference between 3NF and BCNF relations.

Exercise 4.3

Which of the following relations are in 3NF and which are in BCNF?

1. MACHINE-PRODUCTION

SHIFT	MACHINE-NO	NO-ITEMS PRODUCED	MACHINE OPERATOR	DATE
FIRST	M6	60	Joe	June 7
SECOND	M6	69	Joe	June 7
THIRD	M6	72	Bill	June 7
FIRST	M5	63	Joe	June 8
SECOND	M5	58	Bill	June 8
THIRD	M5	71	Jane	June 8

Machine operators work on one machine each day and they can work more than one shift on a day. Only one machine operator uses a machine on a given shift. The number of items produced by each machine on a given shift is recorded.

OPERATOR, DATE → MACHINE
OPERATOR, DATE, SHIFT → NO-ITEMS
MACHINE, DATE, SHIFT → NO-ITEMS, OPERATOR

Exercise 4.3 (continued)

2. BUS-SCHEDULE

BUS-NO	BUS DRIVER	START TIME	DESTINATION
Z201	James	5pm 10 June	SYDNEY
Z309	Mary	5pm 10 June	MELBOURNE
Z201	Kerry	2am 12 June	CANBERRA
Z308	Mary	5pm 12 June	CANBERRA

Each driver drives a bus to its destination. There is only one driver on each trip.

BUS-NO, START-TIME → BUS-DRIVER, DESTINATION
BUS-DRIVER, START-TIME → BUS-NO, DESTINATION

Again you should note that a 3NF relation with one relation key is automatically in BCNF.

NORMAL FORMS AND MULTI-VALUED DEPENDENCIES

It is interesting to note that even BCNF relations can be redundant. All we have used to define BCNF relations is functional dependencies. It is, however, possible for redundancies to arise because of multi-valued dependencies. For example, look at Figure 4.9.

The relation in Figure 4.9 stores the PRODUCT-CLASS of sales responsibility of each representative, and the CUSTOMERS visited by that representative. Thus Joe sells Cosmetics and Haberdashery. Joe has BH Store and Union Bazaar as his customers. You should note that both a person's PRODUCT-CLASS and CUSTOMER may be stored more than once. Thus the fact that Joe has BH Stores and Union Bazaar as customers is stored twice. Yet this relation is in BCNF. It has one key only, namely, {REPRESENTATIVE, CUSTOMER, PRODUCT-CLASS}. It has no non-prime attributes and thus satisfies all the conditions for 3NF and BCNF. The reason for this redundancy is that there are more than two multi-valued dependencies in relation SALES-AREAS. These are:

Figure 4.9 RELATION SALES-AREAS

SALES-AREAS

REPRESENTATIVE	CUSTOMER	PRODUCT-CLASS
Joe	BH Store	Cosmetics
Joe	BH Store	Haberdashery
Helen	Greater Stores	Cosmetics
Helen	Greater Stores	Clothing
Helen	Greater Stores	Shoes
Joe	Union Bazaar	Cosmetics
Joe	Union Bazaar	Haberdashery
Helen	BH Store	Cosmetics
Helen	BH Store	Clothing
Helen	BH Store	Shoes

REPRESENTATIVE →→ CUSTOMER, and
REPRESENTATIVE →→ PRODUCT-CLASS

What is needed is a definition to cater for redundancies that arise from multi-valued dependencies.

Fourth normal form

A relation is in 4NF if for any multi-valued dependency X →→ Y there are no attributes other than those in X and Y.

This is not the case for SALES-AREAS. Here REPRESENTATIVE →→ CUSTOMER is a MVD but there is another attribute, PRODUCT-CLASS, in the relation. Relation SALES-AREAS can be decomposed into the two relations shown in Figure 4.10. Both of these relations are in 4NF.

Figure 4.10 Decomposing SALES-AREAS

REPRESENTATIVES

REPRESENTATIVE	PRODUCT-CLASS
Joe	Cosmetics
Joe	Haberdashery
Helen	Cosmetics
Helen	Clothing
Helen	Shoes

AREAS

REPRESENTATIVE	CUSTOMER
Joe	BH Store
Joe	Union Bazaar
Helen	BH Store
Helen	Greater Stores

Fifth normal form

For a long time 4NF served as the ultimate goal for relational design. However, it was shown that even this definition does not cover all possibilities. Suppose we now add another condition to relation SALES-AREA, namely the PRODUCT-CLASS of goods sold by a store. If BH Store does not sell Haberdashery, and Greater Stores does not sell Cosmetics then rows 2 and 3 are not needed in the relation and the result is the relation in Figure 4.11. This relation still contains redundancies but cannot be decomposed into two relations. It can, however, be decomposed into the three relations shown in Figure 4.12. It is in 4NF but not 5NF.

Figure 4.11 Relation SALES-AREAS

SALES-AREAS

REPRESENTATIVE	CUSTOMER	PRODUCT-CLASS
Joe	BH Store	Cosmetics
~~Joe~~	~~BH Store~~	~~Haberdashery~~
~~Helen~~	~~Greater Stores~~	~~Cosmetics~~
Helen	Greater Stores	Clothing
Helen	Greater Stores	Shoes
Joe	Union Bazaar	Cosmetics
Joe	Union Bazaar	Haberdashery
Helen	BH Store	Cosmetics
Helen	BH Store	Clothing
Helen	BH Store	Shoes

Figure 4.12 Decomposing SALES-AREAS

REPRESENTATIVES

REPRESENTATIVE	PRODUCT-CLASS
Joe	Cosmetics
Joe	Haberdashery
Helen	Cosmetics
Helen	Clothing
Helen	Shoes

AREAS

REPRESENTATIVE	CUSTOMER
Joe	BH Store
Joe	Union Bazaar
Helen	BH Store
Helen	Greater Stores

SELLS

CUSTOMER	PRODUCT-NEEDED
BH Store	Cosmetics
BH Store	Clothing
Greater Stores	Clothing
Greater Stores	Shoes
Union Bazaar	Cosmetics
Union Bazaar	Haberdashery
Greater Stores	Accessories

Finally, suppose we add a further constraint in that not all REPRESENTATIVES of a given PRODUCT-CLASS can sell that PRODUCT-CLASS to a store. For example, suppose we do not want both Joe and Helen to sell cosmetics to BH Store, and assign that responsibility to Joe. The result is the relation shown in Figure 4.13. This relation cannot be decomposed and is in 5NF.

Figure 4.13 Relation RESTRICTED-SALES-AREAS

SALES-AREAS

REPRESENTATIVE	CUSTOMER	PRODUCT-CLASS
Joe	BH Store	Cosmetics
~~Joe~~	~~BH Store~~	~~Haberdashery~~
~~Helen~~	~~Greater Stores~~	~~Cosmetics~~
Helen	Greater Stores	Clothing
Helen	Greater Stores	Shoes
Joe	Union Bazaar	Cosmetics
Joe	Union Bazaar	Haberdashery
~~Helen~~	~~BH Store~~	~~Cosmetics~~
Helen	BH Store	Clothing
Helen	BH Store	Shoes

SUMMARY

This chapter described normal form relations. It made a distinction between two classes of normal forms. The first class uses the idea of functional dependencies only. Its goal is to define relations that contain no redundancies of single-valued facts. Four normal forms were defined here. These were the first, second, third and Boyce-Codd normal forms. Two further normal forms were also defined. These were the fourth and fifth normal forms. These two normal forms do not include any multi-valued redundancies.

Ultimately the design goal is to ensure that all relations in a database are in the highest possible normal form. Design methods that satisfy this goal are described in the following chapters.

5

More on dependencies and relation keys

INTRODUCTION

The previous chapters described all that need be known about relations for most practical database design methodologies. Practical database design commences with a high-level model that is converted to relations close to the highest normal form. Checks like those described in the previous chapters are used to examine these relations and if necessary decompose them to BCNF. In most cases very little decomposition is needed because most relations produced by high-level analysis are in BCNF.

Functional dependencies and relation keys have many additional properties that need not be used in most practical methodologies. These properties concern derivation of relation keys from functional dependencies and derivation of functional dependencies from each other. These properties are needed in those design methodologies that use only relational analysis. They also provide a useful background in practical design through a better understanding of relational processes and better insights to the normalization process.

This chapter covers some additional properties about functional dependencies, their relationship to relation keys and how relation keys can be derived from functional dependencies. The next chapter uses these properties to describe design methods that use relational analysis only. However, if you are interested in practical design methodologies based on high-level semantic models, you can skip this chapter and the next chapter without missing any continuity.

REDUNDANT FUNCTIONAL DEPENDENCIES

In relational database design, relations are constructed from functional dependencies. Any redundant functional dependencies lead to redundancies in the relations. To avoid these redundancies, redundant functional dependencies must be removed before relations are constructed.

Redundant functional dependencies are those dependencies that can be derived from other known dependencies. For example, if it is known that:

REG-NO → MODEL, and
MODEL → NO-CYLINDERS

then we can derive:

REG-NO → NO-CYLINDERS.

This states that if we know the model of the car for a given registration number (REG-NO) and the number of cylinders for the model, then we can derive the number of cylinders for a given REG-NO. A non-redundant set of dependencies would not include any dependency that can be derived from other dependencies in the set. Such a non-redundant set would not include the dependency REG-NO → NO-CYLINDERS. Redundancies can be removed either by:

- examining the dependency diagram for redundant dependencies using a set of inference rules, or by
- using a membership algorithm.

REMOVING DEPENDENCIES BY EXAMINATION

Removal of redundant dependencies through examination uses rules that specify how one dependency can be derived from other dependencies. It turns out there there is a minimum set of such rules needed for this purpose. These rules are known as the inference rules. If we show that one FD, f1, in a set can be derived from other FDs in the set using the inference rules, then f1 is redundant.

Inference rules

There are a number of inference rules. Inference rules are defined in terms of sets of attributes. The definitions refer to such sets using capital letters such as X, Y, Z and so on. We begin by defining the more straightforward rules and then follow with the definition of some of the more complex rules. The first is the union rule.

Union

If X → Z and X → Y then X → ZY.

Figure 5.1 The union rule

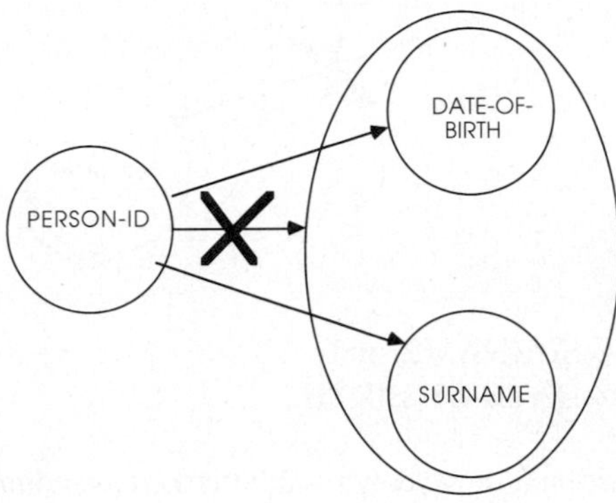

This rule is quite straightforward and is diagramatically illustrated in Figure 5.1. Here the two functional dependencies:

PERSON-ID → DATE-OF-BIRTH, and
PERSON-ID → SURNAME

are replaced by the one functional dependency

PERSON-ID → SURNAME, DATE-OF-BIRTH

This last dependency is thus redundant as shown by the cross in Figure 5.1.

Decomposition

If X → ZY then X → Z and X → Y.

The decomposition rule is opposite to the union rule. This rule states that a functional dependency with a number of attributes on the right-hand side can be replaced by several functional dependencies.

An example is given in Figure 5.2. This example is exactly the opposite of the example in Figure 5.1. Here the functional dependency

PERSON-ID → SURNAME, DATE-OF-BIRTH

is decomposed into two dependencies

Figure 5.2 The decomposition rule

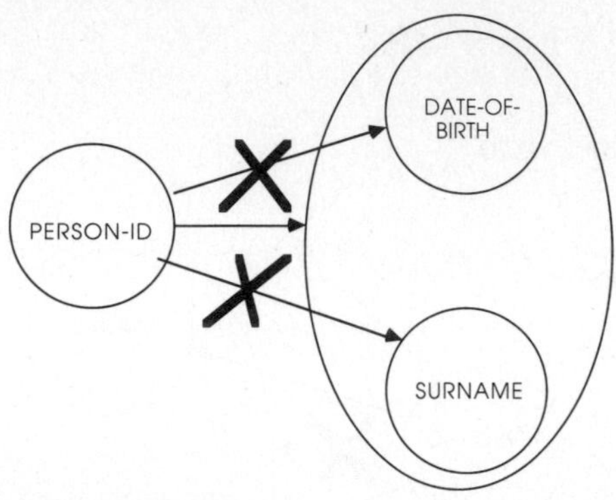

PERSON-ID → SURNAME, and
PERSON-ID → DATE-OF-BIRTH

These last two functional dependencies are marked as redundant in Figure 5.2.

There is also a word of warning to beginners to be careful and not to extend the decomposition to the determinant. It is tempting to extend the decomposition rule and state that if:

AX → Y then

A → Y and X → Y.

This is not true. For example if

PERSON-ID, PROJECT-ID → TIME-SPENT

then neither

PERSON-ID → TIME-SPENT, nor
PROJECT-ID → TIME-SPENT

are true.

Neither of these functional dependencies hold because there may be many different values of TIME-SPENT for a project. There can be a different value of TIME-SPENT for each different person on a given project. Similarly the same person may spend a different amount of time on each project. Designers must therefore remember that decomposition applies to the right-hand side and not the left-hand side of a functional dependency.

Reflexivity

The reflexivity rule states that:

If Y is a subset of X then X → Y.

The functional dependency diagram that represents this rule looks rather strange. As illustrated in Figure 5.3 it doubles back on itself, hence the name reflexivity. The example in Figure 5.3 shows that some of the attributes of a person can be determined by these attributes combined with other person attributes. This is really stating the obvious and is thus redundant.

The reflexivity rule also implies that X → X.

Figure 5.3 Reflexivity

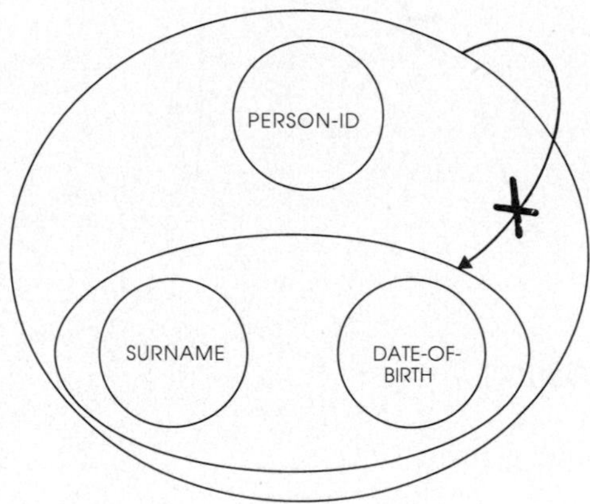

Augmentation

The augmentation rules states that:

If Z is a subset of W and X → Y THEN XW → YZ.

The augmentation rule is very similar to the reflexivity rule, except that the subset is now combined with another functional dependency. A simple example of the augmentation rule is given in Figure 5.4. Here we are given that:

ORDER-NO, PART-NO → QTY-ORDERED.

We can now choose W to be anything, say CUSTOMER. By definition, a null set is a subset of customer and hence Z is the empty set. The augmentation rule then states that:

ORDER-NO, PART-NO, CUSTOMER → QTY-ORDERED.

A more complex example is also shown in Figure 5.4. Now:

W = {CUSTOMER, CUSTOMER-ADDRESS} and

Figure 5.4 Augmentation

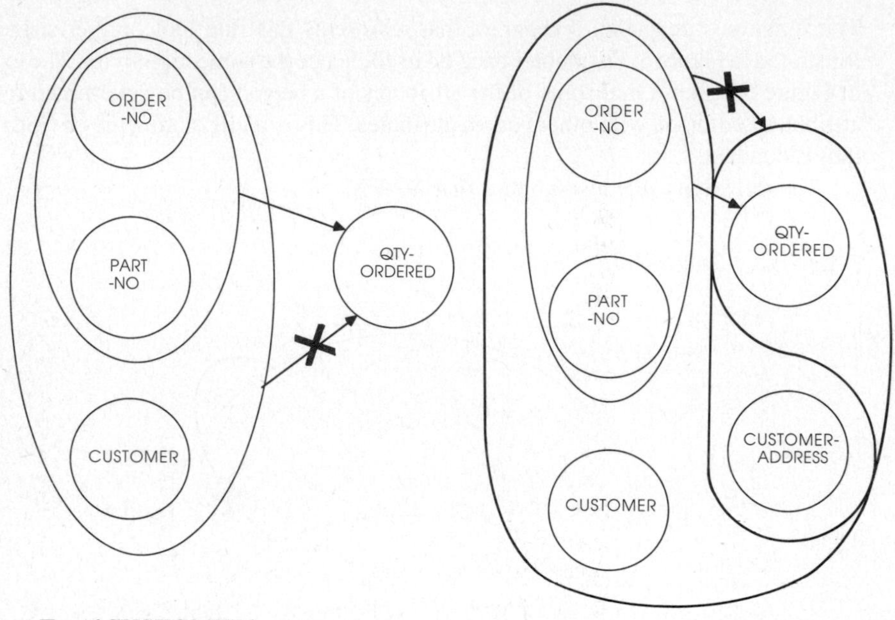

Z = {CUSTOMER}

By augmentation we get:

ORDER-NO, PART-NO, CUSTOMER, CUSTOMER-ADDRESS →
QTY-ORDERED, CUSTOMER-ADDRESS

The next rule is transitivity.

Transitivity

The transitivity rule states that:

If X → Y AND Y → Z THEN X → Z

The idea behind transitivity is illustrated in Figure 5.5 in terms of a concrete example. Here:

PERSON-ID → DATE-OF-BIRTH

DATE-OF-BIRTH → DAY-OF-WEEK

This can be used to derive:

PERSON-ID → DAY-OF-WEEK

Figure 5.5 Transitivity

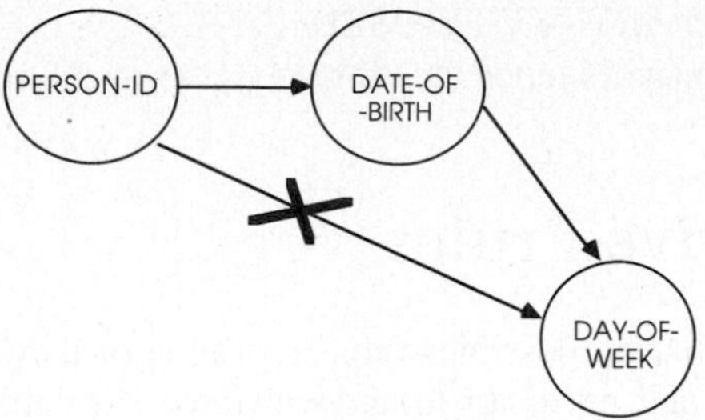

The functional dependency PERSON-ID → DAY-OF-WEEK is redundant because once we know a person's date of birth then we can tell what day of the week the person was born on.

The last of the six rules is pseudo-transitivity.

Pseudo-transitivity

The pseudo-transitivity rule states that:

If A → B AND BC → X THEN AC → X

Figure 5.6 Pseudo-transitivity

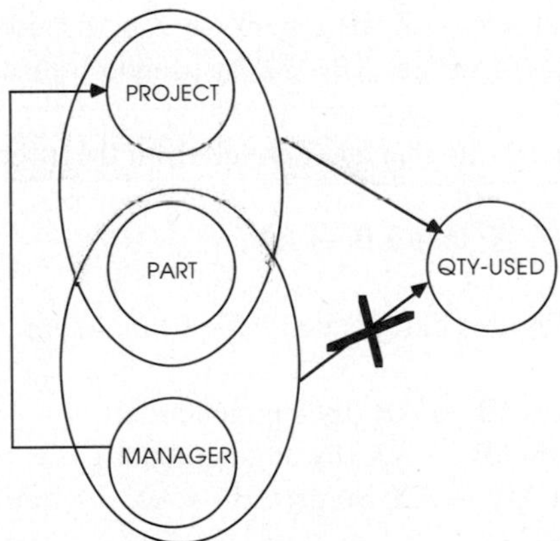

Pseudo-transitivity is illustrated in Figure 5.6 using a more concrete example. Here:

PROJECT, PART → QTY-USED
(a project uses a quantity of given parts)

and

MANAGER → PROJECT
(the project is the only project managed by the manager)

then

MANAGER, PART → QTY-USED
(the manager is reponsible for the use of quantities of given parts)

Some derived rules

You should note that it is possible to construct additional inference rules from those given above. In fact it is only necessary to start with three of the above rules, namely, reflexivity, augmentation and transitivity, and derive the other rules from them. For example, we can derive the pseudo-transitivity rule as follows:

Suppose we are given A → B and BC → X. Then from A → B we get AC → BC by augmentation, and from AC → BC and BC →. X we get AC → X by transitivity.

The reflexivity, augmentation and transitivity rules are sometimes known as the axioms as they can be used to derive all the other rules. Such other useful rules include:

- If A → B and AB → X then A → X by pseudo-transitivity, and
- If A → X and B → Y and XY → Z, then AB → Z.

The second of these rules is simply defined by a double application of the pseudo-transitivity rule as follows:

- From A → X and XY → Z we get AY → Z by pseudo-transitivity, and then from B → Y and AY → Z we get AB → Z by pseudo-transitivity.

A third commonly used rule that can derived from the inference rules is:

- If Z → A and B → X, then ZB → AX.

This rule is almost obvious but it is derivable from the inference rules as follows.

If Z → A (given) then ZB → AB (by augmentation).
If B → X (given) then AB → AX (by augmentation).
From ZB → AB and AB → AX we get ZB → AX (by transitivity).

However, again a word of warning. If you are given AB → AX then you cannot simply 'cancel' A to give B → X.

For example, if:

PERSON-ID, DEPT-NAME → PERSON-ID, DATE-STARTED

then it is not true that:

DEPT-NAME → DATE-STARTED.

Inference rules and multi-valued dependencies

It is important at this stage to point out that inference rules on functional dependencies do not carry over to multi-valued dependencies. For example, it is not true that if:

PERSON-ID →→ PROJECT, SKILL-USED then

PERSON-ID →→ PROJECT, and
PERSON-ID →→ SKILL-USED.

Here the first MVD describes the skills used on projects by persons. It is necessary for the right hand side to include pairs of SKILL-USED and PROJECT because we are determining what skills a person uses on what project. Thus we can have that:

Jill determines (PROJ1, ACCOUNTING) and (PROJ2, COMPUTING)

The decomposition tells us what project a person works on and what skills they possess. In our example, decomposition can show that:

Jill has COMPUTING and ACCOUNTING skills and
Jill works on PROJ1 and PROJ2.

The information on what skills persons apply to projects is now lost.

There is also a set of rules that have been developed for multi-valued dependencies but these are out of the scope of this text because they are not used in practice.

Examining for redundant dependencies

The general idea behind examining sets of dependencies for redundancy is to see whether a functional dependency in a set can be derived from the other functional dependencies using inference rules. If that can be done then that functional dependency is redundant.

Example

Suppose we are given the set of functional dependencies illustrated in Figure 5.7. This set is:

J → K	V → J	VY → W
KZ → W		Y → Z

VY → W is redundant because it can be derived from the other functional dependencies as follows:

V → J and J → K gives V → K by transitivity
V → K and KZ → W gives VZ → W by pseudo-transitivity
Y → Z and VZ → W gives VY → W, by pseudo-transitivity.

Figure 5.7 Applying inference rules

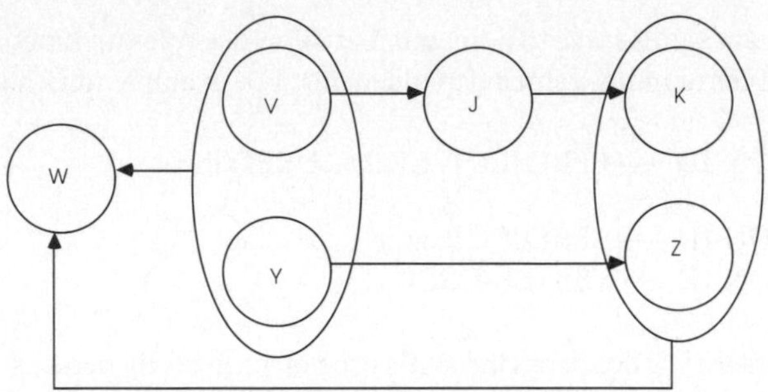

Diagramatically it can be argued that we do not need the functional dependence VY → W because there is an alternative path from VY to W. This paths goes V to K through J by transitivity and from VY to Z. Once KZ is reached then W follows.

At this stage you should attempt Exercise 5.1 to find redundant functional dependencies.

Exercise 5.1

1. Are there any redundant functional dependencies in the following FD diagram?
2. Are there any redundant functional dependencies in the following FD diagram?

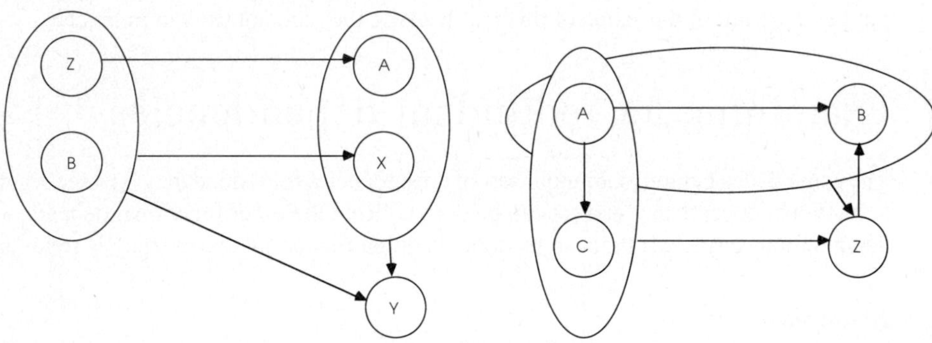

It is by now becoming apparent that it is not always easy to find a redundant functional dependence by examining a set of dependencies in this way. The way to proceed to find a redundant FD is not always clear and one can never be sure that all possibilities have been exhausted. What is needed is a method that is guaranteed to terminate while ensuring that all redundant dependencies have been detected.

This can be done using the membership algorithm.

MEMBERSHIP ALGORITHM

To see if a functional dependency X → Y (where X may be a set of attributes) is redundant, use the following steps:

Step 1 : Set variable T to X. T is a variable that can contain any number of attributes.
Step 2 : Look at each FD to see if its determinant is in T.

If it is, then enter the RHS of the FD into T. If not, then go to Step 4.

Step 3 : Every time the T is changed, repeat Step 2.
Step 4 : To see if X → Y is redundant, check if Y is in T. If it is, then X → Y is redundant.

This algorithm must be repeated in turn for each functional dependency in the set.

Example

Detect any redundant dependencies in the following set:

Z → A, ZB → X, AX → Y, ZB → Y

Each functional dependency must be tested in turn.

Is Z → A redundant?

Step 1 : T = {Z}.
Step 2 : No other FD has its determinant in T.
Step 3 : Go to step 4 as T has not changed.
Step 4 : A is not in T and hence Z → A is not redundant.

Is ZB → X redundant?

Step 1 : T = {Z,B}.
Step 2 : ZB → Y has determinant in T. Hence add Y to T and T = {Z, B, Y}.
Step 3 : Repeat step 2 as T has changed.
Step 2 : Z → A has its determinant in T. Hence add A to T and T = {Z, B, Y, A}.
Step 3 : Repeat step 2 as T has changed.
Step 2 : No other FD has its determinant in T.
Step 3 : Go to step 4 as T has not changed.
Step 4 : X is not in T and hence ZB → X is not redundant.

Is AX → Y redundant?

Step 1 : T = {A,X}.
Step 2 : No other FD has its determinant in T.

Is ZB → Y redundant?

Step 1 : T = {Z,B}.
Step 2 : Z → A has its determinant in T. Hence add A to T and T = {Z, B, A}.
Step 3 : Repeat step 2 as T has changed.
Step 2 : ZB → X has its determinant in T. Hence add X to T and T = {Z, B, A, X}.
Step 3 : Repeat step 2 as T has changed.
Step 2 : AX → Y has its determinant in T. Hence add Y to T and T = {Z, B, A, X, Y).
Step 3 : Repeat step 2 as T has changed.
Step 2 : There are no more FDs to list.
Step 3 : Go to step 4 as T has not changed.
Step 4 : Y is in T and hence ZB → Y is redundant.

Some points about the membership algorithm

1. Note that once T has changed you must look at all the remaining functional dependencies again — even if you have looked at them before.
2. The order in which functional dependencies are examined is not important.
3. You can terminate once the right-hand side of the functional dependency under test becomes part of T.
4. Remember that if you have a functional dependency with two attributes on the right-hand side, you should split up into two functional dependencies and test them one by one.

   Thus A → XY
   becomes A → X and
   A → Y

   and each is tested as a separate functional dependency.

5. After a while you should be able to apply the membership algorithm quickly using a shorthand method. For example, go back to the previous example and take ZB → Y.

T = ZB	A	X	Y	stop
start	add A because Z → A and Z is in T	add X because ZB → X and ZB is in T	add Y because AX → Y and AX is in T	as RHS of ZB → Y is in T and hence ZB → Y is redundant

Exercise 5.2

Find any redundant functional dependencies in each of the following sets.

Set 1	K → MNB	W → J
	J → M	N → W
Set 2	XY → Z	VY → Z
	V → WX	W → Y
Set 3	KL → B	HD → I
	B → C	FG → KI
	G → LH	C → D
	D → KC	
Set 4	AB → CE	BD → A
	F → C	A → D
	FA → E	CD → F
	E → B	

MINIMAL SETS

Often there is more than one redundant functional dependency in a set of functional dependencies. However, it is not possible to remove both of these dependencies from the set because each is redundant only if the other one remains in the set. In that case there is more than one minimal set.

For example, take the set:

BJ → K, K → W, BJ → W, W → K

Here you will find both BJ → K and BJ → W are redundant. However, once BJ → K is removed from the set then BJ → W is no longer redundant. Similarly, if BJ → W is removed from the set then BJ → K is no longer redundant.

Thus there are two sets with no redundant dependencies:

1. BJ → K, K → W and W → K

   and

2. BJ → W, K → W and W → K.

Exercise 5.3

Find minimal sets of functional dependencies for the following sets.

1.	AB → JC J → K	KA → CJ KJ → B
2.	XY → WZ X → K B → Z	WK → BYX WZ → B
3.	QT → U UM → S PQR → ST	SU → T QS → U PT → M
4.	JX → WS B → SX	W → B JB → W
5.	AC → D AE → DC A → X	DX → WE CE → W EX → DA
6.	B → C C → D D → B	CE → A BE → A
7.	JX → B WY → B JW → B	W → X X → W YX → B

Another important definition here is the closure. This is all the dependencies that can be derived from a given set of dependencies. Finally there is the covering, which is the set of all dependencies that can be derived from an initial set using the inference rules.

A WAY TO FIND RELATION KEYS

We now turn to the other important property of relations, namely relation keys. In Chapter 4 relation keys were needed to determine the normal form of a relation. In that chapter relation keys were determined by an examination of the relation given the properties of the information. It is also possible to determine the relation key directly from functional dependencies.

There is an algorithm that can determine a relation key from FDs. This algorithm is illustrated by applying it to the following set of FDs:

$$R = (\{A, B, C, D\}, \{AB \rightarrow C, C \rightarrow D, CB \rightarrow AD, D \rightarrow A\})$$

Algorithm for determining relation keys

The algorithm for deriving relation keys from dependencies is illustrated in Figure 5.8 together with an example. It is made up of the following three steps:

Figure 5.8 Finding relation keys

STEPS USED TO FIND RELATION KEY	EXAMPLE R= ((A, B, C, D), (AB → C, C → D, CB → AD, D → A))
LIST ALL FUNCTIONAL DEPENDENCIES (Include given dependencies as well as any dependencies that can be derived from the given dependencies.)	AB → C C → D CB → AD D → A AB → D BD → C
CREATE A BASE SET OF ALL DETERMINANTS	A, B, C, D
ELIMINATE ATTRIBUTES FROM THE BASE SET. (Any attribute that can be found from other attributes is eliminated from the base set.)	A, B, C, D AB → C: A, B, D C → D: A, B, C D → A: B, C, D A, B, D — AB → D → A, B A, B, C — AB → C → A, B B, C, D — CB → D → B, C

1. List all the functional dependencies between attributes in a relation. This must include any given FDs and any FDs that can be derived from the given FDs.

   [Example: AB → C, C → D, CB → AD, D → A, AB → D, BD → C]

   Note that AB → D and BD → C has been added because it is derived.

2. Create a base set of attributes that is made up of all the determinants of the FDs and any attributes that do not appear in any FD.

   [Example: BASE SET = {ABCD}]

   The base set will also include any attributes that do not appear in any dependency and any attributes that appear in a multi-valued dependency.

3. Eliminate any attributes that can be derived from other attributes in the base set. The new set becomes the new base set.

   Note that there can be more than one elimination sequence. Each such sequence may lead to a different relation key. Two such sequences are shown in Figure 5.8.

   Any attributes that cannot be removed from the base set become the relation key. Thus the relation R has two relation keys, AB and BC.

It is important to note here that all functional dependencies are used in the elimination step. All of these FDs are derived in step 1.

Exercise 5.4

Find the relation keys for the following relations

1. R1 = ({P,Q,R,S}, {PQ → R, R → S})
2. R2 = ({X,Y,Z,W}, {XY → Z, XZ → Y, Y → W})
3. R3 = ({K,L,M,N}, {KL → M, MN → K})
4. R4 = ({J,K,L,M,N}, {JKM → NL, JKN → LM, M → N})
5. R5 = ({A,B,C,D,E,F}, {AB → C, DE → F, F → D, BE → A})
6. R6 = ({F,G,H,I,J}, {FG → H, IJ → H, F → IG, G → JF})
7. R7 = ({A,B,C,D,E}, {AB → C, BC → AD, EC → AB})
8. R8 = ({P,Q,R,S,T}, {PQ → T, T → RS, RS → PQ})

FINDING THE HIGHEST NORMAL FORM OF RELATIONS

Finally the methods described above can be used to formally define a set of steps that can determine the highest normal form of a relation. These are:

1. List all the functional dependencies between attributes in a relation. This includes the given and derived dependencies.
2. Find all the relation keys of a relation.
3. List the prime and non-prime attributes.

4. Are all non-prime attributes fully functionally dependent on each relation key?
   If NO then the relation is 1NF only.
   STOP HERE
   If YES then the relation is at least 2NF. Continue with step 5 to see if normal form higher than 2NF.
5. Are there any functional dependencies between the non-prime attributes?
   If YES then relation is 2NF only.
   STOP HERE
   If NO then relation is at least 3NF. Continue with step 6 to see if normal form is BCNF.
6. If the relation has one relation key then it is in BCNF.
   If it has more than one relation key then do step 7.
7. Are all the determinants found in step 1 also relation key?
   If YES then relation is in BCNF.
   If NO then it is 3NF only.

Exercise 5.5

What is the highest normal form for the following relations?

R1 = ({X,Y,Z,W}, {XY → Z, Z → W})
R2 = ({A,B,C,D}, {AB → C, CD → A})
R3 = ({J,K,L,M,N}, {JKM → NL, JKN → LM})
R4 = ({D,E,F,G,H}, {DEF → G, GH → E, E → H, G → DF, H → F})
R5 = ({ J,K,L,M,N}, {JKM → NL, JKN → LM, M → N})

SUMMARY

This chapter described some of the more advanced issues about functional dependencies and relation keys. You will find that you will not often need to use them. Most practical problems reduce system data into forms that are close to relational using the semantic analysis techniques that are described in the following chapters. All you need to do is check these relations to see if they are BCNF. The methods described in Chapter 4 are sufficient here.

However, the ideas outlined in this chapter should answer many problems that arise in more complex situations.

6

Designing normal relations

INTRODUCTION

The previous chapters defined the goal of relational design. This goal is to construct a set of normal relations that represent user data. The next step is to define the methods that can be used to construct such normal relations. One set of such methods is defined in this chapter.

Design methods can be divided into two kinds. First there are purely relational design methods. Then there are methods that use high-level semantic models. This chapter will describe the relational design methods. Chapter 7 will begin a description of methods based on semantic modeling.

You should note that most practical design methodologies start with high-level semantic analysis rather than relational design. They first identify major system entities. They then associate attributes with these entities and perhaps if needed decompose them. Then relational design is used to normalize the relations derived from the entities.

Nevertheless relational design can sometimes be used on its own without starting with high-level analysis. One case is where the system is small and well defined. It is possible to start here with dependencies and use them to construct relations. The other is where semantic analysis defines groups of attributes. Relational design can then be used to decompose these attributes into normal relations.

Furthermore, even though most practical methodologies start with semantic modeling, the methods described in this chapter will give designers a stronger relational knowledge and thus indirectly improve their understanding of the design process.

However, some practitioners, especially those who are interested in high-level models may wish to skip this and the previous chapter.

The remainder of this chapter describes relational design. Relational design begins by identifying rules in the system and then constructing data dependencies from these rules. These dependencies are then used to construct normal relations.

Once data dependencies are derived, design can proceed in one of two ways: by synthesis or by decomposition. In synthesis, relations are constructed from the functional dependencies. In decomposition, the functional dependencies are used to decompose relations.

RULES AND DEPENDENCIES

The first step in relational design is to find out rules about a system and construct data dependencies from these rules. Rules are simple statements that describe system structure and behavior. Examples of rules include:

- A person has one surname.
- A person works in one department.
- A person is identified by a unique value of PERSON-ID.
- A department has a unique name and one address.

Although the idea behind rules is quite simple it is not always straightforward to find a set of rules that can be easily used in relational design. The main reason for this is that no standards exist for business rules specification. Consequently business rules are of varying levels of complexity. Thus there may be rules that simply state functional dependencies, as for example:

A person has one SURNAME.

There may also be rules that specify more complexity, as for example:

A person applies all their skills to an internal project.

Thus business rules must often be analyzed before they can be used in design. The analysis may require a decomposition of some rules into simpler rules until each rule corresponds to a single dependency. Such rules can then be used in relational design to define relations. These relations are then examined to see if they satisfy normal form conditions, and if not, then they are decomposed into normal form relations. Thus the rules in the example can be used to construct the relation:

PERSONS(PERSON-ID, SURNAME, DEPT-NAME, DEPT-ADDRESS)

This relation is then decomposed into the two relations:

PERSONS(PERSON-ID, SURNAME, DEPT-NAME)
DEPARTMENTS(DEPT-NAME, DEPT-ADDRESS)

An alternative approach is to first use the business rules to construct a dependency diagram and then construct relations from this diagram.

Dependency diagrams

The dependency diagram shows the functional and multi-valued dependencies between attributes.

Figure 6.1 is a simple example of a functional dependency diagram. It shows the attribute PERSON-ID with arrows to all attributes that are functionally dependent on PERSON-ID.

Figure 6.1 Dependencies on one attribute

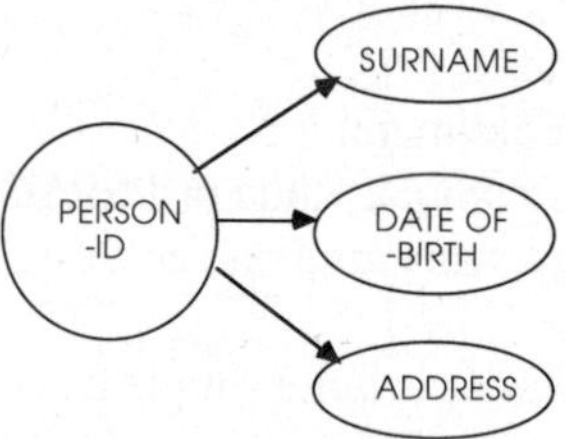

Multi-valued dependencies can also be shown on dependency diagrams. They are shown by double arrows as that in Figure 6.2. Here SKILL is a multi-valued dependency on PERSON-ID because a person can have many skills.

Dependency diagrams can of course include many dependencies. These dependencies may be on one attribute or on many attributes. Figure 6.3 shows a dependency diagram that has many dependencies. It shows that a person has one ADDRESS and DATE-OF-BIRTH. It also shows that a project has one BUDGET and that PERSON-ID and PROJECT-ID determine a unique value of TIME-SPENT. The dependency diagram in Figure 6.3 also includes two multi-value dependencies. One is that a person has many skills and the other that a project uses many parts.

Figure 6.2 Multi-valued dependency

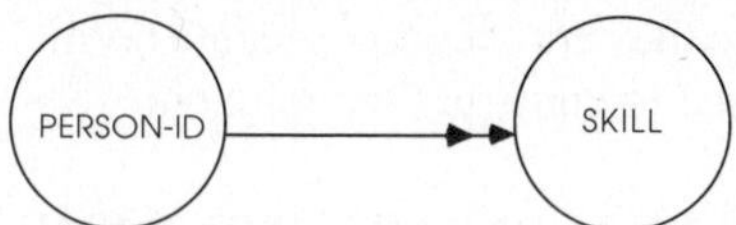

Figure 6.3 Combining a number of dependencies

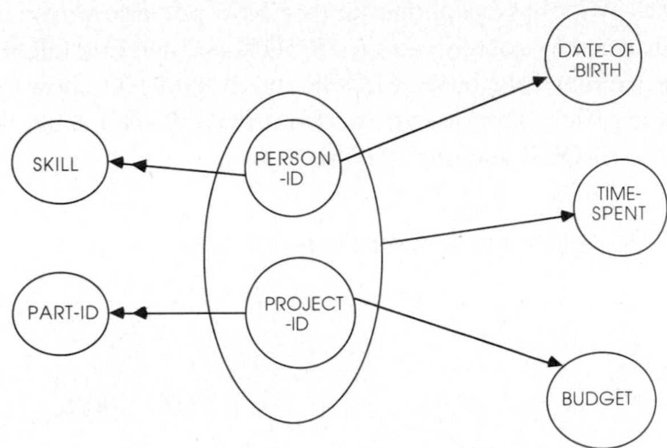

Some dependency diagram techniques

There are number of techniques used in drawing dependency diagrams. One is that each attribute appears at most once on a dependency diagram. Other techniques are used to simplify the dependency diagram. For example, Figure 6.4(a) shows a diagramming technique that combines attributes determined by some other attribute into one circle. This reduces the number of circles in the dependency diagram. However, this idea should not be extended to combining attributes that determine other attributes as shown in Figure 6.4(b). Now it becomes difficult to add dependencies on any one of the attributes in the circle.

Figure 6.4 Modeling techniques

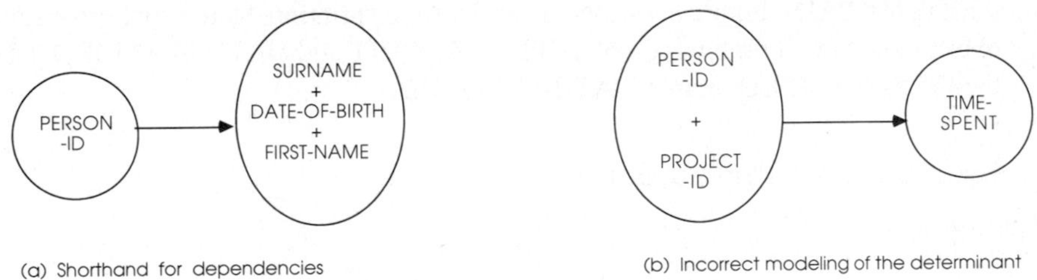

(a) Shorthand for dependencies

(b) Incorrect modeling of the determinant

One-to-one dependencies

One-to-one dependencies can also be shown on dependency diagrams. Figure 6.5(a), for example, shows a one-to-one dependency between managers and projects. Here each project has one manager and each manager manages one project. This one-to-one dependency is shown by the double-headed arrow in Figure 6.5(a). Another case of a one-to-one dependency is shown in Figure 6.5(b). Here each phone number applies to one office and each office has one phone number. Now a double arrow cannot be used because offices are identfied by a combination of ROOM-NO and FLOOR. The arrow to PHONE-NO from the combined attributes, FLOOR and ROOM-NO, show that one phone number appears in one office. The two arrows from PHONE-NO show that that PHONE-NO appears on one FLOOR and one ROOM-NO.

Figure 6.5 Modeling one-to-one dependencies

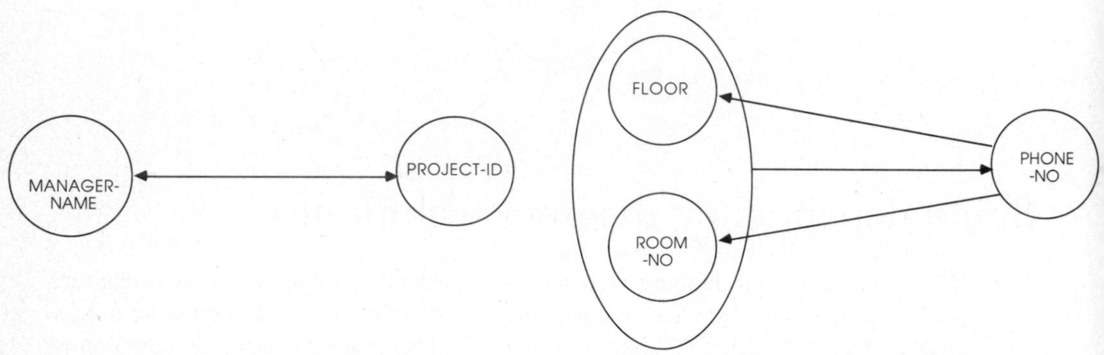

(a) A project has one manager only and one manger manages one project only.

(b) Each room has one phone only and one phone number applies to one room only.

Modeling time variations

Dependencies on time appear in many systems and must be modeled by dependency diagrams. Figure 6.6 shows one such model, where a person identified by a PERSON-ID is paid over time. Here the PERSON-ID and PAY-DATE determine a given value of AMOUNT-PAID. Figure 6.7 shows a similar time variation. Here suppliers supply parts over time. Now a combination of SUPPLIER, PART and DATE-SUPPLIED determine the QTY-SUPPLIED on that DATE-SUPPLIED.

Figure 6.6 Modeling paydates

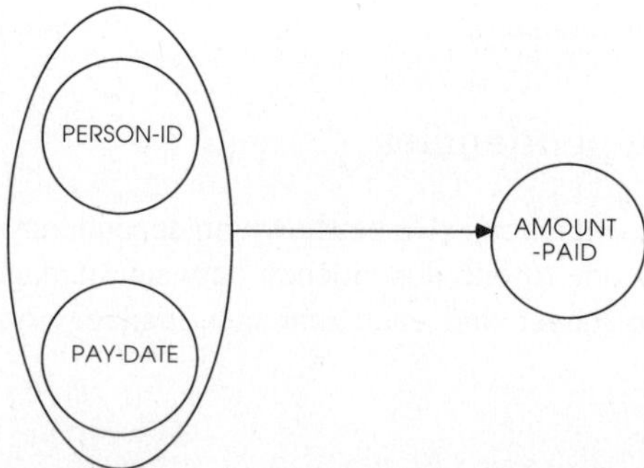

Figure 6.7 Modeling deliveries

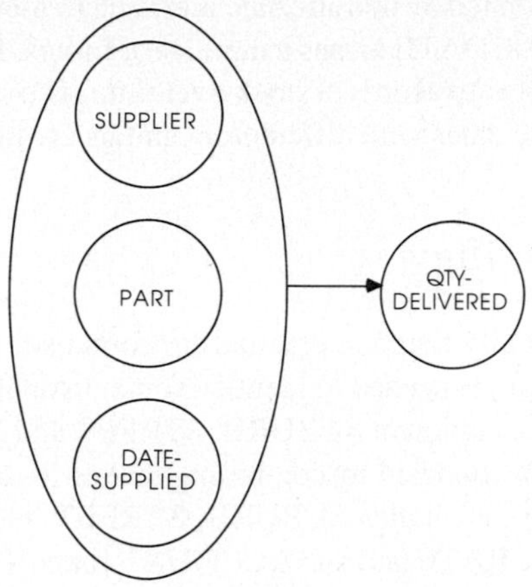

Figure 6.8 Correct modeling of dates

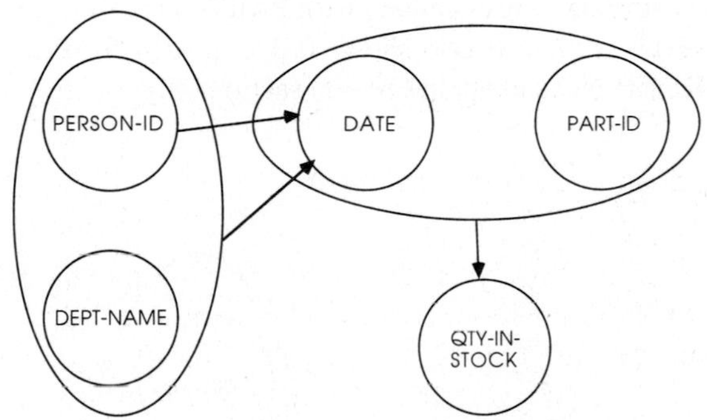

(a) Incorrect model

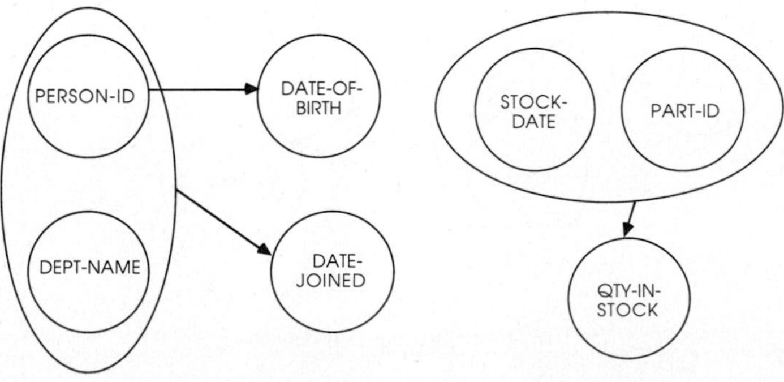

(b) Correct model

One important thing to remember about modeling time is not to use just one attribute for time. For example, the type of FD diagrams shown in Figure 6.8(a) should be avoided. Here DATE is represented by one attribute and used to model a number of dependencies. The one representation DATE means a number of things. It is persons' birth-dates, dates of joining department and records of stock over time. The correct representation is shown in Figure 6.8(b). Here dates with different meanings are modeled by different attributes.

Composite identifiers

Another thing commonly found in practice are composite identifiers. These occur when more than one attribute is needed to identify some distinct object. For example, a house is identified by a combination of SUBURB, STREET and NUMBER. Any dependencies on this object must be modeled by combining the attributes of the composite identifier. Thus in Figure 6.9(a), attributes SUBURB, STREET and NUMBER are combined to show that there is one RATE and one ACCOUNT for each house. The figure also shows that each account is for one house and the amount paid against each account on a given date.

Another example of a composite identifier is shown in Figure 6.9(b). Here a combination of DEPARTMENT and SECTION identify a unique section in the organization. These two attributes are combined with PART-ID to show the quantity of a given part needed by each section. It also shows orders placed for the parts. Each order is identified by ORDER-NO and applies to one section only.

Figure 6.9 Modeling composite identifiers

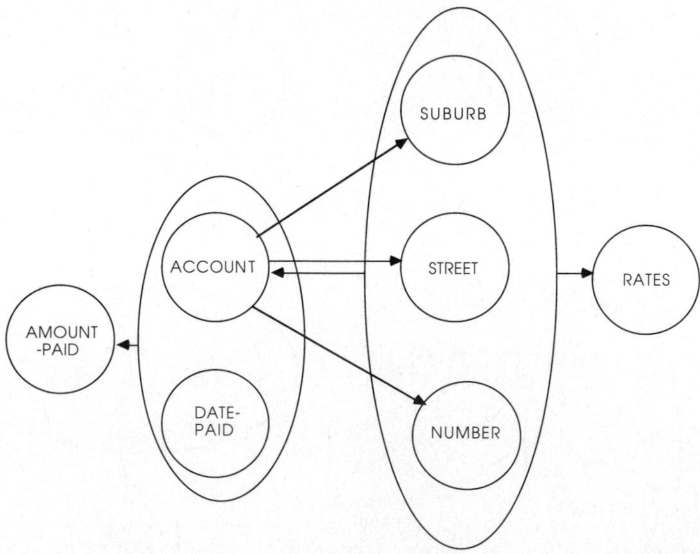

(a) Using addresses as an identifier

Figure 6.9 (continued)

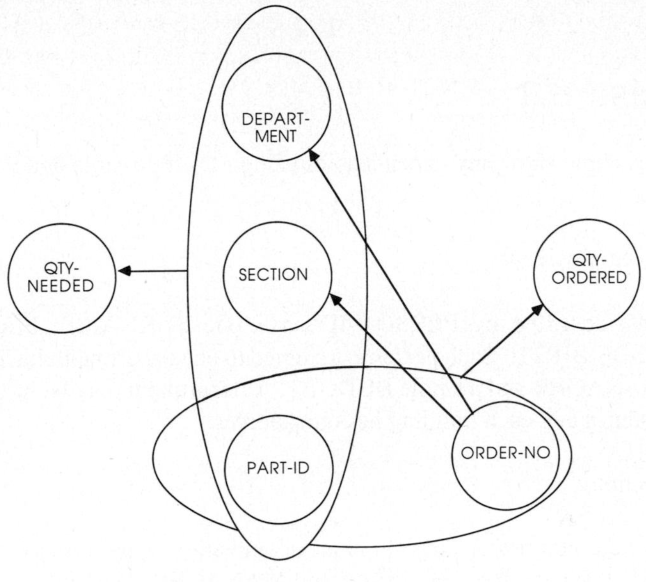

(b) Sections within departments

Figure 6.10 Difference between FDs and MVDs

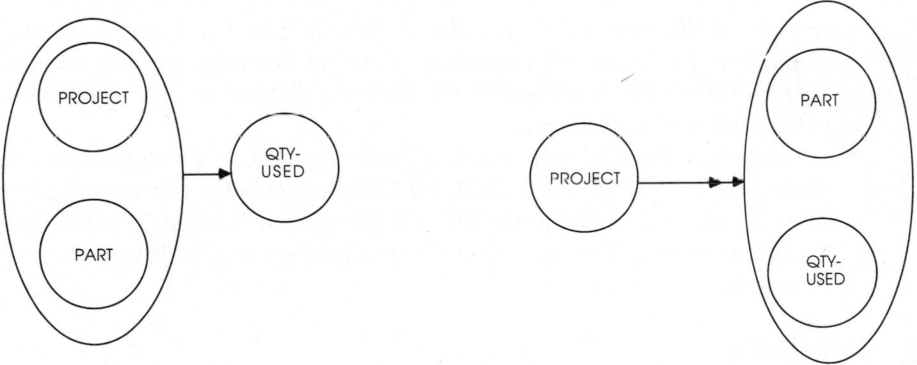

FDs and MVDs in dependency diagrams

You should also recall from Chapter 5 that FDs should be used in preference to MVDs in dependency diagrams. Thus suppose each project uses a given QTY-USED of a given part. This dependence can be shown using the two alternative ways shown in Figure 6.10. Figure 6.10(a) shows a functional dependence, whereas Figure 6.10(b) shows a multi-valued dependence. The rule is to always use the functional dependence in preference to multi-valued dependencies on a dependency diagram.

Exercise 6.1 includes some examples that will help you become more familiar with dependency diagrams.

Exercise 6.1

For each example show any dependencies using FDs if possible and then add MVDs if necessary.

1. Person employment

   Persons identified by PERSON-ID have one SURNAME, FIRST-NAME and DATE-OF-BIRTH. Each person is assigned to one department. Each department has one MANAGER and a single BUDGET. A department may be located in a number of buildings and each building has one address.

2. Requisitions

   There are a number of projects in an organization. Each project is identified by a PROJECT-ID and has a BUDGET and MANAGER. Each project is made up of a number of tasks, identified by TASK-NAME within the project. Each task has a START-DATE.

   Tasks make any number of requisitions for parts. Each requisition is identified by a REQ-NO and is made on a given DATE-MADE. Each requisition is for a number of parts, identified by PART-ID. The QTY-NEEDED of each part is entered in the requisition. Each part in a requisition is ordered from one supplier, identified by SUPPLIER-NAME, at a given PRICE. Different parts in the same requisition can be ordered from different suppliers.

   Deliveries made by suppliers are identified by DEL-NO within supplier and are made at a given DATE-DELIVERED. Each delivery may contain any number of parts. The delivery will state the REQ-NO for the parts and the QTY-DELIVERED for that requisition. Thus parts requested in a delivery may be delivered in a number of separate deliveries.

3. Deliveries

   Deliveries identified by DEL-NO are made to customers. Each customer may have a number of addresses. Each delivery is to one customer at one customer address and there may be many parts in each delivery. There is a QTY-DELIVERED of each part, and each part has one WEIGHT and can have many COLORs. There is one truck (identified by REG-NO) used in each delivery, and one driver (identified by DRIVER-NAME) makes a delivery. Each customer has a unique CUSTOMER-NAME and each part can be identified by PART-NO.

CONSTRUCTING RELATIONS FROM DEPENDENCY DIAGRAMS

Dependency diagrams can be used to construct normal relations. Some simple rules for constructing relations from functional dependency diagrams are shown in Figure 6.11.

Figure 6.11 Some basic conversion rules

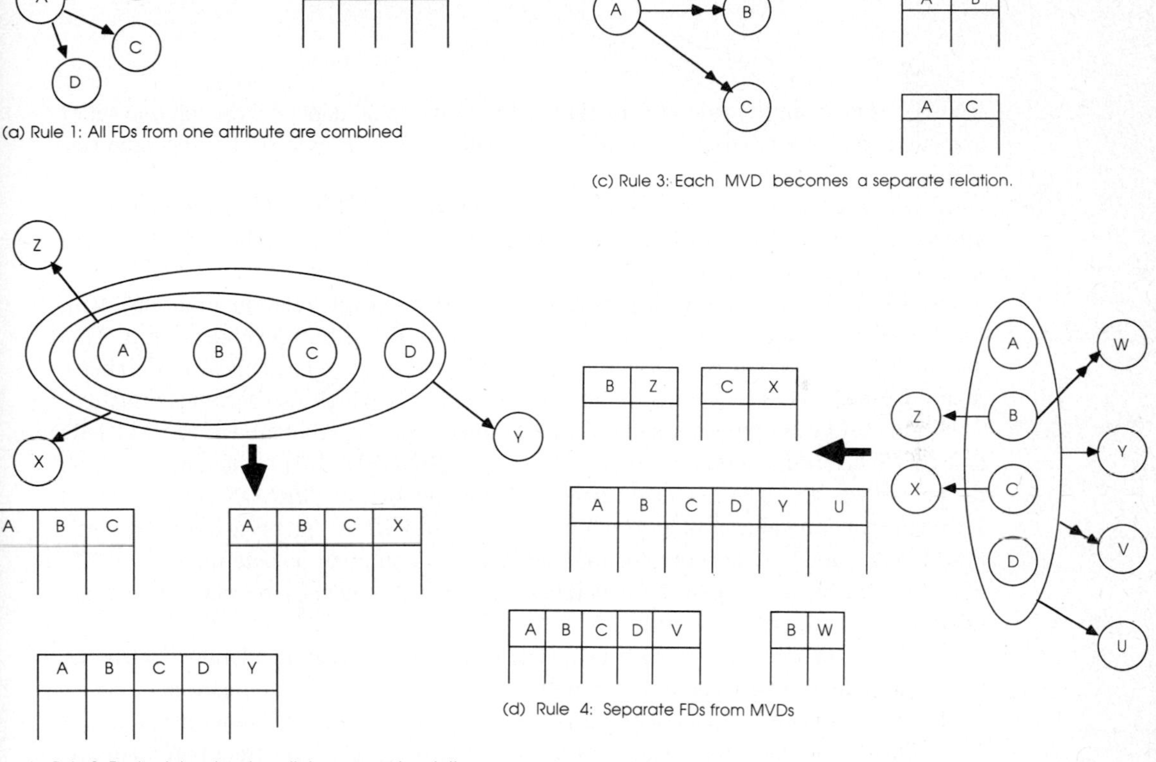

Figure 6.12 Example of Rule 1

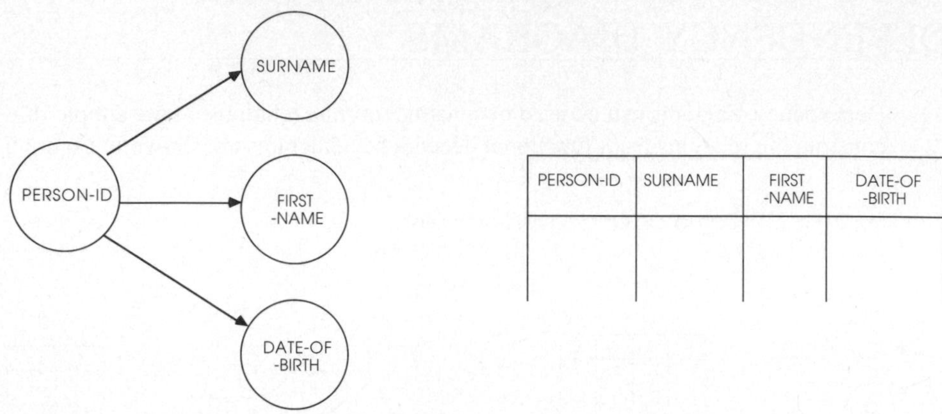

RULE 1 is the simplest rule. It is to place all the functional dependencies on one set of attributes into one relation. Thus all the dependencies in Figure 6.11(a) become one relation.

Figure 6.12 shows an application of this rule. Here PERSON-ID determines three attributes: SURNAME, FIRST-NAME and DATE-OF-BIRTH. All these attributes are used to construct one relation.

RULE 2 requires that each determinant results in a separate relation. Figure 6.11(b), for example, contains three determinants. One is (A, B) with Z dependent on it. This becomes one relation. Another is (A, B, C) with X dependent on it. This also becomes a relation. Finally there is (A, B, C, D) with the dependent Y which also becomes a relation.

Figure 6.13 is an application of this rule. It shows that a combination of PERSON-ID and DEPT determine a unique value of DATE-ASSIGNED. This is the date on which the person was assigned to the department. A combination of PERSON-ID, DEPT and JOB determines a value of time spent on a department JOB by that person. Finally when PART-NO is added to the combination, then the new combination determines the QTY of parts used by that person on that job. Each such dependency becomes a separate relation.

RULE 3 is to convert each multi-valued dependency to a separate relation. Each of the two multi-valued dependencies in Figure 6.11(c) becomes a separate relation.

Figure 6.14 is an application of this rule. Here PERSON-ID determines many values of ADDRESS but also many values of SKILL. This is used to construct two relations. One shows the persons ADDRESSes, and the other shows their SKILLs.

RULE 4 is to separate functional and multi-valued dependencies on the same attributes into different relations. This is illustrated in Figure 6.11(d). In this figure there are two dependencies on B. One is a functional dependency to Z and the other a multi-valued dependency to W. These two dependencies do not appear in the same relation but are converted to two separate relations. Similarly (A, B, C, D) has functional and multi-valued dependencies emanating from it. The functional dependencies are converted to one relation. Each multi-valued dependency is then converted to a separate relation.

Figure 6.15 illustrates an application of this rule. Note that the dependency of SKILL and SURNAME on PERSON-ID has been split into two relations, because one is

Figure 6.13 Example of Rule 2

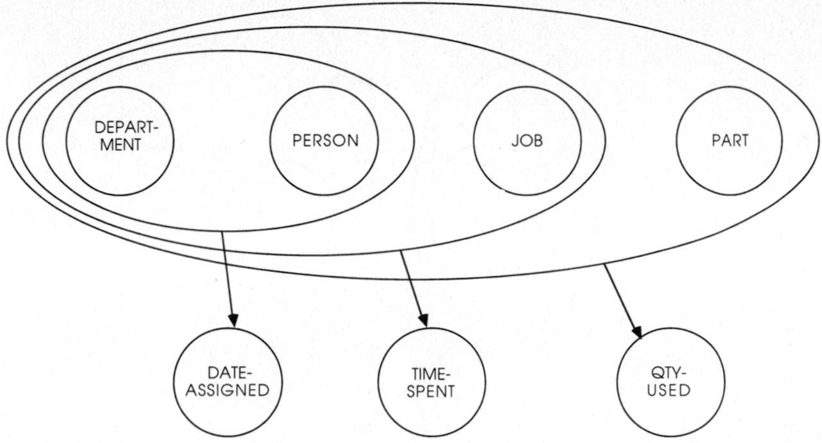

DEPARTMENT	PERSON	DATE -ASSIGNED

DEPARTMENT	PERSON	JOB	TIME -SPENT

DEPARTMENT	PERSON	JOB	PART	QTY-USED

Figure 6.14 Example of Rule 3

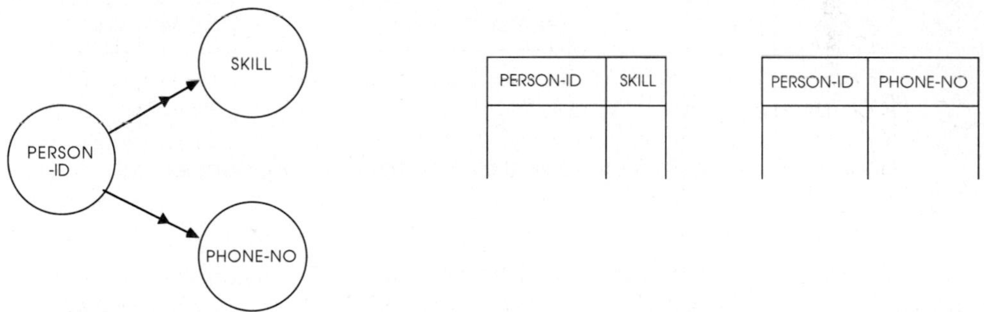

a multi-valued dependency and the other a functional dependency. Similarly the dependencies on PROJECT-NO have become two relations.

What has been described so far in the conversion is relatively straightforward. However, there are many pitfalls in these conversion rules. One is to avoid redundant dependencies because they can result in non-normal relations. For example, in Figure 6.16 the dependency

PERSON-ID → DEPARTMENT-ADDRESS

is redundant.

Figure 6.15 Example of Rule 4

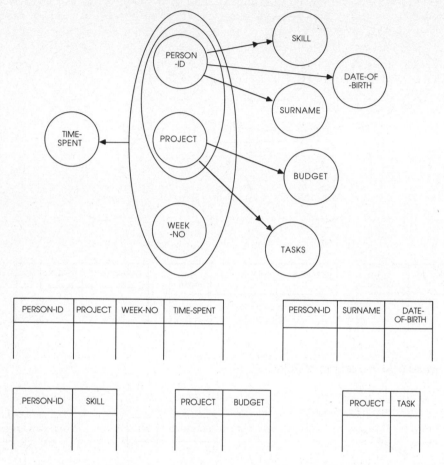

PERSON-ID
PROJECT
WEEK-NO
TIME-SPENT
SKILL
DATE-OF-BIRTH
SURNAME
BUDGET
TASKS

PERSON-ID	PROJECT	WEEK-NO	TIME-SPENT

PERSON-ID	SURNAME	DATE-OF-BIRTH

PERSON-ID	SKILL

PROJECT	BUDGET

PROJECT	TASK

Figure 6.16 Redundancy caused by redundant dependencies

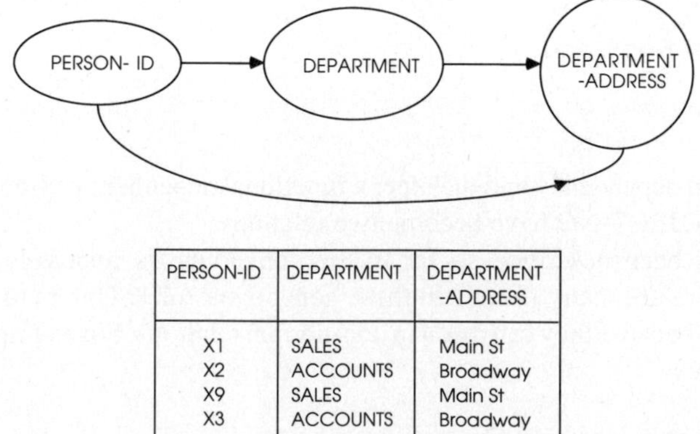

PERSON-ID	DEPARTMENT	DEPARTMENT -ADDRESS
X1	SALES	Main St
X2	ACCOUNTS	Broadway
X9	SALES	Main St
X3	ACCOUNTS	Broadway

As a result, the relation derived from PERSON-ID as a determinant is not in BCNF. It has a dependency between non-prime attributes and is in 2NF only. To avoid this kind of redundancy it is necessary to remove redundant FDs from the set of FDs used to construct relations. This can be done using the techniques described in Chapter 5.

The other pitfall is what is known as equivalent keys, illustrated in Figure 6.17. Here DEPARTMENT and MANAGER are equivalent keys. The following two relations are constructed from this diagram using the above rules.

DEPARTMENTS(DEPARTMENT, MANAGER, DEPARTMENT-ADDRESS)
MANAGERS(MANAGER, DEPARTMENT, DATE-OF-BIRTH)

Figure 6.17 Redundancy caused by equivalent keys

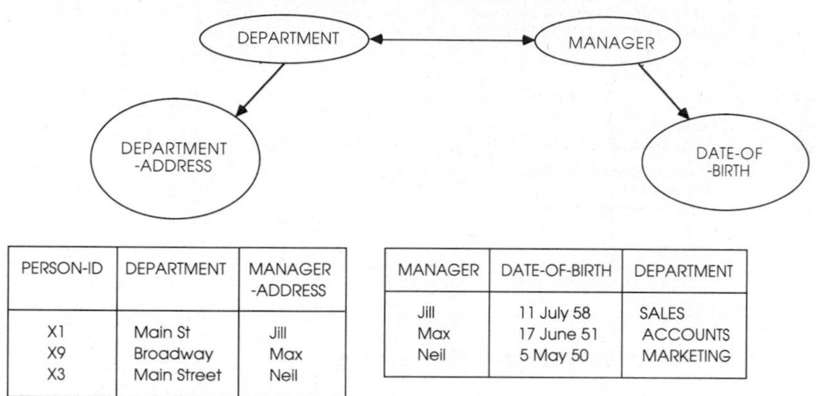

PERSON-ID	DEPARTMENT	MANAGER -ADDRESS
X1	Main St	Jill
X9	Broadway	Max
X3	Main Street	Neil

MANAGER	DATE-OF-BIRTH	DEPARTMENT
Jill	11 July 58	SALES
Max	17 June 51	ACCOUNTS
Neil	5 May 50	MARKETING

These relations store the manager of each department twice, once in each relation.

To remove such redundancies, groups of functional dependencies, dependent on equivalent keys, are often combined to produce one relation only. If this is done in the case of Figure 6.12, then functional dependencies on DEPARTMENT and MANAGER are all converted to the one relation, namely:

DEPARTMENTS(DEPARTMENT, MANAGER, DATE-OF-BIRTH, DEPARTMENT-ADDRESS)

The question is whether an algorithm can be produced to derive a set of relations from a set of FDs. Bernstein [1975] showed an algorithm that can convert a set of FDs to a minimal set of 3NF relations. The idea of this algorithm is illustrated in Figure 6.18. The first step is to find equivalent keys and place all FDs about equivalent keys permanently in the minimal FD set. Any other FDs can then be removed if they are redundant.

To see why FDs about equivalent keys must be in the minimal set, consider the set of FDs in Figure 6.19. Here it can be shown that AB and XY are equivalent keys. $XY \rightarrow AB$ is given and so is $AB \rightarrow X$. However, $AB \rightarrow Y$ is not in the given set. It can, however, be derived from the set as follows:

$AB \rightarrow P \rightarrow C \rightarrow Y$

Figure 6.18 An algorithm for finding a minimal set of 3NF relations

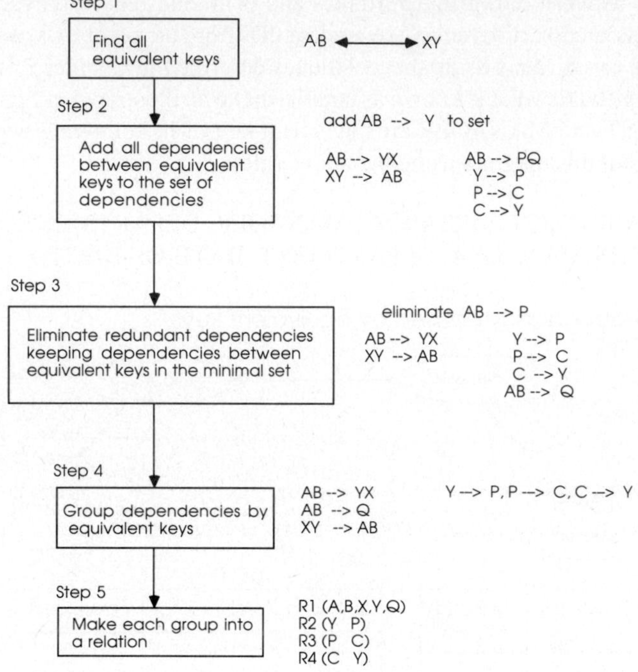
Step 1
Find all equivalent keys
AB ⟷ XY
Step 2
Add all dependencies between equivalent keys to the set of dependencies
add AB --> Y to set
AB --> YX
XY --> AB
AB --> PQ
Y --> P
P --> C
C --> Y
Step 3
Eliminate redundant dependencies keeping dependencies between equivalent keys in the minimal set
eliminate AB --> P
AB --> YX
XY --> AB
Y --> P
P --> C
C --> Y
AB --> Q
Step 4
Group dependencies by equivalent keys
AB --> YX
AB --> Q
XY --> AB
Y --> P, P --> C, C --> Y
Step 5
Make each group into a relation
R1 (A,B,X,Y,Q)
R2 (Y P)
R3 (P C)
R4 (C Y)

Figure 6.19 Set of functional dependencies

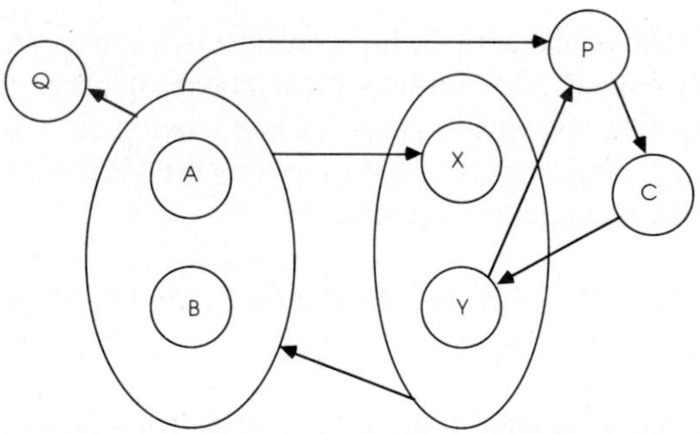
Q
P
A
X
C
B
Y

A set of relations constructed from the set of FDs in Figure 6.19 is not in 3NF. This set is:

R1(A, B, X, Y, Q, P)
R2(Y, P)
R3(P, C)
R4(C, Y)

R1 is not even in 2NF because P, a non-prime attribute, depends on part only of the key XY. You should note that so far AB → Y is not in the set of FDs used to construct these relations. However, once AB → Y is placed into the set, then AB → P becomes redundant and is taken out of the set of FDs used to construct the relations. If this new set of FDs is used then relation R1 becomes:

R1(A, B, X, Y, Q)

which is in 3NF.

How to find equivalent keys

An important part of the algorithm described above is to find equivalent keys. This can be done quite simply. Take each determinant in the given set of FDs and derive all other attributes from it using the same method as in the membership algorithm. Then see if you can find pairs that derive each other.

At this stage you should do Exercise 6.2 to familiarize yourself with the techniques used to construct relations from dependency diagrams.

Exercise 6.2

Construct relations from the following dependency diagrams.

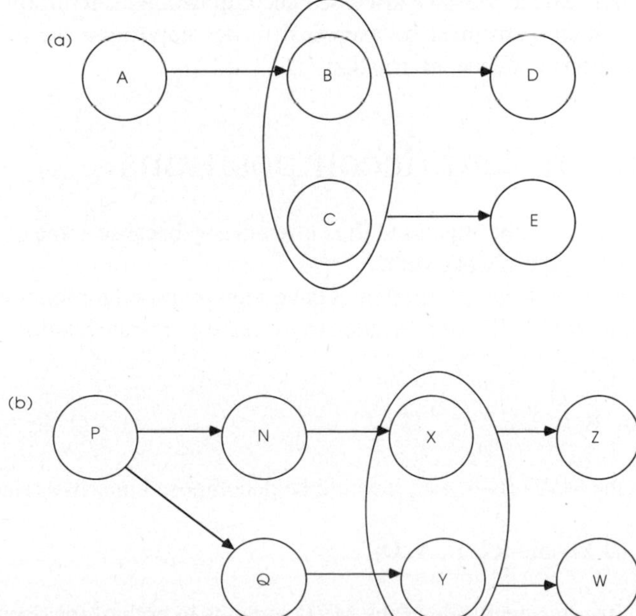

Exercise 6.2 (continued)

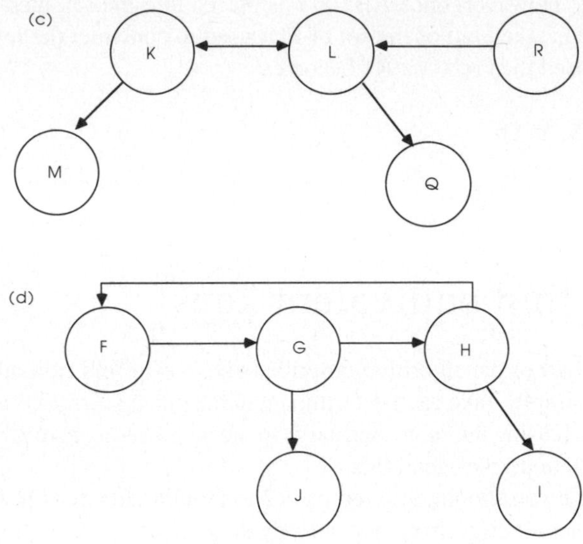

DECOMPOSITION

The alternative to synthesis is decomposition. The theoretical approach here is to place all attributes in one relation and test to see if the relation is normal. If it is not then it is decomposed. So far, we have discussed decomposition in an informal way in Chapter 4. However, some care must be exercised in decomposition, as it is possible to have decompositions that lose information.

Good and bad decompositions

Decomposition is not often used. It is often messy because some of the relations can be large and difficult to work with.

A number of decomposition rules have been proposed for relational design. One is to first take out any MVDs from relations and create a separate relation for each MVD. Thus if a relation

R1 (A, B, C, D)

contains the MVD B →→ C, it would be decomposed into two relations:

R11 (B, C) and R2 (B, A, D)

Note that the left-hand side of the MVD remains in both of the decomposed relations.

Once the MVDs are removed a similar rule can be used to decompose any relation that is still not in BCNF. Again the idea here is to take out a functional dependency from the relation. For example if relation

R1 (X, Y, Z, W)

is not in BCNF because it contains the FD X $\rightarrow$ Y, then it is decomposed into:

R1 (X, Y) and R2 (X, Z, W)

Note that the determinant again appears in both the decomposed relations. If this were not the case then information may be lost. As an example, consider relation ACCOUNTS in Figure 6.20. Here information is stored about accountants responsible for accounts. Accounts are numbered sequentially within a branch. As indicated by the FD diagram, each account has one customer and one accountant. Furthermore each accountant is responsible for accounts in one branch only.

Figure 6.20 Decomposing a relation

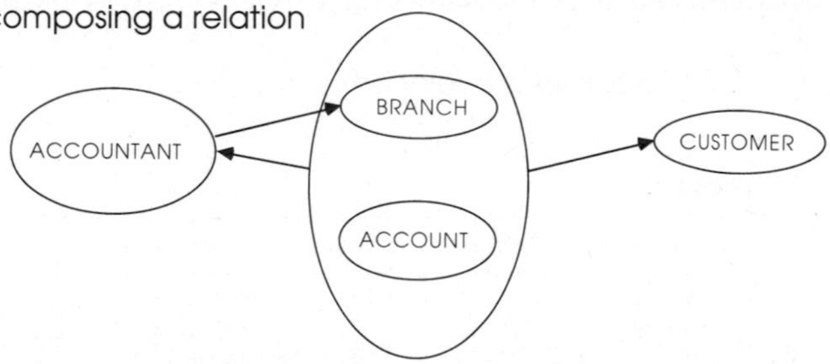

ACCOUNTS

ACCOUNTANT	BRANCH	ACCOUNT	CUSTOMER
Grant	Broadway	1	XYZ Group
Grant	Broadway	3	Acme Corp
Wendy	Broadway	2	Mars Corp
Max	Main	2	Acme Corp
Max	Main	1	Data Technology
Sarah	Main	3	XYZ Group

EMPLOYEES

ACCOUNTANT	BRANCH
Grant	Broadway
Wendy	Broadway
Max	Main
Sarah	Main

ACCOUNTS

BRANCH	ACCOUNT	CUSTOMER
Broadway	1	XYZ Group
Broadway	3	Acme Corp
Broadway	2	Mars Corp
Main	2	Acme Corp
Main	1	Data Technology
Main	3	XYZ Group

Relation ACCOUNTS is not in BCNF. The two relation keys of ACCOUNTS are (ACCOUNTANT, ACCOUNT) and (BRANCH, ACCOUNT) and CUSTOMER is the only non-prime attribute. However, there is a dependency ACCOUNTANT $\rightarrow$ BRANCH, but ACCOUNTANT is not a relation key. Thus relation ACCOUNTS is not in BCNF.

One possible decomposition of relation ACCOUNTS is shown in Figure 6.20. Here a separate relation, EMPLOYEES, has been created to show branches to which accountants are assigned. The remaining relation ACCOUNTS shows the customers for the accounts. Note that the common attribute of the decomposed relations, BRANCH, is not a determinant of any functional dependency. As a result you cannot recreate the information in the original relation from the decomposed relations but get the relation shown in Figure 6.21 instead. There are more rows in this relation than in the original relation. However, information has been lost because it is no longer possible to see who is responsible for particular accounts. For example, who is responsible for account 1 in branch 'Broadway'? It could be either Grant or Wendy, but the original relation specifically stipulated Grant for that account. Thus the decomposition lost this information. This kind of decomposition is said to be 'lossy'.

To avoid lossy decompositions it is necessary to choose a decomposition where the common attributes are a determinant of an FD. Thus a lossless decomposition of ACCOUNTS is:

EMPLOYEES (ACCOUNTANT, BRANCH)
ACCOUNTS (ACCOUNTANT, ACCOUNT, CUSTOMER)

Figure 6.21 Recombined relation

ACCOUNTS

ACCOUNTANT	BRANCH	ACCOUNT	CUSTOMER
Grant	Broadway	1	XYZ Group
Wendy	Broadway	1	XYZ Group
Grant	Broadway	3	Acme Corp
Wendy	Broadway	3	Acme Corp
Grant	Broadway	2	Mars Corp
Wendy	Broadway	2	Mars Corp
Max	Main	2	Acme Corp
Sarah	Main	2	Acme Corp
Max	Main	1	Data Technology
Sarah	Main	1	Data Technology
Max	Main	3	XYZ Group
Sarah	Main	3	XYZ Group

RELATIONAL ANALYSIS USING COMBINATIONS OF METHODS

Most relational design methodologies are ad-hoc and often use a combination of synthesis and decomposition. Thus one might start with a set of rules and use these rules to construct an initial set of relations. Then a set of 'local' dependency diagrams may be drawn for each relation and used to check whether the relation is normal. If it is not, then it is decomposed, taking care not to lose any information.

SOME PROBLEMS WITH USING RELATIONAL DESIGN ONLY

There are a number of problems in using a relational only approach to design large systems. Some of these problems are:

- Dependency diagrams will become large and difficult to manage for large systems.
- A bottom-up rather than a top-down approach is implied by relational analysis. Relational analysis calls for designers to identify attributes as the first step. Analysis of large systems does not usually begin by identifying attributes. Usually analysts prefer to start by identifying larger objects and then look at their attributes.
- Normalization is sometimes difficult, especially when higher normal forms are concerned.

Finally, relational design does not include sufficient guidance for correct semantic representation. This last point is illustrated by considering the dependency diagram in Figure 6.22. This shows that a project has one manager, and each manager manages one project. Each person is assigned to one project and manager. Relational analysis can produce the two alternative designs shown in Figure 6.23.

The first design (Figure 6.23(a)) is more appropriate if persons are assigned to managers. The second (b) is more appropriate if persons are assigned to departments. However, the dependency diagram is the same for both cases and designers cannot use it to make the appropriate choice. For this reason semantic models are often used as a first analysis step to define the basic system semantics.

Figure 6.22 Functional dependencies

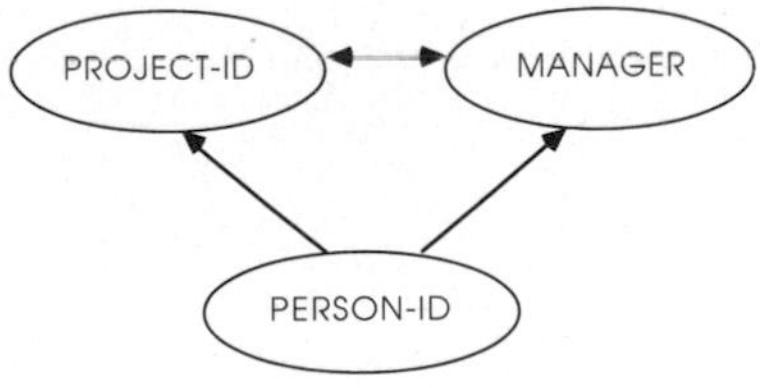

Figure 6.23 Alternative decompositions

PROJECT-ID	MANAGER
PROJ1	Jill
PROJ2	Graham
PROJ3	Nancy

PROJECT-ID	PERSON-ID
PROJ1	PER1
PROJ1	PER2
PROJ2	PER3
PROJ2	PER4
PROJ2	PER5
PROJ3	PER6

(a)

(continued on p. 84)

Figure 6.23 (continued)

PROJECT-ID	MANAGER
PROJ1	Jill
PROJ2	Graham
PROJ3	Nancy

MANAGER	PERSON-ID
Jill	PER1
Jill	PER2
Graham	PER3
Graham	PER4
Graham	PER5
Nancy	PER6

(b)

SUMMARY

This chapter described some methods that can be used to construct normal relations. The methods start with a set of rules, which are converted to dependency diagrams. The dependency diagrams are then converted to relations. Relational analysis on its own is often adequate for smaller systems because of the problem of manipulating a large number of attributes as one group. It may however be suited for a prototyping approach where a small system is built first and then additions are made to it.

Large systems built using the linear approach, however, most often combine relational analysis with other data analysis techniques. This approach is described in subsequent chapters.

7

E-R models

INTRODUCTION

The relational model provides the goal for an ideal database structure. It gives the designer a set of criteria (namely normal forms) to aim for in the design. Designs that satisfy these criteria have no redundancy and remain consistent following simple operations.

However, in large systems, large numbers of attributes make it difficult to begin by using relational analysis only. There are many dependencies between attributes and the analysis task will look daunting if they are treated as a whole. Thus database design is made more difficult by requiring analysts to look at the detail without knowing what the problem is all about.

Thus most practical methodologies start analysis by examining the system at a top level without worrying about dependencies. Such a top-level approach usually arranges attributes into small sets and these sets become the initial relations, which are subsequently normalized.

The top-down approach uses a top-level model that reduces the system in an orderly manner to a relational model. Many methodologies use the entity-relationship (E-R) model for top-level analysis. The E-R model is used to develop a high-level model of a system that describes the major system objects, the interactions between them and their properties. These system objects and interactions are then reduced to normal relations.

ENTITIES AND RELATIONSHIPS

The main idea behind E-R modeling is the entity. Entities are objects that are considered to be important in a system. E-R modeling usually begins by identifying all such major entities and grouping entities with the same properties into entity sets. Figure 7.1 shows the idea of modeling entities. It shows the set of people modeled as an entity set. Thus 'Joe', 'Jill', 'Peter' and 'Mary' are all people in the set and each person is one entity. The set of all persons is represented by the rectangular box with the entity set name, PERSONS, inside the box.

Figure 7.1 An entity set

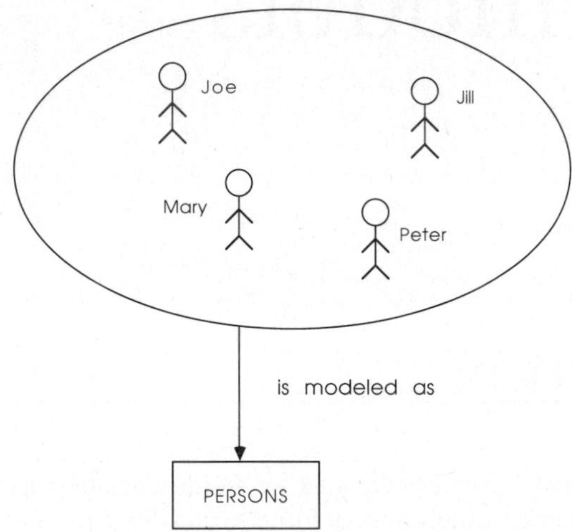

It is important to remember the distinction between entity sets and entities. An entity is one object instance, such as the person named 'Joe'. An entity set is a collection of objects with the same properties.

Things modeled as entities

Different entity sets may model many different types of things. They may model things that can be physically seen and identified, as for example PERSONS, VEHICLES, BUILDINGS, PARTS.

They may also model things that do not exist as physical objects but which serve to identify some organizational entity, as for example, PROJECTS, SECTIONS, DEPARTMENTS, BUDGETS.

They may also model things that happen, as for example, FAULTS, DELIVERIES, APPOINTMENTS, EXAMINATIONS.

Relationship sets

Entity sets on their own cannot model a complete system. They model the things in the system but not what they do or how they interact with each other. To do this, we need relationships. Relationships model interactions between entities. The idea behind relationships is illustrated in Figure 7.2.

Figure 7.2 A relationship set

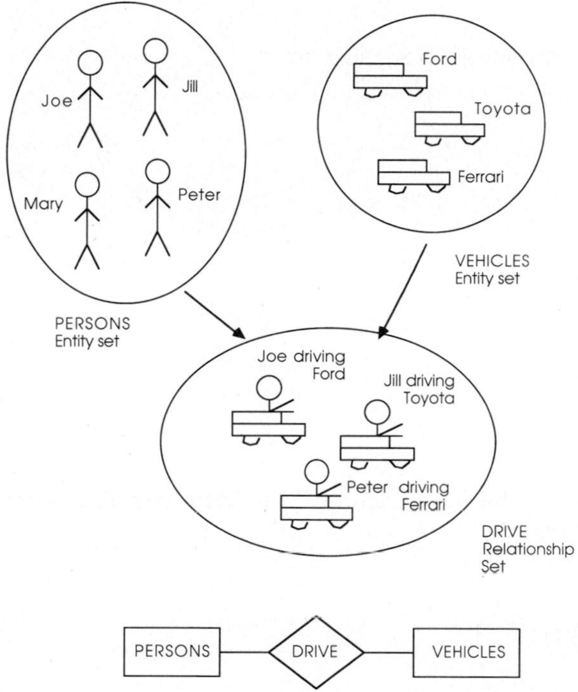

Figure 7.2 shows two entity sets, PERSONS and VEHICLES. They are modeled by rectangular boxes in the E-R diagram. The E-R diagram also shows that persons drive vehicles. This is modeled by a relationship set, DRIVE. Each relationship instance in relationship set, DRIVE, is one person driving one car. Thus 'Joe driving the Ford' is one relationship. 'Jill driving the Toyota' is another. The collection of relationships is called the relationship set. Relationship sets are modeled by diamond-shaped boxes on the E-R diagram.

The distinction between the idea of entities and entity sets also carries across to relationships and relationship sets. Just as one entity is one object, so a relationship is one interaction between two objects. Similarly just as an entity set is a collection of entities, so a relationship set is a collection of relationships.

Occurrence diagrams

Often for illustrative purposes it is necessary to show how entities in a model interact with each other. This can be done using semantic occurrence diagrams. One such diagram is illustrated in Figure 7.3. This is an illustration of persons driving cars. It shows four persons, p1, p2, p3 and p4 and three vehicles, v1, v2 and v3. Lines joining pairs of entities through a relationship show which person drives what car. Thus p1 drives v1, p2 also drives v1, p2 drives v2, and so on. Each point that shows the interaction of a pair of entities is one relationship in DRIVE. Thus Figure 7.3 also illustrates the set of DRIVE relationships.

Figure 7.3 An occurrence diagram

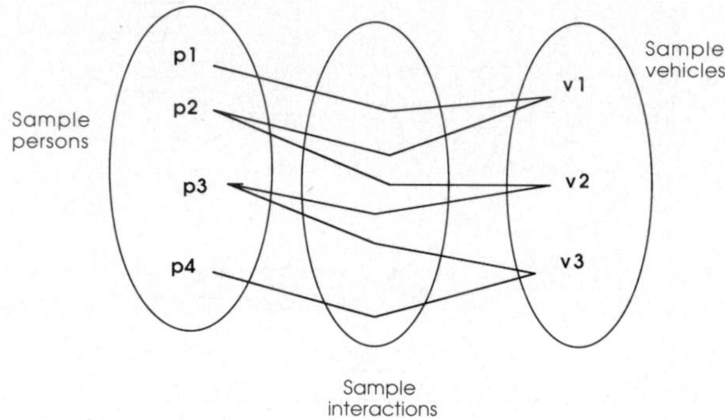

At this stage you should do Exercise 7.1 to become familiar with the idea of entity and relationship sets.

Exercise 7.1

Drawing occurrence diagrams.

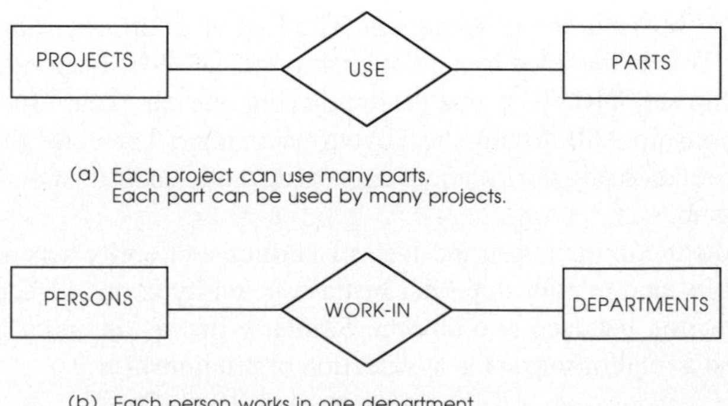

Exercise 7.1 (continued)

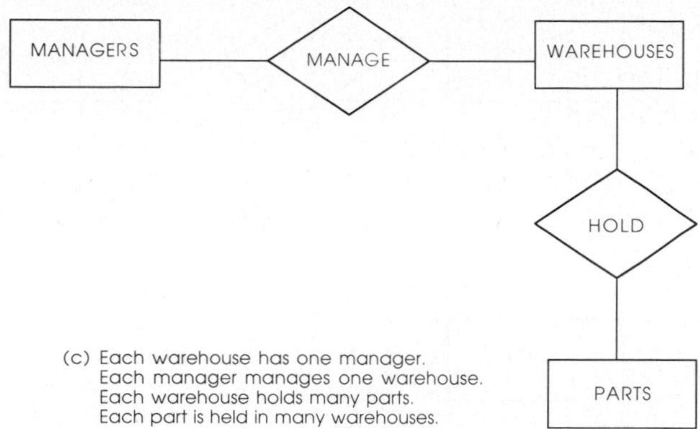

(c) Each warehouse has one manager.
Each manager manages one warehouse.
Each warehouse holds many parts.
Each part is held in many warehouses.

SOME GUIDELINES FOR DRAWING E-R DIAGRAMS

It is not possible to give designers a prescriptive set of steps that guarantee a correct E-R diagram. Analysts must keep a number of criteria in the back of their minds when developing E-R diagrams. One of these is to use the E-R diagram as a communication tool to ensure that all of the system data has been captured and correctly described. The other is to ensure that the E-R diagram structures the data in a way that is amenable to conversion to normal form. How to achieve both of these requires the development of skills that correctly identify entities and relationships and show them in a way that satisfies all criteria.

These skills cannot be prescribed but some guidelines can be given to assist analysts in their early work. Such guidelines include desirable E-R model characteristics as well as the structures to avoid in E-R diagrams. We commence with some of the more obvious characteristics.

Naming

One of the more important considerations in an E-R diagram is that it is a communications tool and every effort should be made to ensure that it is easy to understand. One way to achieve this is to choose names that make an E-R diagram readable.

Entity sets are usually passive and thus named by nouns, whereas relationship sets usually indicate activity and hence are named by verbs. Figure 7.4(a) is one example. Here the three entity sets are PROJECTS, PARTS and MANAGERS. On their own they are static and do not indicate any activity. The two relationships, named by the verbs MANAGE and USE, show the activity of the entities in the entity sets. Thus managers manage projects and projects use parts.

Figure 7.4 Sample E-R diagrams

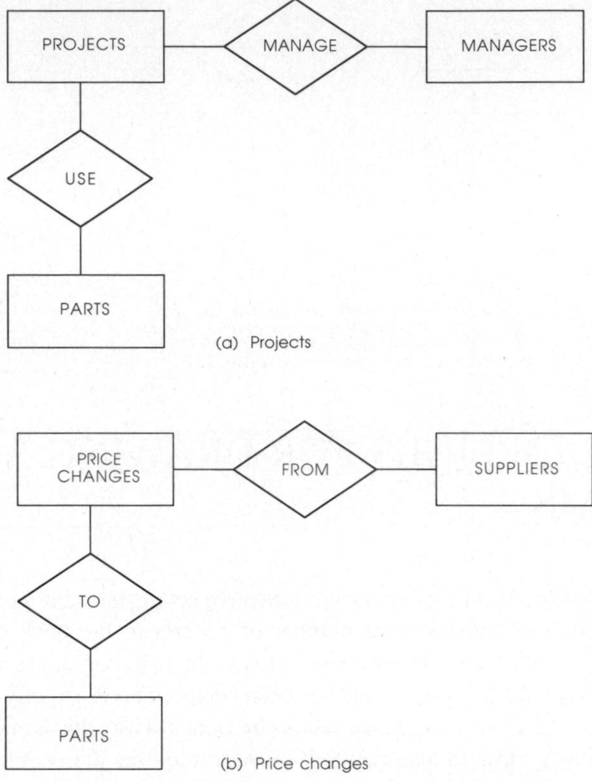

(a) Projects

(b) Price changes

Relationship sets can also be named by prepositions, such as, OF, TO, FOR, ABOUT, IN, and BY. This is useful where some entities are part of other entities or where activities modeled by entities involve other entities. Thus Figure 7.4(b) shows that a price change involves a supplier and a part.

More than one relationship between the same two entity sets

E-R diagrams should be able to help analysts easily describe semantics without placing any unreasonable constraints on the analyst. There is thus no reason to prevent different relationships between entities in two entity sets. Thus Figure 7.5 shows that there are two relationship sets between the entity sets COMPANIES and VEHICLES. Each such relationship set contains relationships with different properties. Thus the property of a LEASES relationship may be the length of lease, whereas the property of an OWNS relationship may be the cost of the vehicle.

Figure 7.5 More than one relationship between the same two entity sets

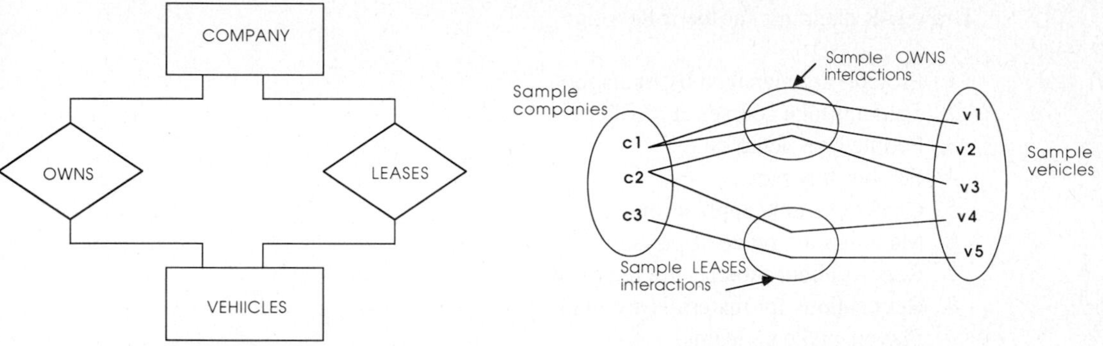

The total system should not be included in the E-R diagram

It is important to remember that the system being modeled should not itself appear in the E-R diagram. Thus Figure 7.6(a) shows an E-R diagram that includes the set BUSINESS, which in fact represents the business that is being modeled. Adding the business itself as an entity can cause confusion because it is now being given the same importance as its own components. Also, there is only one entity in the set BUSINESS and there would have to be a relationship between BUSINESS and every other entity set. The proper model for this system is shown in Figure 7.6(b).

Figure 7.6 Excluding the system

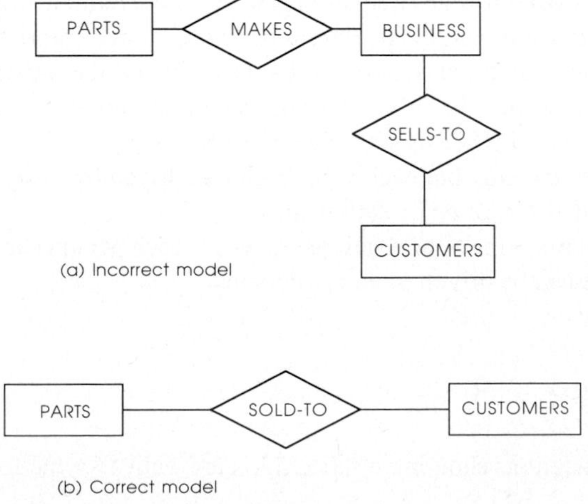

Exercise 7.2

Draw E-R diagrams for the following:

1. Projects are managed by managers.
2. Students take courses at a college.
3. People own vehicles.
4. Persons buy parts.
5. Clerks examine applications.
6. Machines are made of parts.
7. Reports about projects are received.
8. Requisitions for materials are made.
9. Players make up teams.
10. Parts are in stores.

CARDINALITY OF RELATIONSHIPS

Entities and relationships only show some of the information about a system. Although this may be the most important information, there are still additional things to be shown on an E-R model to complete the total picture. One of these is cardinality of relationships.

Cardinality shows the number of relationships in which one entity can appear. The idea of cardinality is perhaps best illustrated diagramatically using occurrence diagrams.

Figure 7.7(a) shows a system where each entity can participate in only one relationship. Here each person can drive only one car and each car can be driven by one person. The 1 on the link between the DRIVE and the PERSONS sets indicates the number of persons that can drive a car. The 1 on the link between the DRIVE and the VEHICLES sets indicates the number of cars that can be driven by one person.

Figure 7.7(b) illustrates a relationship set where entities from one set can participate in more than one relationship. Here a person can drive more than one vehicle. This is shown by the N on the link between the DRIVE and the VEHICLE sets. Each vehicle, however, can at most be driven by one person as shown by the 1 on the link between the DRIVE and PERSONS sets. The converse is Figure 7.7(c) where each person can drive one vehicle only but each vehicle can be driven by many persons. These relationships are called 1:N or N:1 relationships.

Finally there is the N:M relationship where each person can drive many vehicles and each vehicle can be driven by many persons.

Exercise 7.3

Draw E-R diagrams showing relationship cardinality for the following:

Figure 7.7 Cardinality

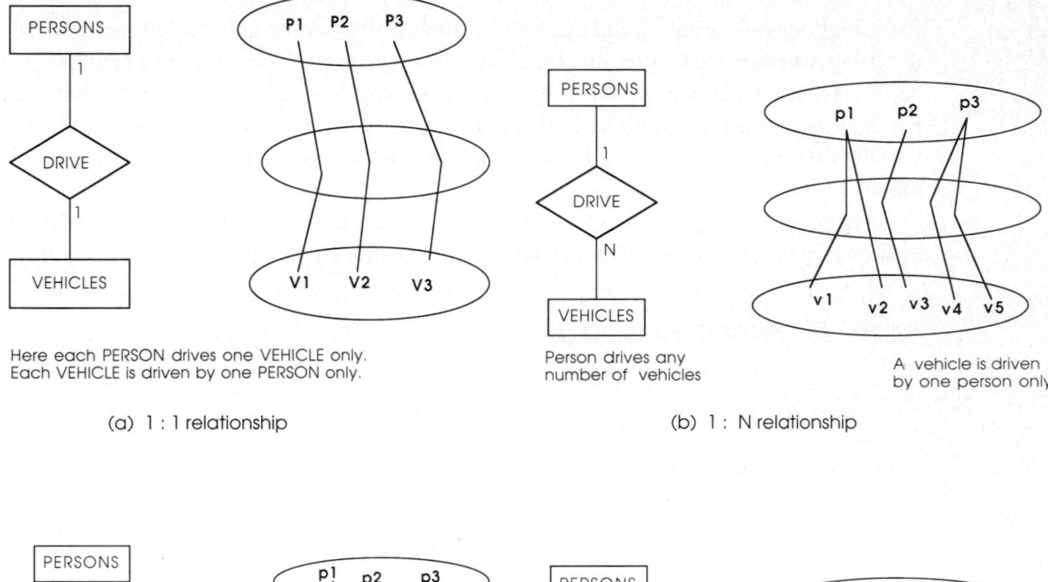

(a) 1 : 1 relationship (b) 1 : N relationship

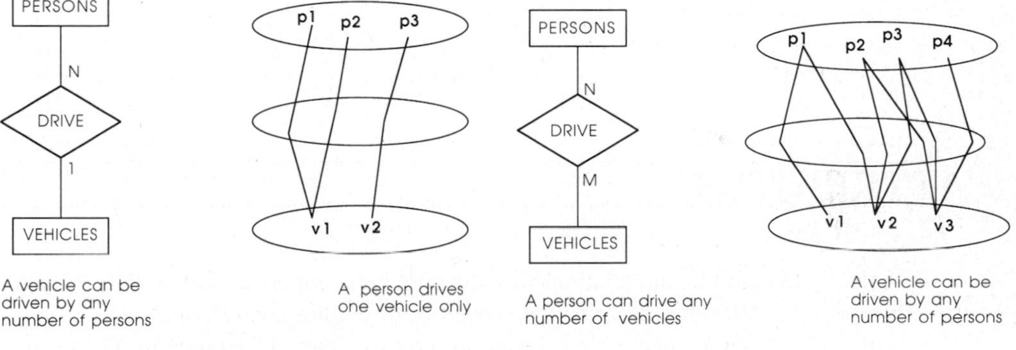

(c) N : 1 relationship (d) N : M relationship

1. An order is made by one project but a project can make many orders.
2. A supplier can supply any number of parts and each part can be supplied by many suppliers.
3. A person works in one department but many people can work in a department.
4. An application is examined by one manager but a manager can examine many applications.
5. A manager manages one project and each project has one manager.
6. A person can take any number of tours and there may be many people on the tour.
7. A team has one manager and many players. A player is on one team but a manager can manage more than one team.

PARTICIPATION

Participation is some additional information that is often stored about relationships. This describes whether each entity in a set must participate in a relationship. For example, we could have a system where each vehicle must be driven by at least one person, but each person need not drive a vehicle. In this case the participation of a person in relationship set DRIVE is optional whereas the participation of each vehicle in relationship DRIVE is mandatory.

Optional participation is indicated by a circle next to the box modeling an entity set as shown in Figure 7.8. Mandatory participation is indicated by the absence of the circle.

Figure 7.8 Adding participation

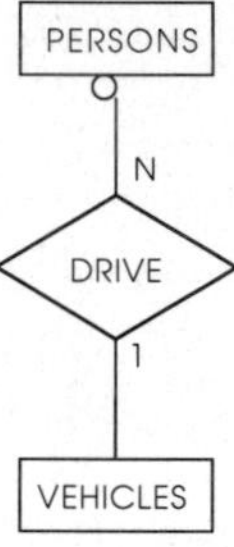

ATTRIBUTES

Perhaps after entities and relationships, the third most important part of an E-R diagram is attributes. Attributes describe the properties of entities and relationships. Each such attribute is given a name which is used to refer to a particular property. For example, entities in entity set PERSONS all have properties such as SURNAME, PERSON-ID, DATE-OF-BIRTH and so on. Thus SURNAME, DATE-OF-BIRTH become attributes of the entity set PERSONS. As shown in Figure 7.9 these attributes appear next to the box that models the entity set.

Relationship attributes

Just like entities, relationships also have properties. These properties describe properties of the interactions between entities. For example, relationship DRIVE has properties such as MILES-DRIVEN, TIME-STARTED and so on. The relationship must also include attributes that describe the entities that participate in a relationship.

Note that in Figure 7.9, TIME-SPENT is a property of the relationship set WORK-ON. Values of TIME-SPENT only arise when a person works on a project.

Figure 7.9 Attributes and identifiers

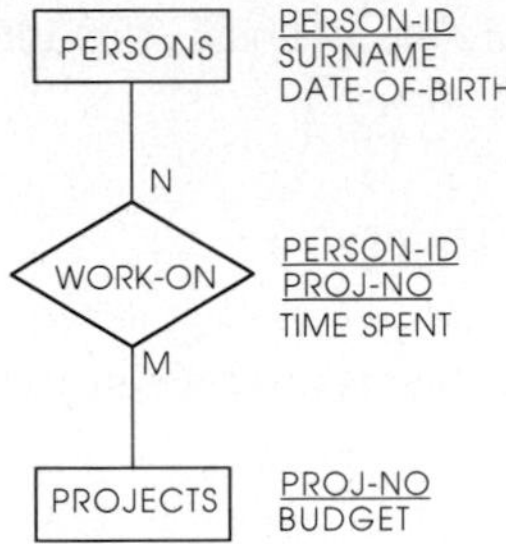

Choosing attribute names

Just like entity and relationship set names, attribute names must also be chosen to make E-R diagrams self-explanatory. Thus in the first instance it is important to choose meaningful names. Second, the same name should not mean different things in different contexts. Thus attribute names should be unique within the system. Finally, all the attributes that describe a particular entity or relationship must be given. Note that this requires each relationship to contain attributes that describe the entities participating in the relationship.

IDENTIFIERS

So far, we have made a distinction between entities and entity sets. E-R diagrams only include sets but not individual entities. However, one requirement of all systems is to be able to identify individual entities without necessarily showing them on the E-R diagram. Such identification is needed to determine the activities carried out by the entities. The usual practice is to identify entities by an entity identifier.

Entity identifiers

An entity identifier is an attribute (or set of attributes) whose values identify a unique entity. Identifiers are often attributes that are specially chosen to identify individual entities. Examples include PERSON-ID to identify persons, or PROJ-NO to identify projects. As shown in Figure 7.9 identifiers are underlined in an E-R diagram.

Relationship identifiers

A relationship identifier is an attribute (or set of attributes) whose values identify a unique relationship. The identifiers are underlined in an E-R diagram. Usually a relationship can be identified by the entities that participate in the relationship. Thus as a general rule, the identifier of a relationship are the attributes that identify the participating entities.

Identifier structure

Identifiers are either unique (that is a single attribute) or composite (that is made up of more than one attribute).

Unique identifiers

Unique identifiers are the preferred alternative especially for entity sets. Sometimes identifiers can be devised to uniquely identify entities. For example, persons can be identified by PERSON-ID, projects by PROJECT-ID, faults by FAULT-ID and so on. Sometimes, however, it is unnatural to make up unique identifiers. For example, a house may be identified by a combination of STREET-NO, STREET-NAME, SUBURB, POSTCODE rather than making up a unique identifier, say, HOUSE-NO. In that case composite identifiers are preferred.

Composite identifiers

Several reasons exist for using composite identifiers. Some we have already come across. One of these is where it is unnatural to use unique identifiers as in identifying houses. Another is in relationships where we prefer to use combinations of identifiers of the interacting entities rather than making up a unique identifier.

There are still other cases where composite identifiers are needed. One case is where some entities are identified within other (parent) entities. For example, suppose a project identified by PROJ-NO has a number of tasks and tasks are numbered within project. The task identifier for the task is made up of PROJ-NO and TASK-NO. TASK-NO on its own would not be sufficient as there may be more than one task with TASK-NO = 1 (but of course each such task is different as each such task is a task in a different project). Another case arises when time-repetitive actions are modeled. For example, there may be a work entity for each week a person works on a project. This work entity is identified by PERSON-ID and WEEK-NO.

Some guidelines for creating identifiers

Just as for relationship and entity sets, it is also possible to provide some guidelines for selecting attributes and choosing identifiers. Some such guidelines follow.

Remember that identifiers uniquely distinguish objects within the system and not the whole universe

Thus a project identifier PROJ-NO identifies projects in the organization being modeled not in the whole country or the whole world.

Similarly a person identifier PERSON-ID in an organization is only unique within that organization.

A street may be identified by STREET-NAME if you are modeling one suburb and all street names are unique within suburbs. On the other hand it will be identified by {SUBURB-NAME, STREET-NAME} if modeling a whole city.

Unlike entities should not be grouped in the same set

Sometimes we are tempted to construct an entity set whose entities may have different identifiers, but appear in the same relationship set. For example, suppose registration of some vehicles is recorded by individuals and others by organizations. One possible way to model this system is as shown in Figure 7.10. Here both individuals and companies register vehicles and are thus placed in the same entity set, namely OWNERS. The question is what do we use to identify OWNER? The identifier depends on whether the owner is an individual (in which case it may be SURNAME) or an organization (where it may be TRADING-NAME). This can then lead to E-R diagrams such as that shown in Figure 7.11. Here both TRADING-NAME and SURNAME are alternate identifiers of OWNERS. But each entity set only has a value for one of these identifiers.

As a general rule E-R diagrams like that in Figure 7.11 should be avoided and all entities in the one set should have the same identifier attribute. If you find yourself nominating different identifiers for a set then you have most probably chosen a bad set.

Whenever a situation like that shown in Figure 7.11 arises, the entity set must be split into two or more entity sets. Each of the new sets should have one identifier. Thus the E-R diagram of Figure 7.11 should be converted to that shown in Figure 7.12. This new E-R diagram now has two relationships for registration. There is an alternative way of modeling this problem that avoids splitting relationship sets. It uses subsets and is described in Chapter 8. This would have OWNER with its own identifier as a role taken by COMPANIES and INDIVIDUALS.

Figure 7.10 Grouping unlike entities

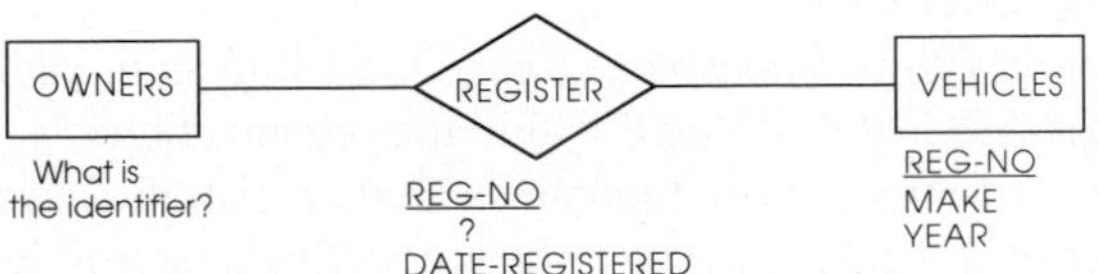

Figure 7.11 Undesirable effects of grouping unlike entities

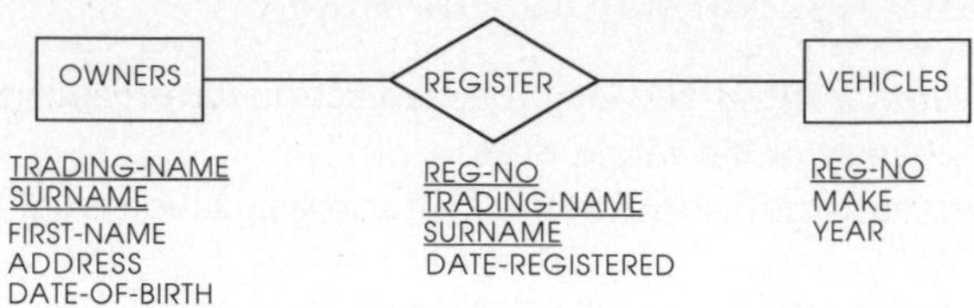

Figure 7.12 Separating unlike entities

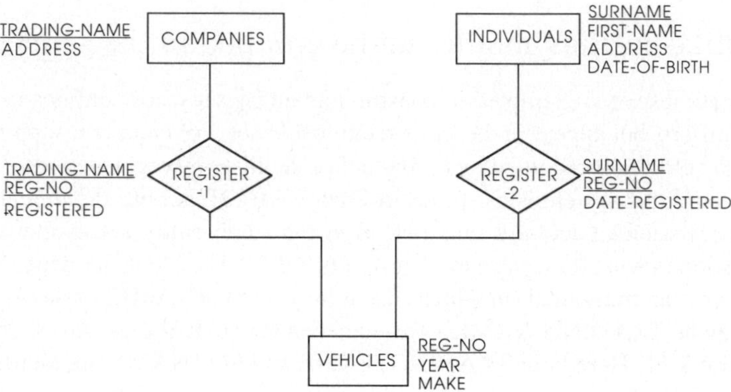

Exercise 7.4

Nominate identifiers for the following:

1. A *refrigerator* made by a *manufacturer* (when modeling a shop that sells refrigeration from many manufacturers). Refrigerators made by a manufacturer have a uniqe FRIDGE-NO within the organization.
2. A *high school* in a state (when modeling all high schools in the country). All high schools have a unique HIGH-SCHOOL-NAME in the *state*.
3. A *student* at a *university* (when modeling the university). The student has a unique STUDENT-ID.
4. A *book* in a *library* (when modeling the library). The book has a unique ACCESSION-NO.
5. *Sections* within *departments* (when modeling an organization). Each section has a unique SECTION-NAME within the organization.
6. A motor *vehicle* (when modeling a state registration system).
7. A person's weekly *payroll* (when modeling a payroll in an organization).
8. An *assignment* in a *subject* (when modeling all subjects in a university). All assignments are sequentially numbered within subjects. Each subject has a SUBJECT-NAME.
9. A *flight* that leaves an airport at the same time every day (when modeling all flights in a country). All flights in the country have a unique FLIGHT-NO.

10. A *bus route* that passes through a number of *suburbs*. Each route has a BUS-ROUTE- NO.
11. The *application* with a given APPLICATION-NO is made by a customer with CUSTOMER-NAME in an APPLICATION-DATE. *Customers* may make a number of applications but each application is made by one customer.
12. An *examination* for a given SUBJECT-NAME that is given on more than one SEMESTER. Students with STUDENT-ID and NAME get GRADES in this examination.
13. A *delivery* made by a driver with a DRIVER-NAME using vehicle registered with REG-NO has a DELIVERY-NO, starts on a given START-DATE and *stops* at a number of locations with a given ADDRESS and leaves quantities of a given ITEM-NO at those locations.
14. A *flight* that has a FLIGHT-NO and may start at an ORIGINATING-AIRPORT and pass through any number of other airports to a terminating airport. *Seats* with SEAT-NO can be occupied by different passengers with a given PASSENGER-NO and NAME between each two airports.
15. A shop has a number of copies of video films that have a FILM-NAME and a COPY-NO. The *copies* are rented to customers on a given RENTAL-DATE and returned on a RETURN-DATE.

SOME MORE GUIDELINES

Apart from choice of identifiers, there are other problems that arise in E-R modeling. These concern choice of entity sets and the placement of attributes.

Choosing entities and attributes

The first guideline here is how to select which objects to make into entities and what should be an attribute. Sometimes it is not clear what should be an attribute or what should be an entity. For example, do we model the COLOR of a PART as an entity or an attribute? The alternatives are shown in Figure 7.13.

Figure 7.13 Choosing attributes and entities

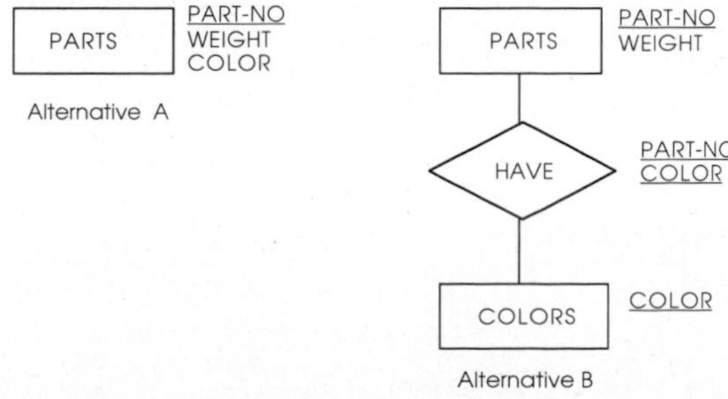

The chosen alternative depends on the analyst's view of the system. If the analyst sees COLOR as a property of PARTS and the system has no control over a part's color, then ALTERNATIVE A may be preferred.

However, in an organization that makes dyes, COLOR may be significant in its own right. Each COLOR will need a new dye and hence may be treated as an entity. In this case ALTERNATIVE B is preferred.

A useful rule here is:

Existence rule: If a value of an attribute is important even though there is no entity with that value as a property then that attribute should be modeled as an entity.

Thus if any COLOR is important even though there is no part with that COLOR, then COLOR should be an ENTITY.

Exercise 7.5

Distinguish between entities and attributes for the following:

1. Film production: Under what circumstances are these alternatives preferred?

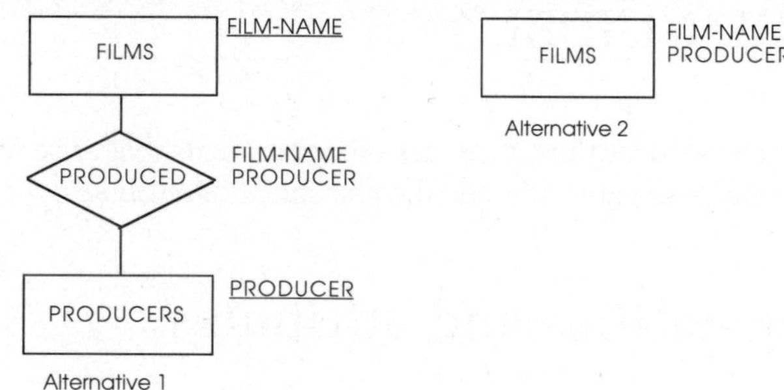

2. Deliveries: A delivery van, numbered VAN-NO, made by a MANUFACTURER, is used for deliveries numbered DEL-NO by the organization. Should the MANUFACTURER be an attribute or an entity?

3. Shop-ownership: Under what circumstances is each of these alternatives preferred?

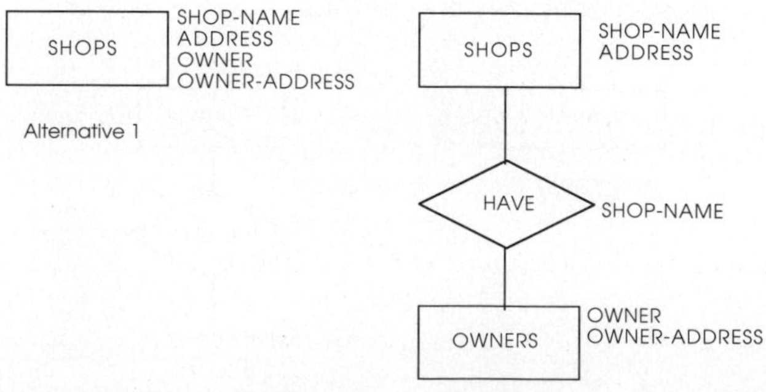

Exercise 7.5 (continued)

4. Paintings: Paintings have PAINTING-NAME and are painted by painters with a given PAINTER-NAME and depict scenes in a given ERA. Which of these three, PAINTER-NAME, PAINTING-NAME and ERA would you expect to identify entity sets and what would be attributes of these entity sets?

Attributes and 1:N relationships

Sometimes in a 1:N relationship it is not clear whether an attribute should be attached to an entity or to the relationship. For example, Figure 7.14 shows two alternative methods for placing an attribute in an E-R diagram. In one DATE-PURCHASED appears in the entity set VEHICLES, in the other it appears in the relationship set OWN. One could argue for alternative 1 because DATE-PURCHASED is the date when the vehicle was purchased and hence is a property of a vehicle. On the other hand DATE-PURCHASED is something that occurs (that is takes a value) because of the action of taking ownership and hence should be part of the relationship. Semantically therefore the second alternative is preferred.

Figure 7.14 Attributes in 1:N relationships

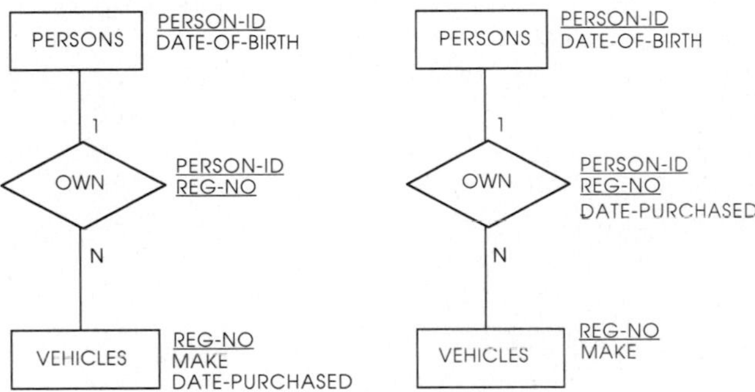

[It turns out later that where the model is converted to relations the file design will be the same irrespective of the choice made because entity and relationship sets in 1:N relationships are combined into the one file.]

Exercise 7.6

Draw an E-R diagram for the following:

An organization uses a number of items of equipment to produce goods. Each item is at one LOCATION, of one TYPE and has a DETAILED-DESCRIPTION.

Faults on the equipment are identified by a unique FAULT-ID and are reported at a TIME-REPORTED. Any number of persons may be assigned to a fault and work on the fault until it is fixed. The TIME-FIXED is recorded as is the TIME-SPENT by each person on a fault.

Any number of parts may be used to a repair a fault. The QTY-USED of each part is recorded against the fault. Each part is identified by a PART-ID, has a given WEIGHT and MAX-DIMENSION and can have any number of COLORs.

Each person is identified by a PERSON-ID, has a SURNAME and FIRST-NAME and any number of QUALIFICATIONS.

SUMMARY

This chapter introduced the idea of high-level semantic modeling. It described the E-R model and how this model can be used to describe systems.

The main components of an E-R model are entity sets and relationship sets. Entity sets model the major objects in the system whereas relationship sets model interactions between the entities. Attributes are used to describe the properties of relationship and entity sets.

The next chapter will introduce some additional E-R semantic constructs for modeling dependence, time variation and subsets.

8

Subsets and dependent entities

INTRODUCTION

Entities, relationships and attributes provide a simple and yet powerful method for modeling systems. They can be used to construct an initial top-level model of most systems. However, it is sometimes difficult to model some system semantics naturally without using additional semantic constructs. Furthermore some additional constructs are often needed to preserve normal correspondence while retaining semantic clarity. For this reason extensions are often made to E-R modeling. The two most widely used extensions are the subset and the dependent entity set.

SUBSETS

There are many situations in systems when some entities are treated the same way for one purpose and differently for other purposes. These situations can be modeled using subsets.

For example, suppose an institution receives loan applications. Some of these loan applications are for personal loans while others are for home mortgage loans. Both of these kinds of applications are usually treated similarly at, say, the loans reception desk. The time of receipt is recorded and perhaps an entry is made in a receipts file. From then on processing may depend on the type of application and personal loan applications are treated differently to mortgage loan applications.

The two types of applications can be modeled by the E-R model shown in Figure 8.1. Here LOAN-APPLICATIONS model all loan applications whereas PERSONAL-LOAN-APPLICATIONS is a subset of LOAN-APPLICATIONS that only includes applications for personal loans. Similarly MORTGAGE LOAN-APPLICATIONS is a subset that only includes applications for mortgage loans.

Figure 8.1 Modeling subsets

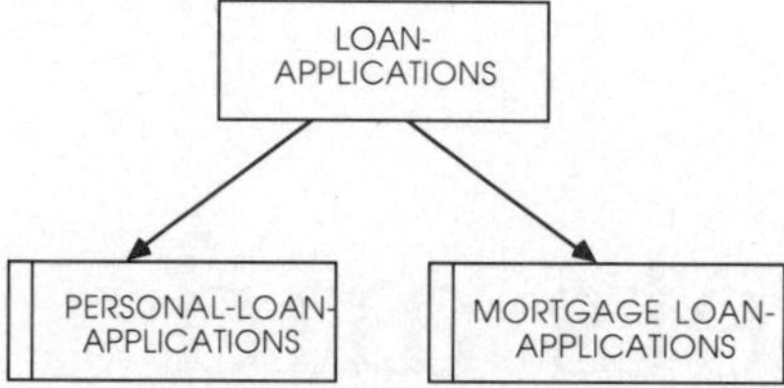

The occurrence diagram in Figure 8.2 illustrates the idea behind subsets. It shows that all objects in the subset must come from another set, which is called the source set of the subset. Thus application, ap1, in PERSONAL LOAN APPLICATIONS comes from LOAN APPLICATIONS, as do all applications in PERSONAL LOAN APPLICATIONS. LOANS-APPLICATIONS is thus the source set of PERSONAL-LOAN and MORTGAGE-LOAN APPLICATIONS.

Figure 8.2 An occurrence diagram for subsets

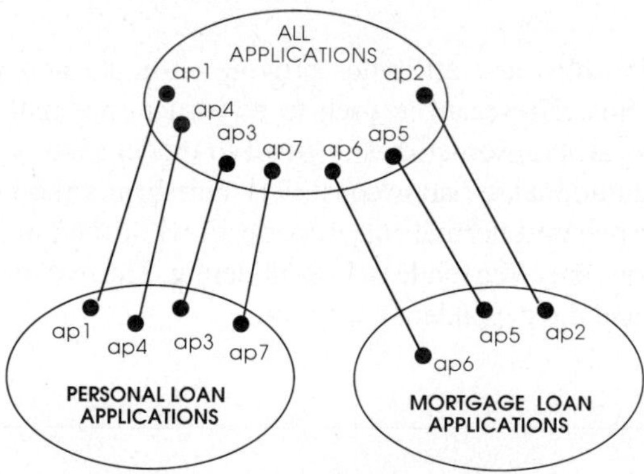

A subset in an E-R diagram appears as a rectangular box with an extra line on the left-hand side. There is an arrow to the subset from its source set. Subset attributes appear next to the box that models the subset.

Figure 8.1 illustrates the idea of dividing a set into a number of subsets. It does not show any differences in the treatment of these subsets. Subsets from the same source can have different attributes and appear in different relationships.

Figure 8.3 is an example that illustrates such differences between subsets. Here assignments are taken by students. Each assignment is identified by ASSIGNMENT-NO and has a DUE-DATE. These assignments may be computer or written assignments. As far as student records are concerned, all assignments are treated the same way. They appear in the TAKEN-BY relationship set with students. This relationship set includes the identifier ASSIGNMENT-NO and STUDENT-ID to show assignments taken by students and GRADE to show the grade obtained by each student.

Figure 8.3 Subsets and relationships

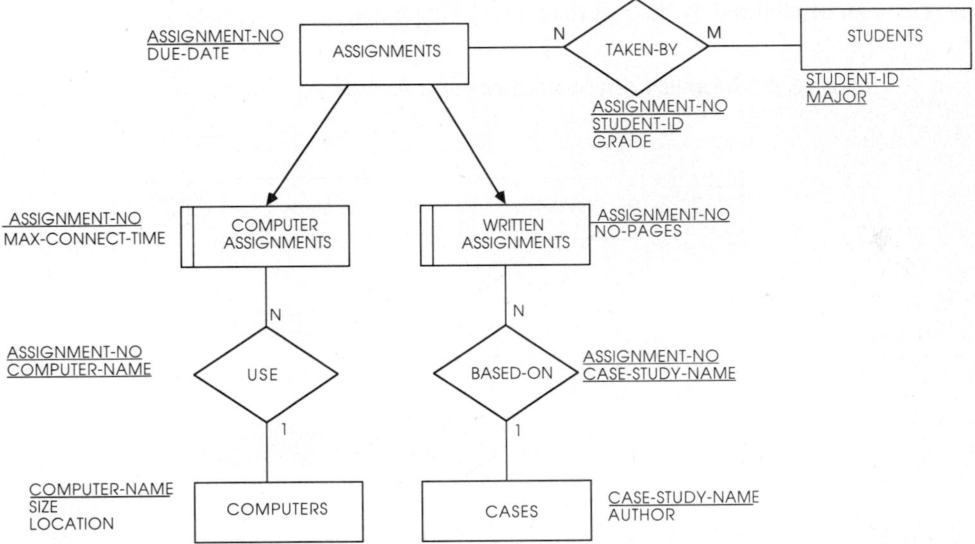

Assignment details arc treated differently for the two kinds of assignments. They have different attributes and appear in different relationships. They are therefore modeled by subsets. Computer assignments arc modeled by the subset COMPUTER-ASSIGNMENTS. This subset has the same identifier as ASSIGNMENTS and an additional attribute, MAX-CONNECT-TIME. Attribute MAX-CONNECT-TIME specifies the maximum terminal time allowed to a student and applies only to computer assignments and not written assignments. Similarly written assignments have the attribute, NO-PAGES, which applies only to written assignments. Furthermore, computer assignments appear in relationship USE with computers used by the assignments. Written assignments appear in relationship set, BASED-ON, with cases used in these assignments.

Subset identifiers

Just like entity sets and relationship sets, subsets also have attributes and some of these attributes are chosen to be the subset identifiers. Subsets whose members all come from the same source set can use the same identifier as the source set. Thus if the identifier of LOAN-APPLICATIONS is APPLICATION-NO then the identifier of PERSONAL-LOAN-APPLICATIONS and MORTGAGE-LOAN-APPLICATIONS can also be

APPLICATION-NO. Similarly the identifier of COMPUTER-ASSIGNMENTS and WRITTEN-ASSIGNMENTS is ASSIGNMENT-NO.

Combining subsets

Sometimes it is convenient to combine subsets from two entity sets (or to combine the entire entity sets). Suppose students and staff are members of a club. Club membership can be modeled by the E-R diagram in Figure 8.4.

Figure 8.4 Subsets from more than one source

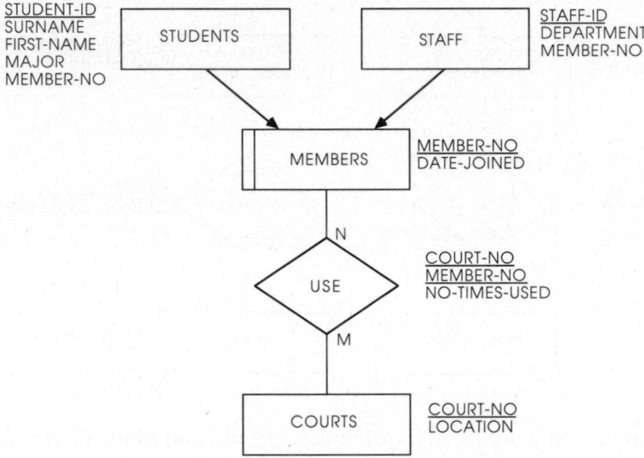

Subsets, whose members come from more than one source set, are sometimes called NON-UNIFORM subsets. Subsets that contain objects from one source only are known as UNIFORM subsets. Computer assignments and written assignments in Figure 8.3 are both uniform subsets.

Identifiers for non-uniform subsets

Non-uniform subsets cannot use the same identifier as their source set because their identifier values may overlap. For example, there may be a student and a staff member with the same numeric value of their identifier. For this reason, a special identifier is often created for the non-uniform subset. In Figure 8.4, MEMBER-NO is such an identifier. It is used to identify MEMBERS. MEMBER-NO is also an attribute of the STUDENTS and STAFF entities. It is needed in those sets to find the membership number for a particular staff member or student.

An alternative way for identifying members of non-uniform subsets is to use composite identifiers. In that case the identifier is made of an attribute TYPE whose value is the name of the source set of the member. The other part of the identifier would be an attribute that takes the same value as the source set identifier. The identifier of subset MEMBERS would thus be made up of:

1. an attribute TYPE whose value would either be 'STUDENT' or 'STAFF';
2. an attribute, say, NUMBER, where NUMBER has the same value as STUDENT-ID if the member is a student or STAFF-ID if the member is a staff member.

You should also note that MEMBER attributes are only those attributes that apply to both staff and students in their role as club members. The only attribute of that kind is DATE-JOINED, the date that a particular member joined the club.

Additional terminology

The idea of participation also applies to subsets. Participation of objects in a source set may be MANDATORY or OPTIONAL in a subset.

A source is MANDATORY to a subset if every member in the source must also appear in the subset. A source is OPTIONAL to a subset if every object in the source may (but need not) appear in the subset.

Of course objects in a set may be mandatory in one subset and optional in another. Alternatively a non-uniform subset may have mandatory and optional subsets participating in it. The example in Figure 8.5, for example, shows that COMPUTER PROGRAMS are mandatory COMPUTER SYSTEM COMPONENTS but optional ASSEMBLY LANGUAGE PROGRAMS.

Figure 8.5 Participation of sources

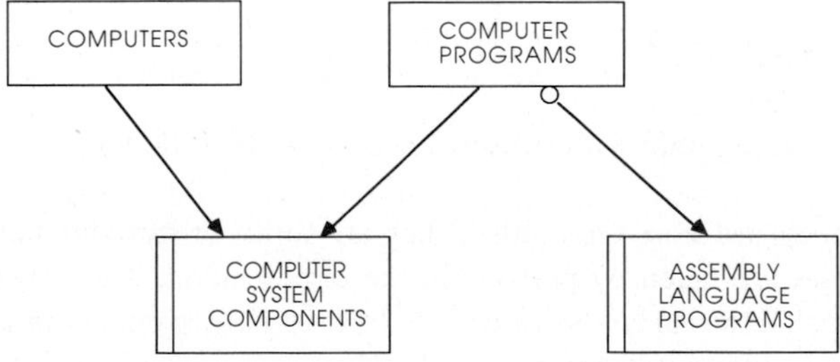

The example in Figure 8.6 shows that STUDENTS have to be members of a student union whereas staff may only elect to do so. In that case STUDENTS are mandatory subset members whereas STAFF are optional subset members.

Figure 8.6 Participation of subsets

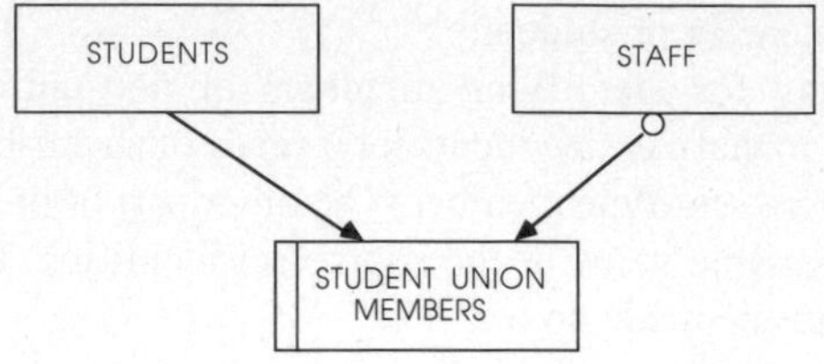

Symmetry

You may by now also have noticed a symmetry about how one goes about modeling subsets. For example, Figure 8.7 shows what appears to be another way of modeling club membership. In this figure club MEMBERS are subdivided into two subsets, STUDENTS and STAFF.

Figure 8.7 Symmetry

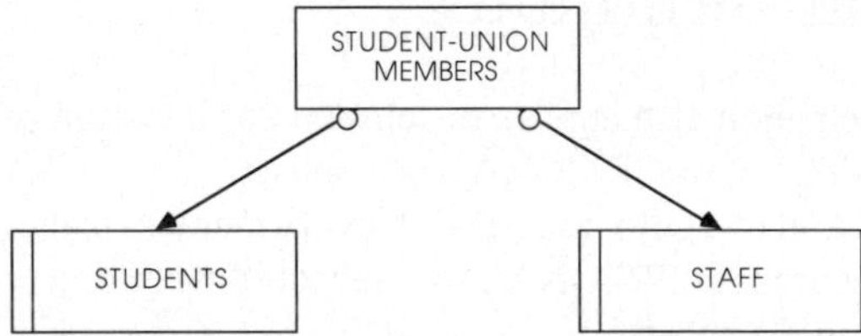

There is a subtle difference between the two models shown in Figures 8.6 and 8.7. The STAFF and STUDENTS in Figure 8.7 will not include those staff and students who are not members. However, in Figure 8.6 these two sets include all the staff and students.

For this reason the model in Figure 8.7 would be used if we are only interested in club members. The model in Figure 8.6 would be used if we are interested in all staff and students.

Exercise 8.1

Draw an E-R diagram with subsets for each of the following.

1. Materials are stored in holds if they are solids or stored in tanks if they are liquid.
2. Courses are taken by persons in the organization. The courses can be external or internal. External courses are given by external organizations and internal courses are given by internal lecturers.
3. Projects, departments and individuals are computer users. The time spent using programs is recorded for each computer user.
4. Deliveries are either handled internally or subcontracted to contractors. Internal deliveries are delivered by company vehicles.

5. Library borrowers may be individuals or other libraries. A record of books borrowed by each borrower is kept.

Use of subsets

Subsets are now increasingly used in conceptual models. They are very useful for organizations that have different types of customers. As shown in Figure 8.8 such customers may be BORROWERS, LENDERS, GUARANTORS and so on. The common information about customers, such as their ADDRESS, may be kept centrally, whereas particular details relevant to their role are kept in a subset. The links from the customer record to all the roles enable profiles on customers to be developed.

Figure 8.8 Classifying entities

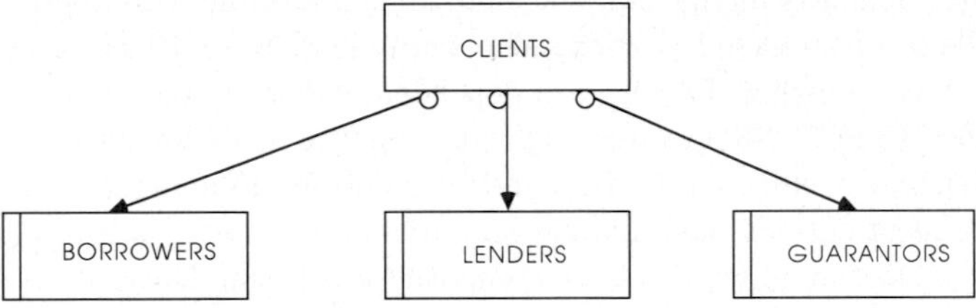

Figure 8.9 Levels of subsets

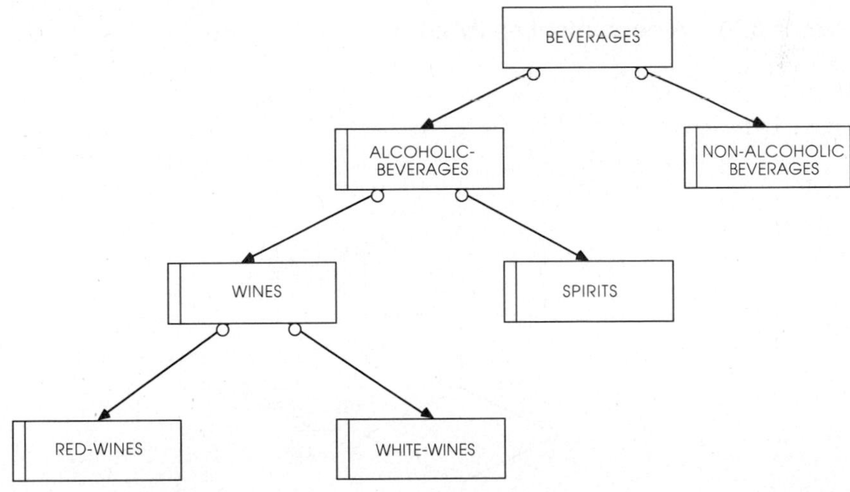

Subset structures can also go to a number of levels. In such structures some subsets are divided up into further subsets and so on. Figure 8.9 illustrates one such structure. Here there is an entity set, BEVERAGES, that models all possible beverages sold in a store. These beverages can now be subdivided into two subsets, ALCOHOLIC-BEVERAGES and NON-ALCOHOLIC-BEVERAGES. The ALCOHOLIC-BEVERAGES can be further subdivided into WINES and SPIRITS. WINES can then be subdivided into WHITE-WINES and RED-WINES, and so on.

DEPENDENT ENTITIES

It is often said that entities are objects that can stand on their own and are not dependent on the existence of other objects. Such objects should have unique identifiers. Thus, for example, persons exist in their own right: so do parts or buildings. Persons have an identifier, say PERSON-ID, whose role is simply to identify persons.

However, there are situations where some entities depend on other entities. For example, suppose a task can only be set up for a project. There cannot be a task without a project. In this case the task is dependent on the project and the project is the parent of the task. Similarly there cannot be an invoice line without an invoice.

The task is modeled as a dependent entity in Figure 8.10. Here the double line on top of the box states that TASKS is a dependent entity set and the arrow on the link from PROJECTS to TASKS expresses the dependence of TASK on PROJECT.

Dependent entities differ from independent entities in the structure of their identifier. Independent entities have unique identifiers whose sole purpose is to identify those entities. Dependent entities have composite identifiers. One part of the identifier is the identifier of the parent and the other is an attribute that identifies a dependent uniquely within a parent.

Figure 8.10 A dependent entity set

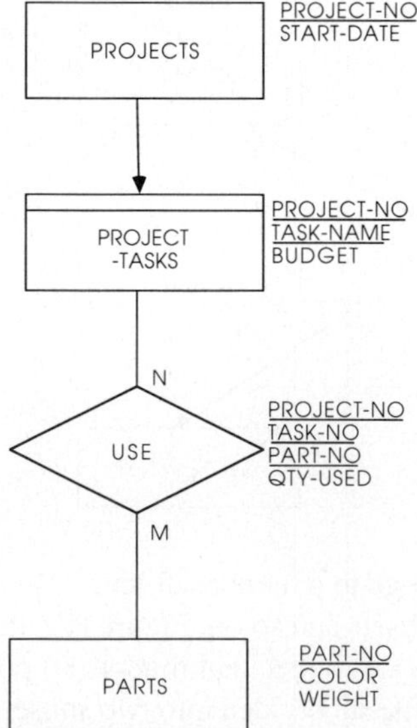

Figure 8.11 Some more examples of dependent entity sets

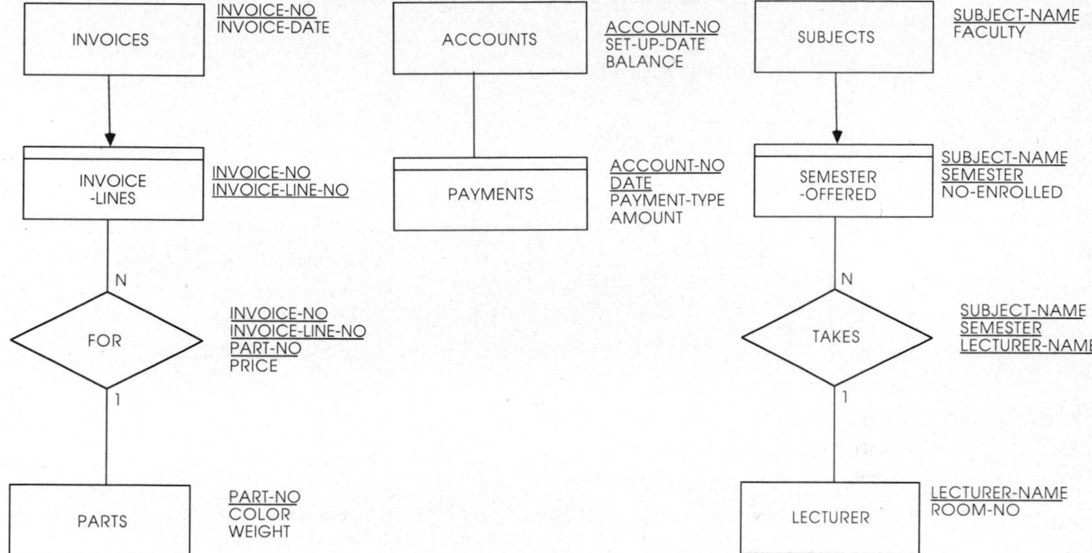

Thus the TASK identifier is (PROJECT-ID, TASK-NO) and tasks are numbered 1,2,3 . . . within projects. There may be more than one task with the same TASK-NO but each of these tasks belongs to a different project.

More examples of dependent entity sets are given in Figure 8.11. Invoice lines, for example, depend on the existence of an invoice. Here the invoice line identifier is made up of the invoice identifier together with a number that identifies a line within an invoice. Similarly payments on an account are identified by the account number together with the time of payment.

The last example in Figure 8.11 is subject offerings. Here a subject may be offered any number of semesters. Each offering is identified by the subject name and the semester offered. Lecturers appear in relationships with the offering. A different lecturer can take the same subject on each offering.

You should note that no cardinality is specified between a dependent entity set and its owner. This is because as a rule each owner can have many dependent entities but each dependent belongs to one owner.

Choosing identifiers for dependent entities

An identifier of a dependent entity should be made up of the identifier of its parent, and an attribute whose sole purpose is to identify dependents within its owner. Some other entity identifier should not be used to identify dependents within its parents. For example, the identifier shown in Figure 8.12(a) should be avoided. Here the identifier of the dependent entity set STOPOVER uses the identifier of another entity set, CITY, to identify dependents within parents. Instead an identifier should be chosen specifically for identifying dependents within an entity set. For example, the attribute STOPOVER-NO in Figure 8.12(b) is used solely for identifying stopovers within trips.

Figure 8.12 Choosing identifiers

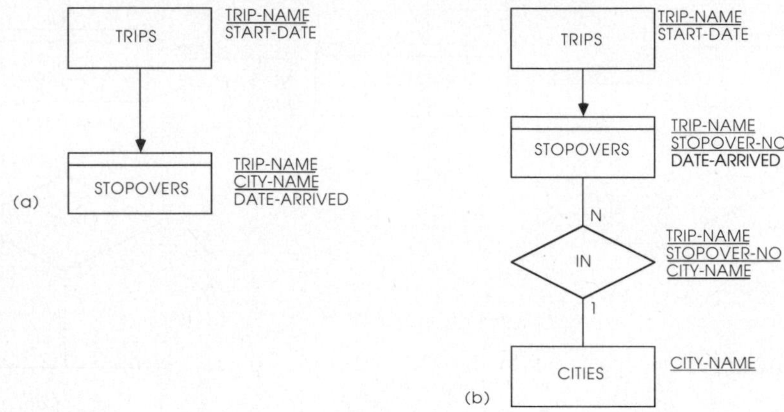

CHOOSING THE CORRECT PARENT

Dependence must always express the natural dependence of one entity on another and not some derived dependence. For example, suppose orders are placed within contracts that have been negotiated with suppliers. Some people may then argue that orders depend on suppliers, because we could not make an order without there being a supplier. The resultant E-R diagram is shown in Figure 8.13.

Here ORDERS is modeled as dependent on CONTRACTS but its composite identifier expresses dependence on supplier. We assume that ORDER-IN-SUPPLIER increments within supplier and not within contract. CONTRACT-NO is included to show the CONTRACT under which the order is made.

Figure 8.13 Improper dependency

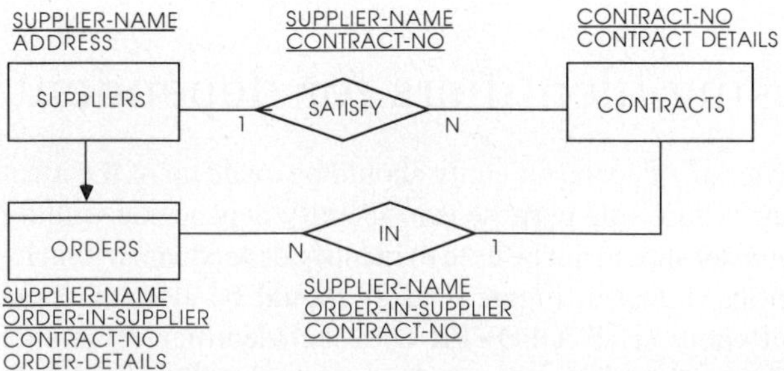

Figure 8.14 Direct dependency

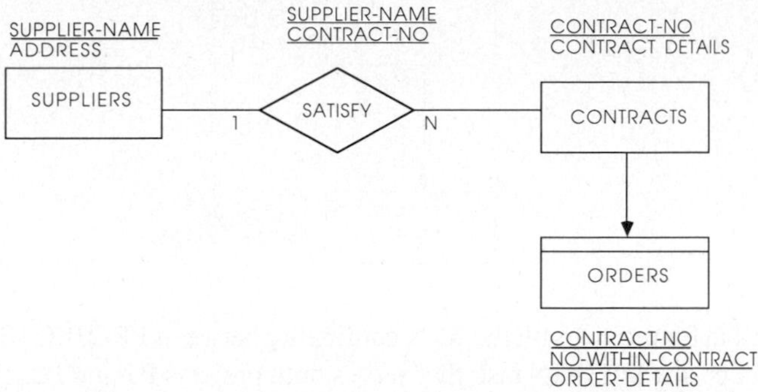

Now suppose ORDERS is converted to the relation

ORDERS (SUPPLIER-NAME, ORDER-IN-SUPPLIER, CONTRACT-NO, ORDER-DETAILS)

This has two relation keys:

{SUPPLIER-NAME, ORDER-IN-SUPPLIER} and
{CONTRACT-NO, ORDER-IN-SUPPLIER}

Now there is a dependency CONTRACT-NO → SUPPLIER but CONTRACT-NO is not the relation key and hence the relation is not BCNF.

The correct way to model dependence here is shown in Figure 8.14. Now the composite identifier of ORDERS shows dependence on contracts. ORDER converts to relation

ORDERS (CONTRACT-NO, NO-WITHIN-CONTRACT, ORDER-DETAILS)

which is in BCNF.

It is thus important to ensure that the identifier of the direct parent is used as part of the dependent entity identifier.

AVOIDING REDUNDANCY WITH DEPENDENT ENTITIES

Such redundancy can occur when one dependent entity has more than one parent. One example of this possibility is shown in Figure 8.15. Here a dependent is identified by the parent's identifier (PROJECT-NO) and the TASK-NAME.

Now suppose there are some tasks that belong to more than one project. This is

Figure 8.15 Possible redundancy

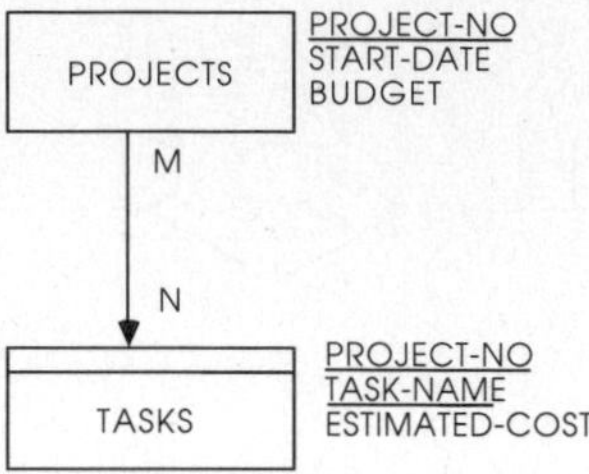

indicated in Figure 8.15 by the M:N cardinality between PROJECTS and TASKS. Thus there can be one DESIGN task that serves both projects P1 and P2. This task can appear twice in the system:

1. once identified by P1, DESIGN; and
2. another time identified as P2, DESIGN.

Both of these occurrences are the same task and have the same ESTIMATED-COST. This redundancy can be removed by converting the dependent entity set to an independent entity set.

Converting dependent entities to non-dependent entities

A dependent entity set can be converted to an entity set by choosing a unique identifier for the dependent entity set and establishing a relationship between the new entity set and its previous parent. The conversion is illustrated in Figure 8.16. Here tasks are given a unique identifier, TASK-ID. Each task in the system now has a unique value for its TASK-ID. Any project that makes use of the task is related to that task through relationship set, HAVE. The value of ESTIMATED-COST will now be only stored once for each task.

Figure 8.16 Converting to entity sets

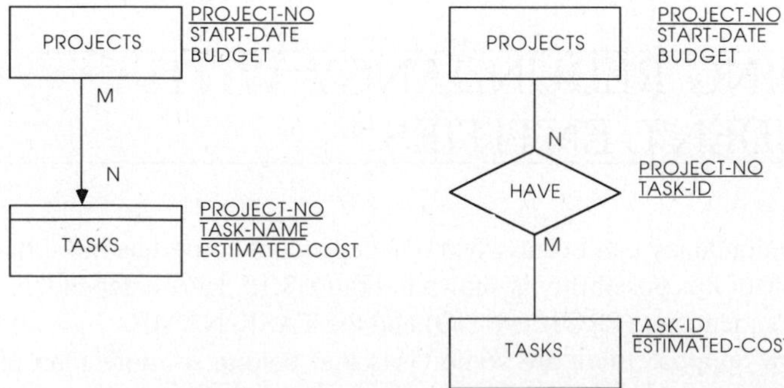

CHOOSING BETWEEN DEPENDENT AND INDEPENDENT SETS

The dependent entity concept is sometimes useful but often introduces uncertainties of whether to model some entity set as an independent set or to model it as dependent on some other set. For example, if persons work in departments then isn't person a dependent of department? After all if we didn't have a department then we need not have that person. The answer to this is that if we abolish the department the person still exists and hence is not a dependent. However, INVOICE-LINE is dependent on INVOICE-NO because if we tear up the invoice the INVOICE-LINE also ceases to exist.

Thus an entity should be modeled as a dependent entity only if it completely disappears and is of no more interest at all in the system once its parent is removed from the system. Another rule is that anything with a unique identifier should not be modeled as a dependent entity. You will find that because of this requirement dependent entities are used infrequently. Thus the general rule is that IF IN DOUBT about making something a dependent then start by making it an entity set rather than a dependent entity set.

Later you may find that your entity set needs a composite identifier. Furthermore, you may find that this composite identifier contains an identifier of another entity set. In that case you should consider making the set with the composite identifier into a dependent entity set.

You may now wish to do Exercise 8.2 to see if you can identify situations where dependent entities should be used.

Exercise 8.2

Examine the following and comment on whether the dependence is valid or should be removed.

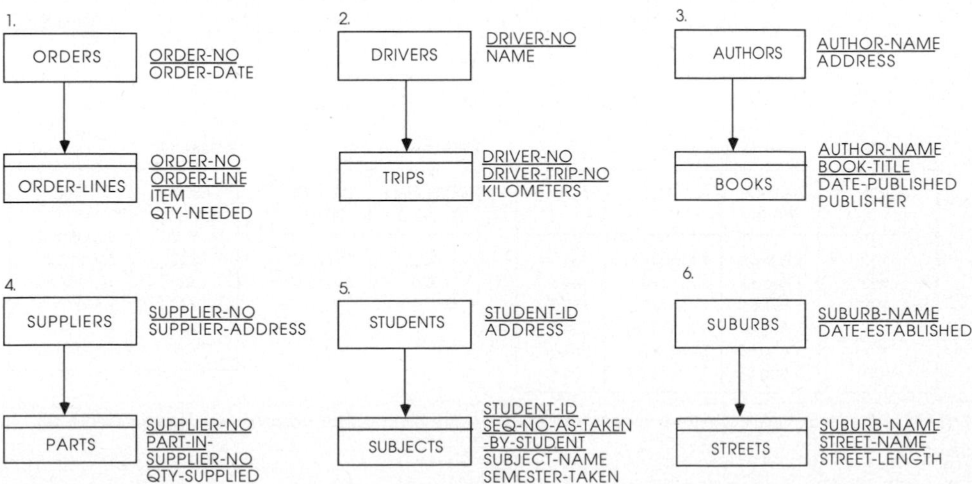

MODELING TIME VARIATIONS

Dependent entity sets can be used to model time variations. Here all time-independent attributes in a set can be stored in the set, whereas the time-dependent attributes become part of a dependent set. There are a number of kinds of time variation. The most common ones are attribute variation, relationship variation and role variation.

Attribute variation

Attribute variation occurs where an object attribute value varies over time. This attribute is sometimes called a historical attribute. An example is keeping track of how a person's WEIGHT changes over time.

Figure 8.17 illustrates a method that can be used to model attribute variations. Figure 8.17(a) models such variations as part of the entity set. As a result that entity set would convert to a relation that is not even in second normal form. Figure 8.17(b) shows how the variation of the attribute WEIGHT is modeled by a separate dependent entity set. The E-R diagram in Figure 8.17(b) can be converted to two relations, both of which are in BCNF. The first relation, PERSONS, models the time-independent properties. The second, WEIGHINGS, models weight variations. There would be one such relation for each historical attribute.

Figure 8.17 Modeling attribute time variation

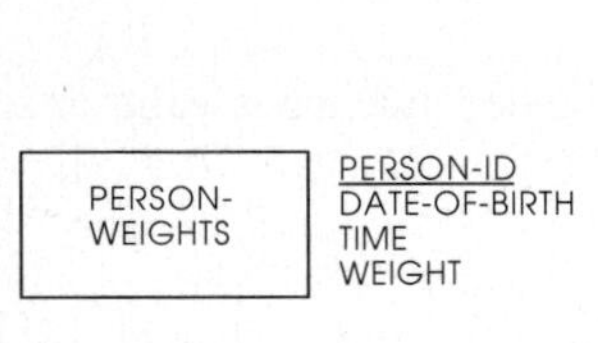

WEIGHINGS

PERSON-ID	DATE-OF BIRTH	TIME	WEIGHT
X22	1 Feb 63	3 March 83	63
X22	1 Feb 63	6 April 83	64.5
X22	1 Feb 63	11 May 83	52.1
X37	3 Aug 63	9 March 83	58.9
X37	3 Aug 63	20 April 83	58.7
X37	3 Aug 63	17 June 83	58.8

(a) Variations in the entity set

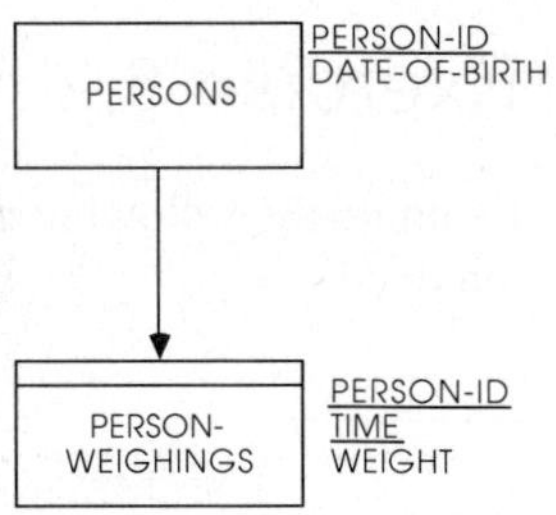

PERSONS

PERSON-ID	DATE-OF BIRTH
X22	1 Feb 63
X37	3 Aug 63

WEIGHINGS

PERSON-ID	TIME	WEIGHT
X22	3 March 83	63
X22	6 April 83	64.5
X22	11 May 83	52.1
X37	9 March 83	58.9
X37	20 April 83	58.7
X37	17 June 83	58.8

(b) Variations in a dependent entity set

Relationship variation

A time variation occurs in relationships between entities in two different sets. An example is a person's movement from one department to another, or changes in ownership of a vehicle.

Another such variation is illustrated in Figure 8.18 where the time spent by persons on projects is recorded on a weekly basis. A person's pay rate is set on a weekly basis and a person can work on many projects in one week. The relationship WORK-ON again does not correspond to a BCNF relation. Here the relation key is (PERSON-ID, PROJECT-NO, WEEK-NO) but PAY-RATE depends on part of this key, namely, (PERSON-ID, WEEK-NO).

Figure 8.18 Representing time variations in relationship

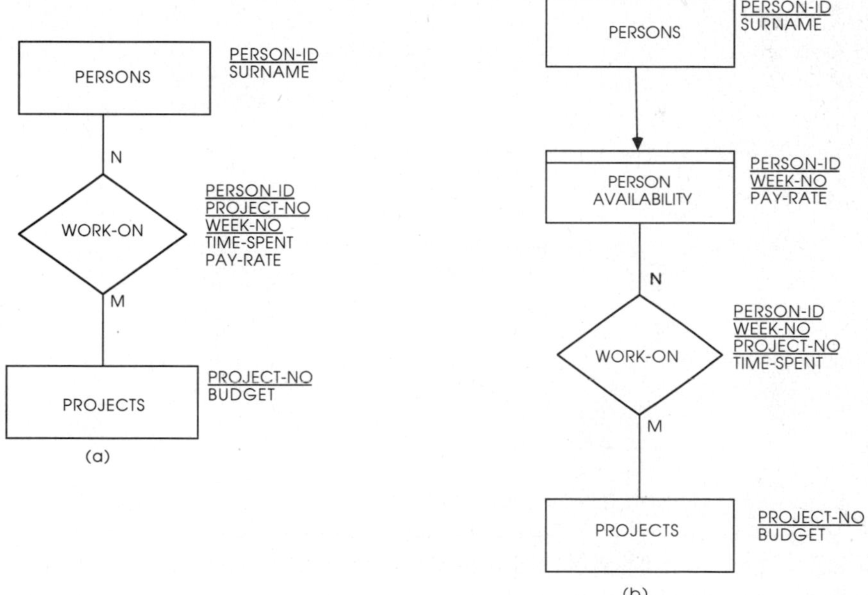

A better model of this system is shown in Figure 8.18(b). Now a dependent entity set, PERSON-AVAILABILITY, models a persons availability and PAY-RATE for a given week. The relationship WORK-ON specifies the projects for that person for the week.

Role variation

A variation in subset appearance can occur. For example, a person may be a casual employee for some periods and a permanent employee for other periods. This kind of time change will be described in the next chapter which covers roles and types.

A method to model this time variation is illustrated in Figure 8.19. Here appointments are modeled by a dependent entity set, APPOINTMENTS. Figure 8.19 also shows that there are two kinds of appointments. These are MANAGERIAL-APPOINTMENTS and ENGINEERING-APPOINTMENTS. In each case the appointment is identified by a combination of PERSON-ID and START-DATE. Both kinds of appointments have different attributes and appear in different relationships. Managerial appointments are made at some level and are made to manage a department. Engineering appointments are made at some salary and are to a selected project.

Figure 8.19 Modeling time variation of roles

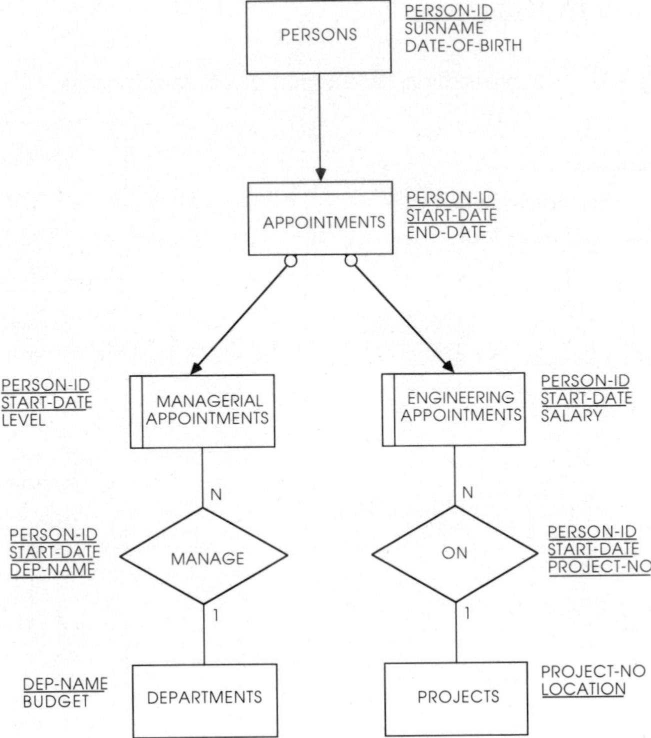

Exercise 8.3

Construct an E-R diagram including any subsets or dependent entity sets for the following systems.

1. An organization's customers may be individual persons or they may be companies. Each customer is given a CUST-ID and has a DATE-JOINED. Persons have a SURNAME and P-ADDRESS. Companies have a TRADING-NAME, T-ADDRESS and PHONE-NO.

2. Customers may be service customers or purchase customers. Purchase customers have a CREDIT-LIMIT stored for them. A customer may be both a service and a purchase customer.
3. Service customers have maintenance contracts arranged for them. Each contract has a CONTRACT-NO, CONTRACT-DATE, COST and EQUIP-DETAILS.
4. Calls made against each contract are recorded. Each call is given a CALL-NO within the contract. The DATE-MADE and DURATION of each call is stored. In addition, the quantity of parts used is stored for each call.
5. Parts used in the organization are identified by PART-ID and have a weight and price.
6. Purchase customers arrange regular orders for parts delivery. Each regular order has a REG-ORDER-NO and REQ-DATE.
7. Each regular order may have any number of components. Each component has a DAY-NO within the order. The DAY-NO identifies the day of the month on which a quantity of parts is to be delivered.
8. Prices of parts vary from time to time. Each price change is recorded with its effective date.
9. The deliveries made for each regular order are recorded. This record includes the actual delivery date, and the quantities of parts delivered on that date. The delivery is identified by the REG-ORDER-NO, the DAY-NO and the actual date.

SUMMARY

This chapter described two extensions often used in E-R modeling. One extension was subsets. These are often used to model entity sets whose objects can be treated similarly for some purposes and differently for other purposes. The other extension was dependent entity sets. These can be used to model entities that depend on other entities. They are also useful in modeling time variations.

9

Converting E-R models to relations

INTRODUCTION

The previous chapters described how to develop E-R and relational models of user data. The next step in database design is to convert these models to a database. Databases are created and maintained using database management systems (DBMS), which are software systems that are used to maintain databases. A DBMS supports a data structure and the database must be specified in terms of that data structure. As a result, the next step of database design is to convert the model of data, which may be an E-R or relational model, into the data structure supported by the DBMS. This conversion depends on the type of structure supported by the DBMS.

The simplest conversion is to DBMS that support relational structures. These DBMS are sometimes known as relational database management systems (RDBMS). In that case, a model specified as a set of relations becomes the data definition to the RDBMS.

A number of criteria must be considered during conversion. One important criterion is preserving correspondence to BCNF relations. Analysts spend a considerable amount getting their relations into the highest normal form to remove data redundancy. It is essential that this non-redundant structure be carried across to the database definition to prevent database redundancy. However, conversions to RDBMS must also satisfy a number of other criteria. They should also maintain integrity constraints and keep the number of files to a minimum.

There is also another set of criteria. These concern performance of transactions that use the database. Transactions are often initiated by users, who expect a relatively quick response. Designers must ensure that their designs result in quick transaction response.

This chapter describes conversion methods from E-R models to RDBMS. It describes conversion criteria and how these criteria are met by conversion processes from E-R models to RDBMS. It also outlines the balance between clarity and normal correspondence at the E-R level and its effect on conversion from E-R models to relations. The chapter then describes how such designs are adjusted to improve transaction performance.

THE IDEAL CONVERSION METHOD

In an ideal conversion, each set in the E-R diagram becomes a relation. The set identifiers become relation keys of these relations. In the ideal case these relations would be in the highest normal form. This ideal can often be reached if proper care is exercised in drawing the E-R diagram. Thus for example the E-R diagram in Figure 9.1 is converted to the three relations:

1. WORK-ON (PERSON-ID, PROJECT-ID, HRS-SPENT)
2. PERSONS (PERSON-ID, DATE-OF-BIRTH, SURNAME)
3. PROJECTS (PROJECT-ID, BUDGET)

Figure 9.1 An E-R diagram

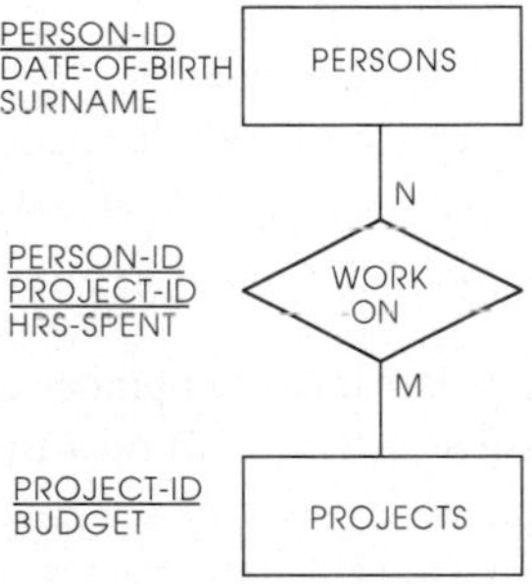

However, there are many cases where this ideal process does not result in BCNF relations. There are two reasons for this. One is errors in the E-R model. The other is where the E-R model includes constructs used to improve clarity in E-R diagrams.

Figure 9.2(a) is an example of an error in the E-R diagram. In this figure, entity set PERSONS includes both details about persons as well as their current department details. Obviously that type of set should be decomposed into the three sets shown in Figure 9.2(b) at the E-R level. The guideline here is to represent each set of facts by a separate relation.

Figure 9.3(a) is an example of an E-R diagram that includes constructs that improve clarity, but which do not convert to BCNF relations. Entity set PERSONS in this figure contains information about persons. One attribute here is PHONE-NO and the

Figure 9.2 Separating concepts

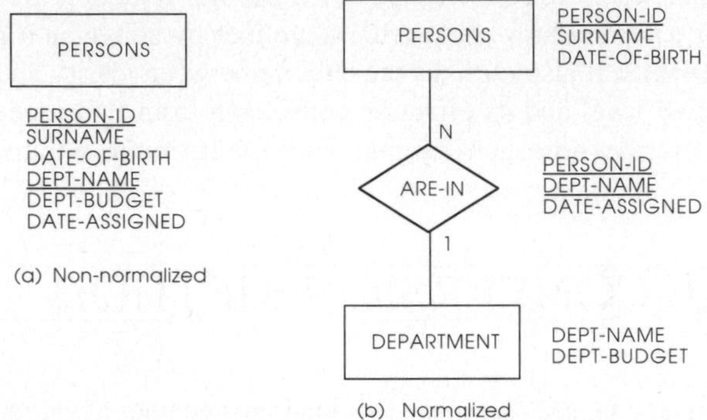

(a) Non-normalized

(b) Normalized

Figure 9.3 Creating entity sets

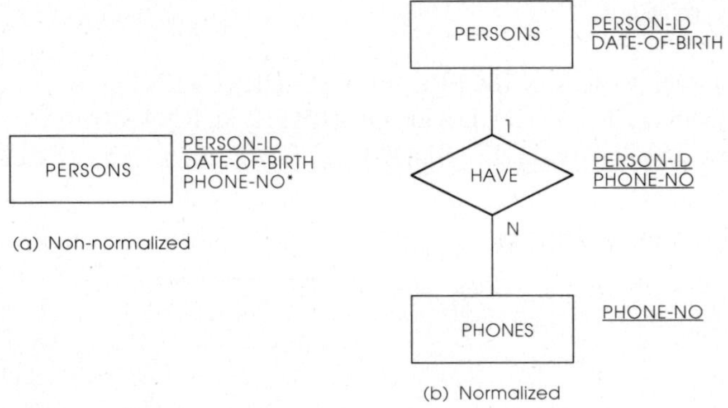

(a) Non-normalized

(b) Normalized

asterisk indicates that this attribute takes a number of values because a person has more than one phone number. PERSONS will not be a BCNF relation. In fact it is not even a normal relation. It could then be argued that the E-R diagram in Figure 9.3(a) should be replaced by that in Figure 9.3(b). This new diagram however is often not acceptable in high-level modeling. Modeling phone numbers by separate entity sets gives them more importance than necessary. As a result many practitioners would accept Figure 9.3(a) and normalize after conversion to relations.

There would be two steps in the conversion. The first conversion step would be to convert PERSONS in Figure 9.3(a) to relation:

PERSONS(PERSON-ID, DATE-OF-BIRTH, PHONE-NO*).

The second step is to normalize PERSONS by decomposing it into the two relations:

PERSONS(PERSON-ID, DATE-OF-BIRTH)
CONTACTS(PERSON-ID, PHONE-NO)

In summary, it is important in E-R modeling to keep a balance between clarity and normality. On the one hand, it is important to separate important objects and concepts into their own sets and incorrect diagrams like that in Figure 9.2(a) should be avoided. However, some less important properties can often stay unormalized at the E-R level and be removed by decomposition following conversion to relations.

For these reasons it is necessary to check relations obtained following any conversion to ensure that they are in the highest normal form and decompose them if necessary. However, the fact that relations are checked for normality after conversion should not become a reason for making bad choices at the E-R level.

Creation of normal relations is only one of the conversion goals. There are also other constraints concerned with date integrity and a need to minimize the number of relations.

Preserving integrity constraints

System integrity is important in any system. It requires all constraints defined during analysis to be preserved in the RDBMS. Some of these constraints appear in the E-R diagram. They include cardinality and participation. The links from object sets to relationships are also a constraint. They state that an entity cannot appear in a relationship unless it is in the entity set. Thus we cannot have a value of PERSON-ID in relation WORK unless that value of PERSON-ID also appears in entity set PERSONS. This constraint is known as *referential integrity*. Still another constraint is defined by set identifiers. This requires that no more than one row in the relation possesses the same value of the identifier.

Direct conversions to relations do not preserve these constraints. For example, there is nothing to stop someone adding a row to relation WORK where that row has a PERSON-ID value that does not exist in relation, PERSONS. Many methodologies do not convert E-R diagrams directly to relations but use an intermediate step that shows such integrity constraints. This intermediate step produces what is sometimes called the logical record structure or the composite logical structure.

Figure 9.4 is an example of a logical record structure. It is produced by conversion from the E-R diagram in Figure 9.1. Here each object set becomes a logical record with the same name as the object set. Links in the E-R diagram are converted to links between logical records in the logical record structure. The links are labeled by those attributes that are common in both sets. The link between PERSONS and WORK is labeled by PERSON-ID because PERSON-ID appears in both PERSONS and WORK. The direction of the link is from WORK to PERSONS. This implies that a value of PERSON-ID must exist in PERSONS before it can be used in WORK.

Each record in the logical structure is then converted to a relation in a RDBMS. The links in the logical structure correspond to the concept of foreign key, which was described in Chapter 3. PERSON-ID is a foreign key in relation WORK but a relation key in relation PERSONS. This implies that values of PERSON-ID in WORK must already exist in relation PERSONS. The link is from a foreign key in one relation to the relation where that foreign key is the relation key. It is the foreign key that appears as the label on the link between the two sets.

Such links would be converted to foreign key definition in a RDBMS that supports

Figure 9.4 Composite diagram

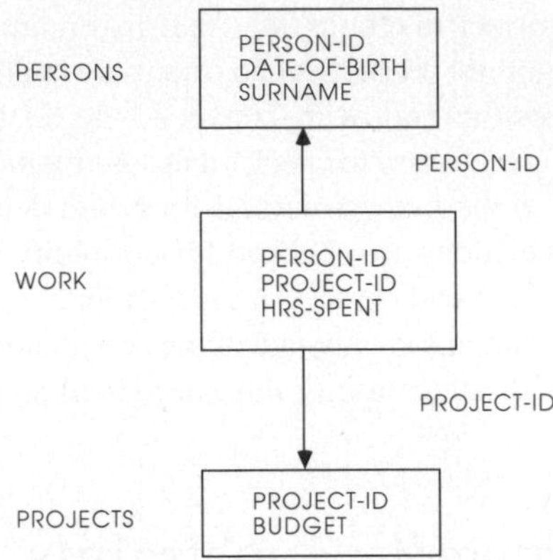

foreign keys. However, it should be pointed out that many RDBMS do not support relation key definitions. Consequently referential integrity constraints must be maintained by application programs.

Minimizing relations

Another conversion criterion is to minimize the number of relations. This is done for obvious reasons. It is to reduce the overheads associated with setting up unnecessary files or relations.

One way to reduce the number of relations is to combine relations with equivalent keys. One such combination combines any entity set, whose entities participate in at most one relationship, with that relationship. The relation key of that entity set and the relationship are the same and thus the relations can be combined. The identifier of the entity that appears in one relationship only becomes the key of the combined relation. One such conversion is illustrated in Figure 9.5. Here there is a 1:N relationship set, WORKS-IN, between PERSONS and DEPARTMENTS. The relation key of WORKS-IN is PERSON-ID because a person works in one department only. The relation key of PERSONS is also PERSON-ID. As a result the entity set DEPARTMENTS and the relationship set, WORKS-IN, are combined and the E-R diagram in Figure 9.5 is converted to the two relations:

PERSONS (PERSON-ID, SURNAME, DATE-OF-BIRTH, DEPT-NAME,
DATE-ASSIGNED)
DEPARTMENTS (DEPT-NAME, BUDGET)

As a rule any 1:N relationship can be combined into one relation. Some writers, however, recommend that combinations be allowed only where entity participation in the relationship set is mandatory. This is proposed to ensure that all foreign keys always have a value in a relation. For example, if participation of PERSONS in WORKS-IN is optional, then some rows in relation PERSONS will have no value for DEPT-NAME, its foreign key.

Figure 9.5 Combining an entity set and a relationship set

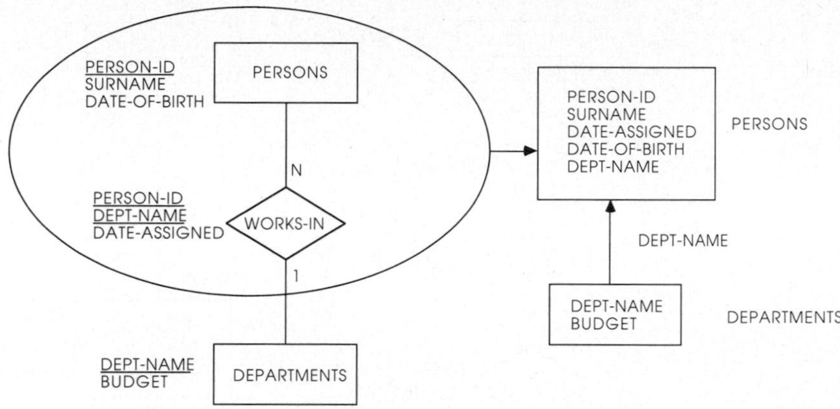

The combination would therefore not take place. However, entity sets with optional participation are combined in systems where minimizing relation is an important criterion.

Combinations that involve more than two entity sets are also possible. Figure 9.6 shows an E-R diagram where each department has one account and each account belongs to one department. The DEPARTMENTS and DEPT-ACCOUNTS entity sets can be combined into the one relation. You may recall from Chapter 6 that relations DEPARTMENTS and DEPT-ACCOUNTS would have equivalent keys. Algorithms discussed in that chapter described how these relations can be combined. Figure 9.7 shows an even more elaborate example. Here five object sets are combined to make the one relation. This is equivalent to combining five relations with equivalent keys.

Figure 9.6 Converting a 1:1 relationship

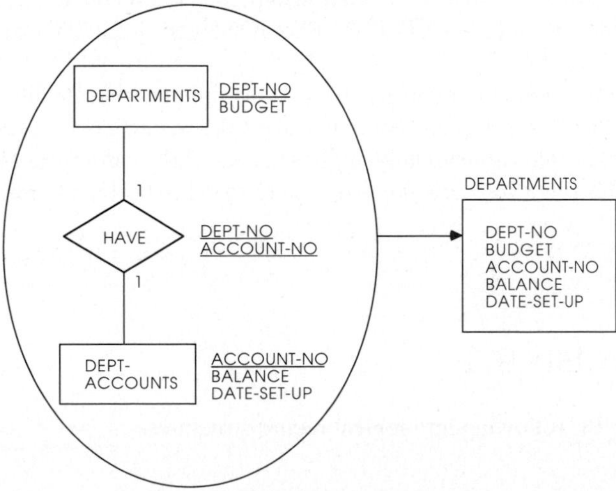

Figure 9.7 Converting sequences of 1:1 relationships

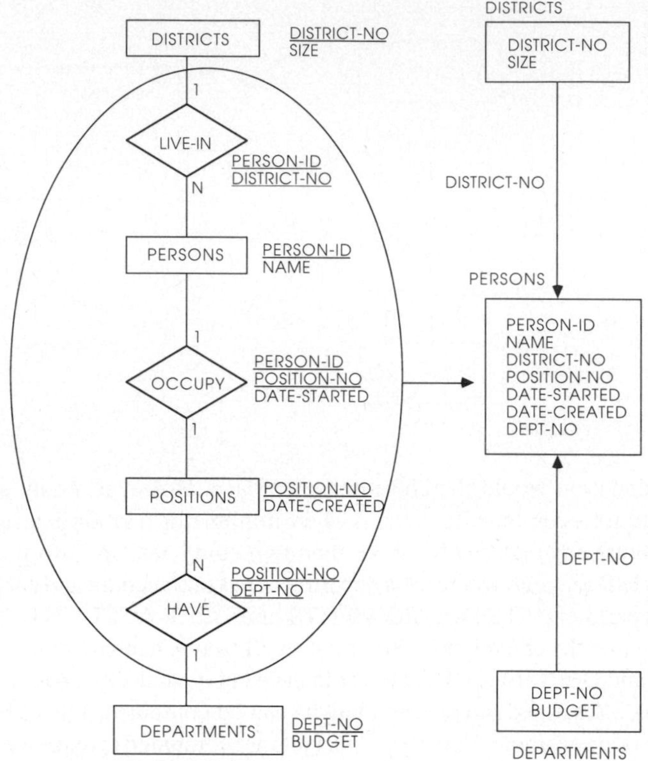

Just as in the previous discussion it is possible to restrict combinations to entities with mandatory participation in the relationship. For example, if POSITIONS participation was optional in the OCCUPY relationship, then POSITIONS and HAVE would be used to construct one relation. LIVE-IN, PERSONS and OCCUPY would be used to construct another relation.

Combination of sets can also be used to implement cardinality constraints. If two sets in an 1:N relationship are combined then the identifier of the entity set becomes the relation key. This immediately implies that the entity can appear in one relationship only.

At this stage you may like to do Exercise 9.1 to become familiar with the conversion method.

Exercise 9.1

Convert the following into logical record structures:

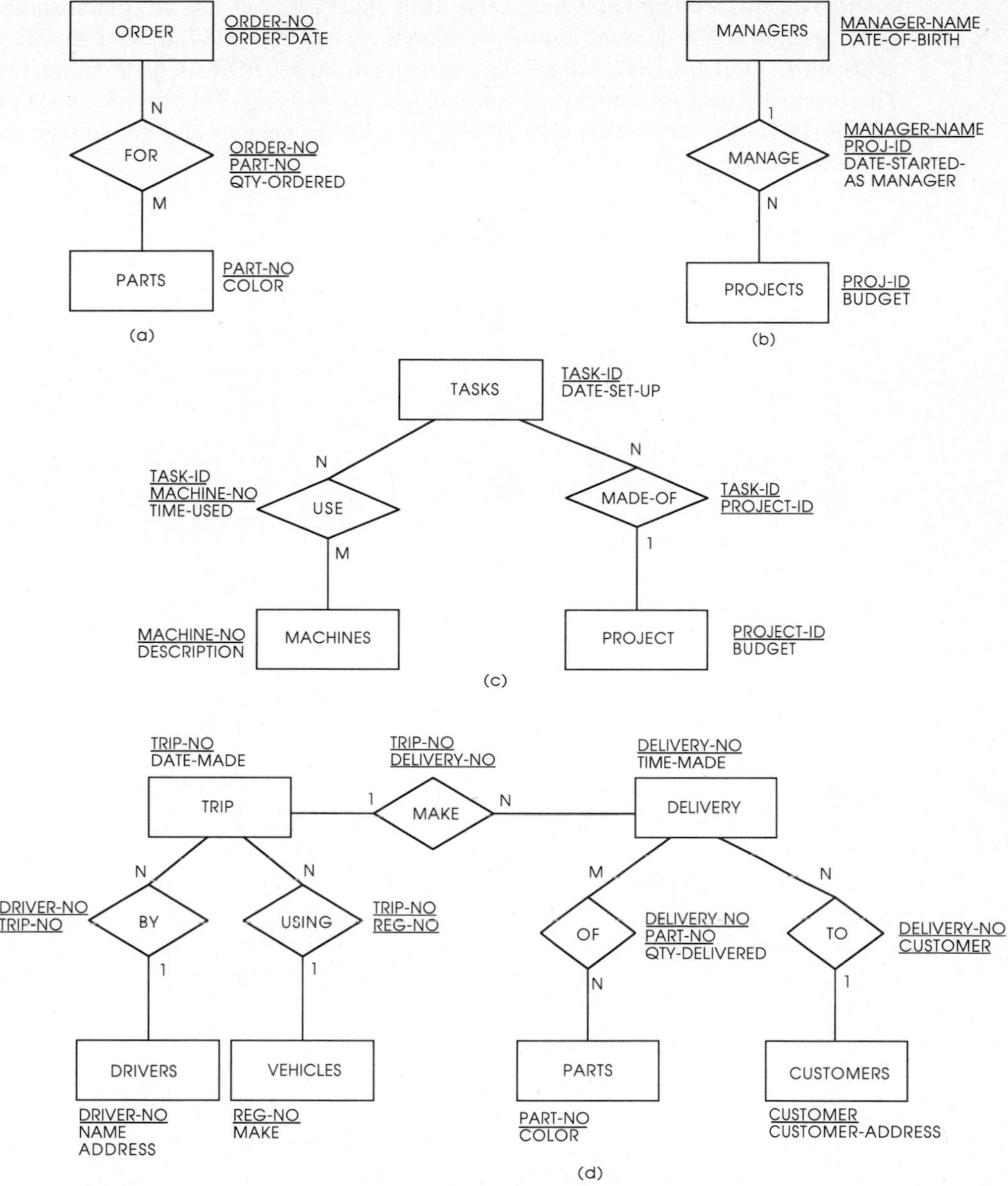

Converting dependent entity sets

So far our conversion examples concentrated on converting entity and relationship sets to relations. Similar ideas can be used to convert dependent entity sets.

Figure 9.8 shows the conversion of a dependent entity set to a relation. Here the set is simply converted to one relation. Dependent entity sets can also be combined with relationship sets to reduce the number of relations. Thus Figure 9.9 shows a dependent entity set, INVOICE-LINES, combining with relationship set, FOR, to create one relation. This is possible because each invoice line includes one part only. Thus the relation key of FOR is (INVOICE-LINE-NO). INVOICE-LINES has the same relation key and can thus be combined with FOR.

Figure 9.8 Converting dependent entity sets

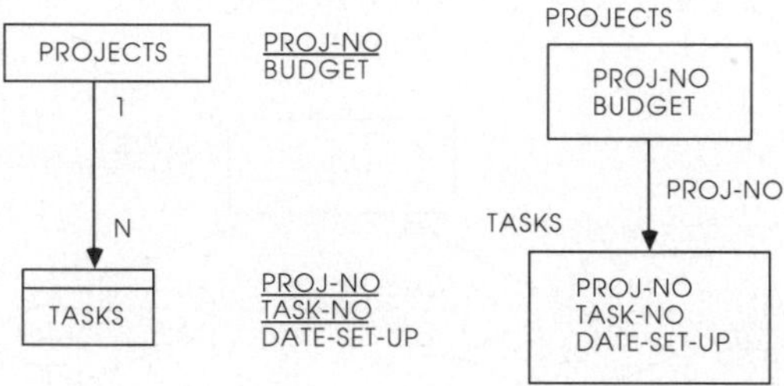

Figure 9.9 A dependent entity set and 1:N relationship

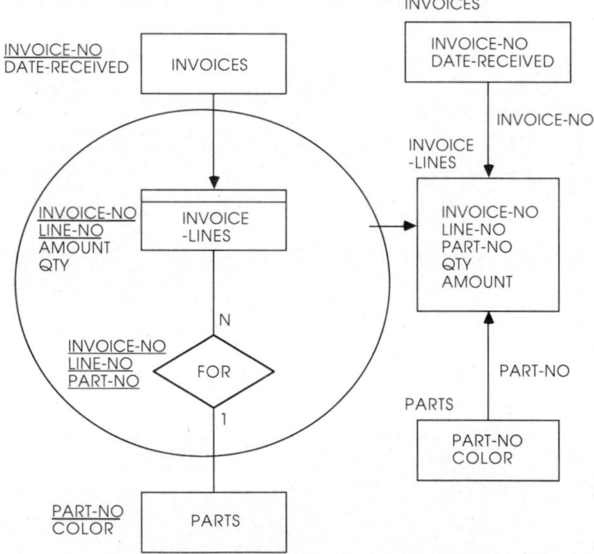

Converting subsets

Converting subsets to relations presents the designer with more alternatives, especially if it is important to reduce the number of relations. The options available include:

1. Convert each subset to a separate relation.
2. Combine the source set into the subset set and make one relation out of them.
3. Combine the subset into the source set and make one relation out of them.

Figure 9.10 illustrates the alternative logical structures that can be generated for uniform sets. Another criterion can be used to choose among these alternatives. This criterion is non-homogeneity — that is relations where some attributes never take values for some rows. For example, consider OPTION 3 in Figure 9.10. Here the subsets have been combined with the source. Each row in the combined relation PERSONS will always have some NULL values. If the person is a manager, then QUALIFICATIONS will be NULL and if the person is an engineer then DATE-ASSIGNED will be NULL. OPTION 3 should thus not be used with uniform sets if non-homogeneity is to be avoided.

Figure 9.10 Converting uniform subsets

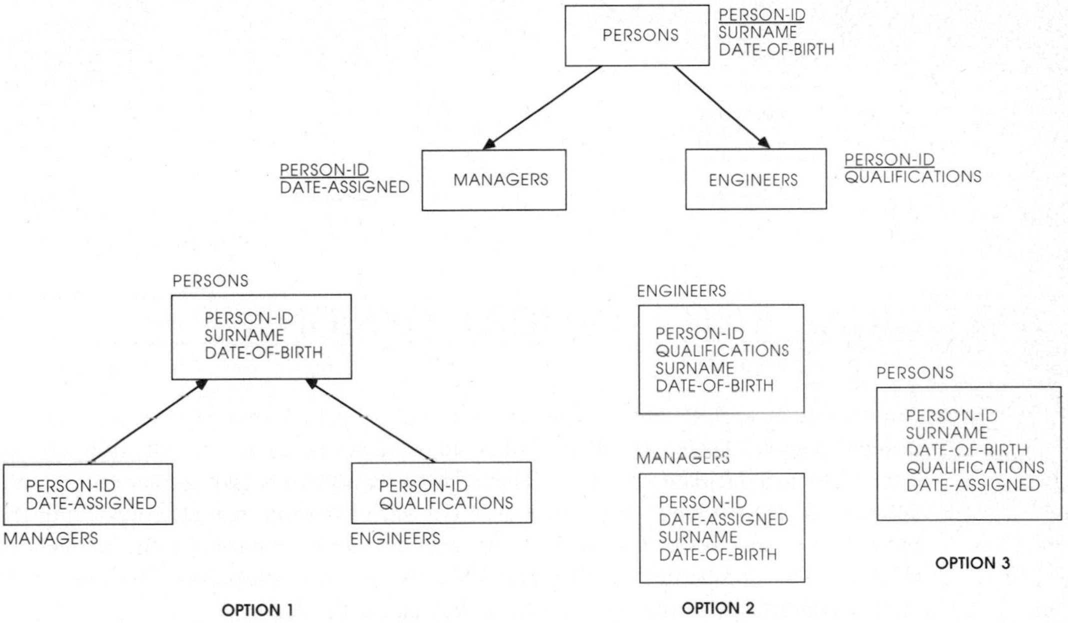

The situation changes with non-uniform sets. An example of the three options with non-uniform sets is illustrated in Figure 9.11. Now OPTION 3 will only have non-homogeneity if participation is optional. However, OPTION 2 will always have non-homogeneity because a member can only be a student or a staff member but not both.

The guidelines that can be used to minimize relations and yet avoid non-homogeneity are:

1. use OPTION 2 for uniform sets, and
2. use OPTION 3 for mandatory non-uniform sets.

Figure 9.11 Converting non-uniform subsets

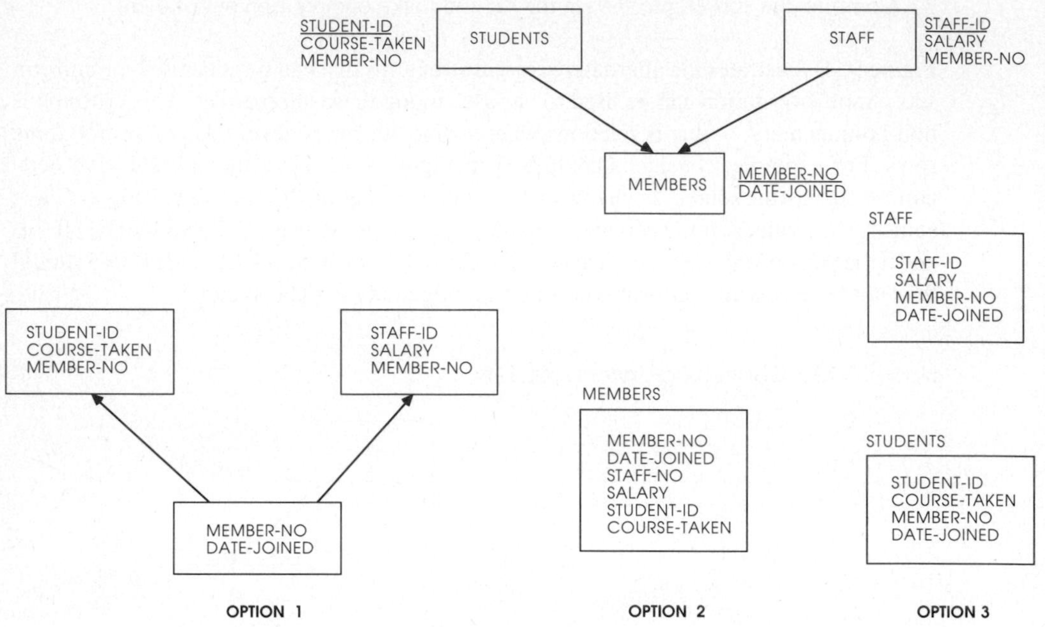

LOGICAL AND PHYSICAL DESIGN

Conversion to logical record structure is usually the first step of conversion to an implementation. There are often further adjustments made to this structure before conversion to a database definition. These further adjustments take further criteria into account. So far we have only considered one set of criteria, namely, preserving the properties of the model obtained during analysis while minimizing the number of relations. These properties included normality and integrity constraints. The other set of criteria concerns performance of transactions that use the database.

Designs that satisfy the first criterion only often do not result in good performance. Transaction performance is usually determined by the number of records that must be accessed by the transaction. Designs that correspond to BCNF relations often require many records to be accessed by transactions.

Performance can be improved in two ways. One is to add indices to the database. Such indices ensure that a transaction can retrieve required records directly rather than by a sequential search through a database. The other is to adjust the normalized design to reduce the number of records that must be accessed by a transaction. This is usually done by introducing some redundancy into the design. Transaction must be analyzed to determine the indices to be added to the database. Some analysis is needed to determine the indices to be added and any logical structure adjustments.

Transaction analysis

Analysis usually begins by choosing the most important transactions, seeing how they use database tables and adding indices to support such use. Important transactions are those that occur very frequently or those that support some critical need.

Transactions are analyzed by plotting access paths against the logical record structure. An access path defines the path followed by a transaction given some input parameter to find the desired output. Figure 9.12 illustrates one such access path.

Figure 9.12 Access paths

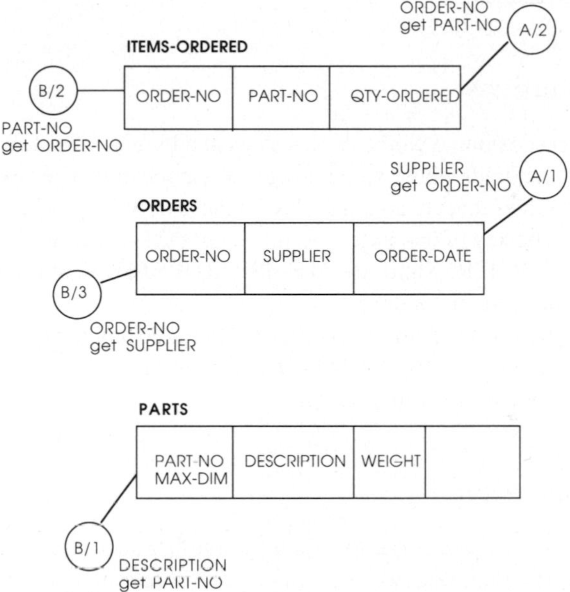

This figure shows a structure made up of three logical records. Record ORDERS shows orders placed by an organization with its suppliers. Record ITEMS-ORDERED shows the quantities of parts in each order. Record PARTS is a description of the parts. Figure 9.12 also shows access paths for the following two transactions:

Transaction A: Find the PART-NO of all parts ever ordered from a given supplier,
Transaction B: Find the suppliers who have supplied parts with a given description.

An access path is plotted for each of these transactions in Figure 9.12. The access path shows the records accessed by each transaction. Each access path is made up of a number of steps. Each step shows one record structure accessed by the transaction and the access step sequence shows the sequence in which these records are accessed.

The access step for transaction A starts with step A/1. This access step uses ORDERS and a known value of SUPPLIER to find the ORDER-NO of all orders made to that supplier. Access step A/2 uses the values of ORDER-NO retrieved by access step A/1 to find the PART-NO of parts ordered from that supplier. Each access step is labeled by an access step number. This number is made up of the transaction identifier, in this case the letter A, and a sequential number. The access step also shows the fields whose values are known at the time of the access step, and the fields whose values are retrieved.

Access path for transaction B shows three steps. The first step finds the value of PART-NO with a given DESCRIPTION from file PARTS. The second step uses the values of PART-NO found in step B/1 to find the values of ORDER-NO of orders that contain those parts from file ITEMS-ORDERED. The third step uses the values of ORDER-NO found in step B/2 to find the value of SUPPLIER for suppliers of those orders from file ORDERS.

These access steps are now used to determine indices and any adjustments made to introduce redundancy.

Adding indices

To add indices, examine all the access steps at a logical record. Each such access step is labeled with the fields whose values are known at the time of access. These fields become the keys of indices that are added to the database definition. Thus ORDERS would have two indices. The key of one index would be ORDER-NO, and the key of the other index would be SUPPLIER. Similarly ITEMS-ORDERED would have two indices, while PARTS would have one index.

The next step is to examine whether further adjustments to the structure are needed. These adjustments usually result in the introduction of redundancy, or what is now becoming known as denormalization.

Denormalization

A first cut at denormalization is to reduce the number of access steps for a transaction. This can be done by examining two successive access steps and placing the field retrieved by the first step into the record accessed by the next step. Thus in Figure 9.12, access step A/1 uses a value of SUPPLIER to retrieve values of ORDER-NO and uses these ORDER-NO values as inputs in access step A/2. Thus a possible adjustment is to add field SUPPLIER to record ITEMS-ORDERED. Now as shown in Figure 9.13 transaction A can be processed using one step only. The number of access steps in transaction B is also reduced by this adjustment. Now access step B/3 is not needed because values of SUPPLIER can be found from file ITEMS-ORDERED. Transaction B can be further improved by adding DESCRIPTION to record ITEMS-ORDERED.

Adding redundancy does not always mean that the performance of the system as a whole is improved. Certainly, performance of transactions that make use of the redundancy is improved. However, performance of some update transactions can now deteriorate because they must add the redundancy to the database. For example, suppose DESCRIPTION is added to ITEMS-ORDERED. Transactions that add records to ITEMS-ORDERED must now look up record PARTS to copy the description of ordered parts.

Figure 9.13 Access paths with denormalized files

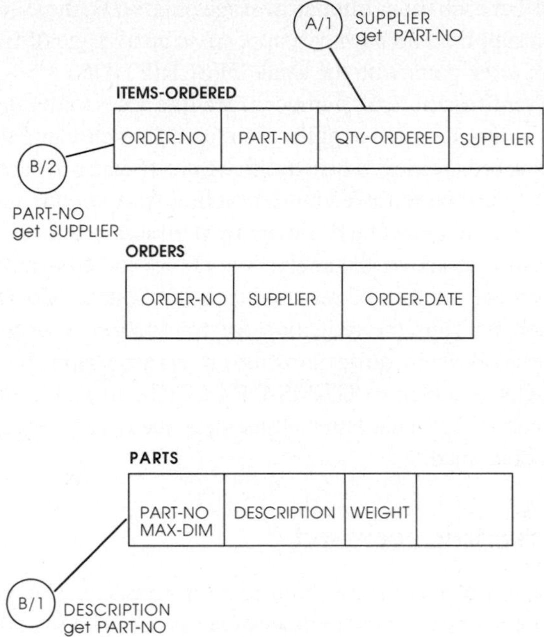

Adding redundancy to reduce the number of access steps can often be deceiving. Although the number of access steps is reduced, the number of records actually retrieved may not be greatly affected. Thus it is often advisable to make some rough computations to determine the number of logical records that are accessed by the alternative designs. This process is called logical record analysis.

Logical record analysis

Logical record analysis determines the number of logical records accessed by each access step. Computation usually proceeds by making an estimate of the number of records retrieved, and entering into a table like that shown in Figure 9.14.

Figure 9.14 Logical record analysis

TRANSACTION	STEP	RECORDS ACCESSED	
A	A/1	50 (orders/supplier)	= 50
A	A/2	50 x 10 (parts/order)	= 500
		TOTAL	= 550
B	B/1	3 (parts with descr.)	= 3
B	B/2	3 x 5 (orders/parts)	= 15
B	B/3	15 x 1 (supplier/order)	= 15
		TOTAL	= 33

(a) Normalized design

TRANSACTION	STEP	RECORDS ACCESSED	
A	A/1	50 x 10 (records/ orders/supplier)	= 500
		TOTAL	= 500
B	B/1	3 (parts/description)	= 3
B	B/2	3 x 5 (orders/parts)	= 15
		TOTAL	= 18

(b) Following denormalization

The following assumptions were made in constructing the table shown in Figure 9.14. It is assumed that each order is for an average of 10 parts, there are an average of 50 orders made to each supplier and each part appears in an average of five orders. There are also an average of three parts with the same DESCRIPTION.

Using this information, the number of records accessed by step A/1 will be 50 because there are 50 orders for each supplier. In step A/2 each value of ORDER-NO retrieved results in 10 records retrieved because there are 10 parts in each order. Thus an average of 550 records must be retrieved by transaction A. A similar computation shows that an average of 33 records must be retrieved by transaction B.

Figure 9.14 also shows the analysis made for the adjusted design shown in Figure 9.13. The average number of records accessed now is 500 for transaction A and 18 for transaction B. Thus the reduction for transaction A is at best marginal, whereas for transaction B it is quite substantial. Transaction B is further improved if DESCRIPTION is added to ITEMS-ORDERED. In that case the number of records accessed becomes 15. This latter adjustment leads to a marginal improvement only, and should not be made.

Physical records accessed

One point should be made here about records accessed. The number of logical records accessed is not necessarily the number of accesses made to disk. Many systems block a number of logical records into one physical record. In that case, all logical records in one block are retrieved in one disk access.

Blocking can improve performance of transactions that retrieve groups of records with a given field value. Thus suppose the physical sequence of records in file ITEMS-ORDERED is in ascending order of ORDER-NO. In that case records, with the same value of ORDER-NO, will be blocked into the same physical records. Performance of transaction A can now be improved because the 500 records retrieved in step A/2 may require many fewer disk accesses. In fact it is possible that all records in the same order are always in the same block. In that case only 50 disk accesses will be needed in step A/2. Furthermore if records in file ORDERS are stored in the physical sequence of SUPPLIER then the number of records retrieved in step A/1 may be much less than 50, in fact it may be one record. Thus only 51 disk accesses may be all that is needed for transaction A.

Note, however, that blocking does not improve performance of all steps at a given logical record. It only improves performance of those steps that retrieve records using the same field values used for physically sequencing records. Thus performance of transaction B is not improved by physically blocking records with the same value of ORDER-NO. Access step B/2 uses PART-NO to access ITEMS-ORDERED, whereas ITEMS-ORDERED blocks records with a common value of ORDER-NO. It also uses ORDER-NO to access file ORDERS, whereas ORDERS blocks records with a common value of SUPPLIER.

Thus a designer has a choice: either block records in the suggested orders and improve transaction A performance only; or make some logical adjustment and improve the performance of both transactions.

Exercise 9.3

You are given the logical structure below. Here projects requisition parts. Each requisition is for one kind of part, identified by PART-NO. The requisition states the QTY-NEEDED of each part. Each requisition can be supplied from more than one warehouse. QTY-SUPPLIED is the quantity of parts in a given requisition that is supplied by a given warehouse.

Plot access paths on this structure for the following transactions:

(a) What is the total of QTY-SUPPLIED for a part with a given PART-NO?
(b) List CITY of the suppliers who supplied parts requisitioned by a given DEPARTMENT.
(c) List the total of QTY-SUPPLIED for a given PART-NO and WAREHOUSE.
(d) List the DEPARTMENTs who were supplied parts from a given WAREHOUSE.

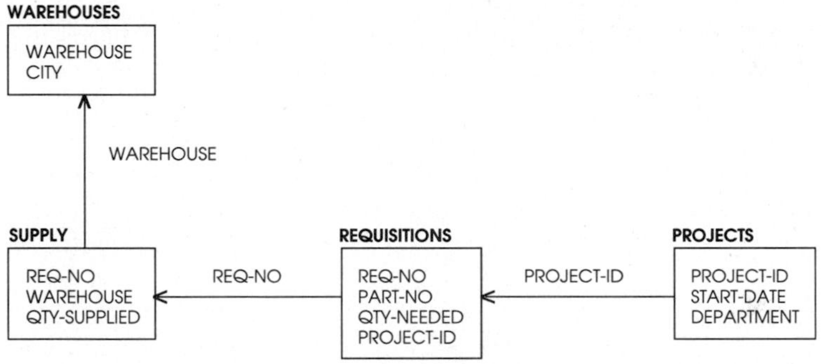

Suggest any possible changes to improve the performance of these transactions. Assume the following:

a. There are an average 400 requisitions per department.
b. Each requisition is supplied by an average of 2 warehouses.
c. Each part appears in an average of 50 requisitions.
d. Each warehouse supplies an average of 2000 requisitions.

SUMMARY

This chapter described conversion from E-R diagrams to relations. It defined criteria to be satisfied by the conversions. One criterion was for the relations to be in the highest normal form. The other two were to preserve integrity constraints and minimize the number of relations.

The chapter discussed some problems of directly converting E-R diagrams to relations. One problem can arise from badly structured E-R diagrams. Another problem can arise from including non-normality at the E-R level to improve clarity.

Methods for combining sets into relations to minimize the number of produced relations were also covered in the chapter. The simplest combination involved entities in 1:N relationships. Difficulties of converting subsets to relations were then outlined and some options described.

Finally the chapter described some adjustments that are often made to normalized designs to improve performance. These adjustments often introduce redundancy and thus are often known as denormalization.

10

Choosing relationships

INTRODUCTION

This chapter contains more guidelines on selecting relationships in E-R diagrams. Most users see choosing relationships as the most difficult task in E-R modeling. This is not just a coincidence. It is because the most important modeling decisions are made when relationships are chosen. It is here that users must identify the basic relationships in the system. These basic relationships are often difficult to identify because users in practice work with interrelated structures and find difficulties in separating them into basic relationships.

One way to view selection of relationships is as the equivalent to decomposition at the relational level. Each normal relation should model one set of basic facts. So should each relationship set. Consequently a major criterion for choosing relationships is to ensure that each relationship set corresponds to a relation in the highest normal form.

Another criterion is to use E-R syntactic guidelines. Unfortunately such guidelines are not sufficient. What is needed is a combination of E-R syntax and normal form definitions. The syntax can be used to identify potential problems and normal form equivalence can then be used to correct the model.

This chapter provides a number of guidelines for choosing correct relationships using this combination. It begins by describing some semantic problems that often arise when choosing relationships and how to check for them. It then continues to show how syntactic structures can often be used to assist modeling and discusses problems caused by multiple and N-ary relationships.

INCOMPLETE RELATIONSHIPS

The term incomplete relationship implies relationships that do not contain all the necessary information about a set of interactions. Loss of information can arise from a number of reasons. One is that all the basic relationships are not included in the model. Another is that the relationships in the model cannot be used to reconstruct all of the system information. This latter case often arises when derived relationships are included in the model.

Derived relationships

A derived relationship is one that can be derived from other relationships in the E-R diagram. One example of a derived relationship is illustrated in Figure 10.1(a).

Figure 10.1 Incomplete relationships

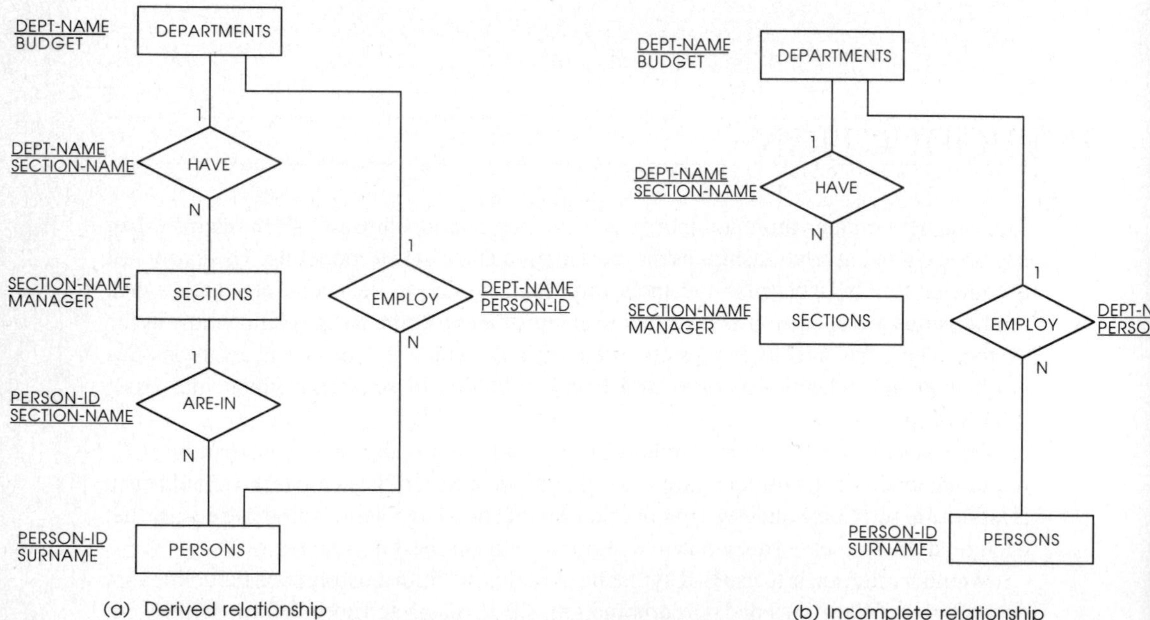

(a) Derived relationship

(b) Incomplete relationship

Figure 10.1(a) shows that departments have sections and persons are in sections. Here, departments employ a person and place that person in one of the department's sections. Figure 10.1(a) also includes the relationship, EMPLOY, to show the person's department. All relationships in relationship set, EMPLOY, can be derived from the other two relationships in the model. This derivation proceeds as follows. Suppose we are given a person. We can find the person's section from relationship set ARE-IN. Once we know the section, we can find the section's department from relationship set, HAVE. This department is the department that employs the person.

The E-R diagram in Figure 10.1(a) is not incomplete or for that matter incorrect. It is simply redundant because it includes information in EMPLOY that can be derived from other relationships in the model. The problem, however, arises when derived relationships are included in the model and basic relationships are left out. This is what happens in Figure 10.1(b). This figure includes the EMPLOY relationship, which shows persons employed by the department. It also includes the HAVE relationship, which shows the sections in a department. We cannot, however, use these two relationships to find the section where that person is located. The diagram in Figure 10.1(b) is now incomplete because it does not include all the information in the system. It is incomplete because it stores a derived relationship at the expense of a basic relationship.

Thus there are two important things to remember about derived relationships. One is that they are redundant and should not be stored in a database. The other is that often analysts make a mistake of storing a derived relationship but leaving out the relationships from which it is derived. In that case the E-R diagram is incomplete because it does not represent some basic data.

Kinds of incomplete relationships

The problem with incomplete relationships is that they often appear very natural to an analyst. For example, take Figure 10.2(a). This figure shows an E-R diagram that models deliveries made by drivers using trucks. It includes two relationship sets. Relationship USE models the trucks used by drivers, and relationship set FOR models the deliveries made by trucks. On a first examination this looks like a correct model. It simply states that drivers USE trucks FOR deliveries. However, careful study of this E-R diagram shows that we cannot tell what driver made what delivery. This is best illustrated by the occurrence diagram shown in Figure 10.2(b).

The occurrence diagram in Figure 10.2(b) shows that both Jill and Richard have used the Ferrari. It also shows that the Ferrari has been used to make deliveries D2 and D3. However, we cannot tell whether it is Richard or Jill who made delivery D2 or delivery D3.

A complete representation of the same information is shown in Figure 10.3. Here there is a relationship MAKE between drivers and deliveries. There is also a relationship USING between trucks and deliveries. The relationship USING is the same as relationship FOR in Figure 10.2(a), whereas relationship MAKE defines the actual deliveries made by drivers. The information about what driver made a delivery now appears in the E-R diagram Figure 10.2(a)). Relationship USE of Figure 10.2 does not appear in Figure 10.3. However, all the information in relationship USE can be derived from the relationships in Figure 10.3. For example, if we know that Richard made delivery D3 and D3 was made by the Ferrari then we know that Richard used the Ferrari.

Figure 10.3 is thus a complete model of the data whereas Figure 10.2 is not. The reason in this case is that Figure 10.2 contains one derived relationship USE. This relationship can be derived from the two basic relationships USING and MAKE in

Figure 10.2 An incomplete relationship

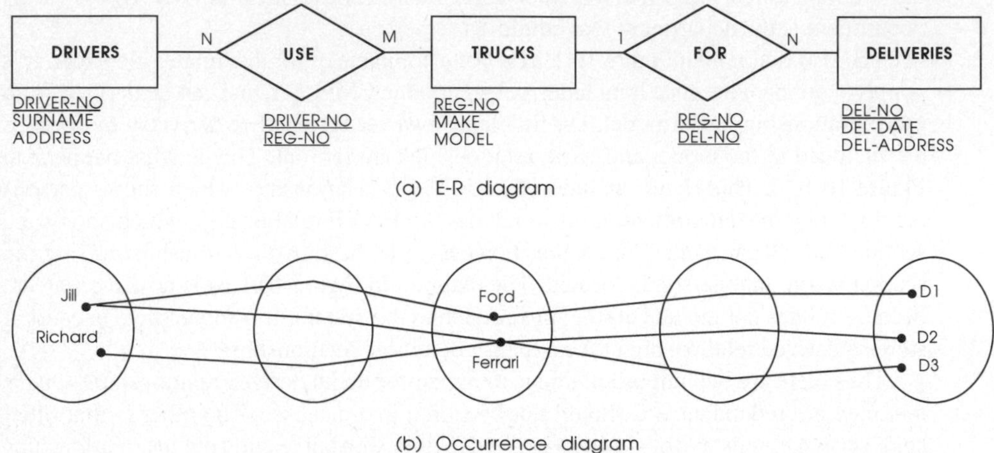

(a) E-R diagram

(b) Occurrence diagram

Figure 10.3 Conversion to a complete relationship

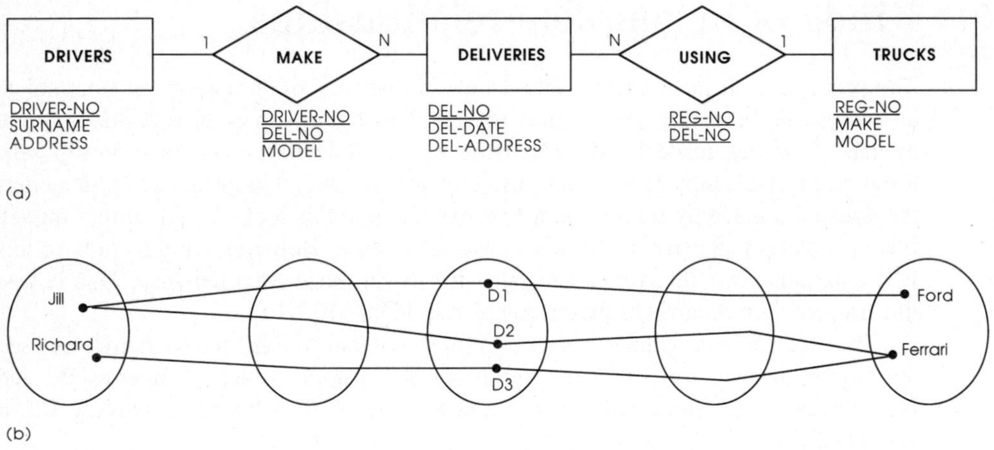

(a)

(b)

Figure 10.2. We could, of course, add MAKE to the E-R diagram in Figure 10.2. This would now make the diagram complete but redundant.

Derived relationships are only one cause of incompleteness in an E-R diagram. It is also possible to draw 'circular' diagrams that do not include all the system information. One example of this kind of model is shown in Figure 10.4. The E-R diagram in Figure 10.4 shows that persons use machines to produce parts. It can then be argued, in the same way as for Figure 10.3, that if only the USE and PRODUCE relationships are included in the model, then we cannot tell what parts a person produced. Relationship MAKE is then added to include this information. However, even with this relationship we still cannot tell what machine a person used to produce particular parts. We know

Figure 10.4 An incomplete circular relationship

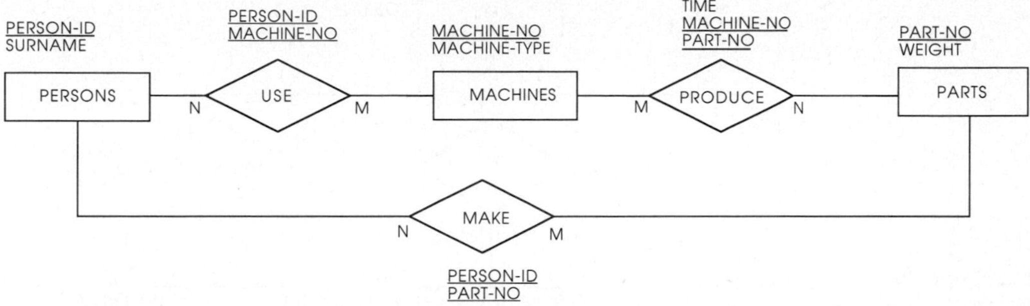

that a person used particular machines and produced particular parts. But we cannot tell what machines the person used to produce what parts.

To include this information it is necessary to add an entity that actually models the activity that involves all the three entity sets in Figure 10.4. One such entity set is JOBS in Figure 10.5(a). Each job includes a person, a machine and a part and thus it is possible to derive any relationships between these three types of entity.

A problem with the model shown in Figure 10.5(a) is that it calls for a new identifier, JOB-NO, to be added to the system. In a practical situation this may often be undesirable in that it would require changes to be introduced into current operation. One way to avoid the introduction of a new identifier is to use dependent entity sets as shown in Figure 10.5(b).

Now the new identifier is not needed because the identifier of jobs is generated by a combination of one of the involved entity identifiers together with an attribute to identify occurrences within that entity. In Figure 10.5(b) such a dependent identifier is generated by a combination of MACHINE-NO and TIME, which is the time when machine use is started. The person and parts involved in machine use at that time are recorded in relationship sets, USE and PRODUCE. Machines used by particular persons to produce a particular part can easily be found using the model shown in Figure 10.5(b). All we need is the time interval at which the person used a machine. This can be found from relationships USE. This time interval and machine is then used to identify the part using relationship set PRODUCE.

Detecting incomplete relationships

The question now is how does one detect incomplete relationships. Ideally we would like to be able to look at an E-R diagram and from its structure determine whether it is complete or incomplete. Many people often argue that loss of information can be determined from cardinality. It can be argued that loss of information occurs whenever the same entity set has a many cardinality with two relationships. Figure 10.6, however, illustrates that this is not the case. The syntactic structure of the E-R diagram in Figure 10.6 is exactly the same

Figure 10.5 Converting incomplete relationships

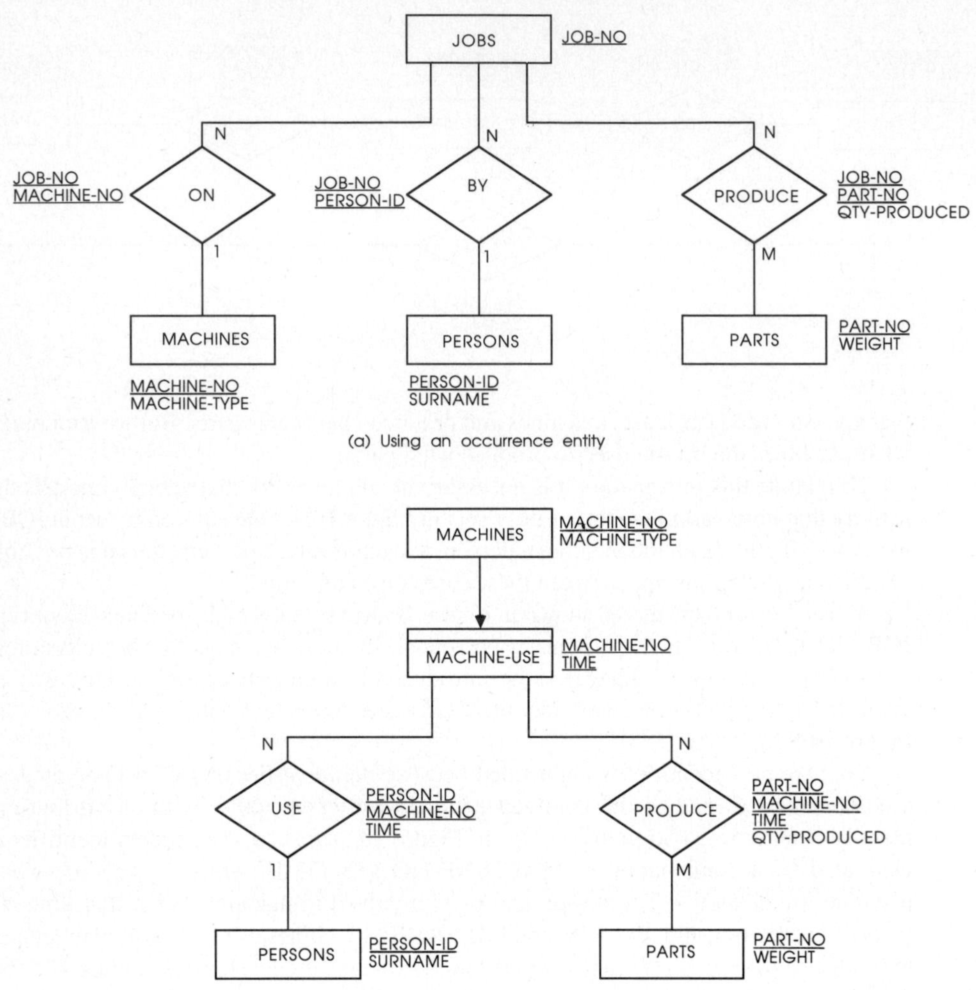

(a) Using an occurrence entity

(b) Using dependent entity sets

as that in Figure 10.2. In both cases an entity set has a many cardinality with two relationships. In Figure 10.2, TRUCKS has a many cardinality with USE and FOR. In Figure 10.6, COMPANIES has a many cardinality with SHAREHOLDERS and BUILDINGS.

However, no information is missing in Figure 10.6 simply because it is not meaningful to have any relationships between SHAREHOLDERS of a company, and BUILDINGS owned by that company. After all, a shareholder does not get a holding in part of a building through the ownership of a company share.

Thus the distinction between a complete and incomplete E-R diagram is semantic and not syntactic. In Figure 10.2 the delivery was described by two relationships, USE and

Figure 10.6 Complete relationships

Figure 10.7 Some complete relationships

FOR, and their combination results in loss of some of the information in a delivery. In Figure 10.6 INVEST and OWN are relationships that cannot be meaningfully combined and are thus the correct basic relationships in the system. Similar comments can apply to circular 1:N relationships like that shown in Figure 10.4. They are incomplete unless there is no meaningful relationship between the three entities.

It is, however, possible to identify some structures that are complete. One is where one of a combination of two relationships through an entity set is such that the entity set has a 1 cardinality with at least one relationship. The E-R diagram in Figure 10.7 is an example of this kind of structure. Here entity set PROJECTS has a 1 cardinality with relationship set, MANAGE. In this diagram it is possible to determine the managers for a person. The projects for a person are found from relationship set WORK-ON. Because each project has one manager it is possible to find the managers of a person's project.

Thus the best that can be done is to provide the following guideline. Whenever an entity set has an N cardinality with two relationships then there is a possibility of incompleteness. Similarly if there are a number of circular relationships incompleteness is possible.

Another guideline is to avoid the kind of circular structure shown in Figure 10.4 by modeling activities by entity sets like JOBS in Figure 10.5(a) rather than by relationships between entities in that activity. Alternatively, dependent entity sets like that in Figure 10.5(b) can be used to replace circular relationships.

Syntactic structure, however, has one useful property. It can give some indication of how to convert an incomplete structure to a complete structure.

Converting to a complete E-R diagram

Previous examples have shown two ways to convert incomplete relationships to complete relationships. One conversion was illustrated in Figure 10.3. This was to remove a derived relationship and replace it by its basic relationships.

Another conversion process was illustrated in Figure 10.5. This was to add a new entity set or dependent entity set to model specific activities. How does one choose the appropriate conversion? One guideline is to always use entity sets to identify activities as was the case in Figure 10.5(a). However, this approach may not always be appropriate.

It calls for the use of additional entity sets with new identifiers. If such an identifier is not natural to the system then two possibilities arise. One such possibility exists where at least one of the participating entity sets has a 1:1 cardinality with a relationship set, as is the case in Figure 10.2. In that case search for a basic relationship and remove a redundant relationship. Otherwise introduce a new entity or dependent entity sets as is the case in Figure 10.5(b).

Exercise 10.1 illustrates relationships some of which may be incomplete. It should give you a feel for identifying such relationships and converting the E-R diagram.

Exercise 10.1

Consider the following relationship sets. Are any of them incomplete? If so, then replace them with E-R diagrams that include all information.

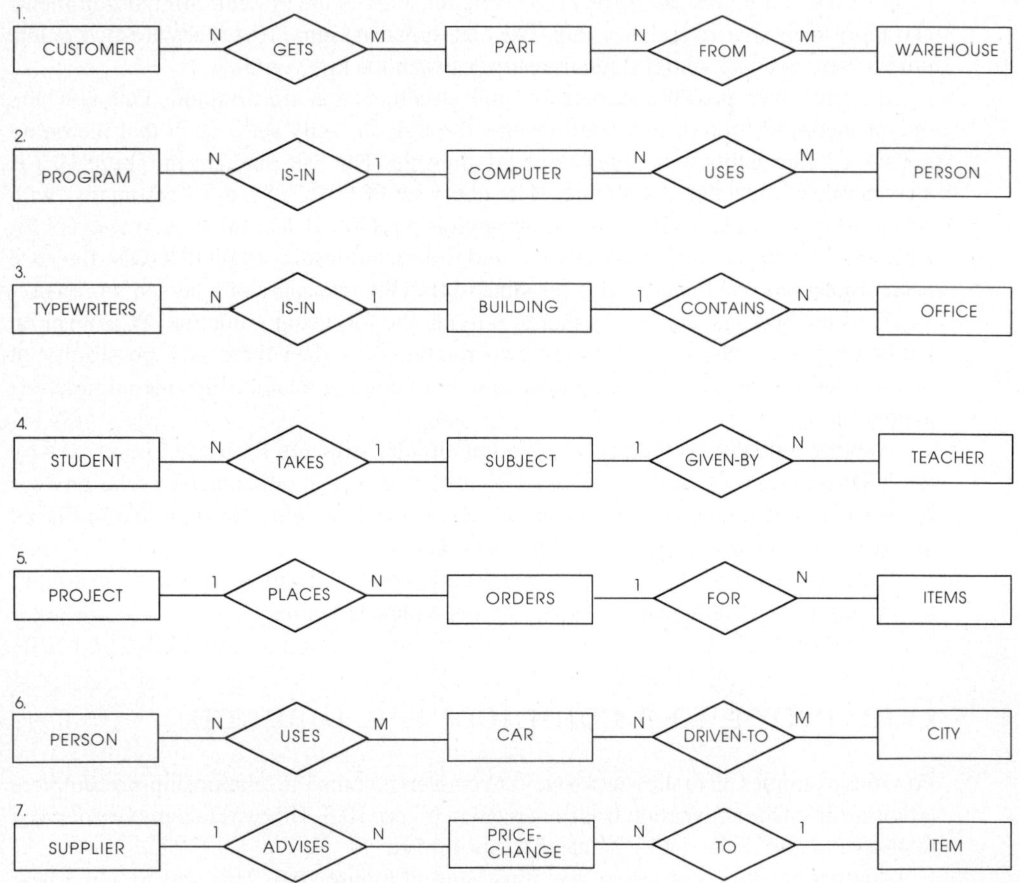

MULTIPLE RELATIONSHIPS

A multiple relationship set is one where the same two entities can participate in more than one relationship in the same relationship set. The E-R diagram in Figure 10.8 is one example of a multiple relationship. Here a given person can participate more than once in a REPAIR relationship set with the same equipment. This would, of course, occur when more than one fault occurs on the same equipment and two, or more, of these faults are repaired by the same person.

Figure 10.8 A multiple relationship

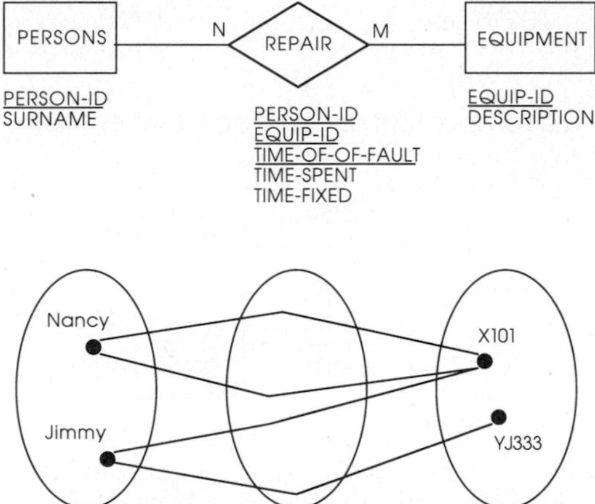

The occurrence diagram in Figure 10.8, for example, shows that Nancy appears in more than one relationship with equipment X101. One such relationship arises between Nancy and X101 every time that Nancy works on a different fault on X101.

The problem with multiple relationships is that they often lead to redundancies when converted to relations. For example, suppose relationship set REPAIR, which describes persons working on the same fault, is converted to a relation. The relation key of relation, REPAIR, will be {PERSON-ID, EQUIP-ID, TIME-OF-FAULT}. TIME-OF-FAULT is included in the relation key to distinguish between different faults on the same equipment. In Figure 10.8 a value of TIME-FIXED is determined by {EQUIP-ID, TIME-OF-FAULT} and hence is determined by part of a relation key. Thus relation REPAIR would not be in the highest normal form.

Multiple relationships should always be converted to relationships that are not multiple. As was the case with incomplete relationships, two types of conversion are possible. One is to create a new entity set that represents the relationship itself. An example is given in Figure 10.9. Here, relationship REPAIR has become the entity set, REPAIR. A new identifier, FAULT-NO, is now created to globally identify faults.

The other way to remove multiple relationships is to create dependent entity sets. This is illustrated in Figure 10.10. Here FAULTS becomes a dependent of EQUIPMENT and

Figure 10.9 A decomposed multiple relationship

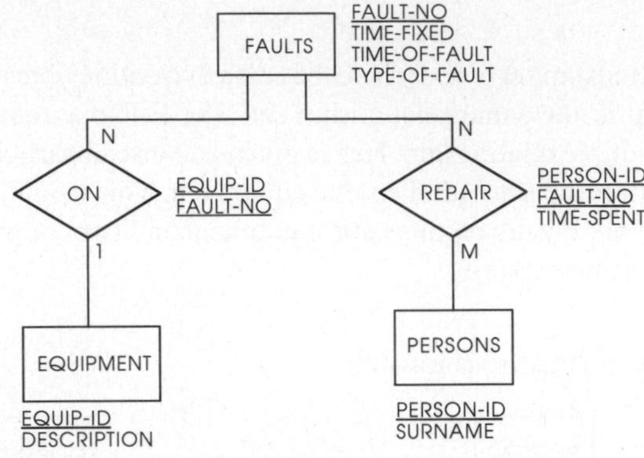

Figure 10.10 Decomposition using dependent entities

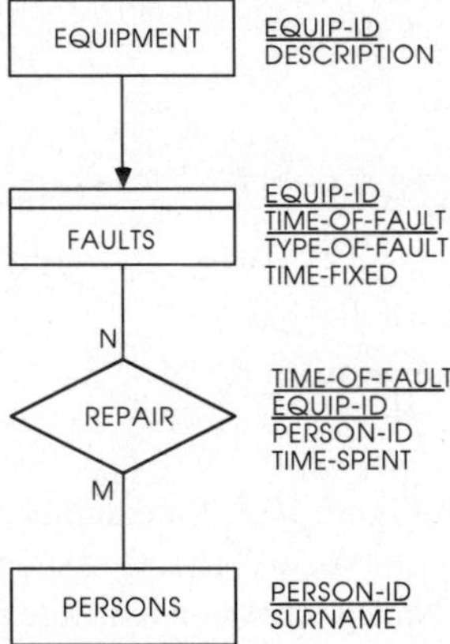

TIME-OF-FAULT distinguishes between dependents (that is, faults) of the same parent (that is, equipment). Attribute TIME-FIXED is now an attribute of faults and is independent of person working on the fault. Both FAULTS and REPAIR in Figure 10.10 can be directly converted to relations that are in BCNF.

Again the question arises on how to detect multiple relationships. In this case there is a syntactic method, which depends on proper choice of identifiers. You should note that in Figure 10.8, PERSON-ID and EQUIP-ID on their own cannot identify one REPAIR relationship because the same two entities can participate in more than one relationship. A third identifier is needed. In Figure 10.8 this is TIME-OF-FAULT. Now the relationship breaks one fundamental rule. Its identifier includes attributes other than the identifiers of the participating entities. Multiple relationships exist whenever such additional identifiers are needed.

You should now try Exercise 10.2 to identify multiple relationships and convert them to non-multiple forms.

Exercise 10.2

Consider the following relationship sets. Do they contain multiple relationships? If so, then convert them to relationship sets that have no multiple relationships.

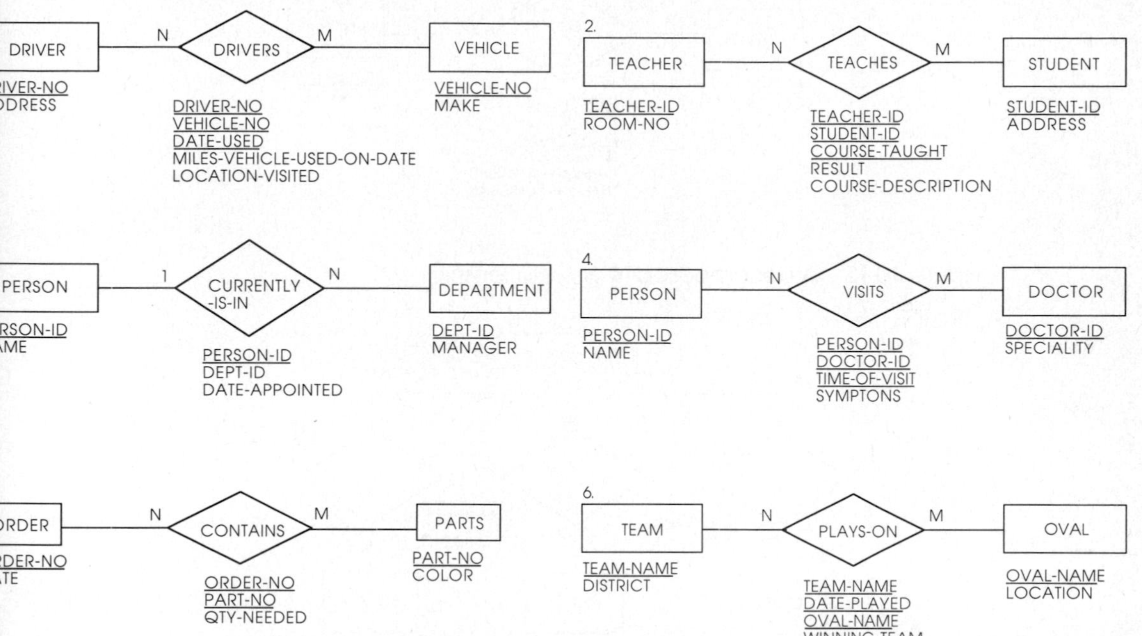

N-ARY RELATIONSHIPS

So far all relationship sets in this book involved two entity sets only. It is, however, possible, and often convenient, to use relationship sets that include more than two entity sets. Such relationship sets are known as N-ary relationship sets. Relationship sets that involve two entity sets only are known as binary relationship sets.

Relationship set, BUY, in Figure 10.11 is an example of an N-ary relationship set. This relationship set models purchases made by persons in any one of an organization's stores. It describes the parts bought by a person from a given store at a given TIME-OF-PURCHASE. Attribute TYPE-OF-PAYMENT has the value CASH or CREDIT and records the manner of paying for a purchase at that time.

Relationship BUY, however, illustrates a problem that exists with many N-ary relationships. It does not correspond to a BCNF relation. The key of relation BUY is {PERSON-ID, PART-ID, STORE-NAME, TIME-OF-PURCHASE}. The value of TYPE-OF-PAYMENT depends on part of that key only, namely {PERSON-ID, STORE-NAME, TIME-OF-PURCHASE}, because all parts purchased at the same time were paid for in the same way.

Figure 10.11 A N-ary relationship

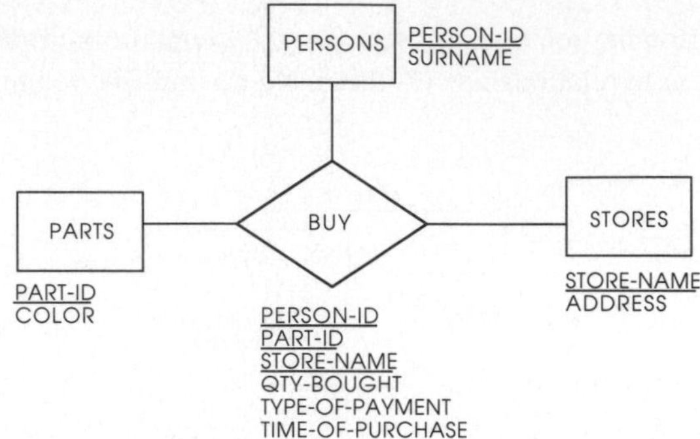

Figure 10.12 A decomposed N-ary relationship

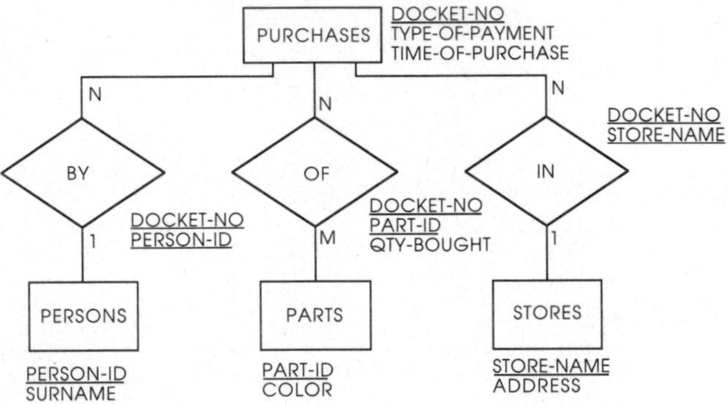

Another problem with N-ary relationship sets is cardinality. If a person shops in one store then the link between BUY and STORES should be labeled 1. But if there are many parts in the store, that same link should be labeled N. But we cannot include two labels on the same link and hence cardinality is not shown on N-ary relationship sets.

As in the earlier examples, two alternative ways exist for converting an N-ary relationship sets to binary relationship sets that correspond to BCNF relations. One is to convert the N-ary relationship set to an entity set. The other is to use dependent entity sets.

Figure 10.12 illustrates the conversion of the N-ary relationship set, BUY, into the entity set, PURCHASES. A new identifier, DOCKET-NO, is introduced to globally identify purchases within the system. Attribute, TYPE-OF-PAYMENT, becomes an attribute of PURCHASES. The entities involved in a purchase are modeled by the three relationship sets, BY, OF and IN.

Figure 10.13 illustrates the conversion using dependent entity sets. Now each purchase is modeled as a dependent of a store. Each purchase within a store is identified by STORE-DOCKET-NO, which is unique within a store. Entity sets involved in a store purchase are modeled by the relationship sets, BY and OF.

Figure 10.13 Decomposing a N-ary relationship using dependent entities

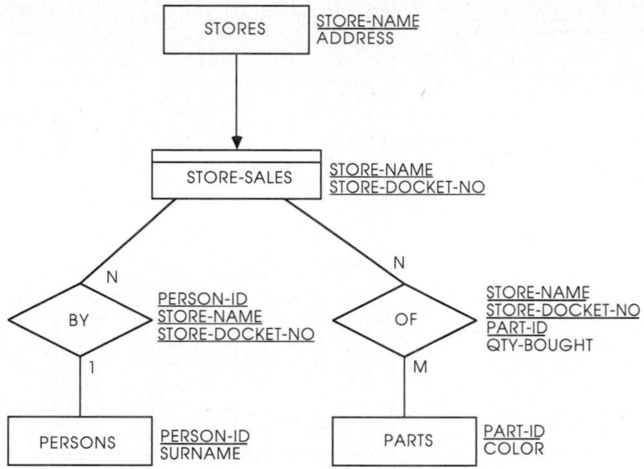

RECURSIVE RELATIONSHIPS

There are many cases where two entities within the same set are related to each other. For example, persons within a set can be related to each other through parentage. Persons in an organization can be related to each other through the supervisory structure within the organization. Parts can be related to each other by the way that some parts are constructed from other parts. This latter structure is often called the BILL-OF-MATERIAL structure and is illustrated in Figure 10.14. The hierarchical tree in Figure 10.14(a) shows the relationship between the parts. For example, Y1 and Y2 are direct components of Z1 whereas X1 and X2 are the direct components of Y1, and so on. It is common to use the terms assembly and component to denote the hierarchical relationships from parts to their direct components. There is one assembly and one component in each link in the tree shown in Figure 10.14(a). For example, Z1 is an assembly and Y1 is a component in the link between Z1 and Y1.

Figure 10.14(b) is an E-R diagram that models this hierarchical relationship. It is made up of an entity set, PARTS, which is the set of all the parts and a relationship set, MADE-OF, that describes the hierarchical relationships between the parts. Each relationship in relationship set MADE-OF represents one link in the hierarchical tree. Two entities are involved in each relationship. One entity is the assembly, the other is the component. Different attributes must be used to identify these entities in the relationship. ASSEMBLY-NO identifies the assembly and COMP-NO identifies the component. The values of these two identifiers are the same as the value of PART-NO of the involved entities.

Figure 10.14(c) is an example of a relation that represents the hierarchical tree. There is one row in the relation for each link in the hierarchical tree.

Recursive structures of the kind shown in Figure 10.14 are sometimes hard to understand. They do not easily show different roles played by entities from the same set in the

Figure 10.14 Bill-of-materials

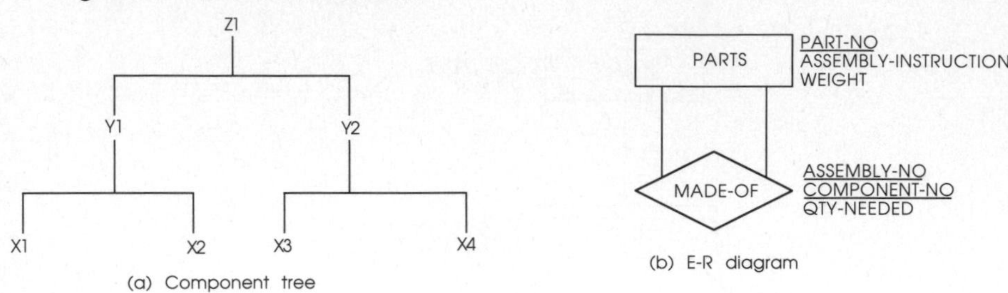

MADE-OF

ASSEMBLY-NO	COMPONENT-NO	QTY-NEEDED
Z1	Y1	9
Z1	Y2	17
Y1	X1	3
Y1	X2	12
Y2	X3	9
Y2	X4	17

(c) Relation

Figure 10.15 Subsets used to model recursive structure

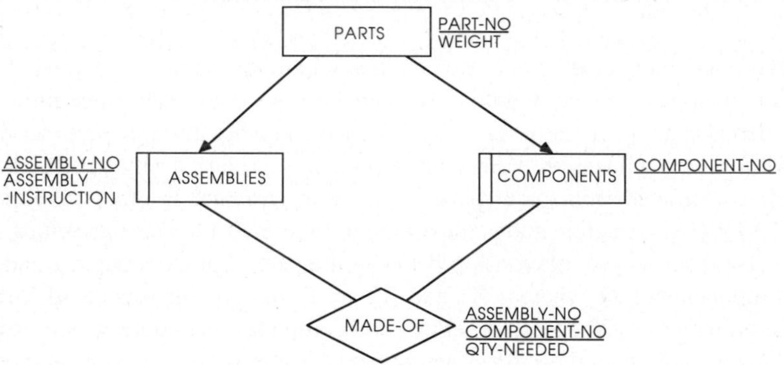

relationship. They can also lead to relations that are not in the highest normal form or to attributes that do not take values in the entity set. For example, suppose the attribute ASSEMBLY-INSTRUCTION is associated with an assembly. If this attribute appears in relationship MADE-OF then MADE-OF will only be in 1NF, because ASSEMBLY-INSTRUCTION depends on ASSEMBLY-NO, which is part of the relation key of MADE-OF. The relation key of MADE-OF is {ASSEMBLY-NO, COMPONENT-NO}. Alternatively, if ASSEMBLY-INSTRUCTION is stored in entity set PARTS, then it will never take a value for those parts that are not an assembly.

There is an alternative method for modeling recursive relationships. It uses subsets. The idea behind subsets is that each entity in a recursive relationship takes a different role. Thus in the MADE-OF relationship, one entity takes the role of an assembly, and the other takes the role of the component. These roles are modeled as subsets in Figure 10.15. Here a part is a member of the ASSEMBLIES subset if it is an assembly, and a member of the COMPONENT subset if it is a component. Attributes such as ASSEMBLY-INSTRUCTION are now included in the ASSEMBLIES subset.

Figure 10.16 is another example of a recursive relationship. It models family trees without using subsets. It has one entity set, PERSONS, that includes all the people in the family tree. It also has a ternary relationship, CONCEIVE, that includes three entities for entity set, PERSONS.

Figure 10.16 Family tree (E-R diagram)

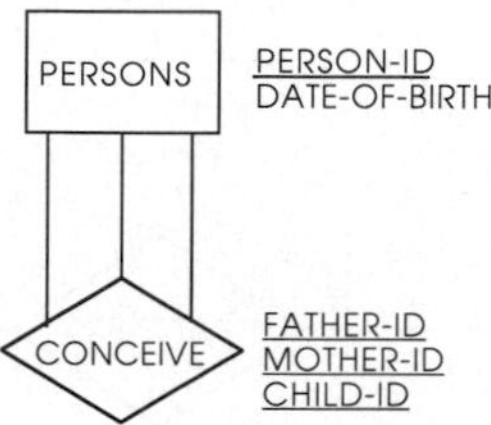

The corresponding model that uses subsets is shown in Figure 10.17. The E-R diagram in Figure 10.17(a) also has one entity set, PERSONS, which models all the persons in the family tree. Each person can be in one of the subsets, MOTHERS or FATHERS. Each person also has one father and one mother. The relationships between persons to their mothers and fathers are modeled by relationship sets, HAS-MOTHER and HAS-FATHER. There is also a separate relationship between fathers and mothers showing their MARRIAGE-DATE.

The E-R diagram in Figure 10.17 can be converted to the relations using techniques described in Chapter 9. One such relation will be the relation, PARENTS, shown in Figure 10.17(c). This relation results from a combination of entity set, PERSONS, with relationship sets, HAS-MOTHER and HAS-FATHER. Each line in relation PARENTS includes all a person's details together with his/her father and mother.

SUMMARY

This chapter illustrated some problems that exist in constructing relationships. It described three kinds of relationship structures: derived, multiple and N-ary relationships. These structures are often convenient to use when developing a top-level model. However, they can result in redundancies when converted to relations.

The chapter also illustrated methods that can be used to convert such relationships to relationships that can be converted to BCNF relations. Two methods were described. In one the relationship set was converted to an entity set. This conversion required an additional identifier to identify activities that involve related entities. The other method used dependent entity sets. In this case occurrences were defined as dependents within one of the related entities.

Figure 10.17 Family tree using subsets

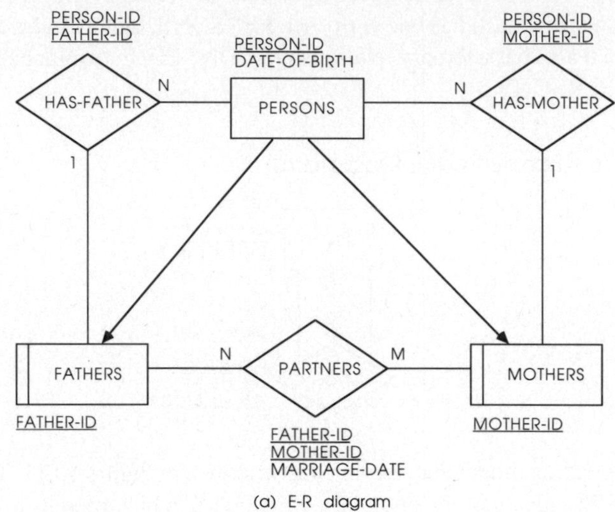

(a) E-R diagram

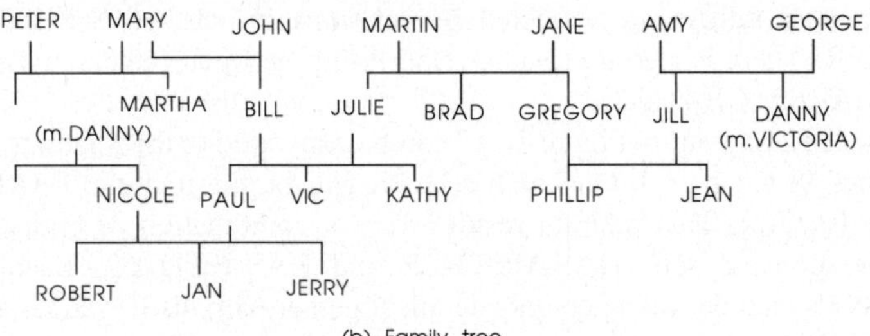

(b) Family tree

PARENTS

FATHER	MOTHER	PERSON	DATE-OF-BIRTH
PETER	MARY	VICTORIA	
PETER	MARY	MARTHA	
JOHN	MARY	BILL	
MARTIN	JANE	JULIE	
MARTIN	JANE	BRAD	
MARTIN	JANE	GREGORY	
GEORGE	AMY	JILL	
GEORGE	AMY	DANNY	
DANNY	VICTORIA	JAMES	
DANNY	VICTORIA	NICOLE	
BILL	JULIE	PAUL	
BILL	JULIE	VIC	
BILL	JULIE	KATHY	
GREGORY	JILL	PHILLIP	
GREGORY	JILL	JEAN	
PAUL	NICOLE	ROBERT	
PAUL	NICOLE	JAN	
PAUL	NICOLE	JERRY	

(c) Table representation

11

Relational systems

INTRODUCTION

Previous chapters described database analysis. They described the steps that are followed to derive a set of relations from user requirements. These steps ensure that the relations are in the highest normal form. These relations must now be implemented on a computer using database management software.

Implementation includes two major activities. The first is to convert the relational design to a database definition. This definition is used by database software to create a database. The second activity is to design and develop the programs necessary to store, update and retrieve data in these databases.

This chapter describes the facilities provided by relational database management systems (RDBMS) for defining databases. It describes the overall structure of RDBMS and the steps used to set up databases on RDBMS. Subsequent chapters will describe how RDBMS facilities are used to develop programs that use these databases.

THE DATABASE ENVIRONMENT

There are a number of ways of using databases in organizations. These are illustrated in Figure 11.1. One is the corporate database, which contains an organization's major data.

Figure 11.1 The database environment

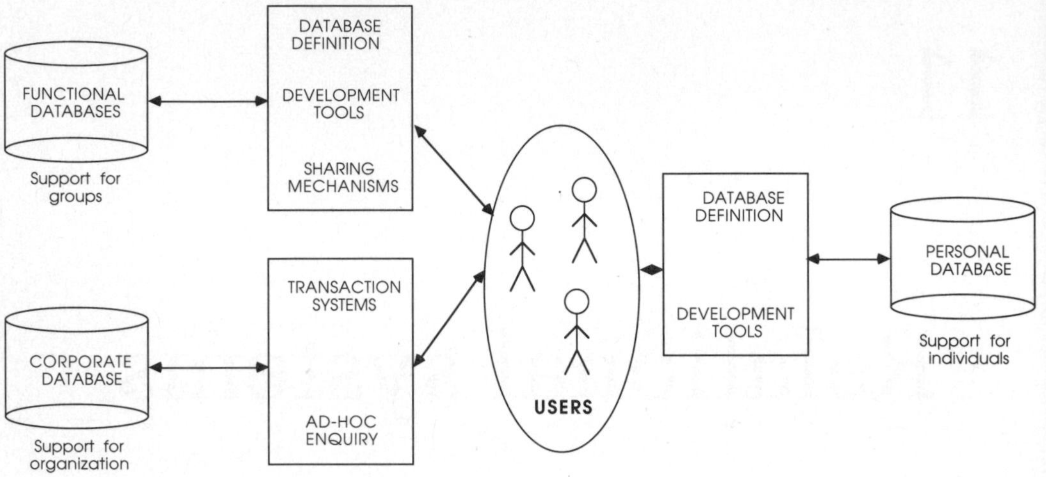

The other is the personal database designed to meet the needs of an individual. There are also functional databases, often designed by end users, to meet the needs of a group of people involved in some well-defined activity.

Corporate databases

Corporate databases contain an organization's critical data. This may be accounts in a bank, store inventories in a warehouse or seat availability for a transport operator. Corporate databases are often set up on centralized machines and controlled by a data administration team. Users access corporate data in two ways. One is through prespecified transactions designed to meet everyday operational needs. Transaction systems satisfy frequently occurring operations in an organization such as updating an account, adding parts to inventory or making a reservation.

There is also an increasing tendency for corporate database users to make ad-hoc access to such databases. Ad-hoc access satisfies infrequently occurring requirements. For example, a marketing manager may need all accounts in a branch with an average balance of over $2000 that increased by over 25% during last month. This data may be retrieved once to pursue some idea and not used again. Rather than developing special programs for such ad-hoc requirements, retrieval languages are provided by RDBMS to formulate ad-hoc queries. These languages can be used to retrieve such data without going through the process of writing programs using a high-level language.

Personal databases

Many users now develop small private databases for their own personal use. These databases are often developed by users on personal computers. Such databases are developed to meet private needs such as local budgets, personal telephone lists or special accounts. These databases are established independently of the corporate database.

Functional databases for groups

Databases that support small functional groups have now become the responsibility of end users. These users often assume responsibility for developing operational systems that use computers. Their responsibility goes beyond simply defining their own personal needs and supporting them with personal computer databases. They more often define the specialized needs of their departments and develop systems that can be used by a number of persons within such departments. Examples of such systems include local inventories, order processing information or resource schedules. In many cases such end users develop systems themselves and make these systems available to other users, who may be cooperating with them.

DBMS FACILITIES

Each of these three kinds of users require different kinds of database facilities. Corporate database users mainly work with prespecified transactions. Important issues in such systems include the ability to handle high volumes of transactions generated at various locations with a quick response time and high accuracy. They also require good interfaces to present these transactions in a simple way.

The personal computer user is not so strongly concerned with performance. The volume of transactions is low and some inaccuracies can be tolerated. Response time is not critical. However, personal computer users do not wish to spend lengthy periods programming computers and do not have access to professional programmers. What is important to them is the ability to set up systems quickly using high-level application generators.

The end user needs a balance of the two. On the one hand they want access to the corporate database with the ability to make ad-hoc retrievals and perhaps to develop report programs. They also need to set up their own databases. Some of these may be on their own personal computers. Others may be as part of the centralized machine that is accessible to other users.

Database integration

In addition to the different kinds of use, there is also an increasing demand for integration of databases developed in separate areas. Such integration requires links between the different kinds of database. Links are now being developed between personal computers and corporate databases and there is increasing integration of specialized departmental systems within the corporate database. This demand is being met by the development of distributed RDBMS. Such RDBMS allow users to set up databases on different computers and allow access to such computers through the network.

Let us now see how relational database management systems cater for such needs.

RELATIONAL SYSTEMS

Relational systems are increasingly able to satisfy the needs of all kinds of database users.

Many RDBMS now include software that supports all kinds of users. A typical relational system, as well as storing data, also includes software development tools needed to develop application programs. Development tools include enquiry languages to support the ad-hoc user who may wish to make occasional enquiries of the database. They also include high-level languages that can be used by programmers to develop applications that support high-volume transactions. They provide report and screen generators that support end users who may wish to develop their own applications.

Figure 11.2 shows the structure used to organize such development tools in a typical RDBMS. The structure is centered around a kernel that manages relational tables. This kernel stores the tables and provides the underlying routines for creating and updating tables. Surrounding the kernel is SQL (Structured Query Language), which has now become the virtual standard language for relational systems.

SQL and the kernel provide the basis for relational systems. They can be used on their own to create and update databases and to make ad-hoc enquiries. This application development support is provided through three classes of facilities. One is support for interactive access using SQL. SQL on its own is usually sufficient to support ad-hoc users or even personal computer users. The SQL language is sufficiently powerful to support any kind of query to the database. Interactive SQL support includes editors to change, save and recall SQL queries.

In addition to supporting interactive access, relational systems also provide facilities for application program development. There are two main classes of product here. One is high-level language support for developing transaction systems. It provides a high-level language interface from programs written in high-level languages such as COBOL, PL/I or C to access the database. Database access is made by SQL statements that are embedded in the high-level languages.

Another kind of development tool are screen and report generators. This kind of support is particularly aimed at end-user development. It allows application programs to be developed in incremental steps.

In addition to these development tools, most RDMS also provide operational support. This kind of support is provided both by the operating system and the RDBMS. The operating system includes support for any networking capabilities and also the kind of support needed for storage devices and on-line access to the system.

The RDBMS also provides various types of operational support. One is provision of system security through database backup. Another is support for sharing and privacy in a multi-user environment. This includes the ability to control database access. It allows database administrators to create new end users and give them abilities to create

Figure 11.2 A relational database management system

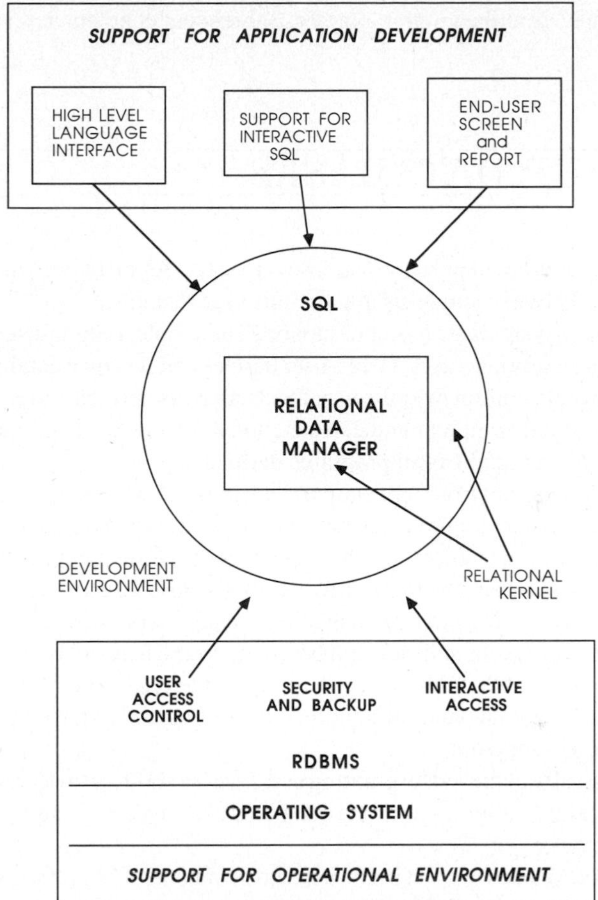

their own databases and share these databases with other users. A group in the organization can use the access controls to set up such databases and authorize users to access them. This group can also authorize end users to develop their own databases. Once they develop these databases, the end users should be able to give other users access to such databases.

RDBMS on personal computers do not include all of the facilities shown in Figure 11.2. For example PC RDBMS would not include transaction processing support or control of sharing. These are not needed by PC users.

You should also note the importance of SQL. SQL has now become the most commonly used language for relational databases. It is now being defined as the standard language for relational database management systems (RDBMS).

The idea behind SQL is to use one declarative statement rather than procedural code to retrieve needed data. You just make a SQL statement that specifies what is to be retrieved. This makes SQL very effective for ad-hoc querying of databases. It can be used to answer an ad-hoc query almost immediately.

However, before a database is set up and application programs developed, a proper database environment must be defined for the database. The method used to set up this environment is described in this chapter. Subsequent chapters describe SQL and how to use it.

SETTING UP DATABASES

There are differences in the way databases are set up for different kinds of user. One clear distinction is between single-user and multi-user systems.

Single-user systems are easier to support. The simplest single-user environment is that of the personal computer user. Here a user defines and sets up a database for personal use. That user has sole control over the way the database is defined and accessed. All that user needs is a personal computer and database software. Once this is available the databases can be created and application programs defined.

The multi-user environment supports a variety of users on one system either as end users or as users of a corporate database. Some of these users may be using the same data but in different ways. Others may be developing their own applications.

Multi-user systems are more difficult to set up because they must support shared access to databases. The environment allows many users to access the system. Each such user may have different abilities in the system. Some users may only be able to retrieve data from certain tables. Other users may be able to create their own data and give other users privileges to that data. Still another class of user may have the ability to give new users access to the system.

This is usually achieved by granting users access abilities to operate within the system. Users can use these abilities to create databases and pass access abilities to their databases to other users.

Most RDBMS can support multi-user environments. They do so using the components illustrated in Figure 11.3. This Figure shows three major components used to set up a shared database. One is the software used to create the database. Another is software used to define database users and define their privileges. Finally there is the software that uses these privileges to control access to databases by these users.

There are two different methods used to support multi-user environments. They differ in how ownership of database tables is defined. One idea is to support centralized ownership. The other is to provide distributed ownership.

Centralized ownership

In the centralized model of ownership, one group is responsible for setting up a database and granting users privileges to the database. All the tables in this database are owned by this central group. This method suits the requirements of corporate databases. Such databases require some control over what actually appears in the database so that overall corporate and performance goals can be met. The database structure thus becomes the

Figure 11.3 A multi-user environment

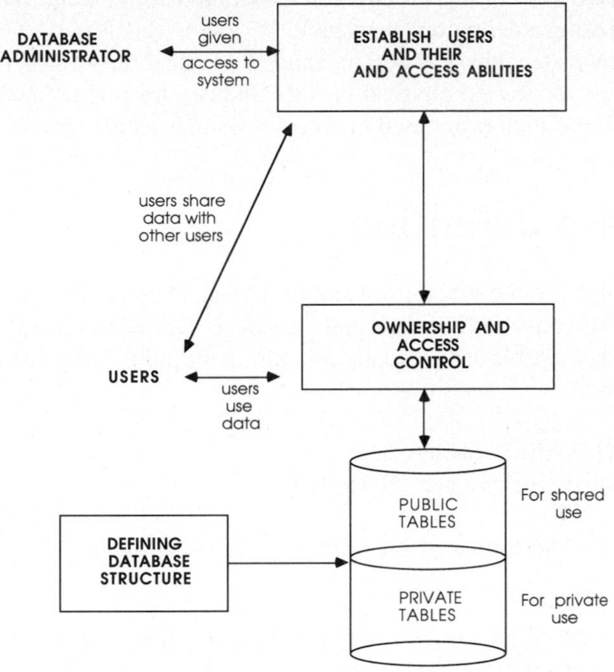

responsibility of the data administration team, which is responsible for developing and maintaining the corporate database.

Distributed ownership

Organizations that support distributed ownership allow individual users to set up their own tables. These users become the owners of these tables can pass privileges on tables owned by them to other users. This environment provides users with a wide degree of freedom and control over database growth. This method is more appropriate for the end-user environment. Here end users can set up their tables and give other users in their group access to selected information in these tables.

The remainder of this chapter will describe how SQL is used to set up and define databases in these environments. We start with the simplest case, namely, the single-user database.

DEFINING THE SINGLE-USER DATABASE

Setting up a single-user database starts where data analysis left off. Data analysis so far has produced a model of data. This was either a relational model or an E-R model. The first step of design is to convert the data model to the data definitions supported by the DBMS.

The conversion method depends on the available DBMS. The simplest conversion is to a relational DBMS. In fact no conversion is required as relations derived during design are defined using a definition language.

The second step, physical design, chooses physical record structures and the placement of these records on physical devices. Indices are also defined to access rows at this stage. These indices are used to access rows in database tables.

Database definition

Logical design is quite straightforward. Each relation derived by the methods described in Chapter 9 is converted to a table and the table is defined using SQL. A table is defined by specifying the table name and the columns in the table. This is done by the following SQL command:

```
CREATE TABLE <table-name>
[<attribute-name> <type> [NOT NULL]]
```

Type specifies the format of the attribute. The SQL standard includes the following types:

CHARACTER, NUMERIC, DECIMAL, INTEGER, SMALLINT, FLOAT, REAL and DOUBLE PRECISION.

NOT NULL is specified for a column if rows in the table must always have a value in that column.

Adding indices

Indices are added to improve performance of database transactions or queries. Transactions are analyzed to determine the indices to be added to the database. Chapter 9 described the methods used to analyze transactions against databases. The result of this analysis is a set of access steps, which show the indices to be defined for the database.

The SQL statement used to define indices is :

```
CREATE [UNIQUE] INDEX <index-name> ON <table-name>
[,<column-name> [ASC:DESC] ]
```

An index may use any number of columns, some in ascending [ASC] and some in descending [DESC] order. If UNIQUE is specified, then no two rows can have the same value of index.

Integrity

At this stage you should note that the definition does not include any of the integrity checks that were discussed in Chapter 9. These constraints particularly include maintenance of semantic links through foreign keys, participation and cardinality.

Very few RDBMS contain direct support for these integrity constraints. Most systems do not contain provisions for defining foreign keys nor establishing links between relations. In such systems semantic links can only be maintained by application programs.

It is possible, however, to use some of the DBMS facilities to support participation and cardinality constraints. Such support is provided by judicious use of the UNIQUE and NOT NULL clauses.

The UNIQUE clause can be used to ensure that no two rows have the same value of the relation key. This is done by defining the columns that make up the relation key to be unique.

There are a number of proposals for extending SQL to support referential integrity. These require extension to define relation keys and foreign keys for tables. A possible extension similar to that adopted in some IBM systems is:

```
CREATE TABLE PERSONS
  RELATION KEY (PERSON-ID)
  (PERSON-ID CHAR(10) NOT NULL,
  SURNAME CHAR(15));

CREATE TABLE WORK-ON
  RELATION KEY (PERSON-ID, PROJECT-NO)
  (PERSON-ID CHAR(10) NOT NULL,
  PROJECT-ID CHAR(4) NOT NULL,
        TIME SPENT INTEGER)
  FOREIGN KEY(PERSON-ID) REFERENCES PERSONS
        NULL NOT ALLOWED ON DELETE CASCADE
```

Here the RELATION KEY clause defines the relation key for a relation. The FOREIGN KEY clause defines the foreign keys for a table. Each foreign key includes a reference to another table through the IDENTIFIES verb. This states that a value of the foreign key must exist in the referenced relation before it can appear in a row in the defined relation. It also states what should be done if an attempt is made to delete a row in the referenced relation. The options are:

RESTRICT: prevents the row in the referenced relation being deleted if it has dependents.
SET NULL: the foreign key value in the dependents is set to NULL.
CASCADE: also delete all dependent rows with the same value of foreign key.

DEFINING SHARED DATABASES

Database definition for environments that support shared ownership proceeds in a similar way to the design of a single-user database. Logical and physical design are used to specify the relations, which are then defined using CREATE TABLE and CREATE INDEX statements. There is one additional activity needed in this environment. This is to define user access abilities to these tables.

There are two important activities in defining such abilities. One is the establishment of system users. The other concerns sharing of tables created by these users. The DBA in this environment is primarily concerned with the first of these activities.

Setting up system users

The database administrator uses SQL to set up the environment. SQL allows the DBA to allocate privileges to users and to give users passwords to enter the system. To set up the environment, the DBA must first enter the system using the command:

CONNECT <dba-name> IDENTIFIED BY <dba-password>

The DBA can now create new users with privileges using the GRANT statement. This statement takes the form:

GRANT <privilege> TO <user> IDENTIFIED BY <password>

Allowable user privileges are:

CONNECT:	allows a user to connect to system only
RESOURCE:	allows a user to acquire own storage space and create tables in that storage space
DBA:	gives the user the same privilege as the DBA

The DBA can also change a privilege or password by repeating the GRANT CONNECT command for the user with a new privilege or password.

Users who have RESOURCE privileges can now create their own tables. They can pass access privileges to their tables to other users.

The DBA can also disconnect users from the system by the command:

REVOKE <privilege> FROM <user>

where privilege is DBA, RESOURCE or CONNECT.

Sharing access to tables

Users who have the ability to create tables can now do so. They can then pass various access abilities to these tables to other users. This is done by using the GRANT command. The format of this command is:

```
GRANT <privilege> ON TABLE <table-name> TO <list of users>
                    [WITH GRANT OPTION]
```

Privileges in this case may be SELECT, INSERT or UPDATE or it may be all of these specified by the word, ALL. The word PUBLIC may be used instead of a list of users to make these privileges available to all users in the database.

There are, of course, variations of this method between systems. Some may require users to acquire spaces.

Acquiring a private dbspace

A RESOURCE user can acquire a private dbspace by:

```
ACQUIRE PRIVATE DBSPACE NAMED <dbspace-name>
```

SETTING UP CORPORATE DATABASES

Corporate databases can be set up using the methods described for shared bases. However, in most cases corporate databases allow users much less flexibility than shared environments. Corporate databases users, for example, cannot set up new relations quickly. Usually such relations are chosen bearing in mind their effect on the rest of the organization and access performance. Consequently a corporate database is often defined once, and changes are not easily made.

This is the proposal in the SQL standard. The idea behind this proposal is to define a schema that contains a number of tables. The definition takes the form:

```
CREATE SCHEMA AUTHORIZATION DEPTA
CREATE TABLE PERSONS . . .
CREATE TABLE PROJECTS . . .
```

Here the first statements identify a schema, whose creator is DEPTA. All database tables are defined within this schema. The tables are defined using the same statements as described earlier.

SECURITY AND PRIVACY

Database definition is one of the major steps of setting up a database. It is the final product of a lot of work that started with the gathering of user data needs and the development of a conceptual model. This was followed by analysis of database use, and detailed design work to adjust the initial model to satisfy performance requirements. Then the database is defined using the CREATE statements described in this chapter.

Two more things still remain to be done. These are concerned with the operational environment rather than with application or database design. A database is an important resource of most organizations. Designers must ensure that this resource is not abused in any way and that it is not inadvertently lost or destroyed. This is where privacy and security come in.

Privacy is necessary to ensure that the database is used in its intended way. Users should be able to get to those parts that they need and carry out their required tasks. It is not necessary for users to have access abilities to those parts of the database that are not needed for their work. Having such access may be beyond user responsibilities and furthermore may result in unnecessary browsing of data or unintended change. For this reason most RDBMS provide facilities to control access to databases.

The other important operational issue is security. A RDBMS must provide facilities that allow recovery should parts of the database be lost or destroyed.

Privacy

Privacy concerns control over database use. The basic premise of privacy is that users should only have access to that part of the database needed for their work. This requires facilities that allow users to access parts of the database only. It also requires facilities to make data available in the most useful form for these users.

Many of the facilities provided to support privacy were discussed earlier in this chapter. The GRANT command can be used to only allow a user to some tables of the database. The database administrator would determine the parts needed by each user and invoke the necessary GRANT commands. This is one facility provided to administrators for privacy control. It is very broad and controls access to entire tables.

Some privacy and sharing requirements call for finer controls. For example, it should also be possible to restrict access to some part of a table or perhaps to a part of the combination of two or more tables. This is where views come in.

Most RDBMS allow designers to define views. A view is a table that contains information derived from some part of a stored table. It may also contain information derived from more than one table. It serves two purposes. One is to restrict access to only part of a table. The other is to present information in a form that may differ from the stored form and thus make it easier for users to use that information. Views are described in detail in Chapter 14.

Security

Security concerns loss or damage to data. Many things can go wrong in a computer system. There can be a failure in the hardware and information may be destroyed. There may be a power surge that stops a transaction half-way through its processing.

A distinction can thus be made between two kinds of error. One is physical loss or destruction of data. The other is an error that may occur during the processing of a transaction, and which leaves the database in an inconsistent state. Different ways are used to cater for these two possibilities.

Recovery from physical loss of information

To recover from physical loss it is necessary to keep duplicate copies of data. One way to do this is to make a copy of the database at regular intervals. This copy is known as the backup copy. Should the working copy be destroyed, then the backup copy is restored as the working copy.

Most recovery procedures also keep copies of transactions since the last copy. These copies can be rerun once a backup is restored to bring the database to the same state as existed at the time of failure.

Recovery from error during processing

Backup copies could also be used to restore the database following this kind of error. However, backup restoration can be lengthy process. If the database is large then it may be necessary to copy many records from the backup medium to the database. This can be a time-consuming process and not feasible in cases other than catastrophic failure.

Errors during transaction processing often affect very few records. It is therefore extremely wasteful in processing time to restore all the records of a database following a very local failure. For this reason an alternative is provided by most RDBMS. This is to use journal files.

The idea of journal files is illustrated in Figure 11.4. The journal file records each database change. A special marker is used to indicate states where the database is inconsistent. Thus, for example, in Figure 11.4 a transaction changed two database records, record 6 and record 4. The first change is to record 6. Both the old copy of record 6 and the new copy of record 6 are recorded on the journal file. Then the old copy and new copy of record 4 are recorded on the journal file. Often old copies of a record are called 'before images' and the new copies of the record are called 'after images'. On completion of the transaction a new marker is placed on the journal file to indicate that the database is again in a consistent state. The changes made by the next transaction are then recorded on the journal file.

Should a failure occur the journal is run backwards against the database to its previous marker. For example, suppose a failure occurred after record 4 was changed but before record 6 is changed. This would leave the database in an inconsistent state. It is now possible to run the journal file backwards replacing all database records by their before images until a marker showing a consistent state is reached. This will restore the database state to that which existed before the transaction began.

Journal files can be used to restore the database to any previous state. Usually the journal file records the time for each transaction and the database can be restored to its state at any selected time. For example, it would be possible to restore the database to its state at the beginning of the day by running the journal file backwards until the first transaction for the day is reached.

Figure 11.4 Backing up a transaction

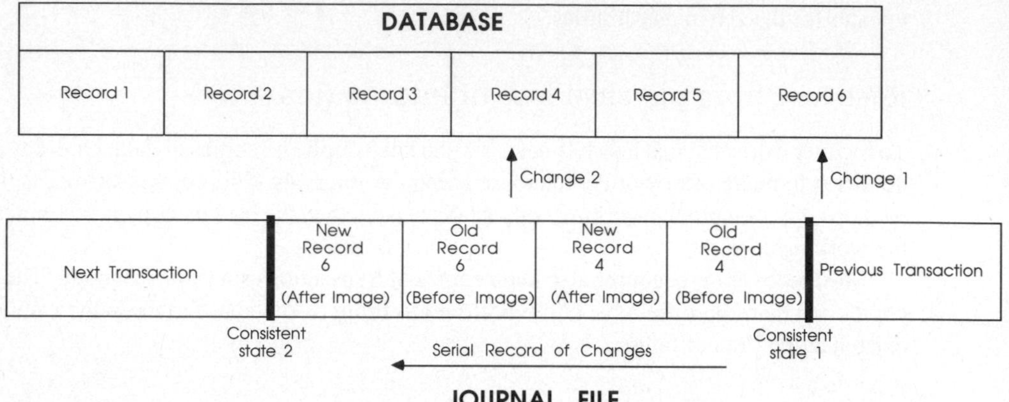

Journal files can be put to many uses. For example it is possible to use them during backup. In that we can start with a backup copy for the beginning of the day. It is then necessary to record any changes made to the contents of records during the day. This can be done by running the journal file forwards and replacing all records by their after images.

SUMMARY

This chapter described relational database management systems and how they can be used to set up databases. It distinguished three kinds of users: the corporate database users, the personal computer users and the end user. It then described the difference between these kinds of use and the methods used to set up databases for each kind of users. Both methods used to define the logical data structure as well as the operational environment were described.

The next few chapters will describe how databases are used in application development.

12

SQL statements

INTRODUCTION

The previous chapter described the role of SQL in relational DBMS. As outlined there, SQL is now the standard language used to access relations in RDBMS. It can be used for ad-hoc retrieval or to update the database. It can be used interactively or embedded in high-level languages. This chapter introduces SQL and describes how SQL statements are used to retrieve data from the database. SQL is a powerful language that can be used to retrieve a variety of data with one statement. It caters for the simple queries that require one row to be retrieved from one relation. It also has the expressive power to formulate queries that retrieve complex relationships between rows in many relations.

Expressive power is only one issue in using SQL. The other important issue is performance. It is possible that some retrievals may require considerable time because they serially search many large tables. Thus some consideration must be given to performance when formulating queries. This chapter considers such performance issues. It describes performance implications of SQL statements and compares effects on performance by using alternate SQL statements for getting the same data.

The chapter uses the database shown in Figure 12.1 to illustrate SQL commands. This database stores requisitions for parts. The requisitions are stored in relation REQUISITIONS and requisition contents are stored in relation REQ-LINES. The requisition data includes the number of the project that made the requisition, the date when the requested items are needed and the location where they are needed. Each row in REQ-LINES represents a line in a requisition. Column REQ-NO defines the requisition, and

Figure 12.1 Sample data

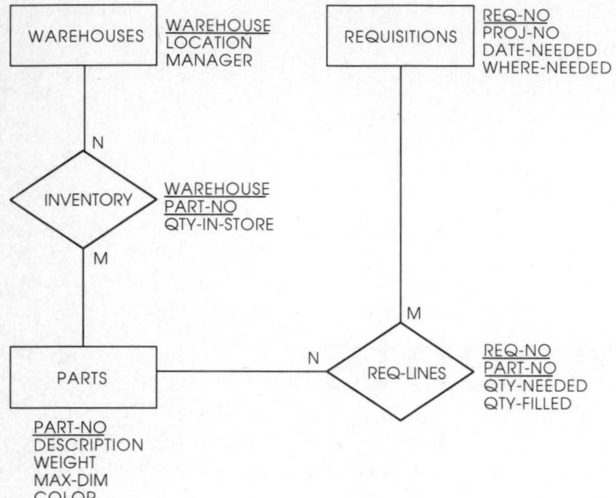

INVENTORY

WAREHOUSE	PART-NO	QTY-IN-STORE
sub1	pc6	100
sub1	mx7	200
sub2	jw3	120
sub2	bb11	83
sub2	pc6	19
center1	mx7	205
center1	jw3	111

PARTS

PART-NO	DESCRIPTION	WEIGHT	MAX-DIM	WEIGHT
px1	Drill	70.0	7.0	blue
pc6	Saw	50.0	12.0	black
mx7	Hammer	90.0	7.0	gray
bb11	Saw	60.0	17.0	brown
jw3	Drill	30.0	15.0	blue

REQUISITIONS

REQ-NO	PROJ-NO	DATE-NEEDED	WHERE-NEEDED
3	pr1	870620	south
4	pr3	870703	north
5	pr1	870612	east
6	pr2	870702	west

WAREHOUSES

WAREHOUSE	LOCATION	MANAGER
sub1	south	J. Black
sub2	west	C. Clarence
center1	north	J. Tran
center2	south	B. Costello

REQ-LINES

REQ-NO	PART-NO	QTY-NEEDED	QTY-FILLED
3	pc6	90	10
3	jw3	30	0
4	pc6	50	0
4	mx7	100	20
5	jw3	40	10
5	bb11	70	0
6	jw3	90	0
5	pc6	22	15

PART-NO defines the part ordered in that line. Each requisition line is for one part and there may be many requisition lines in one requisition. Parts descriptions are stored in relation PARTS. Relation INVENTORY stores the quantity of each part held in the organization's warehouses.

The idea behind this database is that requisitions are made for parts. A search is then made of the inventory relation to determine the warehouses that can deliver these parts.

THE SQL STATEMENT

A SQL statement is entered whenever information is to be retrieved from a database. Such a statement can either be used once, or it can be saved and reused whenever the same information is to be repeatedly retrieved.

The main construct used in SQL is the SELECT statement. The most elementary form of the SELECT statement is:

```
SELECT <columns to be displayed>
FROM <relations that contain the columns>
WHERE <conditions to be satisfied by rows whose column
      values are displayed>
```

The SELECT statement defines rows that are to be retrieved from a relation. It also defines the column values to be displayed for the retrieved rows. The FROM part of the select statement defines the relation whose rows are to be selected; the WHERE part defines conditions to be satisfied by selected rows and the SELECT part defines the columns whose values are to be displayed.

Although simple in idea the select statement can be used to formulate powerful queries. They can display any columns and compute values using standard functions. They can also refer to more than one relation, and specify conditions across relations. This chapter introduces SQL by describing how it can be used to retrieve data from one table and to update a single table. The next chapter will continue by describing how SQL can be used to retrieve data from more than one table.

Retrieving data from one table

The idea of SQL is to examine a table a row at a time, select rows that satisfy the WHERE condition and print out the values of the columns specified by the SELECT condition. SQL provides a variety of methods for specifying the selected rows by WHERE conditions. Perhaps the simplest is where the whole table is to be retrieved. This is specified by:

```
SELECT * FROM PARTS;
```

Here the asterisk (*) specifies that all columns are to be output. The FROM clause specifies that relation PARTS is to be searched. The absence of the WHERE clause implies that all rows are to be output. The WHERE clause must be included to select a subset of rows from a table. For example, all rows with REQ-NO = 3 in relation REQ-LINES are retrieved by:

```
SELECT *
FROM REQ-LINES
WHERE REQ-NO = 3;
```

This statement would display the following rows from REQ-LINES:

REQ-NO	PART-NO	QTY-NEEDED	QTY-FILLED
3	pc6	90	10
3	jw3	30	0

If only some columns are needed in the output, these columns are specified in the SELECT clause. For example, if all that is needed is a list of parts with their PART-NO and their WEIGHT then the following SQL statement is used:

```
SELECT PART-NO, WEIGHT
FROM PARTS;
```

Here only PART-NO and WEIGHT columns of table PARTS appear in the output. It is of course possible to output selected column values in selected rows by specifying the rows in the WHERE clause and the columns in the SELECT. Thus the following SQL statement can be used to find all PART-NO and QTY-NEEDED of parts in one requisition:

```
SELECT PART-NO, QTY-NEEDED
FROM REQ-LINES
WHERE REQ-NO = 3;
```

The output from this statement is:

PART-NO	QTY-NEEDED
pc6	90
jw3	30

Arithmetic expressions can also be included in the SELECT clause. For example, (QTY-NEEDED - QTY-FILLED) could be included in the SELECT clause of the previous statement. This would output the quantity of parts yet to be filled in a requisition.

Ordering and duplicates

Outputs from the previous statements are in the same order that they are stored in the table. If the same values of columns appear in more that one selected row, then those values would appear more than once in the output. SQL includes methods for both controlling the output order and eliminating duplicates from output. Ordering is specified by the ORDER clause as follows:

```
SELECT PART-NO, QTY-NEEDED
FROM REQ-LINES
WHERE REQ-NO = 3
ORDER BY PART-NO;
```

This statement produces the same output as the previous statement but in ascending order of PART-NO. A descending sequence could be obtained by following PART-NO in the ORDER BY clause with DESC.

Duplicates are removed by including DISTINCT in the SELECT clause. For example:

```
SELECT DISTINCT WHERE-NEEDED
FROM REQUISITIONS
WHERE PROJ-NO = 'pr1';
```

The DISTINCT keyword specifies that values of attributes should not be duplicated in the output. Thus, this statement outputs the WHERE-NEEDED locations for a project. A location will only be output once even if there is more than one requisition from project 'pr1' for that location.

If there are more than two columns in the SELECT clause then DISTINCT applies to combinations of values of the columns.

Selection conditions

Selection conditions can include a variety of boolean conditions. The kinds of conditions provided in the standard include arithmetic comparison operators such as greater than (>) or less than(<). They also include the following operators.

BETWEEN

```
WHERE WEIGHT BETWEEN 10 AND 17
```

Selects rows where weight is 10 or greater and 17 or less.

LIKE

```
WHERE DESCRIPTION LIKE 'h%'
```

Selects rows where description starts with the letter 'h'. String matches can be expressed at the start, end or anywhere in the string. Thus %h would find values ending with 'h' and %h% would find values that include 'h' anywhere in the string.

IN and *NOT IN*

```
WHERE DESCRIPTION IN ('Saw', 'Drill')
```

Finds all those rows where description is either 'Saw' or 'Drill' whereas

```
WHERE DESCRIPTION NOT IN ('Saw')
```

Finds all those rows whose description is other than 'Saw'. Remember, however, that SQL tests one row at a time. Thus:

```
SELECT REQ-NO
FROM REQ-LINES
WHERE PART-NO NOT IN ('pc6');
```

does not find requisitions that do not include part ‘pc6’. It finds requisition lines where PART-NO is a value other than ‘pc6’. Alternatively it finds those requisitions that include a requisition line not for ‘pc6’ , or, those requisitions that include at least one part other than ‘PC6’.

AND and OR conditions

Often it is necessary to select rows that satisfy more than one condition. Any number of such conditions can be specified in a SQL statement, separated by AND and OR to specify condition logic. For example:

```
SELECT PART-NO
FROM PARTS
WHERE WEIGHT > 55
AND MAX-DIM > 10;
```

Output all parts heavier than 55 and larger than 10 in their maximum dimension. Another example of using the OR condition is:

```
SELECT PART-NO
FROM PARTS
WHERE DESCRIPTION = 'Saw'
OR DESCRIPTION = 'Hammer';
```

This SQL statement retrieves all parts that are saws or hammers. You should note that another alternative is to use the IN clause — WHERE DESCRIPTION IN (‘Saw’,’Hammer’). A still further alternative is to use the UNION condition, which is discussed later.

There can be any number of AND and OR conditions in a SQL statement. There is a precedence for evaluating AND and OR conditions. They are in fact evaluated in the order that they appear in the SQL statement. Thus if there is a set of conditions C1, C2 and C3 each of which is either true or false, the expression C1 AND C2 OR C3 will be evaluated as follows:

> C1, C2 and C3 will be evaluated to be either true of false. Then (C1 AND C2) is evaluated. This result must also be either true or false. Now the final evaluation is to produce C3 OR (the result of C1 AND C2).

This precedence can be changed by using brackets. Thus C1 AND (C2 OR C3) is evaluated differently. First the result of (C2 OR C3) is found. Then the final evaluation is to evaluate C1 AND (the result of C2 OR C3).

Exercise 12.1

You are given the database shown in Figure 12.2.

Figure 12.2 Problem database (E-R diagram and relations)

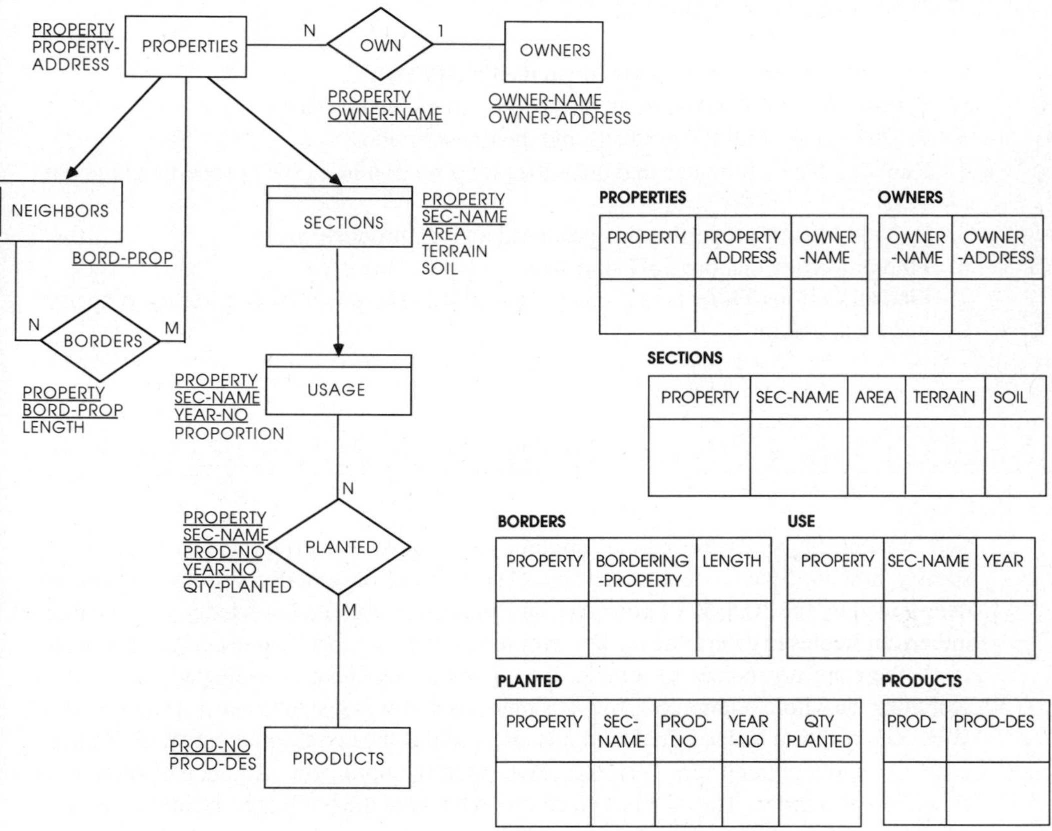

This database stores data collected from a number of owners on the crops grown on their properties. Information about owners is stored in relation, OWNERS, and information about properties is stored in relation PROPERTIES. Relation PROPERTIES is constructed by combining the entity set, PROPERTIES, and the relationship set, OWN, using the rules described in Chapter 9. Each property is divided into sections with information about sections stored in relation, SECTIONS. Each section may be used for plantings in any given year. The dependent entity set, USAGE, models the PROPORTION of a section that was utilized for planting in each year. Records of plantings for each section for each year are kept in relation, PLANTED. The quantity of different products produced in each section for the year is recorded in this relation. Relation PRODUCTS stores information about products of interest in the database. Relation BORDERS stores information about boundaries between properties. It uses the ideas of recursive relations as discussed in Chapter 10. BORDERS is a subset that contains all PROPERTIES. It does not appear as a separate relation but is combined with PROPERTIES using the rules described in Chapter 9. Relationship set, BORDERS, is the recursive relationship that keeps information about borders of adjacent properties. Retrieve the following information from data in the tables shown in Figure 12.2.

1. Select the owner of a property given the PROPERTY.
2. Display the SEC-NAME of all the sections in a given property.
3. Produce a list of all the products and their descriptions.
4. Provide a list of products and quantities for a section in a given property and given year.
5. Provide a list of properties that produced a given product.
6. Find properties that possibly start with the letters 'Ink'.
7. Find all sections whose area is greater than 500 and less than 2000. List their property and section name.

SELECTION CONDITIONS AND PERFORMANCE

SQL statements specify the logical conditions to be satisfied by retrieved data but do not specify how the data is to be retrieved. The method of actually getting the data is determined by the RDBMS optimizer. This optimizer uses its knowledge of available indices and tables to determine the best way to retrieve data specified in a SQL statement.

If there are no indices to a table, then a select statement is evaluated by serially searching the whole relation one row at a time. Each row is tested to see if it satisfies the WHERE condition and selected columns are output if the condition is satisfied. If there is an index to a column in a WHERE clause then the optimizer will decide whether it should use that index. The user has no control over what the optimizer decides to do and whether it will use any indices.

The advantage of this approach is, first, that users need not concern themselves with physical problems of data access. Second, it is possible to change the database by adding indices without having to change the SQL query. These advantages are particularly useful with small tables or databases. The user states the logical requirement and receives an answer. With large databases, however, some consideration must be given to performance when making SQL enquiries.

Improving performance

There are two ways to improve query performance. One is to make indices available to process the query. Then there are also alternative ways of formulating queries.

Choosing indices

The optimizer will process any SQL statement using serial searches if necessary. Such searches of relations can take a long time. Performance can, however, be improved if the selection makes use of table indices. For example, suppose we have the following SQL statement:

```
SELECT PART-NO
FROM PARTS
WHERE DESCRIPTION = 'Hammer';
```

If there is an index that has DESCRIPTION as its key, then a sequential search would not be needed. The system would directly retrieve only those rows whose DESCRIPTION value is 'Hammer'. Updates, however, will become slower with indices because, as well as updating the table, the system must also update the index.

The ideal from a retrieval viewpoint would be to have an index on each column. This ideal, however, is not usually feasible for two reasons. First, indices use storage and creating too many indices could result in prohibitive storage use. Second, update performance is degraded with indices because, as well as updating a table, all indices to that table must also be updated.

Thus considerable care must be exercised when creating indices. Database designers cannot place an index on every field and combinations of fields because the amount of storage used will become large and updating will become slow. They should, however, ensure that the number of queries that require long search times is small. Otherwise the performance of the entire system will be degraded. Thus designers should provide indices at least for the most heavily used queries. They must carefully choose those columns that are frequently used in WHERE clauses and create indices for those columns. Methods for access path analysis that were described in Chapter 9 are used to identify such columns.

Reformulating queries

What you should keep in mind is that the user cannot specify what index, if any, is to be used by a SQL statement. The relational system makes the decision itself. It uses the WHERE clause and its knowledge of indices to select the best way to process a query. It is even possible that SQL may not always use an index on a field even if that field appears in a condition in the WHERE clause. In most cases, indices are used if there is a single value specified for the index key field. The optimizer uses this value to retrieve one index entry. This entry will contain references to rows that contain that value of the index field.

Where a single value of the index field is not given in the WHERE clause, the optimizer may not use the index. It is worthwhile to keep these conditions in mind because sometimes alternative formulations of the same query may make use of the index. It must, however, be pointed out that there is great variability between optimizers in different RDBMS. Thus the following can only be used as guidelines and not as general rules. Particular manuals should be consulted to determine strategies used by particular products. Some conditions that may not use an index are:

SQL statements with OR conditions

This would require an optimizer to do separate searches using two indices and then combine the retrieved records. It is preferable to use the UNION operator (discussed in the next section).

Greater than or less than conditions

These require searches of the index itself. Some optimizers may not carry out such searches.

LIKE conditions

In most cases an index would not be used, although it is possible sometimes where the first letters of a key value are given.

A NOT condition

Usually this is not done by most optimizers because they would have to find all possible values outside the NOT to do the search. Often it is wise to replace a NOT by an equivalent condition that does not include a NOT. For example instead of

WHERE QTY-NEEDED NOT > 85 use
WHERE QTY-NEEDED < 86.

The IN operator

Some optimizers will not use indices with the IN operator. Thus the condition WHERE DESCRIPTION IN ('Saw','Hammer') should not be used. It should be replaced by the UNION operator (discussed in the next section).

Arithmetic conditions in the WHERE clause

An index will not be used if there is an arithmetic expression to the left of a comparison. For example:

WHERE SALARY + 2000 > X

will not result in index use. However, some optimizers may use the index where the condition is stated as:

WHERE SALARY > X -2000

Indices with composite keys

One interesting point is the use of indices with composite attributes; for example, if the index key is made up of three fields (F1, F2, F3). Suppose the WHERE clause only contains F1. Or suppose it contains F1 and F3. Again there is a great variability between optimizers here. Some only use the index if all three fields are specified. Others may use the index if all the higher level fields appear in the WHERE condition. Again it is wise to consult the manufacturer's manual to see whether an index would be used in particular cases.

In summary, the selection of the processing method used to satisfy a query depends on a particular DBMS and its optimizer. There may sometimes be preferred ways of stating a query to ensure index use. However, users must consult their manual to see how their particular query will be executed and what a preferred formulation is.

SOME ADDITIONAL SELECT CONDITIONS

The earlier sections described some of the most common expressions used to retrieve data from single tables. There are also some other constructs that are available in SQL.

UNION — an alternative to OR

UNION presents an alternative way to using OR clauses. It has the advantage in that it can make use of indices that may not be used with an OR clause. Thus the following statement can be used to select parts that are either Saws or heavier than 10:

```
SELECT PART-NO
FROM PARTS
WHERE DESCRIPTION = ‘Saw’;

UNION:

SELECT PART-NO
FROM PARTS
WHERE WEIGHT > 55;
```

The output from this statement is:

PART-NO
pc6
bb11
px1
mx7
bb11

If both DESCRIPTION and WEIGHT are indexed, then these indices would be used by the system. One index would be used in the first part of the statement and the other in the second part. The outputs are then printed out as the combined output for the query.

The indices, however, would not be used in the equivalent OR formulation of the same statement, namely:

```
SELECT PART-NO
FROM PARTS
WHERE DESCRIPTION = 'Saw'
OR WEIGHT > 10;
```

Incidentally, the output from this statement will be:

PART-NO

px1
pc6
mx7
bb11

Note that bb11 now appears once only in the output. When UNION was used the row with bb11 was selected twice, once in each of the SELECT statements. In the statement that used OR, the row was selected once only.

NULL values

There are many times when a value for a particular attribute is not known at a particular instant of time, but is added later. For example, we may not know the WEIGHT of a part but will find it out later. In that case, SQL allows the value of WEIGHT to be NULL. NULL is a special symbol used by SQL for the sole reason of storing values that are not known at a particular instant of time. Furthermore, SQL allows the NULL condition to be specified in the WHERE clause. For example:

```
SELECT PART-NO
FROM PARTS
WHERE DESCRIPTION IS NULL;
```

finds all parts that do not have a DESCRIPTION. It is also possible to use NOT NULL in a comparison. However (=NULL) is not valid construct.

SQL variables comparing two rows from the same table

Sometimes two rows in the same table must be compared. In that case rows can be assigned to SQL variables. The rows assigned to different variables are then compared. For example:

```
SELECT X.PART-NO
FROM PARTS X, PARTS Y
WHERE X.WEIGHT > Y.WEIGHT
AND Y.PART-NO = 'pc6';
```

Here X and Y are SQL variables. Two different rows can be assigned to X and Y. In the example, the row where PART-NO = 'pc6' is assigned to variable Y. Now other rows are assigned to variable X and compared to variable Y. A row in variable X satisfies the WHERE condition when its WEIGHT is greater than the WEIGHT of row Y. The value of PART-NO for the selected row X is output. The output in this case would show part numbers ('px1', 'mx7', 'bb11').

FUNCTIONS IN SQL STATEMENTS

SQL statements can include arithmetic statements, which can include functions such as:

MAX — maximum of a set of values
MIN — minimum of a set of values
SUM — sum of a set of values
AVE — average of a set of values
COUNT — counts the number of rows

These functions can be used in SQL statements. Thus:

```
SELECT COUNT(*)
FROM PARTS;
```

will output the number of rows in relation PARTS, that is, the number of parts, in this case five.

The SELECT clause may contain any arithmetic expression and contain any of the above functions. The SQL statement will select rows from a table and evaluate expressions applying the function to some column in the selected rows. For example:

```
SELECT SUM(QTY-NEEDED)
FROM REQ-LINES
WHERE PART-NO = 'pc6';
```

will find the total number of part 'pc6' that are recorded in REQ-LINES. In our example the output will be 152.

```
SELECT SUM(QTY-NEEDED - QTY-FILLED)
FROM REQ-LINES
WHERE PART-NO = 'pc6';
```

will find the sum of part 'pc6' that still remains to be filled. In our example this will be 137.

It is also possible to group rows in a relation by one column and apply the function to each such group. For example:

```
SELECT PART-NO, SUM(QTY-NEEDED)
FROM REQ-LINES
GROUP BY PART-NO;
```

This query first groups rows. There is one group for each value of PART-NO and all rows in a group have the same value of PART-NO. The function SUM is then applied to each group so that the output contains one row for each PART-NO and the total of that part in inventory. The output from this statement will be:

PART-NO	*SUM(QTY-NEEDED)*
pc6	162
jw3	160
mx7	100
bb11	70

There is one constraint in SQL statements that contain the GROUP phrase. Any column names in the SELECT clause that are not arguments of a function, as for example PART-NO, must appear in the GROUP clause. Thus PART-NO, because it is part of the GROUP clause, can appear in the SELECT clause but DESCRIPTION, WEIGHT or MAX-DIM cannot.

Functions in the WHERE clause

Functions and arithmetic expressions can also appear in the condition clause. This is done by extending the SELECT statement with a HAVING clause. For example the following SQL statement is used to find parts whose total quantity requisitioned exceeds 150:

```
SELECT PART-NO
FROM REQ-LINES
GROUP BY PART-NO
HAVING SUM(QTY-NEEDED> 150;
```

Now all the rows in REQ-LINES are grouped by PART-NO. The sum of quantity requisitioned is evaluated for each group, and the PART-NO output if this sum exceeds 150. In our example this will be 'pc6' and 'jw3'.

Exercise 12.2

Write SQL statements to retrieve the following information from the database in Figure 12.2:

1. The number of properties in the database.

2. The total sum produced of a given product in a given year.
3. A list by product of the total quantities of products.
4. The total area of a given property.
5. A list of properties and their size.
6. Properties that produced more than 10,000 of a given product.
7. Properties larger than 25,000.

SAVING SQL STATEMENTS

Often the same query may be used repeatedly. It then becomes tiresome to have to input it every time it is required. Most SQL editors can save SQL statements. Saved statements can be executed at some later time.

The exact statement used to save and execute saved queries depends on the particular DBMS and its SQL editor. The IBM systems use the statement

```
STORE <statement-name>
```

to store the current SQL statement. The current statement is given the name <statement-name> and then saved.

The saved statement can then be executed by entering

```
START <statement-name>
```

Statements can also be saved with parameters rather than actual values in the WHERE clause. In that case the same statement can be executed selecting different rows each time. Thus suppose we need a statement that will retrieve the PART-NO and QTY-NEEDED for requisitions. Information about different requisitions may be needed each time that the statement is executed. In that case we create the statement:

```
SELECT PART-NO, QTY-NEEDED
FROM REQ-LINES
WHERE REQ-NO = &1;
```

Here &1 is a parameter that may have a different value each time that the statement is executed. This statement is now saved as

```
STORE REQ-DETAILS
```

If we need the details of requisition 1 then we would enter

```
START REQ-DETAILS(1)
```

To get details of requisition 2 we would enter

START REQ-DETAILS(2)

Any number of parameters can appear in a saved SQL statement. They are named &1, &2, &3 and so on. Actual values appear in the START statement in order &1, &2, &3 and so on. The editor simply substitutes the actual value for the parameter. Any para-meters that take string values must be enclosed by quotes in the SQL statement.

UPDATING THE DATABASE

There are a number of ways to change the contents of a table. One way is to use SQL statements to change the database interactively. The other ways are to use programs developed using high-level language or screen-based application generators.

Changing the database using interactive SQL

SQL includes commands to insert new rows into a table, delete rows from a table or change the value of row attributes.

Inserting a new row

To insert a new row it is necessary to specify column names and the values to be assigned to these column names. This is done using the INSERT statement.

```
INSERT INTO REQUISITIONS
(REQ-NO, PROJ-NO, DATE-NEEDED, WHERE-NEEDED)
VALUES (7, 'PR3', 870719, 'east');
```

inserts a new row into relation REQUISITIONS. The names in brackets specify the column names. The values in brackets are values assigned to the attributes. The values are given in the same sequence as the attribute names.

It is also possible to insert rows obtained from a select statement into a table. For example, suppose we have the relation

TEMP (REQ-NO, LOCATION)

and enter the statement

```
INSERT INTO TEMP
SELECT REQ-NO, WHERE-NEEDED
FROM REQUISITIONS
WHERE PROJ-NO = 'pr1';
```

All the rows retrieved by the select statement will be inserted into relation TEMP. Note, however, that you cannot retrieve the rows from one relation and insert them back into the same relation.

This insertion method is used for two reasons. First, it can be used to store results of a retrieval for later use. Second, it can be used to compute new values using some arithmetic expression and store them in a new relation.

Updating a row (or rows)

To change a value of one column it is necessary to define the new value and select the rows to be changed. This is done by the UPDATE statement.

```
UPDATE REQUISITIONS
SET DATE-NEEDED = 870720
WHERE REQ-NO = 3;
```

changes the value of DATE-NEEDED in request 3 to 870720. You should, however, note that an update can change more than one row. It will change all those rows that satisfy the WHERE conditions.

Deleting a row (or rows)

Here it is necessary to select the row to be deleted. This is done by the DELETE statement.

```
DELETE FROM PARTS
WHERE PART-NO = 'pc6';
```

deletes the row whose PART-NO = 'pc6' from relation PARTS. This command can delete any number of rows. It will delete all the rows specified by the WHERE condition.

Insertion of rows using the SQL editor

The INSERT statement described earlier can be cumbersome if a number of rows is to be inserted. The column names must be input every time a new row is entered. Most SQL editors allow such new rows to be entered into the editor without requiring users to continually re-enter column names. The method used depends on the editor. In one system the user simply enters

```
INPUT <table-name>
```

The system will display all the columns for the selected table. The user can enter as many rows as needed. Each row is entered as column values, separated by commas. This continues until all the new rows are input. The user then enters END to terminate the input. Thus to enter a new set of requisition lines begin by:

```
INPUT REQ-LINES
```

The system responds with

```
REQ-NO PART-NO QTY-NEEDED QTY-FILLED
```

The user then enters

```
6,'pc6',12,0
6,'pw3',88,0
6,'px5',79,0
END
```

The result is three new rows entered into table REQ-LINES.

INTERACTIVE UPDATES AND INTEGRITY

It is important to remember that SQL updates do not check integrity. Thus when a part is deleted from relation PARTS, no check is made to ensure that all rows with that part number do not exist in relations INVENTORY or REQ-LINES. It is up to the user to make this check prior to making updates or deletions.

It is also important to remember that commands such as DELETE or UPDATE can affect many rows. It is necessary to be very careful in specifying the WHERE condition to ensure that only the required rows are affected and that no unintended updates or deletions are made. An error in a WHERE condition can cause unwanted changes from which it is not possible to recover.

Example

```
DELETE FROM REQ-LINES
WHERE PART-NO = 'pc6'
AND REQ-NO = 3;
```

This will delete one row in relation REQ-LINES. However, suppose in error, the user forgets the last line — AND REQ-NO = 3. The result is that *all* requisition lines in relation REQ-LINES for part 'pc6' will be deleted. Furthermore, unless back-up copies are kept it will not be possible to restore the erroneously deleted data.

Maintaining integrity

There are two ways to prevent such errors. One is not to allow interactive changes. Instead all changes are made by specially tested programs that check system integrity. The SQL statements are embedded in these programs.

The other is to delay updates. In this case changes specified by a DELETE or UPDATE command are not permanently made to the stored data, but are stored temporarily. The effects of these changes are examined to see if there are any undesirable effects. If no such effects are noted then the change is made permanent. Most systems provide a COMMIT and ROLLBACK function to support this kind of operation. The change is made in two phases. The phases are:

1. Execute an update command and examine the effect of the update command.
2. Commit the update to the database.

The commit is made simply by executing the COMMIT command. If an error is detected, the effect of the temporary update can be undone by executing ROLLBACK. In that case the database is restored to the values that existed at the time of the last COMMIT statement.

Of course the two-phase update is not foolproof. There is a tendency to examine only those rows that should have been changed by the update command and not look any further. This, however, is not a complete check. Rows that should not have been changed should also be checked. This, however, may be very difficult. One difficulty is where a delete is initiated. It will not be possible to determine if unnecessary deletions took place unless the new table contents are checked against the old table contents. This will be almost prohibitive for large tables. In such large databases it is also not possible to examine ALL rows to see if they have been inadvertently changed. Thus it is not possible to guarantee that no unwanted changes took place.

For this reason the two-phase approach is only useful for small tables. The general practice in most operational systems is to allow updates and deletes through specially written programs that check system integrity. Interactive updates are not used during system operation, although they may be used during testing.

SUMMARY

This chapter introduced SQL and described the SQL statement. The SQL statement is made up of the following clauses:

SELECT <columns to be displayed>
FROM <table to be searched>
WHERE <condition to be satisfied>
GROUP BY <where rows are to be grouped>
HAVING <where an arithmetic condition exists>
ORDER BY <columns used to order output>

This chapter described how this statement can be used to retrieve information from one table. It also described interactive update commands and how they must be used with care if database integrity is to be maintained.

SQL statements can also be used to retrieve data from more than one relation. Methods of doing this are described in the next chapter.

This chapter also described some SQL editor functions for saving SQL statements, delaying updates and inputting new rows into a table.

13

The SQL statement: querying many tables

INTRODUCTION

The last chapter described how data can be retrieved from a single relation. However, there are many occasions when data must be retrieved from more than one relation to answer some user query. One way to retrieve data from more than one relation is to first combine two or more relations into one relation, and then use SQL statements to retrieve data from that combined relation. The combination of relations is called a join. It is, of course, possible to actually create and store the newly created relation in the system. However, SQL does not require such a joined relation to be actually created. Instead it has a construct that implies such joining, and the SQL statement can be applied to this implied or virtual join without the table actually being stored during the processing of a SQL statement. Data, however, is retrieved as if such a joined table actually existed.

This chapter describes how joins are used to retrieve data from more than one relation. It then describes some alternatives to joins to retrieve data from more than one relation.

JOINS

A join of two tables, REQ-LINES and PARTS, is illustrated in Figure 13.1. Here each line in REQ-LINES is combined with a row in PARTS that has the same value of PART-NO to create a line in table NEW-REQ-LINES. For example, the first row in REQ-LINES

Figure 13.1 Joining two relations

PARTS

PART-NO	DESCRIPTION	WEIGHT	MAX-DIM	COLOR
px1	Drill	70.0	7.0	blue
pc6	Saw	50.0	12.0	black
mx7	Hammer	90.0	7.0	gray
bb11	Saw	60.0	17.0	brown
jw3	Drill	30.0	15.0	blue

REQ-LINES

REQ-NO	PART-NO	QTY-NEEDED	QTY-FILLED
3	pc6	90	10
3	jw3	30	0
4	pc6	50	0
4	mx7	100	20
5	jw3	40	10
5	bb11	70	0
6	jw3	90	0
5	pc6	12	15

NEW-REQ-LINES

REQ-NO	PART-NO	QTY-NEEDED	QTY-FILLED	WEIGHT	DESCRIPTION	MAX-DIM	COLOR
3	pc6	90	10	50.0	Saw	12.0	black
3	jw3	30	0	30.0	Drill	15.0	blue
4	pc6	50	0	50.0	Saw	12.0	black
4	mx7	100	20	90.0	Hammer	7.0	gray
5	jw3	40	10	30.0	Drill	15.0	blue
5	bb11	70	0	60.0	Saw	17.0	brown
6	jw3	90	0	30.0	Drill	15.0	blue
5	pc6	12	15	50.0	Saw	12.0	black

is combined with the second row in PARTS because they have the same value of PART-NO. The combined rows become the first row in NEW-REQ-LINES. Each join has a join condition. This condition specifies the criteria used to join two rows. In Figure 13.1 the join condition is that the values of PART-NO in the joined rows must be equal. Information can then be retrieved from the joined relation using a SELECT statement.

Joining is implied in a SQL statement by including all the relations to be joined in the FROM clause, and making the join condition one of the conditions in the WHERE clause. An example of the SELECT statement that specifies joining is:

```
SELECT REQ-LINES.REQ-NO, REQ-LINES.PART-NO, PARTS.WEIGHT
FROM PARTS, REQ-LINES
WHERE REQ-LINES.PART-NO = PARTS.PART-NO;
```

Here there are two relations, PARTS and REQ-LINES, in the FROM clause. This specifies that information is to be retrieved from these two relations. The WHERE clause specifies the join condition. The statement REQ-LINES.PART-NO = PARTS.PART-NO specifies that rows in the join combine a line from REQ-LINES with a line with the same PART-NO in PARTS to form one line in the joined table. The SELECT clause specifies the information to be output, in this case REQ-NO and PART-NO from REQ-LINES and WEIGHT from PARTS for that PART-NO.

The output from this SQL statement would be the exact rows shown in table NEW-REQ-LINES in Figure 13.1 without the two columns QTY-NEEDED and QTY-FILLED.

You should note one difference between SQL statements that use one table and those that use more than one table. With more than one table, it is sometimes necessary to use qualifiers to refer to attribute names. Such qualifiers must be used whenever two relations have attributes with the same name. Thus PART-NO was qualified by relation names in the above SQL statement because PART-NO appears in both relations PARTS and REQ-LINES.

Otherwise, the format and options of all the clauses in the SQL statement used for the combined relation is the same as those for a single relation. Thus, for example, to output all the information in each row of the joined relation, the SELECT clause becomes:

```
SELECT *
```

Alternatively, some systems may require the select clause to specifically nominate the relations whose contents are to be output. In that case the SELECT clause becomes:

```
SELECT PARTS.*, REQ-LINES.*
```

This means that all PARTS and all REQ-LINES columns must be output. Joins can, of course, include more than two relations. For example, the following SQL statement uses three relations to find all the projects that ordered saws:

```
SELECT PROJ-NO, REQ-LINES.PART-NO
FROM REQUISITIONS, REQ-LINES, PARTS
WHERE REQUISITIONS.REQ-NO = REQ-LINES.REQ-NO
AND REQ-LINES.PART-NO = PARTS.PART-NO
AND PARTS.DESCRIPTION = 'Saw';
```

Here rows in REQUISITIONS are joined to rows in REQ-LINES with the same REQ-NO. These rows are then joined to rows in PARTS with the same PART-NO. Note that PART-NO is qualified in the select clause, because PART-NO appears in two of the relations in the FROM clause. PROJ-NO, however, does not need to be qualified because it appears in only one relation in the FROM clause.

The output from this SQL statement will be:

PROJ-NO	*REQ-LINES.PART-NO*
pr1	pc6
pr3	pc6
pr1	bb11
pr1	pc6

So far we have assumed that all joins are made by finding rows with equal values of some attributes. Joins can also be made by joining rows whose attributes satisfy conditions other than equal. For example:

```
SELECT REQ-NO, WAREHOUSE, INVENTORY.PART-NO, QTY-NEEDED -
    QTY-FILLED, QTY-IN-STORE
FROM REQ-LINES, INVENTORY
WHERE REQ-LINES.PART-NO = INVENTORY.PART-NO
AND QTY-NEEDED-QTY-FILLED < INVENTORY.QTY-IN-STORE;
```

outputs warehouses that have more parts than needed in a request.

The output from this SQL statement is:

REQ-NO	WAREHOUSE	PART-NO	QTY-NEEDED-QTY-FILLED	QTY-IN-STORE
3	sub1	pc6	80	100
3	sub2	jw3	30	120
3	center1	jw3	30	111
4	sub1	pc6	50	100
4	sub1	mx7	80	200
4	center1	mx7	80	205
5	sub2	jw3	30	120
5	center1	jw3	30	111
5	sub2	bb11	70	83
6	sub2	jw3	90	120
6	center1	jw3	90	111
5	sub1	pc6	7	100
5	sub2	pc6	7	19

Note that a different warehouse may be selected for each line in a requisition. Later on an SQL statement that finds a warehouse to satisfy the whole requisition will be described.

You should note that a qualification is needed whenever an attribute appears in more than one relation in the query. Thus PART-NO is qualified in all cases because it appears in both INVENTORY and REQ-LINES.

Exercise 13.1

Write SQL statements to retrieve the following information from the database shown in Figure 12.2.

1. List all the properties and their AREA for a given owner.
2. List all the properties and their owners with a given product planted in a given year.
3. For a given owner list the owner's property, sections and the area of each section.
4. For a given PROD-DES list all the properties that planted that product in a given year.
5. For a given owner, list the PROD-DES of all the products ever planted on the owner's property.
6. Find the OWNER-ADDRESS of all owners who planted a product with a given PROD-DES in a given year.
7. Find the SEC-NAME of sections that planted a product with a given PROD-DES and are owned by an owner with a given OWNER-NAME.

SUBQUERIES: AN ALTERNATIVE TO JOINS

SQL also includes an alternative to joins for retrieving data from more than one relation. This is to use a subquery. SELECT statements in a subquery are nested to any number of levels. Each level specifies retrieval from one relation. The following SQL statement illustrates a subquery of two levels:

```
SELECT REQ-NO
FROM REQ-LINES
WHERE PART-NO IN
      (SELECT PART-NO
      FROM PARTS
      WHERE DESCRIPTION = 'Saw');
```

This statement finds the REQ-NO of all requisitions that include at least one part with DESCRIPTION 'Saw'. The idea here is to evaluate the inner SQL statement first. This inner statement finds the PART-NO of all parts whose DESCRIPTION is 'Saw'. These PART-NOs are {'pc6', 'bb11'}. These values are now substituted for the inner statement, and then the outer statement is evaluated. This outer statement is now:

```
SELECT REQ-NO
FROM REQ-LINES
WHERE PART-NO IN ('pc6', 'bb11');
```

The output will be:

REQ-NO
3
4
5
5

The information retrieved using a subquery can also be obtained using a join. Thus the REQ-NO of all requisitions can also be found using the following join statement:

```
SELECT REQ-LINES.REQ-NO
FROM REQ-LINES, PARTS
WHERE REQ-LINES.PART-NO = PARTS.PART-NO
AND PARTS.DESCRIPTION = 'Saw';
```

However, note that there is one difference between subqueries and joins. It is not possible to include attributes of the nested relation in the output. For example, in the above query, it is not possible to include any attributes from the PARTS relation in the SELECT clause of the REQ-LINES relation.

Subqueries are sometimes useful because they can retrieve data without introducing variables. For example, it is possible to compare rows in the same relation without variables, as follows:

```
SELECT PART-NO
FROM PARTS
WHERE WEIGHT >
    (SELECT WEIGHT
    FROM PARTS
    WHERE PART-NO = 'pc6');
```

Here the inner statement finds the weight of part 'pc6'. This weight is now used in the WHERE clause of the outer statement to find all parts heavier than 'pc6'. The alternative is to use SQL variables, as was discussed in the previous chapter. You may wish to compare this statement with the corresponding SQL statement in the previous chapter. This earlier statement used SQL variables.

Levels of subqueries

It is possible to have subqueries nested to any level. It is also possible to have more than one subquery at the same level. For example:

```
SELECT REQ-NO
FROM REQUEST-LINES
WHERE PART-NO IN
    (SELECT PART-NO
    FROM PARTS
    WHERE DESCRIPTION = 'Drill')
AND REQ-NO IN
    (SELECT REQ-NO
    FROM REQUISITIONS
    WHERE PROJ-NO = 'pr1');
```

Here there are two subqueries at the same level. Both of these are evaluated before the outer query is evaluated. The first finds all the parts with DESCRIPTION 'Drill'. The second finds the REQ-NO of all the requisitions made by project 'pr1'. The outer query then becomes:

```
SELECT REQ-NO
FROM REQ-LINES
WHERE PART-NO IN ('px1','jw3')
AND REQ-NO IN (3,5);
```

This SQL statement finds all requisitions that include a 'Drill' and are made by project 'pr1'. The output will be:

<u>*REQ-NO*</u>

3
5

There can be an unlimited number of subqueries at the same level. There can also be subqueries to any level.

Mixing joins and subqueries

SQL provides users with considerable flexibility for formulating queries. As well as using subqueries as alternatives to joins, it is also possible to mix joins and subqueries in the same SQL statement. For example:

```
SELECT PROJ-NO
FROM REQUISITIONS, REQ-LINES
WHERE REQUISITIONS.REQ-NO = REQ-LINES.REQ-NO
AND REQ-LINES.PART-NO IN
      (SELECT PART-NO
      FROM PARTS
      WHERE DESCRIPTION = 'Saw');
```

This query finds all projects that have made at least one request that included a saw. The answer will be 'pr1' and 'pr3'.

Exercise 13.2

Repeat Exercise 13.1 using subqueries.

Correlated subqueries

So far we have only described subqueries where the inner query does not refer to attributes in the outer query. However, there are cases where a WHERE condition in the subquery must refer to a column in the top-level query. This column appears in the subquery qualified by the relation name in the top-level query. Such formulations are known as correlated subqueries. An example of a correlated subquery follows.

```
SELECT REQ-NO, PART-NO
FROM REQ-LINES
WHERE PART-NO IN
      (SELECT PART-NO
      FROM INVENTORY
      WHERE QTY-IN-STORE > REQ-LINES.QTY-NEEDED - REQ-LINES.
            QTY-FILLED)
```

This query finds all request lines whose parts can be supplied from the one warehouse. To do this the WHERE condition in the subquery uses column QTY-NEEDED of the relation in the outer query. It does this by qualifying this column by its relation name. This use of outer columns in the inner query makes the subquery a correlated subquery.

However, you should note one limitation of the correlated subquery. It is still not possible to print out column values of columns in the subquery. Thus the attribute WAREHOUSE cannot be displayed because it is not an attribute of the relation in the outer SELECT clause.

Further subquery variations

There are a number of variations possible with subqueries. Rather than using IN in the WHERE clause it is possible to use ANY or EXISTS. Use of ANY in the WHERE clause is to some extent equivalent to using IN in the WHERE clause. For example:

```
SELECT REQ-NO
FROM REQ-LINES
WHERE PART-NO = ANY
      (SELECT PART-NO
      FROM PARTS
      WHERE DESCRIPTION = 'Saw');
```

This SQL statement finds all requisitions that include at least one saw. However, in some cases the use of ANY can lead to some ambiguity. For example:

```
SELECT REQ-NO, PART-NO
FROM REQ-LINES
WHERE QTY-NEEDED > ANY
      (SELECT QTY-NEEDED
      FROM REQ-LINES
      WHERE PART-NO ='pc6');
```

It is possible to interpret ANY to mean one of two things. One is to find REQ-NO and PART-NO with QTY-NEEDED greater than any QTY-NEEDED of part 'pc6'. In this case all the retrieved values are where QTY-NEEDED is greater than the highest value of QTY-NEEDED for 'pc6'. The other is where QTY-NEEDED is greater than ANY one of QTY-NEEDED of 'pc6', that is greater than the smallest value of QTY-NEEDED of 'pc6'. SQL uses the latter interpretation. The answer to this SQL statement would therefore be:

REQ-NO	PART-NO
3	pc6
3	jw3
4	pc6
4	mx7

```
5        jw3
5        bb11
6        jw3
```

It is possible to have levels of subqueries and mix ANY or IN at different levels.

```
SELECT PROJ-NO
FROM REQUISITIONS
WHERE REQ-NO IN
    (SELECT REQ-NO
    FROM REQUEST-LINES
    WHERE PART-NO = ANY
        (SELECT PART-NO
        FROM PARTS
        WHERE DESCRIPTION = 'Saw'));
```

This SQL statement finds all projects that have made at least one request that includes a saw. Alternatively it finds all projects that have ordered at least one saw. You should note that subqueries can go to any depth.

EXISTS and NOT EXISTS

So far, all SQL statements compared values of columns in a relation with some other value. It is also possible to use comparisons that test for the existence of rows that satisfy specified conditions. The EXISTS statement is used to do this. EXISTS is another alternative that can be used in SQL subqueries. It differs from ANY or IN because it does not check individual values but checks for the existence of rows that satisfy particular conditions. It frequently needs to correlate the subquery to the top-level query because such conditions can involve attributes in the top-level relation. For example:

```
SELECT REQ-NO
FROM REQUISITIONS
WHERE EXISTS
    (SELECT *
    FROM REQ-LINES
    AND PART-NO = REQ-LINES.PART-NO)
    AND PART-NO IN (SELECT PART-NO
                    FROM PARTS
                    WHERE DESCRIPTION = 'Saw');
```

This SQL statement is interpreted as follows. Find the requisition with a value of REQ-NO for which there exists a requisition line for a part with description 'saw' and with the same value of REQ-NO. Thus it finds all requisitions that include at least one saw. The output from this SQL statement is:

<u>REQ-NO</u>

3
4
5

It is equivalent to using the subquery:

```
SELECT REQ-NO
FROM REQUISITIONS
WHERE REQ-NO IN (SELECT REQ-NO
                 FROM REQ-LINES
                 WHERE PART IN
                      (SELECT PART-NO
                      FROM PARTS
                      WHERE DESCRIPTION = 'Saw');
```

EXISTS is particularly important not so much for finding existing rows, but for finding the non-existence of rows with particular conditions. Non-existence of rows is specified by using NOT EXISTS. For example:

```
SELECT REQ-NO
FROM REQUISITIONS
WHERE NOT EXISTS
 (SELECT *
 FROM REQ-LINES
 WHERE PART-NO = 'jw3'
 AND REQUISITIONS.REQ-NO = REQ-LINES.REQ-NO);
```

This is interpreted as find requisitions for which there is no requisition line with PART-NO = 'jw3', or alternatively, find all requisitions that do not include part 'jw3'. The output for this SQL statement will be:

<u>REQ-NO</u>

4

You should note that this is the only way to retrieve this information. It is often tempting to use the following statement to find the same information:

```
SELECT REQ-NO
FROM REQUISITIONS
WHERE PART-NO NOT IN ('jw3');
```

This statement, however, finds all those rows that do not have 'jw3' as the value of PART-NO. It will thus find the REQ-NO of all requisitions that include at least one part other than 'jw3'. The answer to this SQL statement will be:

<u>REQ-NO</u>

3
4
5

The EXISTS construct gives users some additional options. One is to compare rows in the same table. The other is to satisfy the ALL predicate.

Comparing rows in the same table using EXISTS

Exists can be used to find rows with the same values of some columns in some table. For example:

```
SELECT PART-NO
FROM REQ-LINES X
WHERE REQ-NO = 3
AND EXISTS
    (SELECT *
    FROM REQ-LINES Y
    WHERE REQ-NO = 4
    AND X.PART-NO = Y.PART-NO);
```

Finds all parts in both requisitions 3 and 4. The query says find the PART-NO in requisition 3 for which there exists a requisition line for requisition 4 with the same PART-NO. The reply to this statement will be:

<u>PART-NO</u>

pc6

There is an alternative SQL for this statement, namely:

```
SELECT PART-NO
FROM REQ-LINES
WHERE REQ-NO = 3
AND PART-NO IN
    (SELECT PART-NO
    FROM REQ-LINES
    WHERE REQ-NO = 4);
```

For set difference NOT EXISTS will be used instead of EXISTS.

Here the query is to find parts in requisition 3 that are also in requisition 4. To find set differences, that is values that appear in one table but not in another, substitute NOT EXISTS for EXISTS or NOT IN for IN in the above two SQL statements. If this were done then 'jw3' would be output because it appears in requisition 3 but not requisition 4.

Satisfying the ALL predicate

Perhaps one of the more interesting uses of NOT EXISTS is to compose SQL statements where the ALL predicate is to be satisfied. SQL cannot include the word ALL or its equivalent and it is necessary to replace ALL queries by a double NOT and formulate them by a SQL statement with two NOT EXISTS phrases.

For example, the query to find requisitions that contain all saws is first restated as 'Find requisitions for which there does not exist a "saw" part, for which there does not exist a requisition line with that request and that part.'

```
SELECT REQ-NO
FROM REQUISITIONS
WHERE NOT EXISTS
      (SELECT *
      FROM PARTS
      WHERE PARTS.DESCRIPTION = 'Saw'
      AND NOT EXISTS
            (SELECT *
            FROM REQ-LINES
            WHERE REQ-LINES.PART-NO = PARTS.PART-NO
            AND REQ-LINES.REQ-NO = REQUISITIONS.REQ-NO));
```

The answer to this SQL statement will be:

REQ-NO
5

because all the saw parts, 'pc6' and 'bb11' appear in requisition 5. Another example is to find all warehouses that contain all saws. This is converted to:

> Find warehouse where there does not exist a part with DESCRIPTION 'Saw' that is not in the warehouse.

This becomes the SQL statement:

```
SELECT WAREHOUSE
FROM INVENTORY X
WHERE NOT EXISTS
      (SELECT *
      FROM PARTS
      WHERE PARTS.DESCRIPTION = 'Saw'
      AND NOT EXISTS
            (SELECT *
            FROM INVENTORY Y
            WHERE Y.PART-NO = PARTS.PART-NO
            AND X.WAREHOUSE = Y.WAREHOUSE));
```

The only warehouse that satisfies this requirement is 'sub2'.

Another example of the ALL query is to find a warehouse that can satisfy an entire requisition. This is converted to find a warehouse where there does not exist a part in the requisition that is not in sufficient quantity in that warehouse.

```
SELECT WAREHOUSE
FROM INVENTORY X
WHERE NOT EXISTS
      (SELECT *
      FROM REQ-LINES
      WHERE REQ-NO =4
      AND NOT EXISTS
            (SELECT *
            FROM INVENTORY Y
            WHERE Y.QTY-IN-STORE > REQ-LINES.QTY-NEEDED -
            REQ-LINES.QTY-FILLED
            AND REQ-LINES.PART-NO = Y.PART-NO
            AND Y.WAREHOUSE = X.WAREHOUSE));
```

The only warehouse that satisfies this condition for requisition 4 is 'sub1' because it contains sufficient of both 'mx7' and 'pc6' to satisfy requisition 4..

Exercise 13.3

Retrieve the following information from the database shown in Figure 12.2.

1. Find all the properties that have never planted a product with a given PROD-NO.
2. Find all owners who do not have a section smaller in area than 100.
3. Find sections owned by a given owner that were not used in a given year.
4. Find the OWNER-NAME of all owners who do not have any properties with a given SOIL.
5. Find properties that planted all products with a given PROD-DES.
6. Find the OWNER-NAME of all owners that have access on their properties to all possible SOILs.
7. Find PRODUCTS that have been planted on all the properties.

FUNCTIONS IN JOIN STATEMENTS

Just like with single relations, functions can be applied to rows that result from the join of two or more relations. These statements can use the GROUP or HAVING construct in a similar way. For example:

```
SELECT INVENTORY.PART-NO, SUM(QTY-IN-STORE)
FROM INVENTORY, PARTS
WHERE INVENTORY.PART-NO = PARTS.PART-NO
AND PARTS.DESCRIPTION = 'Saw'
GROUP BY INVENTORY.PART-NO;
```

This query first joins two relations and selects all rows with part description 'Saw'. It then groups rows by PART-NO and provides a list of the total of each part, which must be a 'saw' in the inventory.

This SQL statement will produce the output:

INVENTORY -PART-NO	SUM(QTY-IN-STORE)
pc6	119
bb11	83

Note that DESCRIPTION need not be qualified here because it appears in one table only. PART-NO, however, must be qualified.

It is also possible to use combinations of attributes to group rows. For example:

```
SELECT REQUISITIONS.PROJ-NO, REQUISITIONS.PART-NO,
    SUM(QTY-NEEDED)
FROM REQUISITIONS, REQ-LINES
WHERE REQUISITIONS.REQ-NO = REQ-LINES.REQ-NO
GROUP BY REQUISITIONS.PROJ-NO, REQ-LINES.PART-NO.
```

This query groups rows with the same value of PROJ-NO and PART-NO and outputs the total of each part required by project.

The output from this SQL statement will be:

REQUISITIONS PROJ-NO	REQUISITIONS PART-NO	SUM(QTY-NEEDED)
pr1	pc6	112
pr1	jw3	70
pr1	bb11	70
pr2	jw3	90
pr3	pc6	50
pr3	mx7	100

FUNCTIONS IN CONDITIONS

There is also further extension of functions with join conditions or subqueries. The biggest difference is where functions generated from one relation are used to compare values in another relation.

A subquery in a comparison

Here the subquery is used to compute a function which is then used in a condition in the outer query.

For example:

```
SELECT WAREHOUSE
FROM INVENTORY
WHERE PART-NO = 'pc6'
AND QTY-IN-STORE >
    (SELECT SUM(QTY-NEEDED - QTY-FILLED)
    FROM REQ-LINES
    WHERE PART-NO = 'pc6');
```

This SQL statement finds warehouses that can supply all of the requisitions for part 'pc6'. The subquery here computes the total number of parts still needed. This total is 137. The reply to this SQL statement will be an empty list because no warehouse contains 137 'pc6' parts. Such comparisons can also be made with correlated subqueries.

Comparison with functions in a correlated subquery

This SQL statement is quite similar to the previous except that the subquery now refers to a column in the outer query. For example:

```
SELECT PART-NO, WAREHOUSE
FROM INVENTORY
WHERE QTY-IN-STORE >
    (SELECT SUM(QTY-NEEDED - QTY-FILLED)
    FROM REQ-LINES
    WHERE REQ-LINES.PART-NO = INVENTORY.PART-NO);
```

This query finds parts and warehouses that can supply all the requisitions for those parts. Thus any part, all of which can be supplied by one warehouse, is output together with that warehouse.

The output from this SQL statement will be:

PART-NO	WAREHOUSE
mx7	sub1
mx7	center1
bb11	sub2

Find rows that satisfy maxima or minima

One reason for using functions in subqueries is to find rows in a relation with maximum column values. For example:

```
SELECT WAREHOUSE, QTY-IN-STORE
FROM INVENTORY
WHERE PART-NO = 'pc6'
AND QTY-IN-STORE =
      (SELECT MAX(QTY-IN-STORE)
      FROM INVENTORY
      WHERE PART-NO = 'pc6');
```

This SQL statement finds the warehouse with the highest number of part 'pc6'. The output will be warehouse 'sub1'. You should note that you cannot get this information using the following SQL statement:

```
SELECT WAREHOUSE, MAX(QTY-IN-STORE)
FROM INVENTORY
WHERE PART-NO = 'pc6';
```

This statement will not be accepted as input in SQL systems and will generate a syntax error.

Functions can appear in one of a number of subqueries in an SQL statement. For example, the following SQL statement finds the earliest request made for part 'pc6':

```
SELECT REQ-NO
FROM REQUISITIONS
WHERE REQ-NO IN
      (SELECT REQ-NO
      FROM REQ-LINES
      WHERE PART-NO = 'pc6')
AND DATE-NEEDED =
      (SELECT MIN(DATE-NEEDED)
      FROM REQUISITIONS
      WHERE REQ-NO IN
            (SELECT REQ-NO
            FROM REQ-LINES
            WHERE PART-NO = 'pc6'));
```

Using a function in a WHERE clause to test groups or rows

Still greater power is provided by combining subquery functions with grouping at the outer level. This gives users the semantic power of comparing values found by grouping rows in the outer query with functions computed in the subquery. For example:

```
SELECT PART-NO
FROM INVENTORY
GROUP BY PART-NO
HAVING SUM(QTY-IN-STORE)
      < (SELECT SUM(QTY-NEEDED - QTY-FILLED)
      FROM REQ-LINES
      WHERE INVENTORY.PART-NO = REQ-LINES.PART-NO);
```

This SQL statement finds those parts whose total quantity in inventory is below the quantity needed in all the requisitions. The output from this SQL statement will be 'pc6'. This is because the total quantity of 'pc6' still needed is 137. The total quantity in all warehouses is only 119. These are the parts that cannot be immediately supplied from inventory.

Exercise 13.4

Find the following information from the database shown in Figure 12.2.

1. Find the total area of all the properties owned by an owner with a given OWNER-NAME.
2. Find the total area used to plant a given PROD-NO in a given year.
3. What is the largest section that has been used to plant a given PROD-NO?
4. Which OWNER planted the greatest QTY-PLANTED of a given PROD-NO in a given year?
5. What is the total QTY-PLANTED of products with a given PROD-DES in a given year?
6. Which owner owns the largest total area with a given SOIL?
7. Which owner planted the smallest amount of a given PROD-NO in a given year?

RECURSION

Chapter 10 introduced recursive relations. You might recall that these relations include relationships between entities from the same set, but in different relationship roles. For this reason, queries addressed to recursive relations must often refer to more than one row in the same relation. To do this, SQL statements must either use variables or subqueries. Each variable in this case refers to a different role. The number of variables or subquery levels that must be used in a SQL statement depends on the depth of the recursive hierarchy in the search.

The simplest case is where the query concerns one level only. In that case, no variables need be used. For example, suppose we have the BILL OF MATERIALS database shown in Figure 10.14 and reproduced in Figure 13.2 for convenience.

Figure 13.2 Bill-of-materials

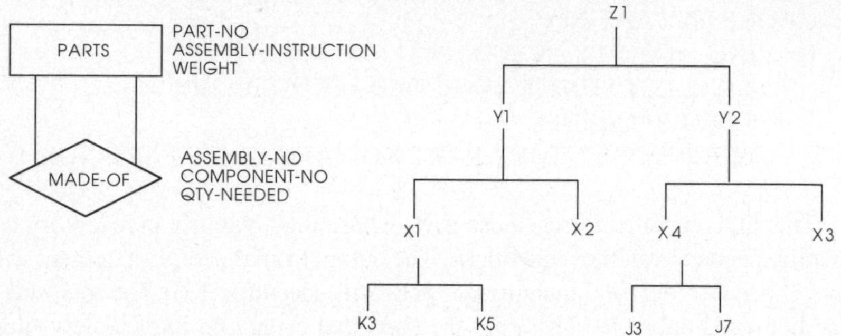

PARTS

ASSEMBLY-NO	COMPONENT-NO	QTY-NEEDED
Z1	Y1	9
Z1	Y2	17
Y1	X1	3
Y1	X2	12
Y2	X3	9
Y2	X4	17
X1	K3	43
X1	K5	17
X4	J3	31
X4	J7	77

Suppose we wish to find the direct components of 'Z1'. They can be found by the following SQL statement:

```
SELECT COMPONENT-NO
FROM MADE-OF
WHERE ASSEMBLY-NO = 'Z1';
```

The output here will be:

<u>COMPONENT-NO</u>

Y1
Y2

Suppose we now want to find all the components of the direct components of 'Z1'. This calls for a search down two levels of a hierarchy and requires the use of one variable. These components can be found by the following SQL statement:

```
SELECT L2.COMPONENT-NO
FROM MADE-OF L1, MADE-OF L2
WHERE L1.ASSEMBLY-NO = 'Z1'
AND L1.COMPONENT-NO = L2.ASSEMBLY-NO;
```

Here L1 is the first level, where the assembly is 'Z1'. L2 is the second level where all the assemblies are the direct components of a 'Z1'. The output from this SQL statement will be:

```
COMPONENT-NO

      X1
      X2
      X3
      X4
```

A similar method can be used to find the components three levels down. Now three variables would have to be used. The problem, however, is that it is not possible to formulate one SQL statement that outputs all of the car's components, that is, all components at all levels that can be reached starting with 'Z1'. The only way to do this is to re-enter new SQL statements going down one more level every time that new components are found. Alternatively, only the SQL statement that goes down one level could be used. In that case intermediate outputs could be recorded manually and re-input to get components at one level.

There is one way to print out such components but it requires using temporary relations to store data retrieved at successive levels. It also requires four SQL statements, called S1, S2, S3 and S4 for convenience.

First, the intermediate relations are defined as follows:

```
CREATE TABLE OUTREL1 (PART CHAR(10), LEVEL INTEGER);
CREATE TABLE OUTREL2 (PART CHAR(10), LEVEL INTEGER);
```

These intermediate relations store parts and the level at which they were found.

The first step of the algorithm is to initialize OUTREL1. This is done using SQL statement S1 as follows:

```
INSERT INTO OUTREL1 (PART, LEVEL)
SELECT COMPONENT-NO, 1
FROM MADE-OF
WHERE ASSEMBLY-NO = 'Z1';
```

OUTREL1 now contains the first level of 'Car' components together with the value 1 for LEVEL. Now a level of components is copied to OUTREL2 by the SQL statement S2 as follows:

```
INSERT INTO OUTREL2
SELECT *
FROM OUTREL1
WHERE LEVEL = &1;
```

The SQL statement is defined using the parameter &1. This parameter is set to successive levels as the algorithm proceeds. S2 is first executed with &1 set to one. The

Figure 13.3 Temporary relations after first step

OUTREL1

PART	LEVEL
y1	1
y2	1

OUTREL2

PART	LEVEL
y1	1
y2	1

contents of OUTREL1 and OUTREL2 following these statements is shown in Figure 13.3.

Now we generate the next level of components into OUTREL1 using SQL statement S3 as follows:

```
INSERT INTO OUTREL1 (PART, LEVEL)
SELECT COMPONENT-NO, &1+1
FROM MADE-OF, OUTREL2
WHERE MADE-OF.LEVEL = &1
AND ASSEMBLY-NO = OUTREL2.PART;
```

If statement S3 is executed with &1 equal to 1 then it will insert all the level 2 components into OUTREL1. The contents of OUTREL1 are now shown in Figure 13.4. They include the first two levels of components. The third level can now be generated by first copying all the second level components from OUTREL1 to OUTREL2 using statement S2 with &1 set to two. Then statement S4 is executed with &1 = 2. This can then be continued by executing statements S2 and S3 with &1 set successively to 3, 4 and so on until no further components are found. Relation OUTREL1 now contains all the components of 'Z1' together with their level and can be printed out by the SQL statement S4 as follows:

```
SELECT * FROM OUTREL1;
```

Figure 13.4 OUTREL1 after second step

OUTREL1

PART	LEVEL
y1	1
y2	1
x1	2
x2	2
x3	2
x4	2

Some further explanation of this procedure concerns the need for two intermediate relations. Two temporary relations instead of one only are needed because SQL does not allow a SQL statement to insert new rows into a relation that also appears in a condition. If we only had one intermediate relation OUTREL1 then it would appear in a condition in statement S3 and statement S3 would also insert new rows into S3. Such inserts are not supported by SQL. For this reason this algorithm needs the second intermediate relation, OUTREL2.

Exercise 13.5

Find the following for the family tree database shown in Figure 10.17:

1. A person's grandfather.
2. A person's siblings (that is, brothers and sisters).
3. All ancestors of a given person.
4. A person's cousins.

For questions 5 to 7 use the database shown in Figure 12.2.

5. Find the OWNER-NAME of all the neighbors of a given person.
6. For a given owner, find the owners of neighboring properties that planted a given PROD-NO.
7. For a given owner, find the largest neighboring property.

SUMMARY

This chapter continued the description of the SQL language. It described how SQL can be used to retrieve data from more than relation. This extension used the idea of joins, which combine a number of relations into one relation. The chapter also described an alternative to joins that uses the idea of subqueries. A number of alternative ways for formulating subqueries were described.

The chapter then described some more difficult queries. These concerned requirements based on the ALL predicate. Methods of using subqueries for this purpose were outlined. Finally the chapter concluded with a discussion of how to use SQL to retrieve information from recursive relationships.

14

The relational environment

INTRODUCTION

The SQL language defined in the previous chapters is sufficient for single-user applications. It allows databases to be populated with data, and for that data to be retrieved as needed. Multi-user environments need more facilities. They require support for data sharing between users and for one user to change the database structure without affecting other users. They should also allow users to examine the data structure by accessing system catalogs. This chapter describes how SQL provides such support.

DATA SHARING

Data sharing has two goals. One goal comes from the longstanding principle of data sharing. This principle states that users of a shared database should only access that part of the database that they need for their particular task. They should not access that part of the database that does not concern them. The need for such a principle is quite obvious. A large database may contain virtually all the data in an organization. It may contain personnel records, orders to suppliers, project budgets and so on. In such environments persons responsible for, say, preparing orders, do not need to access to personnel records. Similarly, persons dealing with personnel records do not require access to ordering data.

Access abilities, of course, may be subdivided on a finer level. For example, perhaps a person should have access to quantities ordered but not prices, or another person have access to persons' addresses but not their medical history.

The other goal is that users should be able to see their data in a form most convenient to them and not in a form forced upon them by other users. The most obvious example concerns data spread over a number of tables. It is much more convenient to see all this data as only one table. Data retrieval because much easier, because users need not concern themselves with joins.

SQL supports data sharing through views. The idea behind views is illustrated in Figure 14.1. Here the database is made up of a number of stored relations. These are the relations that were defined during the design process and created using the CREATE command available with SQL. The database also provides a number of views. These views also appear as tables to users but they are not stored tables. Views are tables that are not stored but tables that are derived from stored tables.

Figure 14.1 Generating views

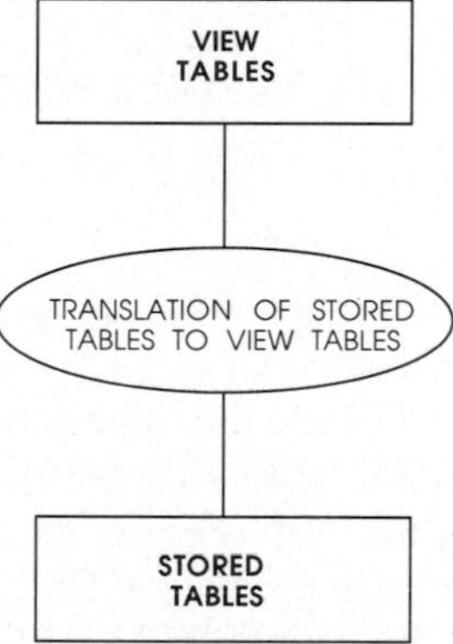

Users can access data in the stored database through views. They use the same SQL language to access views as the language that is used to access stored relations. However, any SQL command that refers to a view is translated to commands on stored tables. For this reason views are sometimes called virtual relations. They are logically accessible to users but are not stored as physical databases.

Views can be used to control access to data. If a user is given access to a view, then that user can only see information that is made available through that view. The view can also be used to control access to the database. The database administrator can create views that only contain the data needed by users to carry out their task.

Defining views

Views are defined using SQL statements. The view definition statement is made up of the following two parts:

```
CREATE VIEW <view-name> (<column-name> . . . <column-name>)
AS <SQL statement>
```

The first part is the clause CREATE VIEW. It defines the view table name and its attributes. The second part defines how the view is derived from the stored relations. This second part is a SELECT statement. Any of the SELECT statements defined in the previous two chapters can be used to define views. In the definition, the column names in the SELECT clause of the SQL statement correspond to the column names in the view. The simplest is where the view is defined as a subset of a relation.

View as a subset of a relation

Here the select statement selects a subset of rows and columns to appear in a view. For example, a view that allows access to all requisitions made by project 'pr1' is defined as follows:

```
CREATE VIEW PROJ1-REQUESTS(REQUEST, DATE-WANTED,
     WHERE-WANTED)
AS SELECT REQ-NO, DATE-NEEDED, WHERE-NEEDED
FROM REQUISITIONS
WHERE PROJ-NO = 'pr1';
```

This view is shown in Figure 14.2. It only contains those rows in table REQUISITIONS with PROJ-NO equal to 'pr1'. The project column does not appear in view table PROJ1-REQUESTS and this table only contains three columns, REQ-NO, DATE-NEEDED and WHERE-NEEDED, which have been renamed REQUEST, DATE-WANTED and WHERE-WANTED in the view. Column REQUEST in view PROJ1-REQUESTS corresponds to column REQ-NO in relation REQUISITIONS, column DATE-WANTED in view PROJ1-REQUESTS corresponds to column DATE-NEEDED in relation REQUISITIONS, and so on.

Information from a view can be retrieved in the same way as from a base relation. Thus all requisitions made by project 'pr1' can be retrieved by the statement:

```
SELECT * FROM PROJ1-REQUESTS.
```

Figure 14.2 View PROJ1-REQUESTS

REQUISITIONS

REQ-NO	PROJ-NO	DATE-NEEDED	WHERE-NEEDED
3	pr1	870620	south
4	pr3	870703	north
5	pr1	870612	east
6	pr2	870702	west

(a) Stored relation

PROJ-1-REQUESTS

REQUEST	DATE-WANTED	WHERE-WANTED
3	870620	south
5	870612	east

(b) View

Furthermore, users who gain access to this view can only obtain information about requisitions made by project 'pr1' and no other projects.

Views from joins of relations

Views can include information from more than one relation. For example, suppose we need a view to retrieve unfilled requisitions for selected projects. This view is defined as:

```
CREATE VIEW UNFILLED-PARTS (REQUEST, PROJECT, PART,
      QTY-TO-BE-FILLED)
AS SELECT REQUISITIONS.REQ-NO, REQUISITIONS.PROJ-NO, PART-NO,
      QTY-NEEDED-QTY-FILLED
FROM REQUISITIONS, REQ-LINES
WHERE REQUISITIONS.REQ-NO = REQ-LINES.REQ-NO
AND QTY-NEEDED > QTY-FILLED;
```

View table UNFILLED-ORDERS is shown in Figure 14.3. It can be used to retrieve details about parts for the one project by one select statement as follows:

```
SELECT REQUEST, PART, QTY-TO-BE-FILLED
FROM UNFILLED-PARTS
WHERE PROJECT = 'pr1';
```

Figure 14.3 View UNFILLED-PARTS

REQUISITIONS

REQ-NO	PROJ-NO	DATE-NEEDED	WHERE-NEEDED
3	pr1	870620	south
4	pr3	870703	north
5	pr1	870612	east
6	pr2	870702	west

REQ-LINES

REQ-NO	PART-NO	QTY-NEEDED	QTY FILLED
3	pc6	90	10
3	jw3	30	0
4	pc6	50	0
4	mx7	100	20
5	jw3	40	10
5	bb11	70	0
6	jw3	90	0
5	pc6	22	15

(a) Stored relations

UNFILLED-PARTS

REQUEST	PROJECT	PART	QTY-TO-BE-FILLED
3	pr1	pc6	80
3	pr1	jw3	30
4	pr3	pc6	50
4	pr3	mx7	80
5	pr1	jw3	30
5	pr1	bb11	70
6	pr2	jw3	90
5	pr1	pc6	7

(b) View

This SQL statement will retrieve all parts yet to be delivered for project pr1. The output from the SQL statement will be:

REQUEST	PART	QTY-TO-BE-FILLED
3	pc6	80
3	jw3	30
5	jw3	30
5	bb11	70
5	pc6	7

View UNFILLED-PARTS was made up from a join of two relations. It is also possible to have views made up from joins of many relations. For example, a view to retrieve warehouses that have sufficient quantities to fill project requisitions is defined as follows:

```
CREATE VIEW PARTS-LOCATION (REQUEST, PART, QTY-TO-BE-FILLED,
                WHERE-AVAILABLE, QTY-AVAILABLE, PROJECT)
AS SELECT REQUISITIONS.REQ-NO, REQ-LINES.PART-NO,
                QTY-NEEDED - QTY-FILLED, INVENTORY.WAREHOUSE,
                INVENTORY.QTY-IN-STORE, REQUESTS.PROJ-NO
FROM REQUISITIONS, REQ-LINES, INVENTORY
WHERE REQUISITIONS.REQ-NO = REQ-LINES.REQ-NO
AND QTY-NEEDED > QTY-FILLED
AND INVENTORY.PART-NO = REQ-LINES.PART-NO
AND INVENTORY.QTY-IN-STORE > QTY-NEEDED - QTY-FILLED;
```

View table PARTS-LOCATION is shown in Figure 14.4. It shows warehouses that contain unfilled parts for requisitions. For example, the first row shows that part ‘pc6’ in requisition 3 can be obtained from warehouse ‘sub1’. This requisition requires 80 of part ‘pc6’ and there are 100 such parts available in this warehouse. The location of parts for a given project can be found by the following SQL statement:

```
SELECT REQUEST, PART, WHERE-AVAILABLE
FROM PARTS-LOCATION
WHERE PROJECT = ‘pr1’;
```

This statement will retrieve the warehouses that contain sufficient parts to meet unfilled requisitions for parts for a given project.

View made from functions

Views can also contain functions. For example, a view that shows the total quantity of parts in all the warehouses is defined as:

```
SELECT HOLDINGS (PART, QUANTITY)
AS SELECT (PART-NO, SUM(QTY-IN-STORE)
FROM INVENTORY
GROUP BY PART-NO;
```

View table HOLDINGS is shown in Figure 14.5. It shows the total quantity of each part held in all the organization's warehouses. The total quantity of a part can be found by the select statement:

SELECT QUANTITY FROM HOLDINGS WHERE PART = 'pc6';

This will respond with the value 119.

Figure 14.4 View PARTS-LOCATION

INVENTORY

WAREHOUSE	PART-NO	QTY-IN-STORE
sub1	pc6	100
sub1	mx7	200
sub2	jw3	120
sub2	bb11	83
sub2	pc6	19
center1	mx7	205
center1	jw3	111

REQUISITIONS

REQ-NO	PROJ-NO	DATE-NEEDED	WHERE-NEEDED
3	pr1	870620	south
4	pr3	870703	norrth
5	pr1	870612	east
6	pr2	870702	west

REQ-LINES

REQ-NO	PART-NO	QTY-NEEDED	QTY FILLED
3	pc6	90	10
3	jw3	30	0
4	pc6	50	0
4	mx7	100	20
5	jw3	40	10
5	bb11	70	0
6	jw3	90	0
5	pc6	22	15

(a) Stored relations

PARTS-LOCATION

REQUEST	PART	QTY-TO-BE FILLED	WHERE-AVAILABLE	QTY AVAILABLE	PROJECT
3	pc6	80	sub1	100	pr1
3	jw3	30	sub2	120	pr1
3	jw3	30	center1	111	pr1
4	pc6	50	sub1	100	pr3
4	mx7	80	sub1	200	pr3
4	mx7	80	center1	205	pr3
5	jw3	30	sub2	120	pr1
5	jw3	30	center1	111	pr1
5	bb11	70	sub2	83	pr1
6	jw3	90	sub2	120	pr2
6	jw3	90	center1	111	pr2
5	pc6	7	sub1	100	pr1
5	pc6	7	sub2	19	pr1

(b) View

Figure 14.5 View HOLDINGS

INVENTORY

WAREHOUSE	PART-NO	QTY-IN-STORE
sub1	pc6	100
sub1	mx7	200
sub2	jw3	120
sub2	bb11	83
sub2	pc6	19
center1	mx7	205
center1	jw3	111

(a) Stored relations

HOLDINGS

PART	QUANTITY
px1	0
pc6	119
mx7	405
bb11	83
jw3	231

(b) View

The advantage of using views

Views can simplify access to a relational database. A user can be presented with a single view table that contains all the data of interest to the user. Consequently SQL statements used to access data through a view will be simpler than the equivalent SQL statement needed to access the same data directly from the stored relations. Users need not then be familiar with concepts such as joins in formulating their queries.

The other advantage of views is that they restrict access to only a part of the database. Thus each user is only provided with abilities to access data that they need, and no additional data.

Views also have one disadvantage when it comes to updating. Many views cannot be updated. Others can be theoretically updated but such updates are not supported by most DBMS systems.

Exercise 14.1

Define views for the following given the database in Figure 12.2:

1. A relation (PROPERTY, SEC-NAME, SOIL) that shows the soil on each section.
2. A relation (OWNER-NAME, OWNER-ADDRESS, PROPERTY, ADDRESS) that shows the owners, their addresses and their properties together with the property address.
3. A relation (OWNERS, PRODUCT) that shows products grown on each owner's properties.
4. A relation (PROPERTY, TOTAL-AREA) that shows the total area of each property.
5. A relation (PRODUCT, SOIL) that shows soils used to plant different products.
6. A subset of relation PLANTED showing plantings for one year only.
7. The relation (PROPERTY, YEAR, PRODUCT) showing the total amounts of products planted by year on each property.

VIEW UPDATABILITY

So far we have only discussed data retrieval from views. Views, however, can only provide users with total flexibility if they can also be used to change database contents. The term 'view updatability' implies such change. In this context this term does not refer to the UPDATE command only. It is a generic term that refers to any changes made to relations. Thus view updatability also requires that deletes and inserts on a view be unambiguously translated to deletes and inserts on the base relations.

However, view tables are not stored tables but are generated from stored tables. Thus any view updates must be converted to updates on the corresponding stored relations. A view update can only be effected by updating the relations that are used to generate the view. Thus update commands issued on a view must be unambiguously converted to updates on the base relations. If such a translation cannot be made then the view cannot be updated.

View HOLDINGS shown in Figure 14.5 is an example of a view that cannot be updated. For example, suppose we issue the command:

```
UPDATE HOLDINGS SET QUANTITY = 123 WHERE PART = 'pc6';
```

The system cannot translate this command to an update on the base relation, INVENTORY. A value of QUANTITY is the sum of the value of QTY-IN-STORE of a number of rows in relation INVENTORY. To change the value of QUANTITY one or more of these rows must be changed. However, an update statement to the view does not specify these rows. Hence the update command to the view cannot be translated into updates on relation, INVENTORY.

As a rule, all views that contain functions or arithmetic statements in the SELECT clause and are generated from one relation are not updatable.

Views that do not include functions or arithmetic expressions in the SELECT clause can often be updated. View updatability is generally possible for views derived from one relation, but frequently not possible for views derived from more than one relation. Some examples of updates on views derived from single relations are described. These are then followed by examples of updates on views derived from more than one relation.

Updating views derived from one relation

The one restriction on changes to views derived from one relation is that it is not possible to insert new rows into a view that does not contain fields defined to be NOT NULL. For example, suppose we generate the following view from relation REQUISITIONS:

```
CREATE VIEW NEW-REQUESTS (PROJECT, DATE)
AS SELECT PROJ-NO, DATE-NEEDED
FROM REQUISITIONS;
```

Suppose now we wish to insert a new row into NEW-REQUESTS by the following INSERT command:

```
INSERT INTO NEW-REQUESTS (PROJECT, DATE)
     VALUES ('pr6',881210);
```

This insertion calls for a new row to be inserted into stored table REQUISITIONS. Table REQUISITIONS contains attribute REQ-NO whose value cannot be NULL. But a value of REQ-NO is not included in the INSERT command. Thus the insert cannot be made into table REQUISITIONS.

Updating views derived from more than one relation

View updatability of views derived from more than one relation is more tricky. There are some views that are theoretically not updatable. There are other views that are theoretically updatable, but the updates cannot be implemented on a DBMS.

Theoretically updatable views

A view is theoretically updatable if any change to the view relations can be unambiguously translated to a change to the base relations. The relation key plays an important role in determining whether a view is theoretically updatable. In general, views that are joins based on a relation key can be updated. Those that are not can often not be updated. The other criterion for determining whether a view is updatable is the condition key of the SQL statement. If that includes the relation key, then the view can be updated. Finally, any attributes defined to be NOT NULL must be included in the view if view insertions are to be allowed. Some of the following examples illustrate these criteria.

Figure 14.6 illustrates two stored relations, NAMES and ADDRESSES, and the view PERSONS created from these two relations. The view is created by the command:

```
CREATE VIEW PERSONS (P-ID, NAME, ADD)
AS SELECT NAMES.PERSON-ID, NAMES.SURNAME,
     ADDRESSES.ADDRESS
FROM NAMES, ADDRESSES
WHERE NAMES.PERSON-ID = ADDRESSES.PERSON-ID;
```

This view is made up of a join of two relations. The join is made on the relation key, that is PERSON-ID, of both of the stored relations. All update and insert commands can be translated unambiguously to updates and inserts on the base relations.

Figure 14.6 View using a relation key to make a join

NAMES

PERSON-ID	SURNAME
P1	Jaras
P2	Grest
P3	Tand
P4	Morwi

ADDRESSES

PERSON-ID	ADDRESS
P1	11 Alma
P2	23 Grove
P3	88 Elm

(a) Stored relations

PERSONS

PERSON-ID	NAME	ADDRESS
P1	Jaras	11 Alma
P1	Grest	23 Grove
P3	Tand	88 Elm
P4	Morwi	-

(b) View

For example:

```
UPDATE PERSONS SET NAME = 'Jack' where P-ID = 'P1'
```

will update one row in base relation, NAMES.

Similarly:

```
INSERT INTO PERSONS (P-ID, NAME, ADD)
      VALUES ('P5', 'GRAST', '^ Rice');
```

should insert one row into relation NAMES and one row into relation, ADDRESSES.

Deletions, however, are not simple to interpret in this case. For example:

```
DELETE FROM PERSONS WHERE ADD = '11 Jara';
```

Should this delete all references to persons who live at '11 Jara', that is, one row in relation ADDRESSES and one in NAMES? Or should it only delete one row from relation ADDRESSES? Various arguments can now be made on the semantics of the delete command. We could say that if the condition clause includes attributes from one base relation only, then a deletion should only be made from that base relation. In that case, how does one interpret this?

```
DELETE FROM PERSONS WHERE ADD = '11 Jara' AND P-ID ='P1';
```

Do we delete from ADDRESSES only or from NAMES as well? Thus even in this simple case some ambiguity exists when interpreting a DELETE statement.

Another example of a view made from a join on a relation key is REQ-DETAILS, which defines the details of each requisition together with the requisition header.

```
CREATE VIEW REQ-DETAILS (REQ, PROJECT, PART, QTY-NEEDED,
      QTY-FILLED)
AS SELECT REQUISITION.REQ-NO, REQUISITIONS.PROJ-NO,
      REQ-LINES.PART-NO,
REQ-LINES.QTY-NEEDED, REQ-LINES.QTY-FILLED
      FROM REQUISITIONS, REQ-LINES
WHERE REQUISITIONS.REQ-NO = REQ-LINES.REQ-NO;
```

Here the join includes a relation key of relation, REQUISITIONS, but not of relation REQ-LINES.

Any updates or insertions on this view can be interpreted. Thus for example:

```
UPDATE REQ-DETAILS SET QTY-NEEDED = 40
      WHERE REQ = 1 AND PART-NO = 'pc6';
```

will update one row in base relation, REQ-LINES.

Similarly:

```
UPDATE REQUISITIONS SET PROJECT = 'pr3' WHERE REQ = 2;
```

will update one row in base relation, REQUISITIONS.

Of course it is possible to cause incorrect updates with views just like with stored relations. For example, consider the following SQL statement:

```
UPDATE REQ-DETAILS SET QTY-NEEDED = 40 WHERE REQ = 1;
```

This statement will set the value of QTY-NEEDED of all rows in the stored relation, REQ-LINES, to 40 whenever REQ-NO = 1. This incorrect result is not a problem of view updatability. As discussed in Chapter 12 such updates can also be caused by SQL statements that use stored relations. Thus the same result would occur if the statement

```
UPDATE REQ-LINES SET QTY-NEEDED = 40 WHERE RERQ-NO =1;
```

were executed against the stored relation.

Thus although the effect of the command on view REQ-DETAILS seems to be incorrect, it is the same effect as would have been obtained by the equivalent command on the base relation. Thus the view is updatable.

Insertions can also be correctly interpreted on this view because all the NOT NULL attributes of the base relations are included in the view.

Deletions pose the same problems as with the previous example. It is sometimes not clear whether a row is to be deleted in one of the base relations or in more than one of these relations. For example:

```
DELETE FROM REQ-DETAILS WHERE REQ = 1 AND PART = 'PC6';
```

Does this mean that only one row in REQ-LINES is to be deleted or that the row with REQ = 1 in REQUISITIONS is also to be deleted. There is a further extension to this problem as illustrated by the next command.

```
DELETE FROM REQ-DETAILS WHERE REQ = 1;
```

This tends to imply that one row in REQUISITIONS is to be deleted only. However, this would leave rows in REQ-LINES for a non-existent requisition.

FILL is an example of a view that only includes parts of relation keys in the join.

```
CREATE VIEW FILL(PART, STORE, QTY-NEEDED, QTY-FILLED,
    QTY-AVAIL)
AS SELECT PART-NO, WAREHOUSE, QTY-NEEDED, QTY-FILLED,
    QTY-IN-STORE
FROM REQ-LINES, INVENTORY
WHERE INVENTORY.PART-NO = REQ-LINES.PART-NO;
```

This view is partly updatable. It is possible to update the base relation INVENTORY but not the base relation REQ-LINES. For example:

```
UPDATE FILL SET QTY-IN-STORE = 10
WHERE STORE = 'sub1' AND PART = 'pc6';
```

results in a change to one row in INVENTORY. The update

```
UPDATE FILL SET QTY-FILLED = 10 WHERE PART = 'pc6';
```

will update all rows in REQ-LINES where the part is 'pc6'. Again this is an incorrect update, but it has the same effect as the corresponding update on the base relation.

Views that are not updatable

Most problems with view updates occur where the relation key of the base relations is not included in the view. One such example is shown in Figure 14.7. Here there are two base relations. Relation ASSIGNMENTS shows departments where persons work, and relation SKILLS shows the skills possessed by persons. View PROFILE is defined as:

```
CREATE VIEW PROFILE (DEP, SKILL)
AS SELECT ASSIGNMENTS.DEPT, SKILLS.SKILL
FROM ASSIGNMENTS, SKILLS
WHERE ASSIGNMENTS.PERSON-ID = SKILLS.PERSON-ID;
```

This view shows skills that exists with the departments. It does not include the complete relation key of either of the two relations.

Figure 14.7 Skill profiles

ASSIGNMENTS

PERSON	DEPARTMENT
Jill	D1
John	D2

SKILLS

PERSON	SKILL
John	Computing
John	Accounting
Jill	Computing

(a) Stored relations

PROFILES

DEPARTMENT	SKILL
D1	Computing
D2	Computing
D2	Accounting

(b) View

View updates on view PROFILE cannot be done. For example, take the update:

```
UPDATE PROFILE SET SKILL = 'French' WHERE DEP = 'D1';
```

This states that there is now someone who knows 'French' in department D1. However, this update cannot be translated to updates on base relations. It would possibly require the addition of new rows that imply that a new person has been assigned to the department or the addition of a new row that shows a new skill gained by a person already in the department. For the same reason the following INSERT command cannot be translated to commands on the base relations.

```
INSERT INTO PROFILE (DEP, SKILL) VALUES ('D1', 'French');
```

Deletes also cannot be readily translated. For example:

```
DELETE FROM PROFILE WHERE DEP = 'D1' and SKILL = 'French';
```

would result in the deletion of all rows with DEPT = 'D1' in ASSIGNMENTS and all rows with SKILL = 'FRENCH' in SKILLS.

Some general comments

View updates in general means that inserts, deletes and updates on a view result in the same effect as the corresponding commands on the base relations. In general, updates on views are supported in all cases where the relation key of at least one relation appears in the view. It may not always be possible to effect a correct update, but certainly the effect will always be the same as on the base relation. Insertions are only possible if all the NOT NULL attributes appear in the view.

Views that do not include the relation key of the base relations cannot be updated or support insertions. They can support deletions but these always result in undesirable effects.

However, although some views are theoretically updatable, it does not mean that such updates are supported by a given DBMS. In fact, most DBMS cannot support updates on joins because they do not include relation keys in their definition. Thus they cannot tell whether a particular view is updatable and hence as a rule do not support updates on views made up of a number of relations.

SQL commands for sharing

SQL includes commands to support sharing. These commands provide users with access abilities to relations in a database. The abilities state both the relations that the user can access and the kinds of access allowed to each relation. Thus a user may obtain the ability to retrieve only information from a relation. It is also possible to allow a user to insert a new row but not update an existing row. Or a user may have the ability only to delete rows. Sharing is achieved through the GRANT and REVOKE commands.

Usually the database administrator controls access to the database. The database administrator first gives users access to the database. Then the database administrator defines access abilities of those users to relations in the database. A new user is created as follows:

```
GRANT CONNECT TO <user-1> IDENTIFIED BY <password-1>
```

Here <password-1> becomes the new user's initial password. The new user can now sign on as

```
CONNECT <user-1> <password-1>
```

Granting access to a user's table

If a user has created a table, that user can give another user, <user-2>, access to that table by:

```
UFI>GRANT <privilege> ON <table> TO <user-2> [WITH GRANT OPTION]:
```

The possible privileges here are:

SELECT — ability to access only
INSERT — ability to insert new rows
UPDATE — ability to update rows
DELETE — ability to delete rows

More than one privilege can be granted to a user.

If the WITH GRANT OPTION clause is included in the grant statement then user <user-2> can pass on the privilege to other users.

Removing access

A privilege is removed from <user-2> by:

```
UFI>REVOKE <privilege> ON <table> FROM <user-2>;
```

Any privileges that user-2 has passed on to other users will also be revoked at this time.

RETRIEVING CATALOG DATA

It is frequently possible for users, especially in volatile shared environments, to lose track of relation names and attributes of these relations. These names are available in system catalogs. Most DBMS systems support access to such catalogs using SQL commands.

The user must know the catalog table names and attributes and can retrieve data from these tables using SQL statements.

CHANGING DATABASE DEFINITIONS

Databases are usually designed for use over extended periods. It is almost certain that over any such period user requirements will change. Such changes will in turn call for changes to the database. Such changes will not only result in changes of the contents of individual relations. They will also call for new relations as well as changes to the structure of existing relations.

SQL allows new relations to be added at any time to a database. They can be added using the CREATE TABLE command. SQL also allows a new attribute to be added to an existing relation. Thus a new column, called PRIORITY, can be added to relation REQUISITIONS using the ALTER command as follows:

```
ALTER TABLE REQUISITIONS ADD PRIORITY CHAR(2);
```

This adds a new field to each row in table REQUISITIONS and sets the value of the field to NULL. It is not possible to delete attributes from existing relations nor to change the relation or attribute names.

SUMMARY

This chapter defined some additional SQL commands. These commands are used to support an environment that supports sharing and database evolution. Sharing is supported through the idea of views that are virtual relations defined on base relations using SQL commands. Views are primarily used to retrieve data. Some problems exist with view updating and it is usually not encouraged in database design.

15

Developing applications

INTRODUCTION

So far Chapters 12 to 14 have described how data is retrieved from a database using interactive SQL and the editors that usually support SQL in a DBMS. These chapters also described how contents of a relation can be changed using insert, delete or update statements. Interactive SQL has all the necessary facilities to set up and use a database. It is thus possible to set up and use a database using SQL commands through an editor. However, applications based on interactive SQL only are not usually acceptable for commercial use.

Such applications often support high-volume transaction applications and require better methods than simply using SQL statements to change one row at a time. What is needed is a screen that supports a transaction. The transaction supports some organizational task. Data generated in this task should be entered in one screen. One such screen entry may change rows in more than one relation. For example, take requisition entry. This will add a new row to table REQUESTS and many rows to table REQ-LINES.

The user in such systems is not required to change one row at a time. The user simply enters the requisition transaction. Once that entry is made, the program will decide what relations are to be changed in the database and initiate the necessary SQL commands to effect such changes.

In addition, commercial systems often need well-presented reports to summarize activities to users. Interactive SQL as described so far does not provide such reports. The output from interactive SQL is a table showing values that satisfy the SQL conditions.

Figure 15.1 A relational database management system

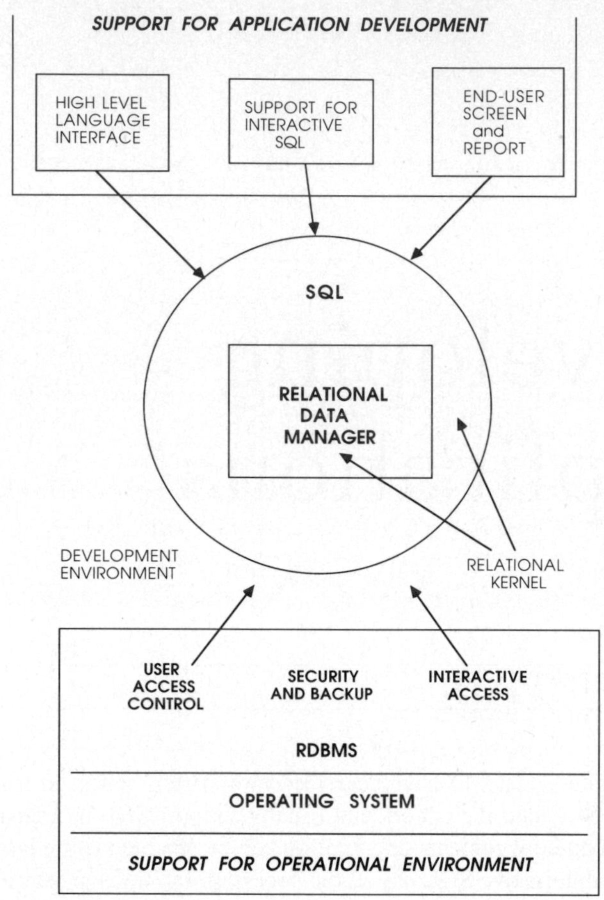

Many applications require better presentation of output. They often require listing in some order in reports with appropriate headings.

Commercial application of this kind can be developed using the facilities shown earlier in Figure 11.2 in Chapter 11 and reproduced in Figure 15.1 for convenience. They are report generators, end-user screen development products and embedded SQL used for transaction support. This chapter will describe report generation. Later chapters will describe the other facilities.

GENERATING REPORTS

Reports may be generated in two ways. One is to use interactive SQL. The other is to use a special report generator.

Using interactive SQL

SQL statements output data values retrieved from a given statement using a standard format provided through the SQL editor. It is also possible to use the SQL editor to specify the detailed layout of this output information. This will present output in a specified report format.

The SQL editor can be used to define some simple report formats. It can be used for the report headings, column headings, page layouts and subtotals. Outputs from SQL statements are presented on the screen using these formats and can be output to the printer. Formatting commands can vary between editors supplied by different manufacturers. Thus a user must consult the manual supplied by the manufacturer before using an interactive report generator. In this book, we will only give some examples of the type of editing commands found in report generators.

Using a special report generator

In an interactive report generator, report formats are defined in a number of steps. First headings are defined, then formats and spacing of each column are defined. Finally any subtotalling is specified.

Report headings

The first part for preparing a report is to determine the report title. Most SQL editors allow a title to be placed at the start and end of a report.

A title can be specified using the command:

```
FORMAT TTITLE 'x'
```

where x is the title of the page.

A title can be added to the rear of the report by the following command:

```
FORMAT BTITLE 'x'
```

where x is the title added to the rear of the report.

Column headings and spacing

The next step in report preparation is to specify the column headings and the spacing of columns on the report. The heading of a column can be changed from its name in the table to some other names as follows:

```
FORMAT COLUMN x NAME y
```

where x is the name of the column in the table and y will be the name of the column in the report. The size of the field can also be changed as follows:

FORMAT COLUMN x y

where x is the name of the column in the table and y is the format specification. The format specification, y, can be any of the following:

DPLACES n — n decimal places
ZEROS OFF — leading zeros off
WIDTH n — the width is n
NULL x — NULL values are replaced by x

Finally there is the separation between columns. This is specified by:

FORMAT SEPARATOR 'x'

'x' is placed between columns in the table. 'x' can be any number of blanks or a combination such as ' *'.

Thus FORMAT SEPARATOR '!' results in ! placed between each column.

Setting session parameters

Some interactive editors allow a user to specify session parameters. These parameters hold for all SQL commands executed during a session. They are particularly useful for setting defaults for NULL or for setting standard separators between columns. The two editor commands used for this purpose are:

1. SET NULL 'x' — NULL be represented by the string 'x' on any display;
2. SET SEPARATOR string — will set the separator between columns for the session.

Computing subtotals

Most reports group rows by certain column values, often separate these groups on the report and may require subtotals on various numeric fields in each group. The first step in specifying such layouts is to specify the columns that will be used to group rows. Then the format of each group and subtotalling is specified.

Selecting columns for grouping

The first step here is to ensure that the SQL statement includes an ORDER BY clause for the columns selected for grouping. For example if a report about ordered items is to be grouped by PART-NO then PART-NO must appear in an ORDER BY clause as follows:

```
SELECT PART-NO, ORDER-NO, QTY-ORDERED
FROM ORDERED-ITEMS
ORDER BY PART-NO;
```

Specifying lists

The appearance of the output can now be changed in a number of ways. First the same value of attribute used to group rows need not be repeated. This can be specified by the command:

FORMAT GROUP (att-name-1)

Repeated values of the column do not now appear.

For example:

FORMAT GROUP(PART-NO)

will mean that the value of PART-NO only appears in a row if it is different from the previous row, as for example in Figure 15.2.

Figure 15.2 Report layouts

PART-NO	ORDER-NO	QTY-ORDERED
pc6	ord 3	70
	ord 4	35
		105
mx7	ord 2	12
	ord 4	99
	ord 3	30
		141

Specifying columns for subtotals or totals

Now a column whose values are to be subtotalled is selected. Suppose this is <att-name-2>. The subtotalling is specified by:

FORMAT SUBTOTAL (att-name-2)

Totalling is specified by:

FORMAT TOTAL(att-name-2)

Thus we can specify subtotals for each part by the command. For example, the following command:

FORMAT SUBTOTAL QTY-ORDERED

will result in the subtotalling shown in Figure 15.2.

Clearing format settings

To clear a title execute:

```
FORMAT TITLE ERASE
```

To clear a compute or break:

```
FORMAT TOTAL ERASE
```

Columns can only be reset by entering a new column heading or format. There is no specific command to go back to the original heading. The only way to do this is:

```
COLUMN x HEADING x
```

SUMMARY

This chapter described methods that can be used to present output reports about data in a database. The two alternatives were to use either the interactive SQL editor or a special report generator.

In contrast to SQL itself, there is no standard for generation products. Users must therefore consult appropriate manuals before using report generators provided by their DBMS supplier. However, some operations are becoming common between products and there are pseudo standards that exist in the field. This chapter described some typical commands that are now being adopted in many interactive report generators.

16

Transaction processing

INTRODUCTION

Earlier chapters showed how SQL can be used to interactively retrieve data from a database, and how report generators can be used to produce reports about information in the database. This chapter will concentrate on how databases are updated in a commercial environment.

So far, we have described only one way to update databases. This was to use SQL commands to insert, delete or change relation rows one at a time. It was also pointed out that such an approach can be quite dangerous and can lead to erroneous updates and loss of integrity to large parts of a database.

Working systems, however, must do all that is possible to maintain database integrity. What is needed are update methods that guarantee database integrity. Such methods must accept one transaction and update all rows affected by that transaction. A user should be able to input a transaction through a screen, and have an update program carry out the necessary updates to the database. These updates may involve more than one row. The update program is written so that it does not violate any integrity constraints in the database. This differs from interactive SQL that updates one row at a time.

This chapter describes how SQL embedded within high-level languages can be used to achieve this goal. Such a language is often called the 'host language' because it is a host to SQL statements. The chapter begins by describing requirements that must be satisfied in database updates.

TRANSACTION REQUIREMENTS

Many corporate databases maintain information that is a vital organization resource. This may be insurance policies, orders in a store, or bank accounts in a bank. Great care must be taken to ensure that this data is always correct and that it cannot be corrupted. A number of steps must be taken to ensure the integrity of such corporate databases. One of these is physical care of the data. This is to prevent loss due to a breakdown in computing equipment, a fire in the organization, or even theft. It calls for elaborate recovery procedures to restore data corrupted by equipment failure. It also requires copies of data to be maintained at different physical locations.

The other important measure is to ensure logical integrity following updates to the database by a transaction. This calls for steps to be taken to ensure that updates only change those parts affected by a transaction, and that the updates do not violate any logical constraints in the data.

Typical transactions include:

1. Make a withdrawal from an account.
2. Change the quantity requested in a requisition.
3. Enter a new insurance policy.
4. Make a reservation on a flight.

Such transactions often change many database rows. As an example, consider a transaction of the second kind applied to the tables shown in Figure 12.1 and reproduced in Figure 16.1 for convenience. This transaction occurs when a requisition is made by a project to withdraw some parts from a warehouse. This transaction will result in a number of changes to the database. These are:

1. Add a new row to table REQUISITIONS.
2. Add two new rows to table REQ-LINES.
3. Change two values in table INVENTORY by subtracting the quantities of withdrawn parts.

All these changes must be made as a group. For example, if two rows are added to REQ-LINES but a change is not made to INVENTORY then the database will be inconsistent. Similarly the two lines in REQ-LINES can only be added together with the new row in REQUISITIONS.

Interactive SQL does provide one facility to group all updates resulting from one transaction. It allows the user to define the point at which the database is known to be consistent. Then a number of changes are specified. These changes, however, do not permanently change the database. They make a number of temporary changes, which can then be made permanent as a group. This is done by the following sequence:

```
SET AUTOCOMMIT OFF
```

Figure 16.1 A transaction

TRANSACTION

REQUISITION

REQ: 20
DATE: 2-7-89
PROJECT: PR9

WAREHOUSE: West

PART-NO	QTY
PX6	22
PX9	72

APPLIED TO →

INVENTORY

WAREHOUSE	PART-NO	QTY-IN-STORE
West	px6	100
West	px9	150
East	px9	30
East	px7	90
East	px11	83

HOLDINGS

REQ-NO	DATE NEEDED	PROJ-NO	WHERE NEEDED
20	2-7-89	pr9	West

PROJECTS

PROJ-NO	BUDGET
pr9	100,000
pr56	230,000
pr87	88,000

WAREHOUSES

WAREHOUSE	LOCATION	MANAGER
West	Main St.	Jackson
East	Third Ave.	Tan

PARTS

PART-NO	DESCRIPTION	WEIGHT	MAX-DIM	COLOR
px6	saw	70.6	7.0	blue
px9	drill	19.6	3.5	green
px7	hammer	17.9	7.9	purple
px11	saw	12.8	8.3	green
px3	drill	88.4	7.7	white

REQ-LINES

REQ-NO	PART-NO	QTY-NEEDED	QTY-FILLED
20	px6	22	0
20	px9	62	0

```
INSERT INTO REQUISITIONS(REQ-NO, DATE-NEEDED, PROJ-NO,
        WHERE-NEEDED) VALUES(20,'2-7-89', pr9, 'West');

INSERT INTO REQ-LINES(REQ-NO, PART-NO, QTY-NEEDED)
        VALUES(20, 'px6', 22);

INSERT INTO REQ-LINES(REQ-NO, PART-NO, QTY-NEEDED)
        VALUES(20,'px9',62);

UPDATE INVENTORY SET QTY-IN-STORE = 78
    WHERE WAREHOUSE = 'West' AND PART-NO = 'px6';

UPDATE INVENTORY SET QTY-IN-STORE = 88
    WHERE WAREHOUSE = 'West' AND PART-NO = 'px9';

COMMIT
```

Here the command SET AUTOCOMMIT OFF tells the system not to carry out any following database changes permanently. Then six SQL commands are input. These statements result in temporary changes to the database. The user can then examine to see what the database looks like with these changes. This examination is made using any SQL retrieval commands. If the user is happy with the change then COMMIT is entered. COMMIT makes the changes permanent. If the changes were found to incorrect at any stage then the database can be restored to its last commit state by the command

ROLLBACK.

The COMMIT facility is the only means provided to interactive users to ensure database consistency. It relies on users remembering to use the commit command and make adequate checks of the database state before executing COMMIT. Such checks must be made to ensure that SQL commands did not inadvertently change some rows that should not be affected by a given transaction. Obviously in a large database with many users one cannot rely on this procedure always being followed. Some users in a hurry may avoid using COMMIT. Others, especially when looking at a large table, may not be able to check all changes before executing COMMIT. For these reasons, interactive SQL cannot be used to maintain logical consistency.

What is needed is a method that combines the power of SQL statements with program logic to ensure that the SQL statements do not lead to database inconsistencies. Such program logic also uses the same procedure to process a transaction. This procedure includes consistency checks. In most relational systems this is done by embedding SQL statements in a high-level procedural language.

EMBEDDED SQL

Transaction processing using embedded SQL follows the steps illustrated in Figure 16.2. An embedded SQL program first reads in the transaction input data. This read may be performed interactively through a screen or it may be part of a batch program. The program then checks whether the data in the input is consistent with the data currently in the database. Inconsistencies may include both field errors as well as detecting states that prevent a transaction. Typical field errors include an account number that does not exist, an invalid part number, and so on. Typical database state inconsistencies may be:

1. A withdrawal cannot be made because there are insufficient funds in the account to cover it.
2. There are insufficient parts in the warehouse to meet the requisition.
3. There are no seats on the flight.

The transaction program first accesses the database to make the consistency checks. It then executes SQL statements to read the database and carry out any consistency checks. Then it uses SQL to insert, delete or change table rows.

Any inconsistencies will be reported and the transaction invalidated. If the data in the transaction is consistent with the database then a permanent change will be made to the database.

Use of embedded SQL programs ensures that any database change is made by pretested SQL statements. It differs substantially from changes made using interactive

Figure 16.2 An update procedure

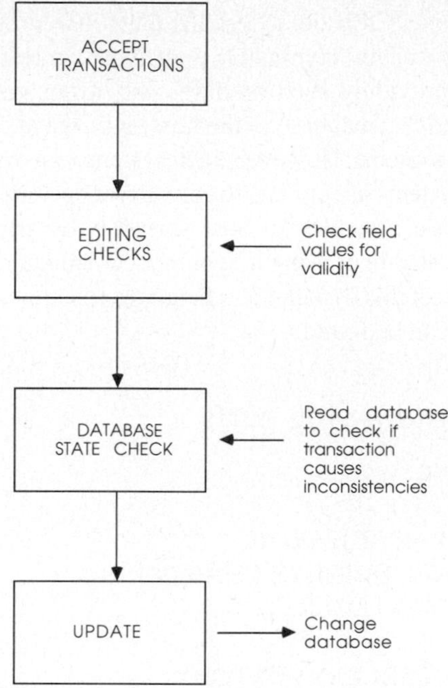

SQL. With interactive SQL a change can be made with an untested SQL statement and can sometimes lead to unintended database changes.

Most relational systems support embedded SQL statements with a number of languages. It is often possible to embed SQL in COBOL, PL/1, C and other languages. An embedded SQL statement takes the same form in a high-level language as in interactive use. However, there must be some means of matching SQL variables to variables in the procedural program.

SQL statements in high-level languages

Embedded SQL programs use procedural host language statements for input, output and arithmetic computations. Variables defined by high-level language hold values that are used in the computation. The programs use database commands to retrieve values from the database and move them to the high-level level language variables. Any required computations can then be carried out on the values and results stored back into the database.

An embedded system must provide links between the host language variables and table and column names. There must be a way for defining database tables to the procedural host language program. There must also be a way for moving values between table rows and host language variables.

Apart from syntactic issues there is also one semantic difference between SQL commands and host languages. SQL commands can operate on sets. Thus an SQL retrieval command may retrieve a set of rows. Procedural host languages operate on one record or row at a time. Embedded systems must then provide a match between a set SQL retrieval and procedural commands in the host language.

The method of providing such bindings vary from system to system. The actual command used to define a database in the host language and bind them to tables will be different in different systems. However, such systems also have many common features. For example, most systems use cursors to convert set operations to procedural code. Most systems bind database variables to host variables by using special prefixes. These techniques are illustrated here using a hypothetical language.

The first example of this hypothetical language illustrates how the quantity of a given part in a warehouse can be found.

Example 1 Withdrawing parts

```
DECLARATIONS

DCL NEEDED-PART CHAR(10);
DCL NEEDED-WAREHOUSE CHAR(20);
DCL QUANTITY INTEGER;

SQL DECLARE TABLE INVENTORY
        (WAREHOUSE CHAR(20),
        PART-NO CHAR(10),
        QTY-IN-STORE INTEGER);

PROCEDURE

ACCEPT NEEDED-WAREHOUSE, NEEDED-PART;
EXEC SQL SELECT QTY-IN-STORE INTO :QUANTITY
        FROM INVENTORY
        WHERE WAREHOUSE = :NEEDED-WAREHOUSE
        AND PART-NO = :NEEDED-PART;
OUTPUT QUANTITY;
```

The program here is made up of two parts. The first part is the declarations. Here both host language variables and database tables are defined. The DCL statement is used to define the host program variables, and the SQL statement is used to define the database tables.

The second part of the program is the procedure. It defines the process to be carried out. The first statement in the procedure is ACCEPT. This statement is used to read the values of the warehouse and part of interest. This read can be made from an interactive terminal or as a batch read from some other media.

The second statement is the SQL statement. It is preceded by the keyword EXEC, which lets the compiler know that a SQL statement follows. Then the SQL retrieval statement follows. The syntax of the retrieval statement is the same as defined in earlier chapters but now it also contains bindings to high-level language variables. These bindings are made by including the host language variables in the SQL statement. The variable, however, is preceded by the character ':' to indicate that it is a host language variable. Thus, for example, in the SQL statement the retrieved row has a value of PART-NO equal to the value stored in variable NEEDED-PART.

There are two reasons for such binding. One is to use values in the host language to select rows in the relation. These variables are included in the WHERE clause. For example, NEEDED-WAREHOUSE and NEEDED-PART are used in the WHERE clause to select a row with a given value of warehouse and part. The other is variables that receive values from the database. These variables are included in the new INTO clause that now follows the SELECT clause. For example, QUANTITY receives the value of QTY-IN-STORE in the selected row.

The previous example showed a SQL statement that retrieves only one row from a table. It is often necessary, however, to retrieve more than one row from a table. For example, suppose we wanted to know the quantity of a given part in each warehouse. The following SQL statement can be used to retrieve this information:

```
SELECT WAREHOUSE, QTY-IN-STORE
FROM INVENTORY
WHERE PART-NO = 'pc6';
```

This statement can retrieve more than one row. Each row contains the quantity of a part held in one warehouse. If this statement is embedded in a procedural language then it will also retrieve more than one row. Some means must be provided to use this set of retrieved rows in the procedural language. Embedded SQL uses cursors to procedurally process sets of rows. The idea behind cursors is illustrated in the following example.

Example 2 Displaying holdings of a part

```
DECLARATIONS

DCL NEEDED-PART CHAR(10);
DCL NEEDED-WAREHOUSE CHAR(20);
DCL QUANTITY INTEGER;

SQL DECLARE TABLE INVENTORY
        (WAREHOUSE CHAR(20),
        PART-NO CHAR(10),
        QTY-IN-STORE INTEGER);

DECLARE WAREHOUSE-LIST CURSOR
        SELECT WAREHOUSE, QTY-IN-STORE
        FROM INVENTORY
        WHERE PART-NO = :NEEDED-PART;

PROCEDURE
```

```
ACCEPT NEEDED-PART;
OPEN WAREHOUSE-LIST;
REPEAT SUBPROC NEXT-WAREHOUSE UNTIL STATUS = 0;
SUBPROC NEXT-WAREHOUSE

BEGIN
FETCH WAREHOUSE-LIST INTO :NEEDED-WAREHOUSE, :QUANTITY;
IF STATUS = 0 THEN EXIT;
IF STATUS > 0 THEN OUTPUT NEEDED-WAREHOUSE, QUANTITY;
END;
```

This program differs from the earlier program because it includes an additional definition. This definition declares a cursor named WAREHOUSE-LIST. The SQL statement attached to the cursor retrieves all the rows in INVENTORY with a given value of PART. This SQL statement is executed at the time when the OPEN WAREHOUSE-LIST command is reached in the procedure. All the rows are retrieved at this time and are now available to the program.

The rows are made available to the program one at a time using the FETCH statement. The next row in the set of rows is made available every time that the FETCH statement is executed. A STATUS variable is set to zero when all the retrieved rows have been made available to the program.

The FETCH statement is placed in subprocess NEXT-WAREHOUSE, which is defined by the SUBPROC statement in our hypothetical language. Statements in a subprocess are bracketed by the BEGIN and END statements. The subprocess is executed in a LOOP, which performs the SUBPROC NEXT-WAREHOUSE procedure as many times as there are retrieved rows. The retrieved values in a row are placed into NEEDED-WAREHOUSE and QUANTITY and then output. The STATUS indicator is set to zero when there are no more rows to be fetched.

A program for a transaction

The syntax described above can be used to process an entire transaction. This includes editing and checking for integrity as well as updating any tables. For example, suppose we return to the transaction that enters a new requisition. This would be programmed as follows.

```
DECLARATIONS

DCL NEEDED-PART CHAR(10);
DCL NEW-REQ-NO INTEGER;
DCL REQUESTING-PROJECT CHAR(15);
DCL WHEN-NEEDED CHAR(10);
DCL LOCATION-NEEDED CHAR(15);
DCL SOURCE-WAREHOUSE CHAR(20);
DCL QUANTITY INTEGER;
DCL NEEDED-QUANTITY INTEGER;
```

```
SQL DECLARE TABLE INVENTORY
        (WAREHOUSE CHAR(20),
        PART-NO CHAR(10),
        QTY-IN-STORE INTEGER);

SQL DECLARE TABLE REQUISITIONS

        (REQ-NO INTEGER;
        REQ-DATE INTEGER;
        PROJ-NO CHAR(15))
        DATE-NEEDED CHAR(10)
        WHERE-NEEDED CHAR(15));

SQL DECLARE TABLE REQ-LINES

        (REQ-NO INTEGER;
        PART-NO CHAR(10);
        QTY-NEEDED INTEGER)
        QTY-FILLED INTEGER));

SQL DECLARE TABLE WAREHOUSES
        (WAREHOUSE CHAR(20);
        LOCATION CHAR(30)
        MANAGER CHAR(20));

SQL DECLARE TABLE PARTS
        (PART-NO CHAR(10);
        DESCRIPTION CHAR(20);
        WEIGHT INTEGER;
        MAX-DIM INTEGER;
        COLOR CHAR(10));

PROCEDURE

ACCEPT NEW-REQ-NO, REQUESTING-PROJECT, WHEN-NEEDED,
LOCATION-NEEDED;
CHECK-PROJECT;
IF ERRMES = 0
        THEN BEGIN OUTPUT ('INCORRECT PROJECT'); EXIT; END;
ACCEPT SOURCE-WAREHOUSE;
CHECK-WAREHOUSE;
IF ERRMES = 0
        THEN BEGIN OUTPUT('INCORRECT WAREHOUSE'); EXIT; END;
BEGIN TRANSACTION.
EXEC SQL INSERT REQUISITIONS (REQ-NO, PROJ-NO,
        DATE-NEEDED, WHERE-NEEDED)
FROM :NEW-REQ-NO, :REQUESTING-PROJECT, :WHEN-NEEDED,
                :LOCATION-NEEDED)
```

```
REPEAT GET-PART UNTIL NO-MORE-PARTS = 0;
END TRANSACTION.

SUBPROC GET-PART;
BEGIN
ACCEPT NEEDED-PART, NEEDED-QUANTITY;
IF NEEDED-PART = ' ' THEN NO-MORE-PARTS = 0;
IF NO-MORE-PARTS = 0 THEN EXIT;
CHECK-PART;
IF ERRMES = 0 THEN EXIT;
END;

SUBPROC CHECK-PART;
BEGIN
EXEC SQL GET PART-NO FROM PARTS
        WHERE PART-NO = : NEEDED-PART;
IF STATUS = 0 THEN
        BEGIN OUTPUT('THERE IS NO SUCH PART'); EXIT; END;
EXEC SQL SELECT QTY-IN-STORE INTO :QUANTITY FROM
        INVENTORY
        WHERE WAREHOUSE = :SOURCE-WAREHOUSE
        AND PART-NO = :NEEDED-PART;
IF (QUANTITY < NEEDED-QUANTITY) THEN
BEGIN OUTPUT('INSUFFICIENT PARTS'); EXIT; END;
EXEC SQL INSERT REQ-LINES (REQ-NO, PART-NO, QTY-NEEDED);
        FROM (:NEW-REQ-NO, :NEEDED-PART, :NEEDED-QUANTITY);
EXEC SQL UPDATE INVENTORY
        SET QTY-IN-STORE = QTY-IN-STORE - :NEEDED-QUANTITY
        WHERE WAREHOUSE = :SOURCE-WAREHOUSE
        AND PART-NO = :NEEDED-PART;

END;

SUBPROC CHECK-PROJECT;
BEGIN
EXEC SQL SELECT PROJECT FROM PROJECTS
        WHERE PROJECT = :REQUESTING-PROJECT;
IF STATUS = 0 THEN ERRMES = 0; EXIT;
END;

SUBPROC CHECK-WAREHOUSE;
BEGIN
EXEC SQL SELECT WAREHOUSE FROM WAREHOUSES
        WHERE WAREHOUSE = : SOURCE-WAREHOUSE;
IF STATUS = 0 THEN ERRMES = 0; EXIT;
END;
```

This program, written in our hypothetical language, illustrates several points. First, INSERT, UPDATE and DELETE statements can be included in an embedded program. All changes to the database are bracketed by the BEGIN TRANSACTION and END TRANSACTION statements. The changes are not made permanent until the END TRANSACTION statement is executed. If the system fails during transaction execution, the database is rolled to the state that existed when the BEGIN TRANSACTION statement was executed. The illustrated program is to some extent oversimplified. It terminates whenever a non-existent project or warehouse is entered. Most systems are programmed to allow the user another try, or to display lists of valid item values. Any such error procedure can be included in the program using the procedural language.

Implementing embedded SQL

Programs that contain embedded SQL statements must be compiled before they can be executed. Compilation usually goes through the two stages shown in Figure 16.3. First there is a precompilation phase. In this phase SQL statements in the high-level program

Figure 16.3 Precompilation of embedded commands

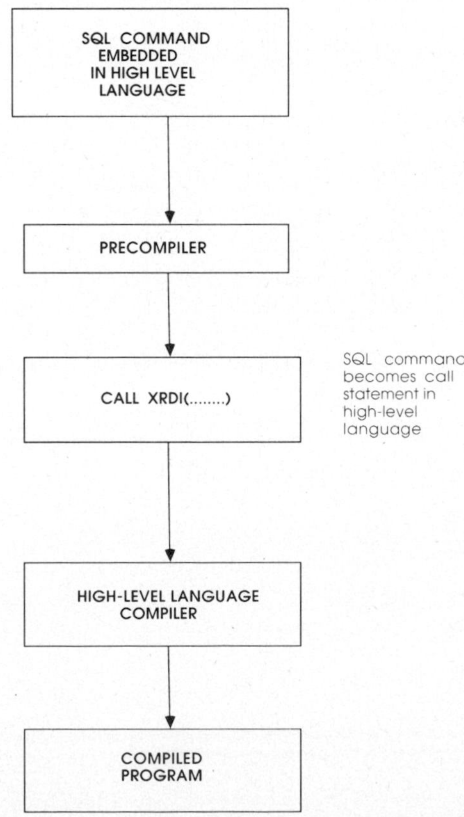

are converted into statements acceptable by the compiler. This usually means that each SQL statement is converted to procedure calls in the high-level languages.

The program with the converted statements is then compiled using the compiler provided for the high-level language. The compiled code can then be executed.

SUMMARY

Transaction processing in an operational environment calls for a number of criteria to be satisfied. Primarily these criteria require that database consistency be always maintained. Interactive SQL cannot satisfy these criteria because it cannot guarantee that transactions are checked against the current database state to ensure that any changes are consistent with this state.

This chapter described a method for implementing transaction processing that satisfies these criteria. It uses a procedural language with SQL statements embedded in this language. The procedural language programs ensure that all the necessary checks are made before a database is updated. The method used to embed SQL in a high-level language depends on particular implementations.

17

Application generators

INTRODUCTION

The previous chapter addressed one important issue in relational system design. It concerned updates to large corporate commercial relational databases. The method described in Chapter 16 used embedded SQL to support transaction processing. This method satisfies a number of requirements. It can ensure database integrity by making pretested procedural checks to the database before any database changes. It can also yield good performance because it uses compiled procedural, rather than interpretive, code.

However, embedded SQL programs have a number of disadvantages that make them unsuitable for end-user environments. Users in such environments develop applications to support small groups of people. These applications usually support much lower transaction volumes and may not need the same level of performance as do large corporate databases. The transactions are usually developed gradually and call for frequent changes to transaction programs. Using procedural code is inappropriate in such environments. In the first instance, they require end-users to learn and become familiar with the procedural language. Procedural language programs are often tedious to develop because they have to be compiled before they are executed. In addition, procedural code is harder to change and thus does not fit into the more volatile end-user environment.

Consequently embedded SQL procedural programs are primarily used for transaction processing with large corporate databases. In such environments, embedded SQL programs are usually written by professional programmers. Once checked and compiled, the programs can provide fast interactive processing of large numbers of standard transactions.

Many users in end-user environments would be happy with interactive SQL. However, they cannot use interactive SQL because such environments call for logical database consistency and interactive SQL cannot be relied upon to provide it. What is needed is some method that can be used to define transaction programs without the detailed procedural programming called for by high-level procedural languages, but which at the same time can guarantee database consistency. This is where application generators come in. They provide a method for supporting transaction processing without resorting to procedural code.

There is no such thing as a standard application generator. Each manufacturer supplies one or more products that can be used in conjunction with the manufacturer's relational system to generate end-user applications. However, most application generators follow the same idea. This is to support end-user development by providing generalized facilities for defining and processing transactions. This chapter describes the general idea behind application generators and some of the common facilities provided by them.

APPLICATION GENERATOR STRUCTURE

The idea behind application generators is quite simple. It is to allow end-users to set up the application by defining the database tables and transactions that update these tables. Once set up, the application generator accepts and processes the defined transactions. Consequently application generators are made up of the two major parts shown in Figure 17.1. The development part is used to develop the application. The other part, the use part, provides the methods to use the application. The developers must use the development facilities to structure the use facilities in the best way for the application.

The usual operation supported by application generators is for users to enter transactions through prespecified screens. Such screens provide fields to accept user inputs, point out any errors or inconsistencies in this input, and then change the database as required by the transaction. These transactions build up a functional database, which can be interrogated using an enquiry language or by generating reports.

Development facilities

The development part usually includes the following components:

1. A database definition language to define a database that contains the application data. Many application generators now use relational database systems. The user is usually provided with an interactive facility to define the relations that make up this database.
2. A method for defining the screen layout. A 'screen painter' is usually provided for this purpose. The screen painter allows a user to define the screen, the position of any fields and names for these fields. The fields will hold the values to be input as part of the

Figure 17.1 Application generation activities

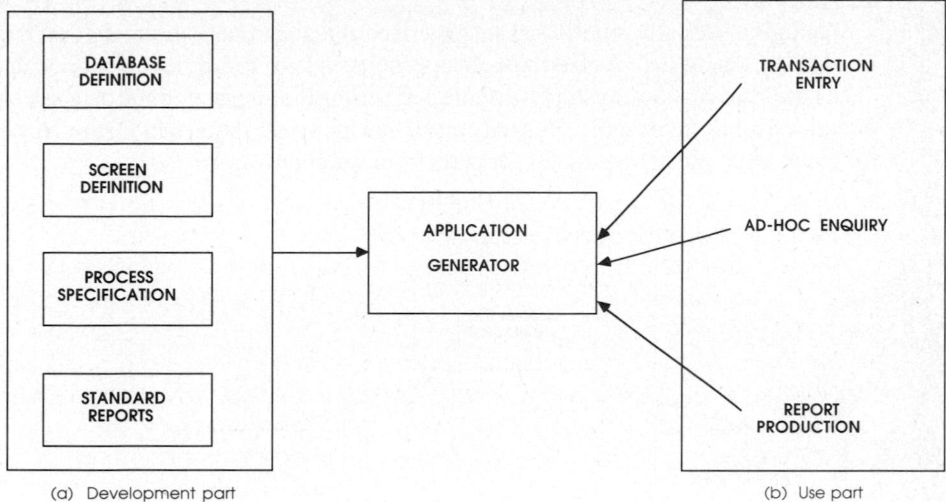

transaction. The screen painter also allows users to define any text that is to appear on the screen.

3. Methods for specifying transaction processing. These methods specify the computations on any data input through the screen. These specifications are linked to the screen or to fields on the screen and are used to check whether data is correctly entered in each screen field and that this data is consistent with the database. They also specify any required database changes. A command programming language is usually provided to write the programs that carry out these computations.

The use part includes:

1. A report generator to produce output reports.
2. An enquiry language that can be used to answer ad-hoc queries about the status of the database.
3. A method for entering transactions using the defined screens.

DEFINING APPLICATIONS

The usual way to set up an application is illustrated in Figure 17.2. The first step is to define the data needed by the application. Methods described in earlier chapters are used to develop a model of user data and convert it to a database definition. Then application inputs and outputs are defined.

Inputs are usually transactions that include data used to update the database. Each transaction is defined by one or more screens. The designer identifies the screen fields and permitted values in each screen. The designer also defines checks to be made on these fields, any output messages produced and how the field values will be used to change the database.

Outputs are usually reports that are generated at regular intervals or on a user request. In addition, output is provided through an enquiry system for retrieving ad-hoc data.

These steps are now illustrated in more detail using the transaction and database shown in Figure 16.1 as an example. You may recall that the system shown in Figure 16.1 caters for requisitions made by projects for parts from warehouses.

Figure 17.2 Steps for defining applications

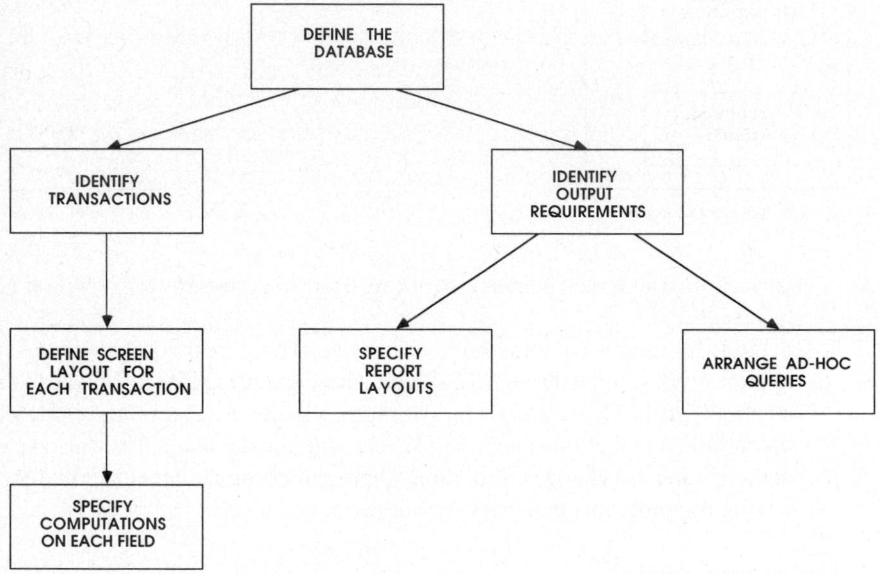

Defining the database

The first step for defining this application would be to define the tables shown in Figure 16.1. In a relational system such tables would be defined using CREATE TABLE statements. There would be one such statement for each table shown in Figure 16.1. Then the transactions are defined.

Defining the transactions

Normally an application has many kinds of transactions. In our example, such transaction kinds include adding a new part or warehouse or changing warehouse or part details. Each requisition is also a transaction in this system. Each transaction kind is implemented by defining one or more input screens to receive the transaction input.

Designing screens

Generally a transaction is defined by the layout of transaction fields on a screen and the values permitted in these fields. There are a number of alternatives for designing screens for system transactions. The major choice is between using one screen only for the transaction, or to use more than one screen for the one transaction.

For the requisition transaction, the choice is between one screen that holds the transaction header and all parts needed in that requisition, or to have one screen for the header and another screen for each requisition line. The first alternative is described here. This alternative for a requisition must somehow cater for a variable number of requisition lines. Figure 17.3 illustrates a screen using the first alternative. Here the screen is made up of four major fields that make up the transaction heading. These fields are given internal names and also have text next to them to indicate the information to be input into the field. This textual information identifies four fields that make up the requisition header. These are 'REQUISITION', 'REQUESTING-PROJECT', 'DATE-NEEDED' and 'WAREHOUSE'. The user enters the requisition number, project number, required date and warehouse name into these fields during transaction processing.

Figure 17.3 A screen layout for the requisition transaction

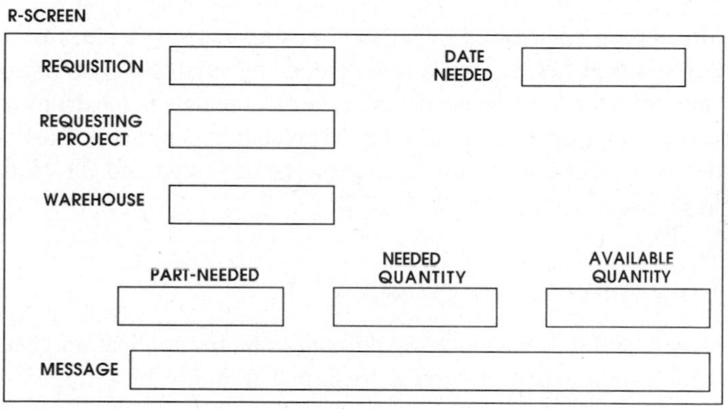

The screen also contains an additional line for each requisitioned part. Parts are entered one at a time into this line. The three fields here are:

1. 'PART-NEEDED', which defines the requested part;
2. 'NEEDED-QUANTITY', which is the requested quantity of the part;
3. 'AVAILABLE-QUANTITY', which is the quantity of the part available in the selected warehouse.

There is also an additional field, named MESSAGE, to display any messages to the user. As each part is accepted the line is cleared to receive the next part.

Defining screens

The layout of the screen is defined using the screen painter. First the screen is given a name. In our example, we assume that the screen shown in Figure 17.3 is called R-SCREEN. The designer must then define all the screen fields, their size and the format of data that they can receive. Each field must be given an internal name as well as an external name, which is displayed as text next to the field. In this chapter we assume that the field internal names are the same as the external names on the screen.

The way that fields are defined depends on the particular application generator. The possibilities are:

1. The user places a cursor on a field position and pushes a function key to define that position to be field. The system then asks the user for the field name, type and size.
2. The user specifies field positions, sizes and names as a command language or in answer to a dialog with the system.

Methods and languages for doing this vary widely between different application generators.

Programs associated with screens

Apart from the screen layout, the designers must also specify what is to be done with values entered into screen fields. This is usually done by small programs associated with each field. These programs can be used to retrieve or store data in the database and to carry out any necessary computations on this data. Application generators must provide means for both specifying when such programs are to be activated and for writing the programs themselves.

Initiating transaction programs

The standard method for supporting programming for application generators is through triggers associated with each screen. As shown in Figure 17.4 triggers can be associated with different parts of the screen and are activated when these components are used. Triggers, when activated, initiate programs that are associated with each trigger. Triggers can be associated with various screen components and are activated in various ways. The most common are:

1. a PRE-TRIGGER, which is activated when the screen is initialized;
2. a POST-TRIGGER, which is activated when a screen terminates;
3. a PRE-FIELD trigger, which is activated when the cursor enters the screen field;
4. a POST-FIELD trigger, which is activated when the cursor leaves the screen field.

Languages for writing trigger programs

Triggers require the application generator to provide a method for writing programs associated with each trigger. One possibility here is the same as discussed in the previous

Figure 17.4 Screen triggers

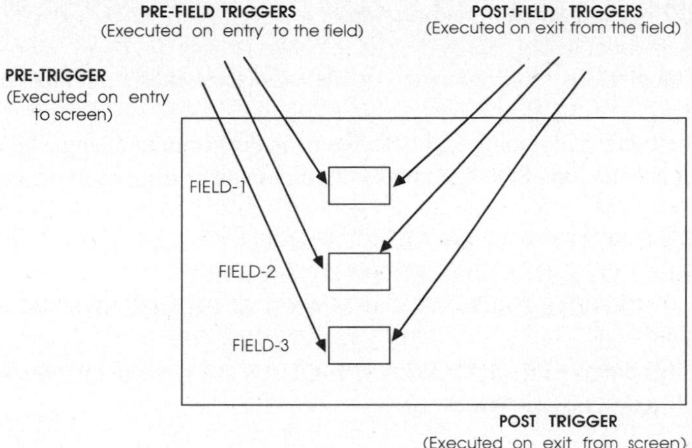

chapter. It is to use a high-level procedural language with SQL statements embedded in it. Programs written using this language are attached to a field and activated by triggers associated with the field. Many application generators support this approach, allowing trigger programs to be written using procedural languages such as C.

Other application generators, however, try to avoid long procedural codes for screen programs. The application generator, after all, is intended for end-users, who should not be required to learn a high-level language. Consequently many systems attempt to provide a more command-oriented method for programming triggers.

A method based on a simple command language is feasible because trigger programs do not have to be exceptionally long. Each such program does one simple task usually associated with one screen field. Usually the trigger is required to make one test and carry out some imperative commands depending on the outcome of the test. In comparison, the embedded SQL program must often process the whole screen.

The next part of this chapter will endeavour to give an idea of the kinds of commands usually provided by application generators. It does this by using a hypothetical language and showing how this language can be used to define the requisition transaction.

An effective language for writing triggers must include:

1. A method of referencing form fields.

   This is usually achieved by prefixing field names with a special symbol such as #. Thus #R-SCREEN.REQUESTING-PROJECT will refer to the REQUESTING-PROJECT field in the R-SCREEN screen.

2. A method of placing the cursor in a given field.

   MOVE CURSOR <field-name> places cursor on the defined field position.

3. A method for placing values into selected fields.

This is usually accomplished by a special command, such as:

FSET <field-name> = <expression>

which places a value computed by the expression in the field named field-name.

4. A method for including SQL statements in the command language expressions. The goal is to include SQL statements directly in an arithmetic expression, for example:

   FSET R-SCREEN.AVAILABLE-QUANTITY =
   SELECT QTY-IN-STORE FROM INVENTORY
   WHERE PART-NO = 'pc6' AND WAREHOUSE = 'West';

   will set the form field AVAILABLE-QUANTITY to the quantity of part 'pc6' held in warehouse 'West'.

5. A method for handling SQL statements that retrieve a variable number of rows.

   This is done using the same technique as used with embedded SQL. First the SQL statement is executed and assigned to a cursor by the statement:

   FASSIGN <label> <SQL statement>

   Then the retrieved rows are made available using a command such as:

   SCROLL <label> to get the next row retrieved by the SQL statement associated with this label.

6. A method for specifying decisions and following alternative paths.

   This is usually achieved by using an IF statement. For example:

   IF (SELECT QTY-IN-STORE FROM INVENTORY WHERE PART-NO = 'px6'
   AND WAREHOUSE = 'West') < 20
   THEN <statement-1>
   ELSE <statement-2>

   Here the condition clause includes an SQL statement. If the condition is true, that is there are less than 20 of the required parts in the selected warehouse, then the statements that follow THEN are executed, in this case statement-1. Otherwise the commands that follow the ELSE are executed, in this case statement-2.

   If more than one statement is to be executed following a condition test, then all these statements are enclosed by a BEGIN ...... END pair.

7. A method for tying decisions to keyboard keys.

This is often done by first reading the keyboard and then testing the character read as follows:

```
READ KBD <char>
IF <char> = F1 THEN <statement-1>
IF <char> = F2 THEN <statement-2>
```

Here the keyboard is read. If F1 is pressed then statement-1 is executed, and if F2 is pressed then statement-2 is executed.

An example

As an example of this hypothetical system let us consider the transaction shown in Figure 17.3. You may recall that this transaction is designed to enter a new requisition for a project. Furthermore the transaction nominates a warehouse to supply the parts. One important part of transaction processing is to check that the entered values of project and warehouse exist in the database. This is done using post-triggers associated with the project and warehouse fields. These trigger programs are used during editing to check field validity as well as checking whether a transaction can be processed without violating system integrity.

For example, the post-trigger for field REQUESTING-PROJECT could be defined as:

```
IF
  (SELECT * FROM PROJECTS WHERE PROJECT=#R-
        SCREEN.REQUESTING-PROJECT)
THEN MOVE CURSOR R-SCREEN.WAREHOUSE
ELSE BEGIN FSET R-SCREEN.MESSAGE = 'NON EXISTENT PROJECT'
        MOVE CURSOR R-SCREEN.REQUESTING-PROJECT; END;
```

Here the SELECT statement is enclosed within an IF command and returns True if a row is found and False if no row is found by the SQL statement. R-SCREEN is the screen name and prefixes screen field names. The IF will thus return False if there is no project in TABLE PROJECTS with the same name as currently appears in field REQUESTING-PROJECT. If the value just entered into the project field is found, the cursor moves on to the WAREHOUSE field. Otherwise an error message is displayed and the cursor returns to the REQUESTING-PROJECT field.

Simple code of this type can be attached to all post-triggers where fields have to be checked for validity.

Transaction designers must define all these trigger routines, give them a name and specify conditions under which they are executed. Such conditions are usually specified interactively to the application generator using a table like that illustrated in Figure 17.5. This table shows the trigger routines that are used with the requisition transaction. It shows the trigger programs that apply to each field. You should note that some fields can have more than one trigger associated with them whereas others have no associated triggers. In addition it has the following triggers:

Figure 17.5 A trigger table

PRE-TRIGGER - NEW-REQ

FIELD	PRE TRIGGERS	POST TRIGGERS
REQUISITION		
REQUESTING-PROJECT		CHECK-PROJECT
WAREHOUSE		CHECK-WAREHOUSE INSERT-REQ
PART-NEEDED		CHECK-PART SHOW-AVAIL
NEEDED-QUANTITY		CHECK-QUANTITY INSERT-REQ-LINE

POST-TRIGGER Commits updates

1. a pre-trigger, NEW-REQ, on the whole form to generate the next requisition number;
2. a post-trigger, CHECK-PROJECT, on field REQUESTING-PROJECT to check whether a valid project value has been input;
3. a post-trigger, CHECK-WAREHOUSE, on field WAREHOUSE to check whether the warehouse is a valid warehouse;
4. another post-trigger, INSERT-REQ, on field WAREHOUSE to generate the new requisition into relation REQUISITIONS;
5. a post-trigger on field PART-NEEDED to check whether a valid part has been input;
6. another post-trigger, SHOW-AVAIL, on field PART-NEEDED to display, in field AVAILABLE-QUANTITY, the quantity of a part available in the chosen warehouse;
7. a post-trigger on field NEEDED-QUANTITY to check if the requested quantity is within the available limit and to insert a new row for that part in REQ-LINES;
8. a post-trigger on the whole form to commit the changes to the database.

Figure 17.5 defines the kind of processing to be carried out on each field. It shows that the transaction changes the database at a number of points. A new line is inserted into table REQUISITIONS when a warehouse is accepted. New rows are inserted into REQ-LINES every time that a new part is accepted. However, all these updates are not committed to the database until the entire screen is successfully completed. Successful screen completion is indicated by pressing some selected key combination, for example, Cntrl-End. The screen can also be aborted by pressing some other combination, for example, Cntrl-Esc.

Figure 17.5 also illustrates some of the purposes for which trigger programs can be used. We have already illustrated how trigger programs can be used to check field validity. Another reason for using a trigger is to display existing data to guide the user in their input.

For example, a post-trigger for a part request displays the quantity of the requested part in a given warehouse. This is done by using the FSET command as follows:

```
FSET #R-SCREEN.AVAILABLE-QUANTITY =
        SELECT QTY-IN-STORE FROM INVENTORY WHERE
        WAREHOUSE = R-SCREEN.WAREHOUSE
        AND PART-NO = R-SCREEN.PART-NEEDED).
```

Change to the database is illustrated by the program that inserts a new requisition line. This takes the form:

```
IF #R-SCREEN.NEEDED-QUANTITY < #R-SCREEN.AVAILABLE-QUANTITY
    THEN BEGIN
          INSERT (#R-SCREEN.REQNO, #R-SCREEN.PART-NEEDED,
                 #R-SCREEN.NEEDED-QUANTITY)
                 INTO REQ-LINES (REQ-NO, PART-NO, QTY-NEEDED)
          UPDATE INVENTORY
                 SET QTY-IN-STORE =
                    QTY-IN-STORE - #R-SCREEN.NEEDED-QUANTITY
                 WHERE WAREHOUSE = #R-SCREEN.WAREHOUSE
                 AND PART-NO = #R-SCREEN.PART-NEEDED
          END.
```

This program as well as inserting a new requisition line, also updates the inventory table to reflect the withdrawn parts.

Triggers can do more than simply carry out the checks, change the database or displaying values. They can also be used to help users select some value by scrolling through a set of values. For example, suppose a user has forgotten the warehouse names. Such warehouse names can be displayed one at a time as follows:

```
FASSIGN WAREHOUSE-LIST =
        SELECT WAREHOUSE INTO #R-SCREEN.WAREHOUSE
        FROM WAREHOUSES.

STEP1.
IF (SCROLL WAREHOUSE-LIST)
THEN
        READ KBD DECKEY
        IF DECKEY = F1 THEN GOTO STEP2
        IF DECKEY = F2 THEN GOTO STEP1
STEP2.
```

In this example, every time that SCROLL is executed a new warehouse name is placed in the warehouse file. The user can select this warehouse by pressing F1 or get the next warehouse by pressing F2.

SUMMARY

This chapter defined methods that are provided to relational database designers for developing applications that support low-volume transactions.

This support is provided through application generators. Such generators allow users to first define a database. Then a number of database transactions are defined. Each transaction is defined as a screen that receives transaction data. Triggers are associated with the screen itself as well as the screen fields. These triggers can activate programs to check database consistency, and make any changes to the database. Special command languages are usually provided for this purpose and this chapter described one such hypothetical language.

The application generators also contain facilities for ad-hoc enquiry to the database and report generation.

18

Distributed databases

INTRODUCTION

All the chapters so far assumed that the database is stored at the one location. Recent database trends, however, have placed greater emphasis on databases that may be distributed over a number of locations. The idea of a distributed database is illustrated in Figure 18.1. Here there are a number of sites, each with its own computer and database management software. Each site maintains its own database and supports a number of users through terminals. The computers at different sites are connected to each other through a communications network. Users at each site can either access the data at their site or access data at other sites through the communications network.

It is common to distinguish between two kinds of distributed database systems. One kind is known as heterogeneous systems. Here different DBMS are used at each site. The other kind are homogeneous systems where the same DBMS is used at each site. In practice, the distinction between heterogeneous and homogeneous systems is important because using common software makes it easier to establish and maintain a homogeneous rather than a heterogeneous database.

Heterogeneous systems often arise where a large amount of data already exists at different locations in an organization. This information may currently be stored at different sites, on different machines and using different database management software. Should new applications that must use data at more than one location be proposed, then links must be developed between different sites to allow such access . Users' application programs use these links to access data at many sites. In heterogeneous systems, such links

Figure 18.1 A distributed database

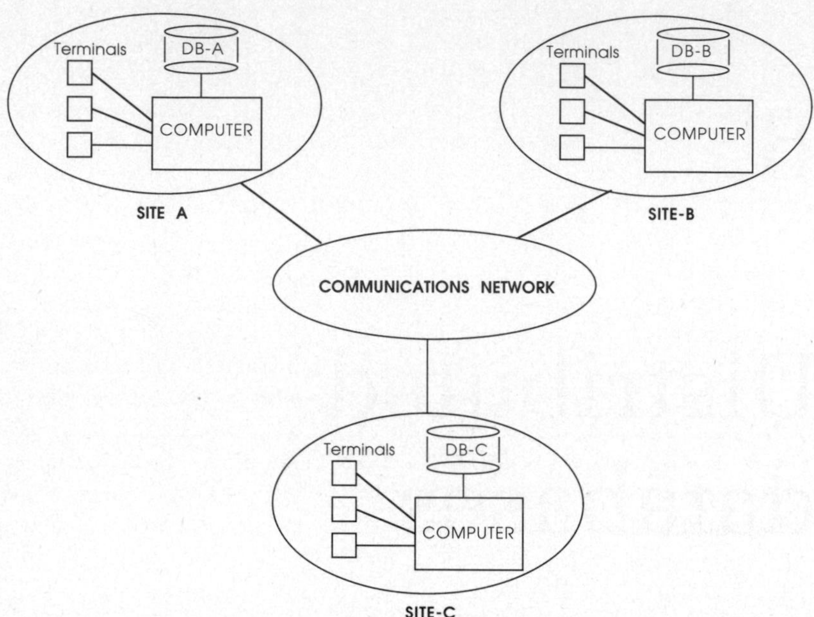

must convert data formats used by a DBMS at one site into formats acceptable to a DBMS at another site. Alternatively, users must write programs that use more than one DBMS.

It is of course easier to provide links between sites in homogeneous systems. In such systems no format conversion is needed and it is only necessary to move the data between sites. Often such movement can be accomplished using DBMS facilities and no special programs need be written by the user. For this reason homogeneous systems are preferred when a totally new application is developed.

This chapter describes some alternative ways of distributing databases and how users access data in such distributed databases. However, before doing so, some advantages and disadvantages of distribution are described.

WHY DISTRIBUTE?

A number of advantages are quoted for data distribution. The most important is that data is stored close to its point of use thus reducing communication time and cost during data access. Another advantage is that greater security is provided because data is stored at a number of locations. A failure at one location only affects part of the database. Finally there is local autonomy. It enables users at each site to determine applications that are important to them. They can use their local knowledge of data to structure the database at their site into a form that is most useful for their applications.

However, there are also some disadvantages in distributing data, most of which concern the extra processing needed to move data between locations. This includes both the time needed to set up an application and the extra processing time needed to move data while the application is running.

In distributed systems, users may need to become concerned with the physical movement of data, which has really nothing to do with the actual application problem. For example, a user program will have to include actual commands that move data or send messages to other sites as well as commands needed by the application program logic. The problem becomes even more acute if the program needs to determine the location of data for each access command. This is often achieved using the method illustrated in Figure 18.2. Here a directory stores the location of each data part. Programs must use this directory to find the data location and then send a message to that location to get the data. Finally a message must be sent to update data at distant sites. The disadvantage is that a user, who is only concerned with using data, also has to worry about finding its location. Many systems overcome this problem by delegating data location to DBMS software. Such software accepts a user command that specifies the data needed by the user. It then finds the location of the data, retrieves it and makes it available to the user.

Another disadvantage of distributed data is the additional time that is needed to access the data. This time includes transmission of messages to distant sites and transmission of needed data from those sites.

Figure 18.2 Program structure

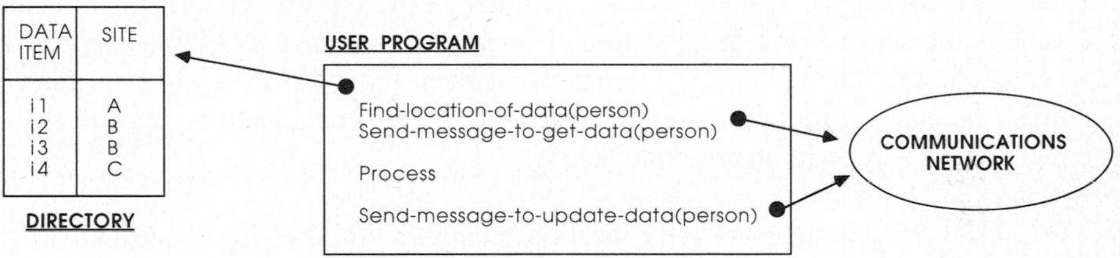

In addition, distributed systems pose greater problems of controlling concurrency over a number of locations. Most corporate databases allow more than one user to access the database at the same time. Concurrent access by many users requires some central control to ensure that concurrent updates of the same data items do not lead to inconsistencies in the database. This is fairly easy to do in a central database as the control is at the one site. It is, however, much more difficult to control redundancy over a number of sites. Control can no longer be centralized and messages must be passed between different sites before an update is allowed, again adding to the processing time.

Effective use of distributed database systems requires software that makes data easy to access, and design procedures which produce distributions that minimize total transmission time. Both of these are based on well-defined principles. There are two sets of such principles. One concerns the design principles that must be followed to ensure that data is stored in the most appropriate locations. The other are principles concerned with database use. These must ensure that distribution has minimal impact on application programs that use the database. We first describe the second set of principles and cover design principles later in this chapter.

PRINCIPLES FOR DATABASE USE

One overriding principle of distributed database use is that it should not make the database more difficult to use. The whole idea behind SQL has been to simplify access to all kinds of users. One does not now want to take this advantage away by distributing the database.

Two conditions must be satisfied if simplicity is to be preserved. One is to make users unaware of database location, and address queries as if the database is local. It is then possible to move a part of a database without affecting any programs that use it. This is known as 'location transparency'. The other condition must ensure that users at one site can work independently of users at other sites. To do this, DBMS must support concurrent access to the database from many locations.

Location transparency

Location transparency exists where a program can refer to data independently of the location of the data. If this is the case, then data can be moved from one location to another without affecting programs that use this data. Location transparency is easier to provide in homogeneous systems. In such systems, the DBMS automatically determines the location of data for a given database command. The DBMS supports the directory and automatically finds the data location given any user command. All the user has to do is enter an SQL statement using some global names, and the DBMS will determine how to find the data. As far as the user is concerned the data could have been local.

Thus the overriding principle here is:

- Users must be unaware of the location of data when addressing enquiries to a database writing application programs.

Concurrency

Concurrency allows more than one user to access the database at the same time. It must be possible for multiple database updates from many locations to be supported while maintaining database correctness.

To do this, a DBMS must propagate updates to all copies of a table. It must first lock all copies of tables affected by a transaction, then change each copy and then unlock each copy. Obviously this can be quite a lengthy process. Apart from the time involved, it also means that other users will not have access to any copy of a table while the update is in progress.

A number of algorithms have been proposed for minimizing the effect of updates on database performance. A good initial description of the principles for algorithms for concurrent updates can be found in Bernstein (1975). You will find that these algorithms are often difficult to implement and require considerable communications and processing time. Consequently they are not provided at this stage by many commercial systems.

The overriding principle here is that:

- User programs need not be affected by the presence of other users in the system.

Let us now look at how databases are set up and controlled.

METHODS FOR DISTRIBUTING DATA

Designers of distributed databases must consider a number of factors. These factors include the way that users expect to use the database and the capabilities of distributed database software. Given these two sets of factors, the designer must then choose the method for distributing the database.

There are many ways to distribute a database. Some methods for distribution allow any operation on each copy of any part of a database. Others restrict users to only a restricted set of operations on each copy. The simplest case is where copies of a database are created for retrieval purposes only.

Local copies for retrieval

Figure 18.3 shows a distribution method where there is a central database with copies of the central database made available at distant locations. These copies may be complete relations, or they may be parts of relations. In Figure 18.3 a copy of the CUSTOMER table is stored at SITE-A and a copy of the SALES table is stored at SITE-B. Users at those sites can only retrieve data from these copies. The advantage here is that retrievals do not require any communications time. Thus they are quicker and also cheaper.

Figure 18.3 Local copies

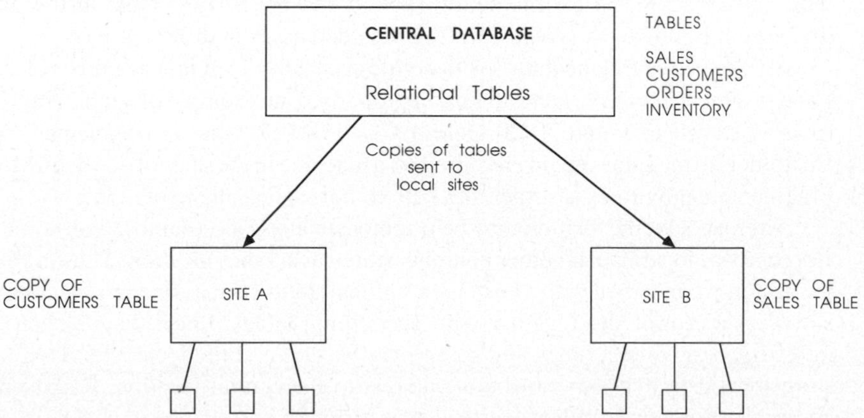

Local copies are frequently used in heterogeneous systems. In these cases software used at a local site may be different to that used at the central site. A format conversion program is used to convert the database into a form acceptable by the software at the local site.

The method of distribution shown in Figure 18.3 has one obvious disadvantage. A copy of data at the distant locations will become out of date as soon as an update is made to the central copy. Thus copies at a distant site must be refreshed at regular intervals to ensure that data is not too much out of date. Consequently replenishment algorithms are needed to change copies following a change to the central database. Replenishment may itself result in additional traffic on the network especially if the database is highly volatile.

To avoid such replenishment an alternative distribution method may be used. This is to divide the database into disjoint parts and store each part at a different location. If each part is stored at a location of most use then replenishment overheads may be reduced.

Storing database parts at different locations

Division of a database into parts is often called 'fragmentation'. There are a number of alternatives for fragmenting databases. Designers must first choose a fragmentation alternative and then choose the location for each fragment. The process of choosing locations for fragments is called allocation. Let us now look at alternative ways for fragmenting a database.

Fragmentation of the database

The simplest way to fragment a database is to make each table into a separate fragment. Each table can then be stored at different locations. This alternative is illustrated in Figure 18.4. In Figure 18.4 there are three tables, each of which becomes a database fragment. Each fragment may be stored at a different site. In Figure 18.4 the INVENTORY table will be stored on a machine in the warehouse, the CUSTOMER table on a machine in the marketing section and the SALES table in the purchasing division. It is, however, possible to fragment databases in different ways.

An alternative fragmentation is to divide each table itself into a number of fragments. Each fragment may have some common property. One example of a table fragmented by rows is shown in Figure 18.5. Here a CUSTOMER table is fragmented by region. Customers in the same region are stored on a machine in the sales office within the region. Fragmentation by rows is sometimes called 'horizontal fragmentation'.

Alternatively, the relation may be fragmented along its columns, with some columns stored at one location, and other columns stored at another location. Thus in Figure 18.6 the columns concerned with a customer's global status such as financial accounts may be stored at a central site together with accounting tables. Local details such as phone numbers, best contact times and so on may be stored at the local site. Such local sites store local data that may not be of interest to the central location. Fragmentation by columns is sometimes called 'vertical fragmentation'.

Figure 18.4 Fragmentation by tables

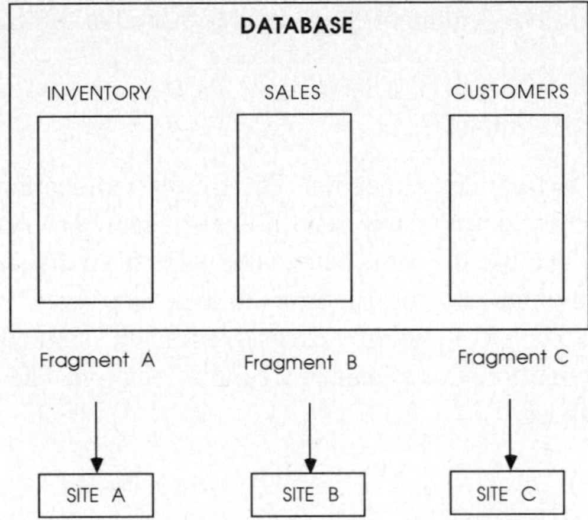

Figure 18.5 Fragmentation by rows

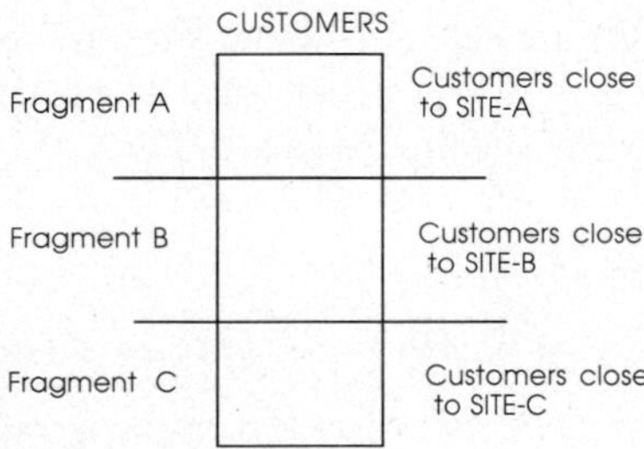

Figure 18.6 Fragmentation by columns

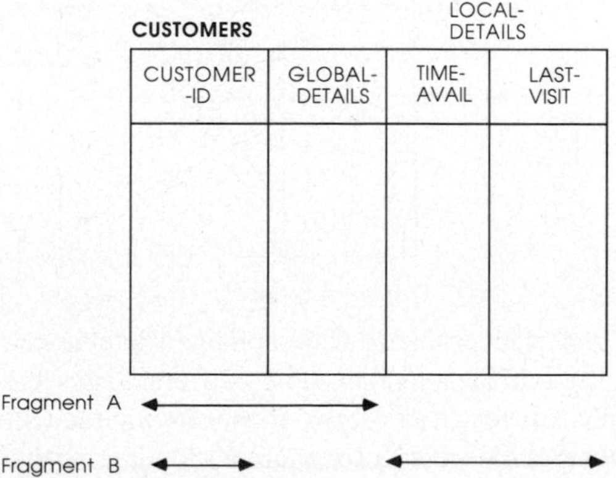

It is, of course, possible to have a fragmentation that employs a mix of each of these three alternatives. In that case, some tables may be fragmented both vertically and horizontally. Different fragments may then be stored at different sites.

Fragment allocation

Let us now turn to fragment allocation. The simplest allocation is to store each fragment at one location only. Such allocation can, however, cause problems if users from more than one location wish to use the same data. Now users from distant locations use communications lines and obtain slower responses to their queries.

There are two ways of avoiding excessive transmission costs in such environments. One is to keep commonly used data at a central location. The other is to replicate some parts of the database.

Database replication

Replication exists when some parts of a database are stored at more than one location. It is illustrated in Figure 18.7. In this figure there are three warehouses each at a different site. Inventory records are recorded for each warehouse at the warehouse site, and copies of inventories at one site are kept at all other sites. Users at any site can easily find the location of a particular part. However, historical data that is not often needed at local sites is only stored at the central site, in this case SITE-A.

Figure 18.7 Replication

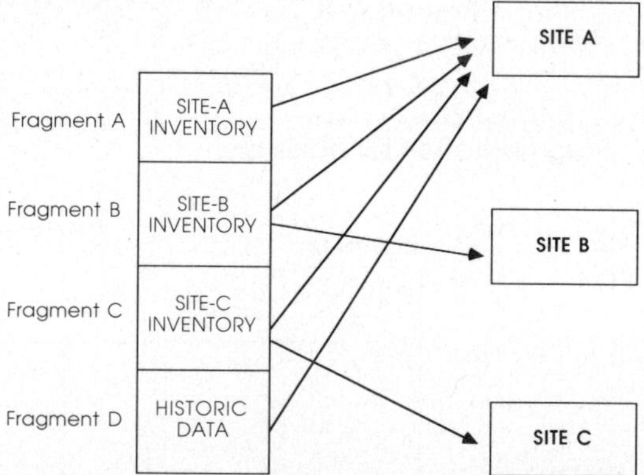

One of the more important problems with replicated databases is support for concurrency. What happens when two persons each at two different sites want to update the same data item? For example, suppose users at two locations want to withdraw the same part from the same warehouse? It is necessary to ensure that updates to that part are made in the same sequence at all sites.

One of the most common ways to control updates emanating from a number of sites is to designate one site as the primary site. All updates are then directed to that site. Copies at other sites are refreshed at different intervals. Obviously replication becomes less desirable as the ratio of updates to enquiries increases.

SOFTWARE TO SUPPORT DISTRIBUTION

Distributed database management systems must allow users to place fragments of databases at various locations and support such distribution by providing location transparency and controlling concurrency. Such support cannot be easily provided in heterogeneous systems. In such systems users must provide the necessary conversion software to convert data between different systems.

However, DBMS software is now becoming available to support database distribution in homogeneous environments. These systems require all data to be stored under the control of one database management system. Such distributed DBMS must provide commands to enable users to define data and its location, move data between locations and access this data.

Controlling distributed databases

Managers of a distributed database must be able to monitor database use and move parts of a database from one location to another.

To do this SQL must be extended to include a COPY command. This command allows the user to select a database fragment and move it from one location to another.

The copy command can be very similar to a view definition. It defines a new stored table name and its column names. This is followed by a SELECT statement that defines the source for this table. For example, suppose a database central site stores a table of customer data:

```
CUSTOMER-DATA(CUSTOMER-NAME, CUSTOMER-ADDRESS,
        POSTCODE, ACCOUNT-NO, CREDIT)
```

A site now wishes to get a copy of the address of the customers within its local area. This can be done by the command:

```
COPY AS LOCAL-CUSTOMERS(NAME, ADDRESS, POSTCODE) FROM
        SELECT CUSTOMER-NAME, CUSTOMER-ADDRESS, POSTCODE
        FROM CUSTOMERS
        WHERE POSTCODE IS BETWEEN 2000 AND 2100.
```

Now a new table is created at the local site. This table, named LOCAL-CUSTOMERS, contains the names and addresses of all customers local to the site.

There is as yet no standard method for copying parts of a database and each DBMS has its own specific facilities. However, most of them follow the idea illustrated by this COPY command.

Accessing distributed databases

Two issues arise in accessing data in distributed database systems. One is how to name data tables and columns. The other is how to access these tables. In a distributed system, names are assigned to tables and attributes as these are created. Different users at different sites may wish to use names convenient to their particular location.

Most distributed DBMS allow sites to name database parts by names most appropriate for their site. Again different DBMS provide different facilities for doing so. The COPY command illustrated one possibility. Here new names were defined when the copy was created. It is also possible to have special commands that define synonyms for database names.

The other accessing issue is location transparency. Here users can access independently of its location. Many distributed DBMS, however, still have limitations and do not fully support location transparency. Such support would have to cater for any possible effect of updates on a distributed database. Such updates have all kinds of effects. For example, updates to a horizontally fragmented table may require rows to be transmitted from one location to another. Thus should a customer move from one location to another, then, given the fragmentation in Figure 18.4, a customer's record must also be moved from one location to another. Total location transparency should cater for situations of this kind. However, many distributed DBMS are limited in their support of location transparency. Consequently databases that are volatile are often not distributed.

DESIGNING DISTRIBUTED DATABASES

The goal of distributed database design is to somehow get the advantages of distribution, without these being outweighed by the disadvantages. To do this requires a proper method of distributing the data, and the right software.

Design of distributed databases proceeds in a similar way to designing centralized databases. It has, however, one additional step during logical design. This step was suggested by Ceri and is called 'distribution design'. Its position in the design cycle is illustrated in Figure 18.8. It begins after a global logical record structure is defined.

Distribution design

Distribution design determines the fragmentation of the database and allocation of fragments to database sites. During distribution design, designers examine access requirements and choose a design that minimizes the number of records transmitted between sites. In most cases this is done on a trial and error basis. A trial fragmentation and a non-

Figure 18.8 Procedure for distributed database design

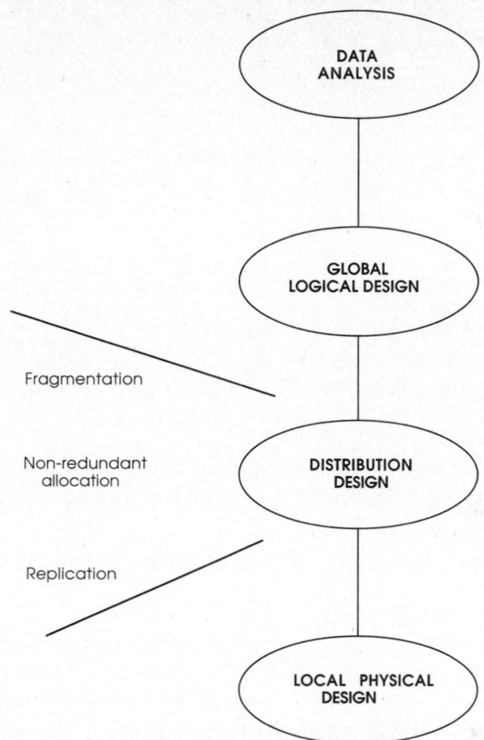

redundant allocation is made by examining the access requirements. The trial allocation is analyzed and adjusted if necessary. Once a suitable fragmentation and non-redundant allocation is found, replication is considered.

This trial and error process is illustrated using the simple example shown in Figure 18.9. This figure shows a database made up of one table, called PERSONS. This table contains a number of columns about the person's details. The two columns important in this example are PERSON-ID, which identifies each person, and ADDRESS, which is a person's current address. There is only one transaction kind made to this database. This transaction is made of one access step (step A/1) illustrated in Figure 18.9(a). This step uses a value of PERSON-ID as the access key to find details about the person identified by that key.

Trial design

Distribution design begins with a trial fragmentation and distribution. The objective of a trial design is to place records at those locations that most need them. Trial fragmentations are often based on one or more attributes of a table. Usually these attributes are those with values of interest in the transaction. If it is known that transactions at one site usually refer to rows whose attribute values fall into a range, then all rows in that range are allocated to that site. In our case, ADDRESS is a good candidate for a trial fragmentation because

Figure 18.9 A simple example

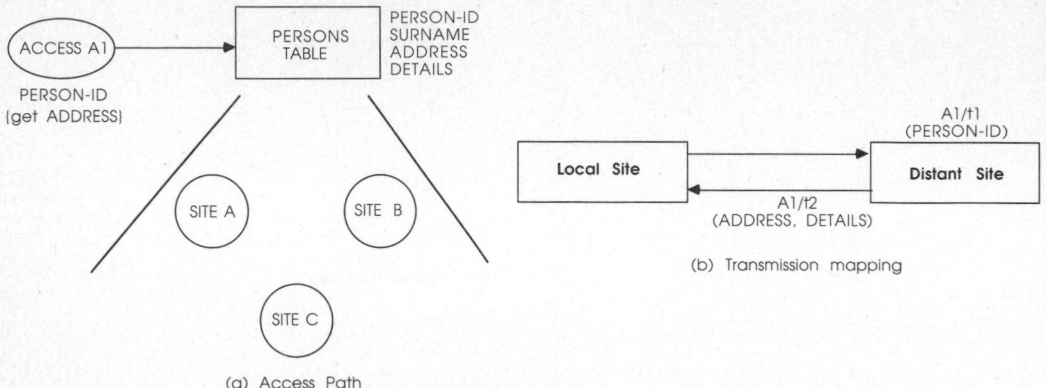

(a) Access Path

(b) Transmission mapping

enquiries at sites are usually about people close to the site. We assume that the PERSONS table is fragmented by ADDRESS. Each site is allocated a fragment made up of a range of addresses within the site boundary.

Analysis starts following the trial fragmentation and allocation.

Analysis

Analysis proceeds by constructing access paths as in centralized design. The one access step for our transaction is illustrated in Figure 18.9(a). The access paths are extended to show how logical records may be transmitted during an access step. This is done by plotting transmission paths. Such a transmission path is illustrated in Figure 18.9(b). It shows that access step A1 is made up of two transmission steps. Step A1(t1) sends the value of PERSON-ID to a distant site. Step A1(t2) sends the value of ADDRESS and DETAILS back to the local site. The goal of distribution design is to minimize the number of records transmitted. Designers must therefore compare transmission volumes for alternative distribution strategies. To do this, it is necessary to estimate numbers of records transmitted for alternative strategies and select the strategy with least transmitted records.

Transmission estimates require information about locations at which queries occur and the location of records required by these queries. This information can then be used to estimate the number of transmitted records for a particular distribution strategy.

The estimating method is now illustrated by using the example shown in Figure 18.9. It is assumed that there are three sites available for storing the PERSONS table. These sites are here called SITE-A, SITE-B and SITE-C and the number of transactions at each site is:

1. SITE-A 500 queries
2. SITE-B 100 queries
3. SITE-C 100 queries

The next step is to find out whether transactions at each site require records of persons closest to the site or whether they require records from other sites. Analysis to find this information is known as logical polarization.

Logical polarization

Logical polarization analysis assumes a trial fragmentation and allocation. It then determines for each access step, the fraction of accesses that can be satisfied locally and the fraction that requires record transmissions.

The results of this analysis are shown on a logical polarization table. This table is illustrated in Figure 18.10(a). It has one row for each site and one column for each fragment. In our example, we call these fragments F(A), F(B) and F(C). Fragment F(A) is allocated to SITE-A, fragment F(B) to SITE-B and so on. Each row shows the fraction of transactions at that row site that need new records from fragments at this and other sites. Thus 0.85 of accesses at SITE-A need records from fragment F(A), 0.1 need records from fragment F(B) and 0.05 from fragment F(C). The notation p(i,j) means the fraction of queries at the site in row i that require records from the fragment in column j.

Figure 18.10 Records transmitted

Site \ Fragment	F(A)	F(B)	F(C)
A	0.85	0.10	0.05
B	0.05	0.90	0.05
C	0.10	0.15	0.75

(a) Logical polarization

Fragment \ Site	A	B	C
F(A)	1.0	0	0
F(B)	0	1.0	0
F(C)	0	0	1.0

(b) Allocation

SITE	Number of records	Records transmitted from site (A1/t1)	Records transmitted to site (A1/t2)
A	500	500(0.85 x (1–1) + 0.10 x (1–0) + 0.05 x (1–0)0 = 75	75
B	100	100(0.05(1–0) + 0.90(1–1) + 0.05(1–0)) = 10	10
C	100	100(0.10(1–0 + 0.15(1–0) + 0.75(1–1)) = 25	25
		TOTAL = 110	TOTAL = 110

(c) Records transmitted

Allocation analysis

Transmission analysis also uses an allocation. Allocations are shown on an allocation table. The allocation table for the trial design is shown in Figure 18.10(b). There is one row for each fragment and one column for each site. The entry in the table shows the fraction of the fragment allocated to the site. In Figure 18.10(b) the whole fragment for an area is allocated to a site of that area. The notation a(i, j) shows the fraction of the fragment in row i allocated to the site in column j.

Transmission estimates

Transmission estimates can begin once we have a polarization and allocation table. These estimates compute the total number of records transmitted given this polarization and allocation and using the transmission path shown in Figure 18.9(b). The computations are shown in Figure 18.10(c).

The table in Figure 18.10(c) has one row for each site. It shows the number of records needed at each site, and the number of records transmitted to and from the site. There is one column in the table for each transmission step shown in Figure 18.9(b).

Transmission will occur at SITE-A whenever records needed by queries at SITE-A can only be found at some other site. This number can be computed from the transaction frequency, the polarization table and the allocation table. It is the number of records needed from each fragment by queries at SITE-A multiplied by the fraction of that fragment at sites other than SITE-A.

The best way to determine the number of records to be transmitted at a site in row i is as follows:

1. From the access and transmission tables find the total number of transactions and records that are needed at the site.
2. For each fragment(j):

   (a) Find, from the polarization table, the fraction of transactions [p(i,j)] at the site that need the fragment.
   (b) Find, from the allocation table, the fraction of the fragment [1 - a(j,i)] that is not stored at the site.
   (c) Multiply this total by the fraction that need this fragment and then multiply by the fraction of the fragment at the site.

3. Repeat step 2 for each fragment to find the total records transmitted at the site. The general formula here is that records transmitted for an access step at site i is given by the formula:

   number of transmitted records x sum over all fragments (j) [p(i,j) x (1 - a(j,i)]

The records transmitted at SITE-A are then computed as follows. The total number of transactions is 500 and the number of records needed is 500 because each access step retrieves one ADDRESS. Thus there is the potential to transmit 500 records out of the site (step A1(t1)) and to receive 500 records (step A1(t2)).

Now we examine each fragment in turn. Of the 500 records, 0.85(500) refer to fragment F(A), which is stored at SITE-A and do not require any transmission. 0.10(500) refer to records in fragment F(B). This fragment is wholly stored at SITE-B and hence there will 50 transmissions to SITE-B and 50 from SITE-B. 0.05(500) transactions refer to fragment F(C), which is wholly stored at SITE-C. They will result in 25 records transmitted to and from SITE-A. The total number of records transmitted to and from this site will therefore be 75.

The records transmitted from and to SITE-B can be computed in a similar way, using the above formula. This number will be:

$$100(0.05(1-0) + 0.90(1-1) + 0.05(1-0)) = 10$$

All the record transfers can then be summarized in the table shown in Figure 18.10(c). This table shows the total number of record transfers for the polarization and allocation chosen in Figures 18.10(a) and 18.10(b). It shows that this allocation results in a total transmission of 220 records.

Designers should of course try more than one allocation. Two alternative allocations are shown in Figures 18.11 and 18.12. One such alternative, shown in Figure 18.11, is an allocation where all fragments are stored at SITE-A. No records are kept at SITE-A and SITE-B. The transmissions are now shown in Figure 18.11(b). You should note, that transactions at SITE-A do not result in any transmissions because all the fragments are stored at SITE-A. Similarly all transactions at the other site result in one record transmitted to and from this site. The total number of records transmitted is now 400.

Figure 18.12 shows another allocation. This allocation involves some replication. The allocation table in Figure 18.12(a) shows that all fragments are available at SITE-A.

Figure 18.11 All fragments at site A

Fragment \ Site	A	B	C
F(A)	1.0	0	0
F(B)	1.0	0	0
F(C)	1.0	0	1.0

(a) Allocation table

SITE	Number of records	Records transmitted from site (A1/t1)	Records transmitted to site (A1/t2)
A	500	500(0.85 x (1–1) + 0.10 x (1–1) + 0.05 x (1–1)0 = 0	0
B	100	100(0.05(1–0) + 0.90(1–0) + 0.05(1–0)) = 100	100
C	100	100(0.10(1–0) + 0.15(1–0) + 0.75(1–0)) = 100	100
		TOTAL = 200	TOTAL = 200

(b) Records transmitted

Figure 18.12 Introducing replication

Site \ Fragment	F(A)	F(B)	F(C)
A	0.85	0.10	0.05
B	0.05	0.90	0.05
C	0.10	0.15	0.75

(a) Logical polarization

Fragment \ Site	A	B	C
F(A)	1.0	0	0
F(B)	1.0	1.0	0
F(C)	1.0	0	1.0

(b) Allocation

SITE	Number of records	Records transmitted from site (A1/t1)	Records transmitted to site (A1/t2)
A	500	500(0.85 x (1–1) + 0.10 x (1–1) + 0.05 x (1–1)0 = 0	0
B	100	100(0.05(1–0) + 0.90(1–1) + 0.05(1–0)) = 10	10
C	100	100(0.10(1–0 + 0.15(1–0) + 0.75(1–1)) = 25	25
		TOTAL = 35	TOTAL = 35

(c) Records transmitted

In addition fragments F(B) and F(C) are replicated at sites B and C respectively. The total number of record transmissions for this allocation is 70.

In summary the estimated total record transmissions for the three trial allocations are:

1. Alternative A: (distribute) Figure 18.10 — 220 records transmitted.
2. Alternative B: (centralize) Figure 18.11 — 400 records transmitted.
3. Alternative C: (replicate) Figure 18.12 — 70 records transmitted.

This suggests that we should choose either alternative A or C. The choice, however, must also consider other factors. For example, if the data is very volatile alternative C may not be suitable because of update problems. What would have to be done here in fact is to carry out the distribution analysis for the update as well and make a choice based on the sum of transmissions for all queries. Also the extra storage needed at SITE-A may prohibit alternative C.

You should also note that the choice will depend on the transaction polarization. So far we have assumed the polarization shown in Figure 18.10(a). Suppose, however, the polarization were different. Let us, for example, assume the polarization shown in Figure 18.13(a). Now a transaction is equally likely to require a record from each site. Here there is an equal probability of records needed from any site.

Analysis for this polarization is now repeated for the three distribution alternatives. Figure 18.13 shows the alternative where each fragment appears at one site only. The total number of records transmitted is now 465.

Figure 18.14 shows estimates made for the centralized allocation. All fragments are now stored at SITE-A. The estimated number of records transmitted is now 200.

Figure 18.15 shows the analysis for the replication option. The total records transmitted is now 264.

In summary the estimated total record transmissions for the three trial allocations given equal distribution are:

Figure 18.13 Change of polarization

Fragment

Site		F(A)	F(B)	F(C)
	A	0.33	0.33	0.33
	B	0.33	0.33	0.33
	C	0.33	0.33	0.33

(a) Logical polarization

Site

Fragment		A	B	C
	F(A)	1.0	0	0
	F(B)	0	1.0	0
	F(C)	0	0	1.0

(b) Allocation

SITE	Number of records	Records transmitted from site (A1/t1)	Records transmitted to site (A1/t2)
A	500	500(0.33 x (1–1) + 0.33 x (1–0) + 0.33 x (1–0)0 = 333	333
B	100	100(0.33(1–0) + 0.33(1–1) + 0.33(1–0)) = 66	66
C	100	100(0.33(1–0 + 0.33(1–0) + 0.33(1–1)) = 66	66
		TOTAL = 465	TOTAL = 465

(c) Records transmitted

Figure 18.14 Changed polarization with all fragments at SITE-A

Fragment

	A	B	C
F(A)	1.0	0	0
F(B)	1.0	0	0
F(C)	1.0	0	1.0

(a) Allocation

SITE	Number of records	Records transmitted from site (A1/t1)	Records transmitted to site (A1/t2)
A	500	500(0.33 x (1–1) + 0.33 x (1–1) + 0.33 x (1–1)0 = 0	0
B	100	100(0.33(1–0) + 0.33(1–0) + 0.33(1–0)) = 100	100
C	100	100(0.33(1–0) + 0.33(1–0) + 0.33(1–0)) = 100	100
		TOTAL = 200	TOTAL = 200

(b) Records transmitted

Figure 18.15 Changed polarization with replication

Fragment

	A	B	C
F(A)	1.0	0	0
F(B)	1.0	1.0	0
F(C)	1.0	0	1.0

(a) Allocation

SITE	Number of records	Records transmitted from site (A1/t1)	Records transmitted to site (A1/t2)
A	500	500(0.33 x (1–1) + 0.33 x (1–1) + 0.33 x (1–1)0 = 0	0
B	100	100(0.33(1–0) + 0.33(1–1) + 0.33(1–0)) = 66	10
C	100	100(0.33(1–0 + 0.33(1–0) + 0.33(1–1)) = 66	25
		TOTAL = 132	TOTAL = 132

(b) Records transmitted

1. Alternative A: (distribute) Figure 18.10 — 9305 records transmitted.
2. Alternative B: (centralize) Figure 18.11 — 400 records transmitted.
3. Alternative C: (replicate) Figure 18.12 — 264 records transmitted.

You should note that now alternative B is preferred over alternative A. This is because most transactions occur at SITE-A and centralization at that site reduces the total number of transmissions.

The computations so far have illustrated the idea of comparing alternative distributions. The computations are relatively straightforward if only one table is concerned. They become more involved with a large number of tables and transactions with a large number of steps. We illustrate some of this complexity in the next section.

Choosing distributions in the design cycle

In larger systems, design again commences in the same way as for centralized design. Initially an E-R model of the system is developed. This model is shown in Figure 18.16(a). It describes an employment agency, which finds employees for vacancies notified by employers. The agency has a number of offices and each office covers a different area. Each office maintains LISTINGS of vacancies notified by employers. A listing contains a DESCRIPTION of the vacancy, its LOCATION, possible SALARY as well as the qualifications needed. In addition each office also stores information about APPLICANTS. This information includes the applicant's personal details and address, their qualifications as well as their preferred location for employment. Each applicant may have more than one qualification and any number of preferred locations.

The agency matches its applicants to available vacancies, arranges interviews after some preliminary discussion and attempts to secure placement of the applicants. The interviews are arranged by offices that may not be the same office that has the listing. The subset INTERVIEWING OFFICES models these offices. The agency receives a commission from employers for successful placements. A record is kept of all interviews as well as any placements.

So far Figure 18.16(a) is a conceptual model that would be developed irrespective of whether the database is distributed or not. Figure 18.16(b) is the logical structure obtained from the E-R diagram using the methods described in Chapter 9. Note that logical record INTERVIEWS is made up of object sets, WITH, INTERVIEWS, BY and ARRANGED-BY. Both INTERVIEWS and BY have the attribute OFFICE-NAME, but each such office may be a different office. The OFFICE-NAME in ARRANGED-BY refers to the office that arranged the interview. OFFICE-NAME in INTERVIEWS refers to the office that has the listing. Different names are used in logical record INTERVIEWS to distinguish between these offices. In the logical record INTERVIEWS, OFFICE-WHERE refers to the arranging office and OFFICE-NAME to the listing office. The logical record structure in Figure 18.16(b) is independent of any data distribution.

The design then proceeds in a way similar to that described in Chapter 9. Access paths are plotted on the logical record structure. Some such access paths are shown on Figure 18.16(b). These are access paths for the following transactions:

A. Find all the vacancies to suit a particular applicant.
B. Find applicants with QUALIFICATION that match those of a given vacancy and have the same preferred location as the vacancy.
C. Create an interview record.
D. List all interviews arranged for an organization for a given time interval.
E. Look up interview and applicant details for a given INTERVIEW-TIME and arranged at a given office.

So far the process has been the same as for a centralized database. We could now carry out any necessary denormalization. For example, it may be worthwhile to add COMPANY-NAME to INTERVIEWS to improve transaction D. Currently we must look up all records for a given interview time using step D/1. Step D/2 is then necessary to

Figure 18.16 Model of placements *(continued next page)*

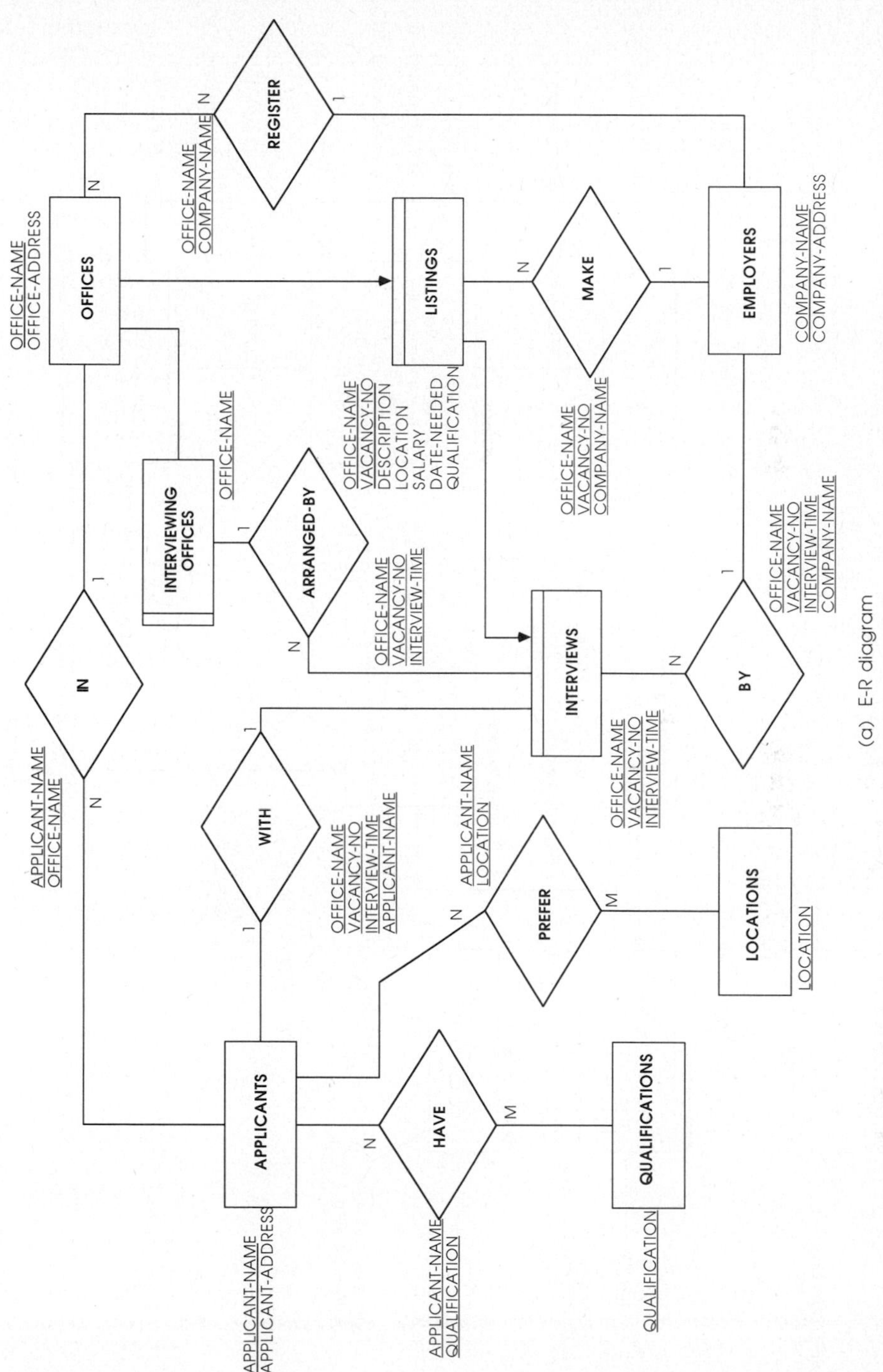

(a) E-R diagram

Figure 18.16 Model of placements *(continued)*

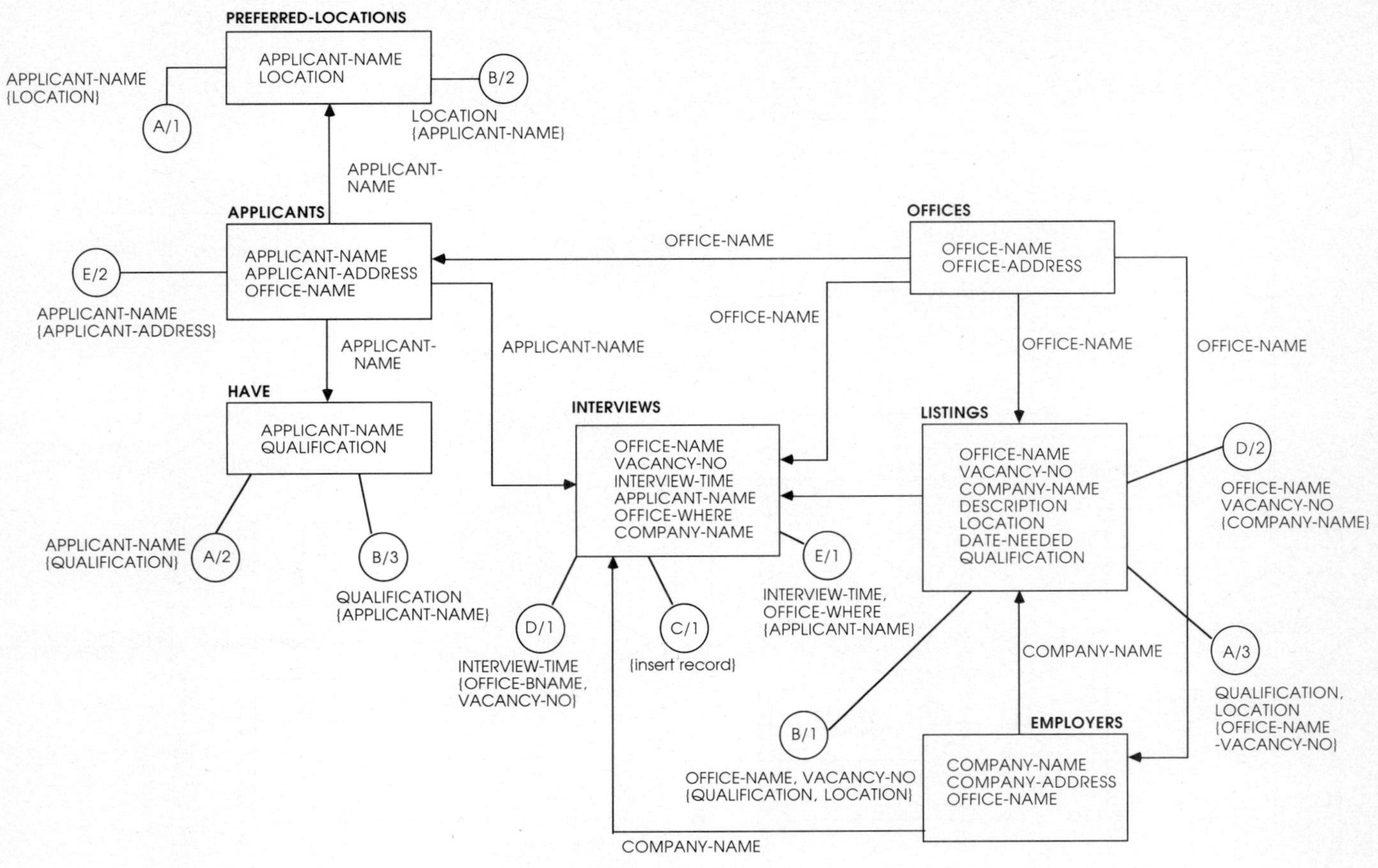

(b) Logical record structure for placements

check the COMPANY-NAME for each interview. It uses OFFICE-NAME and VACANCY-NO to retrieve the COMPANY-NAME from logical record LISTINGS. Adding COMPANY-NAME to INTERVIEWS eliminates step D/2. Distribution analysis commences following denormalization.

Distribution analysis proceeds in the same way as for the simpler example illustrated in Figure 18.9. A transmission path is developed for each transaction and number of records transmitted is estimated for each access step given a trial fragmentation and allocation.

The transmission diagram for transaction A is shown in Figure 18.17. It makes one simplifying assumption. This is that the output from each access step is brought back to the site at which the transaction was initiated.

Figure 18.17 Transmission path for access A

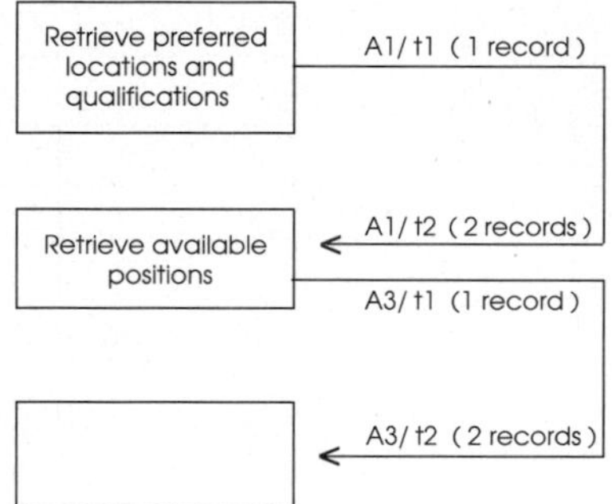

Figure 18.18 Access frequencies

Sites

		S1	S2	S3
Transactions	A	10,000	20,000	5,000
	B	20,000	35,000	7,000
	C	3,000	200	100
	D	200	200	300
	E	100	100	100

As in the previous example, analysis begins by determining the total number of transactions at each site. These totals are given in Figure 18.18. It shows that transaction A occurs 10,000 times at site S1, 20,000 times at site S2 and so on.

Now a trial fragmentation is made. The idea of the initial fragmentation is to store data so that most transactions are local. Access paths assist designers to choose such fragmentations. A number of possibilities exist in our example. One, for example, is to fragment APPLICANTS by their address. Another is to fragment them by their preferred working position. Similarly LISTINGS can be fragmented by their local office or by the vacancy location. Suppose the following choice is made: APPLICANTS is fragmented by the applicants location, and LISTINGS is fragmented by the actual location of the vacancy.

These fragments are then allocated to sites closest to the location. The allocation tables for these fragments are shown in Figure 18.19.

Now polarization analysis begins to determine the location of data needed by transactions at each site. A polarization table is constructed for each access step of each transaction during distribution analysis but our example only illustrates the analysis for transaction A. The polarization of each access step of this transaction is shown in Figure 18.20. Figure 18.20(a) shows polarization for access steps A1 and A2. It shows that 98% of the transaction are made at the applicant's location. Figure 18.20(b) shows the polarization for access step A3. It shows that 70% of applicants at S1 are searching for positions at S1, 25% are searching for positions at S2 and 5% for positions at S3. Access paths also suggest possible replications.

Figure 18.19 Allocations

Fragment \ Site	S1	S2	S3
1	1	0	0
2	0	1	0
3	0	0	1

(a) Allocation of LISTINGS

Fragment \ Site	S1	S2	S3
1	1	0	0
2	0	1	0
3	0	0	1

(b) Allocation of APPLICANTS

Figure 18.20 Polarization for access A

Site \ Fragment	1	2	3
S1	0.98	0.01	0.01
S2	0.01	0.98	0.01
S3	0.01	0.01	0.98

(a) Polarization for access steps A1 and A2

Site \ Fragment	1	2	3
S1	0.70	0.25	0.05
S2	0.05	0.90	0.05
S3	0.05	0.05	0.80

(b) Polarization for access steps A3

Transmission analysis for this polarization is shown in Figure 18.21. There is one estimates table for each access step. Figure 18.21(a) shows the estimates for access step A1. There is an estimate made for each transmission path shown in Figure 18.17. Figure 18.21 assumes that there are two preferred locations for each applicant. As a result there are two records returned for each record transmitted. The total number of records transmitted for this access step is 2100. Access step A2 results in a similar analysis. It is assumed that each applicant has an average of 2.5 skills and as a result 2.5 records (instead of 2 records) would be returned in step A2(t2) for each transmitted record. The result would be 500 transmitted records for step A2(t2) for site S1 (instead of 400 for step A1(t2)), 1000 (instead of 800) for site S2 and 250 (instead of 200) for site S3. The total records transmitted for step A2(t2) would be 1750. Adding this to 700 records transmitted in step A2(t1) gives a total of 2450 transmitted records for step A2.

Figure 18.21(b) shows transmission analysis for access step A3. The number of

Figure 18.21 Distribution analysis for access A

SITE	Step A1(t1)		Step A1(t2)		TOTAL
	Records		Records		
S1	10,000	10,000(0.98(0) + 0.10(1) + 0.01(1)) = 200	10,000 x 2 = 20,000	20,000(0.98(0) + 0.10(1) + 0.01(1)) = 400	600
S2	20,000	20,000(0.01(1) + 0.98(0) + 0.01(1)) = 400	20,000 x 2 = 40,000	40,000(0.01(1) + 0.98(0) + 0.01(1)) = 800	1200
S3	5,000	5,000(0.01(1) + 0.01(1) + 0.98(0)) = 100	5,000 x 2 = 10,000	10,000(0.01(1) + 0.01(1) + 0.98(0)) = 200	300

(a) Records transmitted, step A1 TOTAL 2100

SITE	Step A1(t1)		Step A1(t2)		TOTAL
	Records		Records		
S1	20,000	20,000(0.70(0) + 0.25(1) + 0.05(1)) = 6,000	20,000 x 5 = 100,000	100,000(0.70(0) + 0.25(1) + 0.05(1)) = 30,000	36,000
S2	40,000	40,000(0.05(1) + 0.90(0) + 0.05(1)) = 4,000	40,000 x 5 = 200,000	200,000(0.05(1) + 0.90(0) + 0.05(1)) = 20,000	24,000
S3	10,000	10,000(0.05(1) + 0.15(1) + 0.80(0)) = 2,000	10,000 x 5 = 50,000	50,000(0.05(1) + 0.15(1) + 0.80(0)) = 10,000	12,000

(b) Records transmitted, step A3 TOTAL 72,000

records transmitted is now twice the number of transactions because each applicant has two preferred locations. Also it is assumed that on an average there will be five vacancies for each preference. Thus the number of records returned is five times the number of records sent. The result is a total of 12,000 records sent, and a total of 60,000 records returned, giving a total of 72,000 transmitted records for access step A3.

The total records transmitted for the access requirement is the total of records transmitted for each access step. For transaction A this total will bc (2100 + 2450 + 72,000) = 76,550 records.

There are of course ways of reducing the number of records transmitted. For example, applicants may be replicated by their preferred locations. Thus an applicant will be stored not cause many problems because applicant data is fairly stable and is not frequently changed. However, it will not result in a substantial reduction of records transmitted because all vacancies will still have to be transmitted back to the transaction site. The only way to reduce the transmission of vacancies is to replicate them at each site.

SUMMARY

This chapter described the idea behind distributed databases. It outlined some advantages of database distribution, and defined the principles that must be satisfied to provide a good environment for distributed systems. The chapter then described some of the facilities that must be provided by software to satisfy these principles.

The chapter then outlined how design methodologies must be extended to support distributed systems. Such extensions include an additional distribution step. This step begins by proposing possible database fragmentation and then determines the allocation for each fragment.

19

Design environments and support tools

INTRODUCTION

This book has described techniques used to analyze, design and build a database and its associated applications. Effective use of the techniques calls for considerable computation and documentation especially in large systems. In large systems, the models themselves can be made up of many object sets and each object set can have many attributes. Furthermore, such models can undergo considerable change and amendment as analysis proceeds. Then, once design begins, access paths must be plotted and performance estimates made. The model may then be amended, and this amended model converted to a logical database definition. The volume of work and documentation during design can be quite great, especially in contemporary information systems, which are characterized by ever-growing complexity of relationships between system components.

There is an increasing tendency to use computer support to assist designers in their work. The computer tools used for this purpose are generically referred to as Computer Assisted Software Engineering (CASE) tools. They are increasingly needed in the complex environments of contemporary information systems to keep track of the development process. As well as documentation support, some CASE tools also provide design support for the more detailed design tasks.

This chapter covers CASE tool support for database design. Before doing this, however, the chapter more clearly identifies some of the design environments where CASE tools are applied. The report then continues by summarizing the current status of CASE tools.

DESIGN ENVIRONMENTS

So far we have assumed that database design proceeds in one design environment, namely, the design of new systems. There are, however, many different situations that arise in design environments. These include redesign of an existing system, and integrating two separate systems into an integrated system.

Redesigning systems

Applications are often redeveloped to improve their quality. Such quality can be improved by increasing the application functionality, improving its accuracy or performance.

The first redesign step is to find out the current structure of databases. Thus, the analysis usually proceeds in a reverse manner, sometimes called reverse engineering. The database definitions are now used to develop the E-R model rather than using the E-R model to generate a database. The E-R model developed in this way is carefully analyzed against current user needs.

The analysis identifies any changes needed to satisfy current requirements and produces a more precise model. This new E-R model is then used to identify changes in the existing system, which in turn lead to changes to the current database definition.

Often such analysis is used to study possible integration of existing systems or to add new functionality to an existing computer system.

System integration

System integration is often a special case of redesign. Many redesigns require closer integration between existing applications. This arises when new applications need to use data and programs in two or more existing systems.

The redesign process again begins by analyzing the structure of the two current systems and developing models for the systems. The separate models for each application must be combined into a single model. This combination serves to indicate how the applications should be integrated and leads to a revised database definition.

CASE TOOL SUPPORT

CASE tools should be able to provide support in all these design environments. However, different support facilities are needed in different environments. For example, redesign requires support that produces trial E-R diagrams from database definitions, or integrates E-R models. Design of new systems, on the other hand, needs more emphasis on generating database definitions from E-R models.

Most CASE tools assist designers in two major ways. The simplest and most obvious way is as a repository of system documentation. Here the CASE tool stores the system models and relieves designers from tedious manual tasks of drawing and changing models as the design evolves. Such a repository of models ensures that an up-to-date version of a system description is always readily available for designers.

The other CASE tool role is at a more detailed design level as a design assistant. This assists designers to check their models, normalize them, carry out design computations and convert models to database definitions using the rules described in Chapter 9. The power and functionality of CASE design assistants is in the sophistication of models that they support, and the design assistance that they can provide.

The type of support provided by contemporary CASE tools, both as documentation repositories and as design assistants, varies from system to system. CASE tools must support a variety of activities to effectively support designers in these design environments. These activities include:

Documentation

Here the CASE tool stores all data about the system. Such data includes all object sets in the E-R model together with their attributes and any other information about them. It can readily display these models or provide reports needed by system designers. Often models can be changed interactively on a display screen. This kind of support is needed in all design environments.

System modeling

The CASE tool, as well as acting as a repository of a system model, also assists users to develop and check this model. There is a range of support that is provided by CASE tools at the E-R level. Some may simply check simple model syntax such as whether a set has an identifier. Others may give suggestions on changes to be made to a current model. Still others provide assistance with data normalization.

Generating E-R models from database definitions

Here the E-R model is generated from a logical definition. Usually the definition would be first converted to logical record stuctures. Then common record fields can identify foreign keys, which in turn identify semantic links in the E-R model. This support is useful in system redesign.

Generating database definitions

CASE tools can generate data definitions from existing E-R models giving users a variety of options for combining object sets into logical records. Some assistance may be provided here in access path analysis to amend record structures and construct indices.

Modifying a definition

The CASE tool is used in the same way as in design. However, now it generates commands to amend an existing database definition, rather than construct a new definition.

Model comparison

Compares two E-R models and describes their differences. Assists redesign during conversion. A model of an existing system is developed to measure its precision against current requirements. Changes to the system can then be suggested.

System integration

This combines two or more E-R models into a single model. The models are then examined for commonality and integrated into a corporate model. The integration process must resolve any naming ambiguities in the two models and add relationships between components in the two existing models.

EXTENDING SUPPORT TO OTHER MODELS AND STAGES

CASE tools are not only used for database design. They are also used for modeling other components of a system. These may include system functions and dataflows. CASE tools can also be used at all levels of system development.

Use in conjunction with other models

Apart from a data model such as an E-R model a designer may also wish to use functional and dataflow models. These are illustrated in Figure 19.1. This figure shows a dataflow diagram (DFD). DFDs are made up of four main components. First there are external entities, which represent entities outside the system. The system may interchange information with these external entities. Figure 19.1 shows two such external entities, PROJECTS and SUPPLIERS. Projects place requisitions with the system whereas orders are sent to suppliers.

The other DFD components are processes, data stores and dataflows. Data stores represent repositories of data. They are represented by lines on the dataflow diagram. Figure 19.1 contains one such data store, REQUISITIONS. This contains all the information about requisitions. Processes are represented by circles on a DFD and dataflows are represented by lines that represent flow of data between processes. Dataflows occur between processes or between processes and external entities or dataflows. Each dataflow is given a unique name on the DFD.

Figure 19.1 A dataflow diagram for withdrawing parts

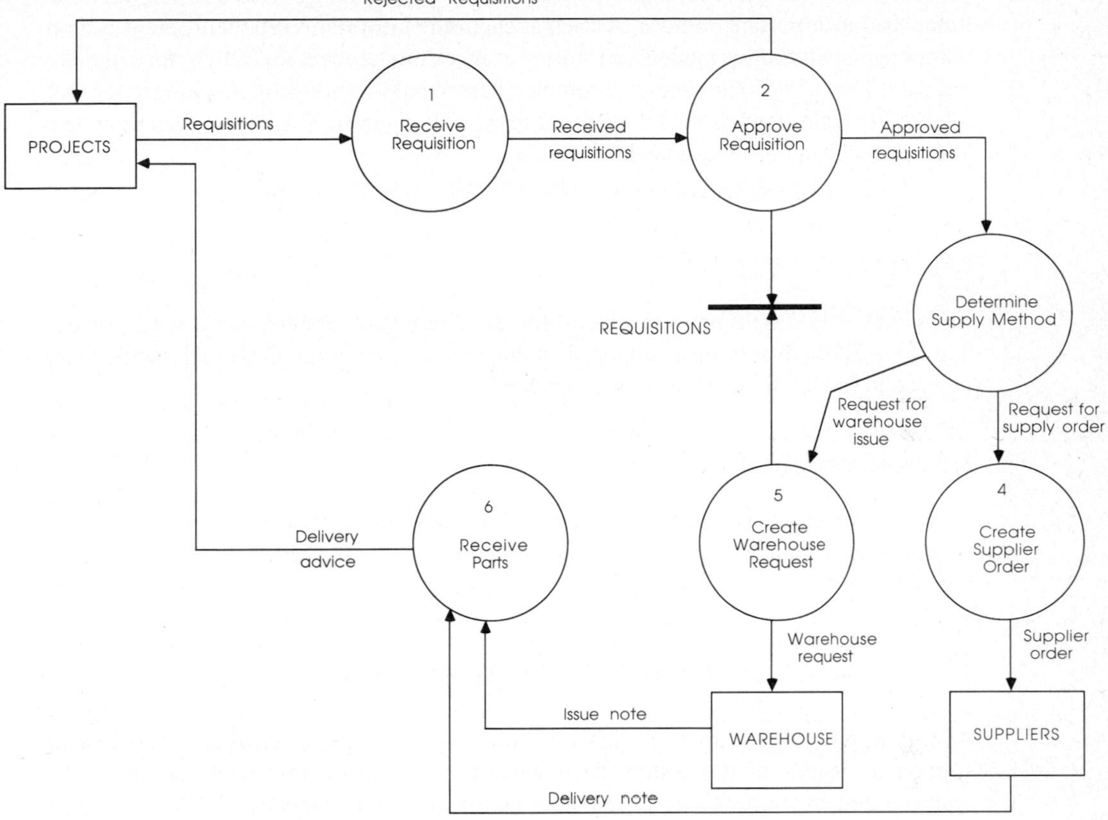

Each process on the DFD is given a unique number. In Figure 19.1, process 1 is called 'Receive Requisitions'. It receives requisitions from projects and sends them on to the next process, 'Approve Requisitions'. Approved requisitions are sent on to the next process to determine how they are to be met. Rejected requisitions are sent back to the projects. Process 3 decides whether a requisition is to be met from a warehouse or from an external supplier and sends a message to either process 4 or process 5. Process 6, 'Receive Parts' receives deliveries from warehouses or suppliers. On receipt of a delivery, it notifies the project by a delivery note and notes the requisition as completed.

Any process in the DFD can be expanded out into a more detailed dataflow diagram. Thus we could take 'Received Requisition' and draw a detailed DFD of the processes that make up 'Receive Requisition'. This could include processes to check the data in the requisition or make an estimate of total cost of requisitioned parts.

Often DFDs are used in conjunction with E-R diagrams. A DFD is drawn first. It identifies the major processes and data entities. E-R analysis is then used to expand the data stores into more detail.

CASE tool must support all modeling methods used in a design methodology. Thus if a design methodology uses DFDs in conjunction with an E-R model, then a CASE tool that supports both these models is needed by the methodology. Use of more than one model has an important purpose. As well as capturing information about different system components, alternative models can be used to check model accuracy. DFDs, for example, use data. Thus a DFD can check the completeness of an E-R model by checking to see that all data elements used by the DFD appear in the E-R diagram. CASE tools can provide a very thorough consistency check.

To do this CASE tools support additional activities. These are:

Multi model support

The CASE tool should provide support for all system components, that is data, process and flow. To do this, it must support than one modeling method. Each such method can be used to model different system components.

System verification

Checks a model for correctness. Can be used as a syntactic check or as a check between two models. This check ensures that all data references in the function model appear in the data model.

Extension to other design stages

As well as providing support for different modeling techniques, CASE tools should also support all stages of the system development cycle. So far this book has primarily concentrated on analysis and design once a particular need is identified. This is usually preceded by long-term planning that identifies such needs.

Long-term planning calls for the understanding of the total corporate system and how information systems can support corporate goals. It begins with a clear definition of corporate goals, and continues by identifying the broad system functions and data needed to realize these goals. The relative importance of the goals can then be used to set priorities for information systems development. These priorities indicate the sequence for application development. This sequence then becomes part of the strategic plan.

The strategic plan identifies any redevelopment or integration of existing systems and proposals for the development of totally new systems. It also produces a strategic model for the organization's information system showing major entities and application programs. Parts of this model become particular applications. It is only when these long-term goals are defined that database design and application development begins.

CASE tools sometimes provide support for developing strategic plans and the strategic corporate information system models that make up these plans. Parts of the corporate model can then be used to initiate individual applications.

EVALUATING CASE TOOLS

There are three criteria that can be used to evaluate CASE tools. One is their functionality in terms of the models and processes that they support. Another is the user interface that they provide for designers. Then there are the activities that they support. An evaluation method must consider all these criteria.

The models and processes used

CASE tools can use any of the modeling techniques currently available for systems analysis and design. These include dataflow diagrams, data modeling or structured design. The particular techniques can be identified by placing their names on the evaluation grid.

The user interface

The user interface is more qualitative than functional. It is often concerned with the level of graphics provided for model input and the kinds of reports that can be generated by the CASE tool. Important factors here are graphics quality, level of intelligence in help screens and ability to manipulate models directly on the screen.

Activities supported

The activities supported by CASE tools have been defined earlier. Now all these criteria must be combined to evaluate a particular tool.

Combining the criteria

One useful chart for describing and comparing tools is shown in Figure 19.2. It shows the domain of a CASE tool in two dimensions. One is the models supported by a CASE tool. These can be DFDs, Entity-Relationship diagrams or other diagramming techniques that are used at various life cycle stages. The second dimension on the chart is the life cycle stage applicable to the tool.

The third dimension of this comparison chart is the activities that are supported by particular tools. This dimension uses the classification of activity levels described above. It then becomes possible to place a CASE tool somewhere in this chart.

Figure 19.2 Positioning a CASE tool

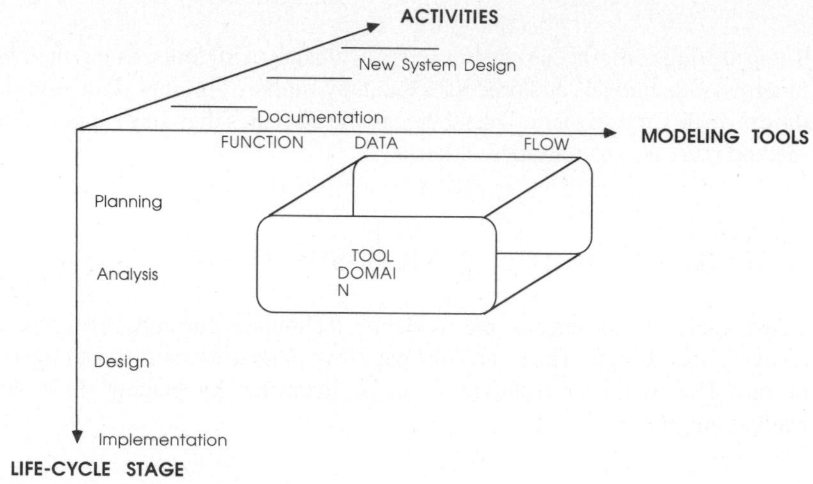

Some current tools

There is a great variety of CASE tools on the market and as yet no clear standard exists. However, there are some common characteristics possessed by many CASE tools. One is that there is a trend for CASE tools to evolve in a modular manner. Thus many CASE tools are now combinations of modules, where each module supports a set of activities using a modeling method at a life cycle stage. A combination of such modules provides support for a large part of the chart shown in Figure 19.2.

The CASE tool or system integrates these modules to produce a complete design environment over the entire life cycle. Two common ways of integrations are vertical and horizontal integration.

In horizontal integration different models are used to check each other. Thus for example an E-R model can be checked against a DFD. The check ensures that all data elements found in dataflow modeling also appear in the E-R diagram.

In vertical integration, a model at one level is converted to a model at the next level of the life cycle. Thus, for example, a logical database definition can be generated from the E-R model.

A typical tool that supports the modular approach is the Information Engineering Workbench. This is more a design methodology than a CASE tool and provides support for all stages of the system development cycle. The tool itself is very comprehensive and cannot be described here in any detail. The intention here is to simply give you an idea of the structure and facilities provided by such tools rather than providing a detailed user manual.

The IEW is structured in the way shown in Figure 19.3. It is made up of three workstations, where each workstation provides a set of diagramming tools appropriate to that stage. Each tool supports one system diagram and information about all diagrams is

Figure 19.3 Information engineering workbench

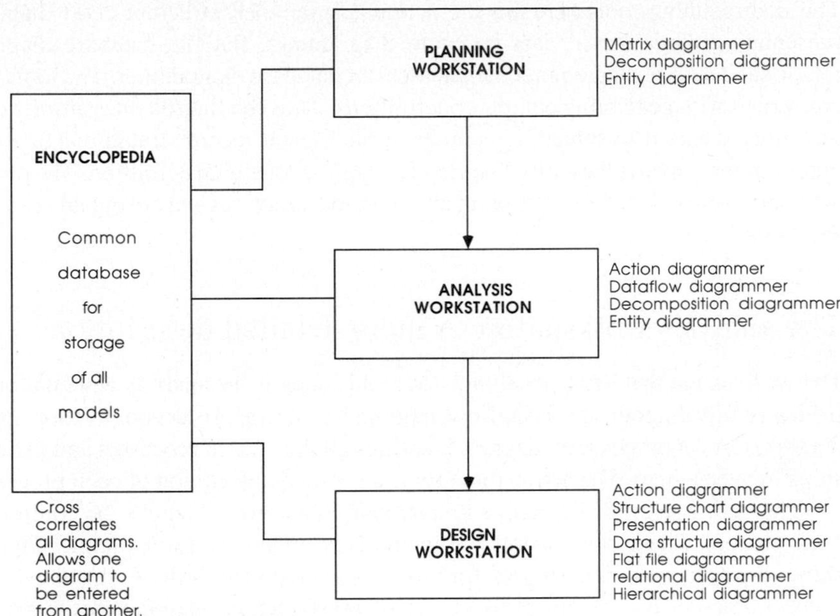

kept in an integrated database, or an encyclopedia, using IEW terminology. Such a common encyclopedia makes it possible to cross correlate information stored using the various diagrams. In fact it is possible to work on one diagram and from this diagram open other diagrams.

The three workstations support thc following diagramming tools:

Planning workstation

This workstation supports initial system planning. It provides three diagramming tools, the matrix diagrammer, the decomposition diagrammer and the entity diagrammer. The decomposition diagrammer models the system processes and the entity diagrammer is used to develop a top-level entity diagram. The entity diagram in this case is very similar to the E-R diagram.

The analysis workstation

The analysis workstation supports system modeling. It is oriented around the dataflow diagram and entity modeling and provides the diagramming tools to supports this. The diagramming tools here are the action diagrammer, the dataflow diagrammer, the decomposition diagrammer and the entity diagrammer. The dataflow and entity diagrammer support DFDs and entity models. The decomposition diagrammer and action diagrammer support process specifications.

The design workstation

The diagramming tools here are the action diagrammer, structure chart diagrammer, presentation diagrammer, data structure diagrammer, flat file database diagrammer, relational database diagrammer and hierachical database diagrammer. The tools here are concerned with generating computer definitions. Thus the flat file diagrammer converts the entity diagram to something similar to the logical record structure. The relational diagrammer converts the entity diagram to a logical relational definition. The other tools are concerned with defining program modules and structures and are outside the scope of this book.

The analysis workstation: A more detailed description

The workstation that most closely relates to this book is the analysis workstation. Apart from an entity diagram and a dataflow diagram it also supports decomposition and action diagrams. A decomposition diagram identifies all the system processes and the relationships between them. The action diagram is a detailed description of each process.

The decomposition diagram is hierarchical in nature and shows the components of each process. These components are themselves processes. For example, Figure 19.4 shows the decomposition diagram for product development. It shows that the three main processes needed to develop a product are to plan production, manufacture the product and distribute this product. Each of these processes themselves is made up of more detailed processes. Thus manufacture is made up of parts maintenance, machine allocation and assembly. Parts maintenance is made up of withdrawing parts, purchasing parts and inventory stocktake. Withdraw parts is the process described by the DFD in Figure 19.1 and its components on the decomposition diagram are the processes shown on that DFD.

The action diagram specifies the logic of each process including the computations carried out by a process. Figure 19.4 includes the action diagram for process 'Receive requisition'. It shows the sequence of computations within the process, together with any loops or decisions. Any components of the process also appear in the action diagram. Thus the three components, 'Check Project', 'Check Warehouse', and 'Check Part' all appear as processes in the action diagram.

All the diagrams produced for a system are closely related because, after all, they represent the same system. Thus designers should be able to start with any diagram but at any time enter a related diagram. The term opening a diagram is used in IEW. An analyst can open one diagram from another. Figure 19.5 illustrates how this relationship between diagrams works for the analysis workstation.

From the decomposition diagram you can open up any other diagram. For example, you can select a process in the decomposition diagram and do any of the following:

1. Open up a DFD that shows all the component processes of the selected process. Thus 'Withdraw parts' would open up to the DFD shown in Figure 19.1.
2. Open up an action diagram that describes the selected process. Thus opening up 'Receive requisition' would shown the action diagram shown in Figure 19.4.
3. Open up an entity diagram that describes the data used by the process.

Figure 19.4 Decomposition and action diagrams

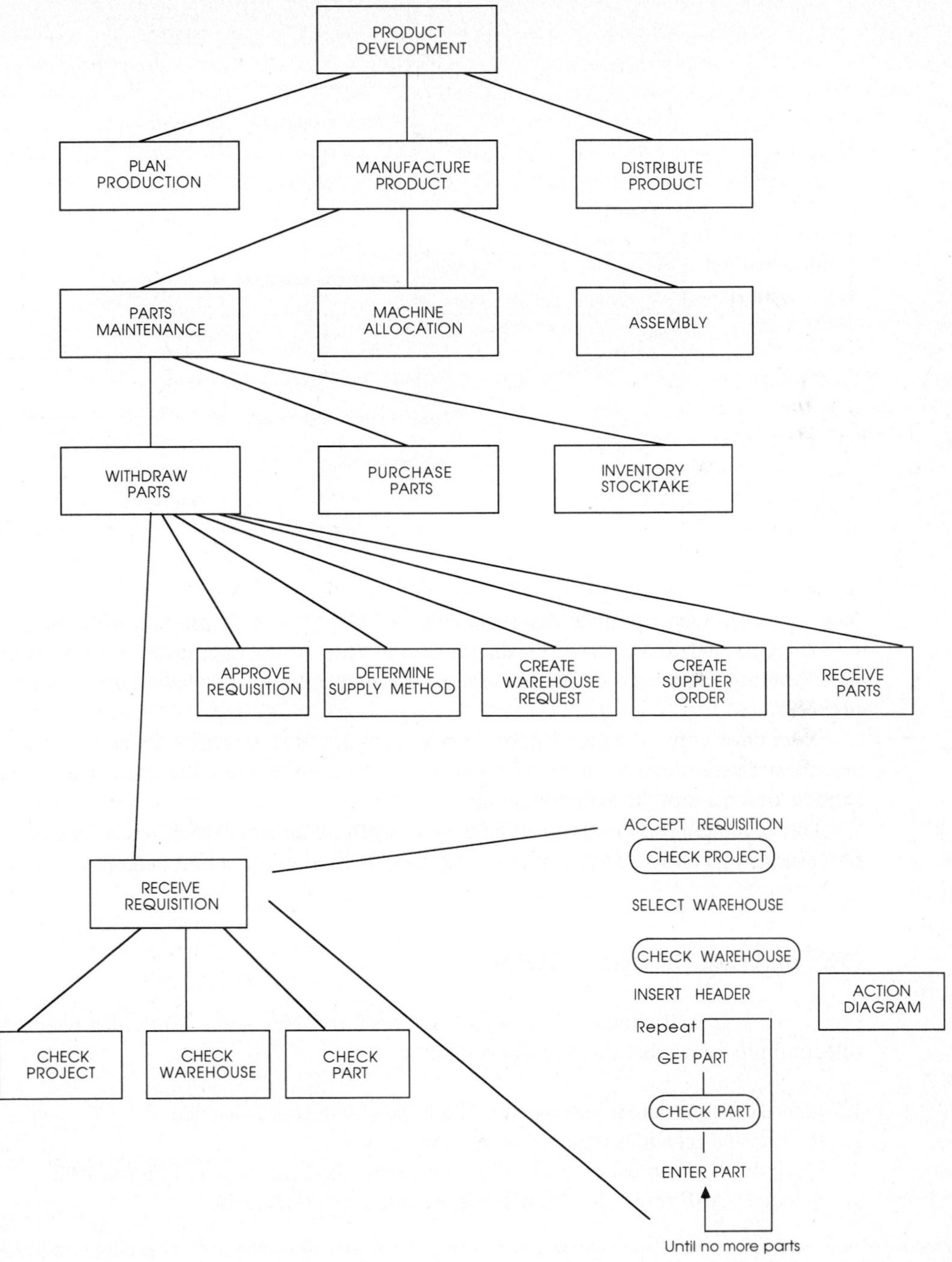

Figure 19.5 Some relationahips between diagrams in the IEW

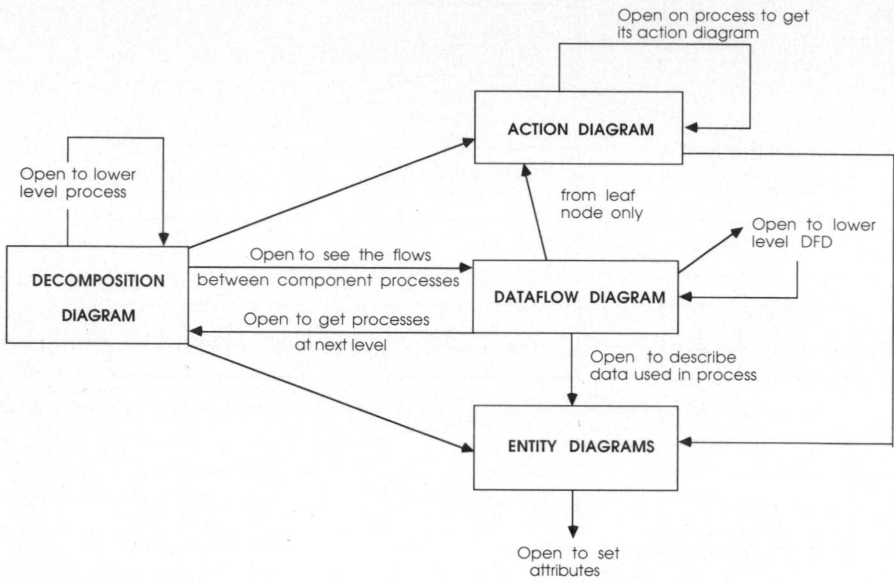

You can also open up other diagrams from a DFD. You can, for example, select a DFD process, and open up an action diagram for it. You can also open up an entity diagram that shows the data used by the process, or you can open a lower level DFD from the process.

A set on an entity diagram can be opened up to describe the attributes in the set, and an action diagram can be opened into an entity diagram to show the data used by the process described in the action diagram.

The action diagram in turn can be used to open up an action diagram of any of its processes, or an entity diagram that shows the data used in the action diagram.

Selecting a case tool

Users are frequently required to select a CASE tool for some particular need. A selection procedure that can be followed is:

1. Identify the particular purpose for which the CASE tool is needed.
2. Identify the activities required within the purpose.
3. Place the requirement on the CASE tool evaluation grid shown in Figure 19.2.
4. Select a CASE tool that falls within the same area on the grid.

POSSIBLE FUTURE DEVELOPMENTS

The future for CASE tools can perhaps be viewed as one of closer integration of all processes. There is currently considerable effort to keep track of the different components and ensure that they are all properly coordinated at all design levels. There is also a trend towards adding intelligence to systems. This suggests modeling methods where databases define certain states. Rules are then defined to initiate actions given these states.

Perhaps what we are looking for in the future is a support tool that only requires users to define their requirements as a precise model of the system. This model defines system components and rules about the behavior of these components.

The user would simply specify this model. Applications would then be identified as parts of the model. The components that make up these parts are then used to generate the application.

The model may only need to have two parts here — the object structure together with rules about the behavior of this structure.

SUMMARY

This chapter described how design activities are supported in practical environments. It outlined several design environments and the type of support that can be provided by CASE (Computer Assisted Software Engineering) tools. It described the facilities provided by such tools, outlined some contemporary tools and gave some guidelines for selecting a CASE tool.

Case study: Requisition system

This case study is included here for use in those chapters concerned with application development. It includes an E-R model that describes requisitioning of parts by projects in organizations. The requisitions are modeled as entity sets made up of any number of requisition lines. These requisition lines are modeled by dependent entity sets. Each requisition line is for any quantity of any one part.

Each requisition line is then used to make up an order line in an order. It should be noted that the whole of the quantity of parts in one requisition line is placed in the same order line. The order line, however, can be made up of any number of requisition lines. The orders are then placed with suppliers.

Eventually deliveries are made by suppliers. Deliveries are modeled as dependent entities on suppliers and are identified by a delivery number, DEL-NO, within SUPPLIER-NAME. Each delivery is made up of any number of delivery lines, with each line corresponding to one order line. You should note that the parts in one order line can be delivered as more than one delivery line. As a delivery is received, the parts in a delivery line are distributed between the requisitions that make up the order line that corresponds to the delivery line. The distributed parts are added to the value QTY-FILLED in the requisition line.

The E-R model is converted to the following relations.

- PARTS (<u>PART-NO</u>, WEIGHT)

  A list of parts.

Case study E-R diagram

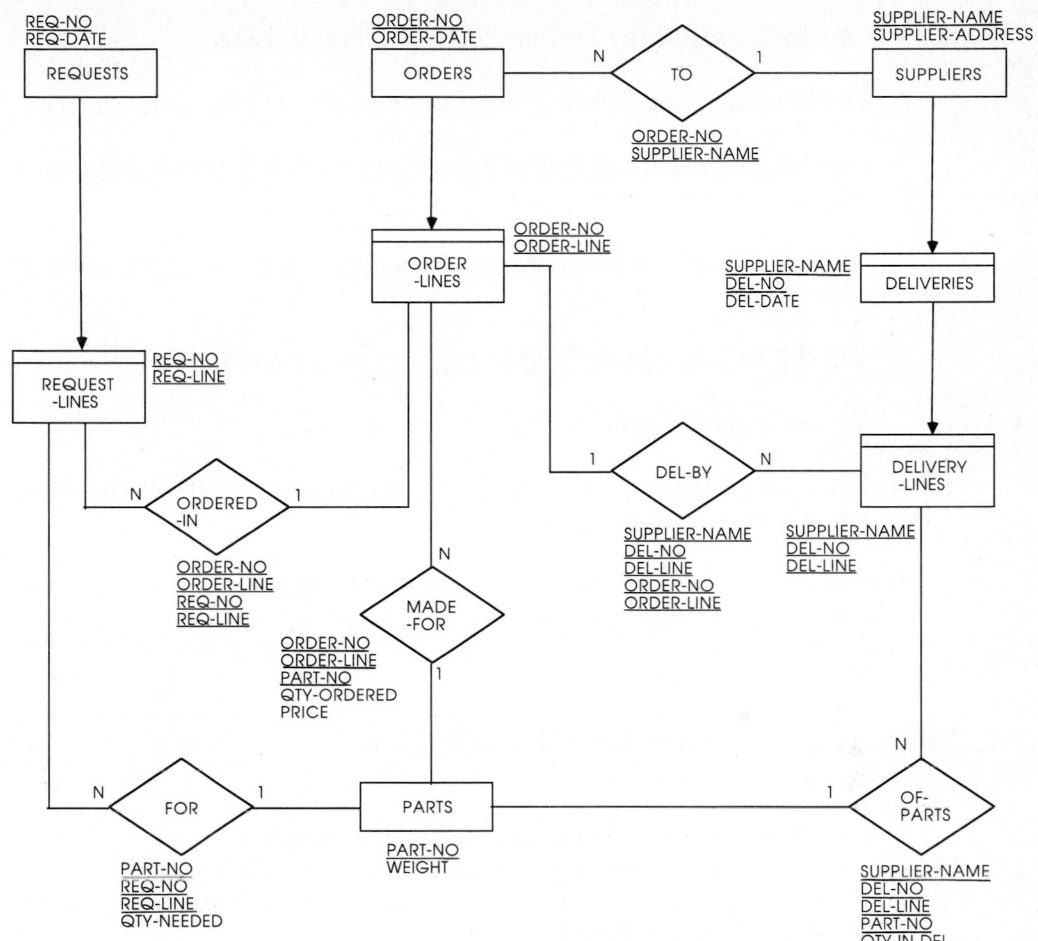

- SUPPLIERS (<u>SUPPLIER-NAME</u>, SUPPLIER-ADDRESS)

  A list of suppliers and their addresses.

- REQUISITIONS (<u>REQ-NO</u>, REQ-DATE)

  Details of each requisition.

- REQUISITION-LINES (<u>REQ-NO, REQ-LINE</u>, PART-NO, QTY-NEEDED, ORDER-NO, ORDER-LINE)

Identifies a requisition line and the order line used to order parts requested in the requisition line. Combines sets REQUEST-LINES, ORDERED-IN and FOR.

- ORDERS (ORDER-NO, ORDER-DATE, SUPPLIER-NAME)

  Details of each order. Combines entity set ORDERS and relationship set, TO.

- ORDER-LINES (ORDER-NO, ORDER-LINE, PART-NO, QTY-ORDERED, PRICE)

  Identifies an order line and its details. Combines sets ORDER-LINES and MADE-FOR.

- DELIVERIES (SUPPLIER-NAME, DEL-NO, DEL-DATE)

  Deliveries and their delivery dates.

- DELIVERY-LINES (SUPPLIER-NAME, DEL-NO, DEL-LINE, ORDER-NO, ORDER-LINE, PART-NO, QTY-IN-DEL)

Identifies each delivery line, the part it includes and the order line that it meets. Combines sets DELIVERY-LINES, DEL-BY and OF-PARTS.

APPLICATION DEVELOPMENT

You should develop the following applications for this database.

Placing a requisition

A project places a requisition. The application should allow a requisition to be made up of any number of lines and check the validity of parts entered in each line.

Making up an order

This proceeds by first making a summary of all parts in unordered requisition lines. The order clerk should then be able to select some of these parts and make an order of them. The order is made up one line at a time and each line is for one part. The order line can include any of the requisition lines for that part.

Distributing a delivery

A delivery is first entered into the system. Each delivery line in a delivery is then examined to find its order line. Requisition lines in that order line are then examined, and the quantity of parts in the delivery line is distributed between these lines.

DESIGNING THE APPLICATION

The first design step should be to convert the E-R diagram to a logical record structure. Access paths for all of the above activities should then be plotted and the logical structure ammended if necessary. You can assume the following in any computations:

1. On an average there are four (4) lines in each requisition.
2. On an average there are six (6) lines in an order.
3. On an average there are about six (6) lines in each delivery.

There are about twice as many orders as there are requisitions. There are about as many deliveries as there are orders.

Bibliography

BERNSTEIN, P. A., 1976. "Synthesizing Third Normal Relations from Functional Dependencies", ACM Transactions on Database Systems, vol. 1, no. 4.

CERI, S., PELAGATTI, G., 1984. *Distributed Database Systems: Principles and Systems*. McGraw-Hill.

CHEN, P. P., 1976. "The Entity-Relationship Model — Toward a Unified View of Data", ACM Transactions on Database Systems, vol. 6, no. 1.

CODD, E. F., 1971. "A Relational Model for Large Data Banks", Communications of the ACM, vol. 13, no. 6, June 1971.

DATE, C. J., 1984. *A Guide to DB2*, Addison-Wesley.

DATE, C. J., 1986. *Introduction to Database Systems*, 4th edn., Addison-Wesley.

HAWRYSZKIEWYCZ, I. T., 1990. *Introduction to Systems Analysis and Design*, 2nd edn., Prentice Hall Australia.

HAWRYSZKIEWYCZ, I. T., 1984. *Database Analysis and Design*, Macmillan.

JACKSON, G. A., 1988. *Relational Database Design with Microcomputer Applications*, Prentice Hall Australia.

KENT, W., 1983. "A Simple Guide to Five Normal Forms in Relational Database Theory", Communications of the ACM, vol. 26, no. 2, February.

KROENKE, D., 1983. *Database Processing*, 2nd edn., Science Research Associates.

MACIASZEK, L. A., 1990. *Database Design and Implementation*, Prentice Hall Australia.

PECKHAM, J., MARYANSKI, F., 1988. "Semantic Data Models", ACM Computing Surveys, vol. 20, no. 3, September.

RICHE, N., 1988. *Database Design Fundamentals*, Prentice Hall Australia.

VAN DER LANS, R., 1989. *Introduction to SQL*, Addison-Wesley.

Index